# DATA ANALYSIS

# FOR CONTINUOUS

# SCHOOL IMPROVEMENT

## THIRD EDITION

BY

VICTORIA L. BERNHARDT, Ph.D.
**Executive Director**
**Education for the Future Initiative**
**Professor**
**College of Communication and Education**
**California State University, Chico, CA**

**Routledge**
Taylor & Francis Group
LONDON AND NEW YORK

First published 2013 by Eye on Education

Published 2013 by Routledge
2 Park Square, Milton Park, Abingdon, Oxon OX14 4RN
711 Third Avenue, New York, NY, 10017, USA

*Routledge is an imprint of the Taylor & Francis Group, an informa business*

Copyright © 2013 Taylor & Francis

Notices
No responsibility is assumed by the publisher for any injury and/or damage to persons or property as a matter of products liability, negligence or otherwise, or from any use of operation of any methods, products, instructions or ideas contained in the material herein.

Practitioners and researchers must always rely on their own experience and knowledge in evaluating and using any information, methods, compounds, or experiments described herein. In using such information or methods they should be mindful of their own safety and the safety of others, including parties for whom they have a professional responsibility.

Product or corporate names may be trademarks or registered trademarks, and are used only for identification and explanation without intent to infringe.

## Library of Congress Cataloging-in-Publication Data

Bernhardt, Victoria L., 1952-
    Data analysis for continuous school improvement / by Victoria L. Bernhardt, Ph.D., Executive Director, Education for the Future Initiative, Professor, College of Communication and Education, California State University, Chico, CA — Third edition.
    pages cm
    ISBN 978-1-59667-252-9
    1. Computer managed instruction—United States. 2. School improvement programs—United States—Data processing. 3. Educational planning—United States—Statistical methods. I. Title.
    LB1028.46.B47 2013
    371.33'4--dc23
                                    2013013734

ISBN 13: 978-1-59667-252-9 (pbk)

# ACKNOWLEDGEMENTS

I feel honored, thankful, and humbled to write this acknowledgement for the people who helped me create this work. I am honored to be connected to these wonderful people whom I trust will give me information to make my drafts better, more powerful, and better able to serve our collective clients' needs. I am thankful because they not only made the manuscript better, they gave me the confidence to keep going. I am humbled by these reviewers' understandings, experiences, and insights. The following people have had profound impacts on the content of the text in front of you:

Sergé Boulé
> Statistical Consultant, Ottawa, Canada

Chuck Breithaupt
> Educational Consultant for VersiFit
> Longitudinal Data Systems, Wisconsin

Robert Dunn
> Retired Superintendent, Ontario, Canada

Diane Findlay
> Manager, Compass for Success, Ontario, Canada

Brad Geise
> Education for the Future Staff, California

Robert Geise
> Retired Businessman, California

Connie Hébert
> Educational Consultant, Cape Girardeau, Missouri
> Director, Southeast Missouri State University
> Autism Center for Diagnosis and Treatment

Mary Hooper
> Director, Leadership Academy, University of
> West Georgia, Carrolltown, Georgia

Kathy Miller
> Director of Instructional Services, Regional ESD,
> Corunna, Michigan

Joy Rose
> Retired High School Principal, Columbus, Ohio

Patsy Schutz
> Education for the Future Staff, California

Cheryl Tibbals
> Common Core State Standards
> Consultant, Lafayette, California

Phyllis Unebasami
> Division Director, Literacy Instruction and
> Support, Kamehameha Schools, Hawaii

Jody Wood
> Assistant Professor, Educational Leadership,
> Saint Louis University, Missouri

Kathy McConnachie
> Principal, Dryden High School,
> Ontario, Canada

Special appreciation go to Brad Geise, Bob Geise, Mary Hooper, and Joy Rose for reviewing multiple drafts. Joy continuously read and edited drafts throughout the process. She is always there for me. Brad was there to read and encourage a "punch" here and there. Joy and Brad served as continual sounding boards for changes and improvements. Bob and Mary helpfully read chapter revisions. I am extremely thankful for our small, committed *Education for the Future* staff—Lynn Swaim, Brad Geise, Patsy Schutz, Sally Withuhn, and Hugh Hammond—who will do whatever it takes for us to produce workshops, presentations, and institutes of highest quality. A huge thank you goes to Lynn Swaim who did a phenomenal job of creating the layout of this book, and keeping me sane throughout the process. Lynn is always there when I need her.

Thank you MC², especially Brian Curtis and Robert Vargas for the cover work. Thank you to VersiFit for automating the data profile. Schools that want to jump start their comprehensive data analysis work can get their data profiles done quickly and easily.

A huge thank you also to my husband, Jim Richmond, who does an outstanding job of tolerating the writing process, putting weekend pleasures on hold, and taking care of the house and forest.

Thank you to the readers for using my other books for the benefit of all students in your schools. May you find this book to be clear, helpful, and provide that information you need to continuously improve your learning organizations. I hope this book exceeds your expectations, and if it does, it is because of the continuous improvement that has resulted from your insights, direction, and support along the way.

In appreciation for all the support,

*Vickie Bernhardt*
April 2013

# ABOUT THE AUTHOR

Victoria L. Bernhardt, Ph.D., is Executive Director of the *Education for the Future Initiative*, a not-for-profit organization, whose mission is to build the capacity of all learning organizations at all levels to gather, analyze, and use data to continuously improve learning for all students. She is also a Professor (currently on leave) in the College of Communication and Education, at California State University, Chico. Dr. Bernhardt is the author, or co-author, of the following books:

◆ *Response to Intervention (RtI) and Continuous School Improvement (CSI): Using Data, Vision, and Leadership to Design, Implement, and Evaluate a Schoolwide Prevention System* (2011) shows schools how to create, implement, and evaluate RtI processes that will improve student learning for all students, by starting with continuous school improvement planning (co-authored with Connie L. Hébert).

◆ *From Questions to Actions: Using Questionnaire Data for Continuous School Improvement* (2009) describes how to create, administer, analyze, and use questionnaires as a tool to improve teaching strategies, programs, and learning organizations (co-authored with Bradley J. Geise).

◆ *Data, Data Everywhere: Bringing All the Data Together for Continuous School Improvement* (2009) is an easy-to-read primer that is conversational and accessible. This book will help your faculty and staff become comfortable with using data to drive continuous school improvement.

◆ *Translating Data into Information to Improve Teaching and Learning* (2007) helps educators think through the selection of meaningful data elements and effective data tools and strengthens their understanding of how to increase the quality of data and data reports at each educational level.

◆ A four-book collection of using data to improve student learning—*Using Data to Improve Student Learning in Elementary Schools* (2003); *Using Data to Improve Student Learning in Middle Schools* (2004); *Using Data to Improve Student Learning in High Schools* (2005); and *Using Data to Improve Student Learning in School Districts* (2006). Each book shows real analyses focused on one education organizational level and provides templates on an accompanying CD-Rom for leaders to use for gathering, graphing, and analyzing data in their own learning organizations.

◆ *The School Portfolio Toolkit: A Planning, Implementation, and Evaluation Guide for Continuous School Improvement*, and CD-Rom (2002), is a compilation of over 500 examples, suggestions, activities, tools, strategies, and templates for producing school portfolios that will lead to continuous school improvement.

◆ *The School Portfolio: A Comprehensive Framework for School Improvement* (First Edition, 1994; Second Edition, 1999) assists schools with clarifying the purpose and vision of their learning organizations as they develop their school portfolios.

Dr. Bernhardt is passionate about her mission of helping all educators continuously improve student learning in their classrooms, their schools, their districts, and states by gathering, analyzing, and using actual data—as opposed to using hunches and "gut-level" feelings. She conducts workshops on comprehensive data analysis, and continuous school improvement, and consults with learning organizations at local, state, regional, national, and international levels.

Dr. Bernhardt can be reached at:

Victoria L. Bernhardt
Executive Director
*Education for the Future Initiative*
400 West First Street, Chico, CA 95929-0230
Tel: 530-898-4482 ~ Fax: 530-898-4484
E-mail: *vbernhardt@csuchico.edu*
Website: *http://eff.csuchico.edu*

# TABLE OF CONTENTS

# FROM COMPLIANCE TO COMMITMENT:
## USING DATA FOR CONTINUOUS SCHOOL IMPROVEMENT

*You cannot force commitment. What you can do...*
*you nudge a little here, inspire a little there,*
*and provide a role model. Your primary*
*influence is the environment you create.*

Peter M. Senge
Author, *The Fifth Discipline*

I have started many workshops in my multi-decade consulting career by asking participants, "What would it take to get learning growth for every student, every year, in your school?" After deliberation with teammates, teachers and administrators tell me these things need to be in place:

*What would it take to get learning growth for every student, every year, in your school?*

1. Teachers and administrators must *honestly* review and use their data— ALL their data, not just study a gap here or there.

2. Teachers and administrators must truly *believe* that *all* children can learn, or learning cannot and will not happen.

3. There must be *one vision* for the school—we have to get everyone on the same page and moving forward together.

4. *One plan* to implement the school vision must be in place. We cannot implement multiple unrelated plans.

5. Curriculum, instructional strategies, and assessments must be *aligned* to *student learning standards*. We will only spin in circles if we do not have this alignment.

6. Staff need to *collaborate* and *use* student, classroom, grade level, and school level data. Teachers need to work together to determine what they need to do to ensure *every* student's learning.

7. Staff need *professional learning* to work differently when the data tell them they are not getting the results they want or that they might not be getting the results they expect. (Professional learning refers to ongoing, job-embedded, results-oriented learning for professional educators.)

8. Schools need to rethink their current structures as opposed to *adding on* to what is existing. (Structures include how curriculum and instruction are delivered. Add-ons are programs and interventions added to close a gap.)

What I do *not* hear is: "We have to study our gaps in performance using summative tests so we can make adequate yearly progress." Educators know, intuitively and experientially, that focusing only on gaps in performance on one summative test will not get student learning improvements for all students, yet it is easy to get caught up in trying to make the work simpler. When asked what is the hardest to do of the eight things listed above, most school staff members say, "It is all hard; it all needs to be done. We don't know how to do it *all*; therefore, we never have." Then they say, "If we had to pick one thing that is the hardest, it would be *honestly* reviewing and using all our data, then making the appropriate changes."

It seems many schools do not have "working structures" in place to systematically and honestly review and then to use all their data to impact student learning results. Without a system or structure to review all the data, mostly external student learning compliance data are used. When only some data are used, the focus is typically on the gaps and improving individual students who are not achieving on that one measure that is used for compliance, and not on what or how teachers are teaching, or how to improve learning for *all* students. Without a system, structure, or vision in place to guide the use of all data, there is no new learning to change teacher attitudes, behaviors, or instruction—and ultimately improve student learning.

What would it look like if a school did all eight elements above? And what would be the outcomes? How can school staff do all these things within the confines of a school year? In order to get school staff to do all these things, we need to shift staff thinking about data use from simple compliance to a true commitment to improvement.

## MOVING AWAY FROM A SINGULAR FOCUS ON COMPLIANCE, TOWARD A COMMITMENT TO CONTINUOUS IMPROVEMENT

When schools focus primarily on compliance, they tend to concentrate their school improvement efforts on what and how they are being measured. Consider, for example, elementary schools in the United States when the No Child Left Behind (NCLB) accountability laws came into being in the early 2000s. Schools were measured on English Language Arts and Mathematics, only. Many schools believed that if they did well in Reading, everything else would follow. School days were reorganized to provide blocks of time for Language Arts. Many schools made incredible improvements in Language Arts because of that focus; however, Mathematics scores stayed pretty stagnant during that time. A few years later, many

*When only some data are used, the focus is typically on the gaps and improving individual students who are not achieving on the one measure that is used for compliance, and not on what or how teachers are teaching, or how to improve learning for ALL students.*

*When schools focus primarily on compliance, they tend to concentrate their school improvement efforts on what and how they are being measured.*

states changed their Mathematics tests to require students to show how they came up with their answers. To meet these new accountability requirements, schools scrambled to teach writing, math vocabulary, and math concepts. With the new focus, those scores improved. Sadly, the Language Arts scores tended to go down.

Fast forward a decade later. Schools were accountable, for the first time, in Language Arts, Mathematics, Science, and Social Studies. Guess what we found? Science and Social Studies had not been taught in some schools in the previous ten years.

When schools focus only on one part of student learning, the others parts will fall apart. Similar scenarios were created when schools focused on specific subgroups of students not making proficiency, or on the "Bubble Kids." "Bubble Kids" are students who perform just below proficiency. The thought is that by focusing on moving these students to proficiency, the school is sure to make Adequate Yearly Progress. Unfortunately, when schools focus only on a small group of students, the other students do not benefit.

Although efforts focused on one area or one student group caused increases to the detriment to other areas, many good things came from NCLB. Needs of student groups who never succeeded before were being met. Teachers learned they have to work together to get schoolwide gains—improvement in one grade level builds on the improvement of the previous grade levels. Schools learned that although they were being measured by one test, it takes more than just improving the results on that one test to get improvement throughout the school.

And now where are we? Schools are in great need of a framework for continuous school improvement and an assessment tool to tell them where they are in the process to help them stay focused on systemic improvement. When schools use a framework for continuous school improvement along with comprehensive data analysis, they understand how they are getting their results—what is working, and what is not working. They know the structures to have in place for continuous school improvement. When schools use a continuous school improvement self-assessment tool they know where they are in the process and how to get all their staff moving forward together.

Figure 1.1 shows the differences in actions on important measures between schools focused on compliance for accountability and schools that commit to using comprehensive data analysis for continuous school improvement.

Most of all, schools committed to using comprehensive data analysis to continuously improve their learning organization are able to blend creativity with discipline to create their future. Schools focused only on gaps and compliance can neither innovate nor create a future that looks different from the status quo. Such an approach inhibits systemic improvement and limits progress towards excellence and real equity.

*When schools use a framework for continuous school improvement, along with comprehensive data analysis, they understand how they are getting their results—what is working, and what is not working.*

Figure 1.1
DIFFERENCES IN ACTIONS BETWEEN SCHOOLS FOCUSED ON COMPLIANCE AND SCHOOLS
COMMITTED TO USING DATA ONLY FOR CONTINUOUS SCHOOL IMPROVEMENT

| Key Components | Schools Focused on Compliance for Accountability... | Schools Committed to Using Data for Continuous School Improvement... |
|---|---|---|
| **Data Analysis** | Blame students for poor results (e.g., our results are not very good because our population lives in poverty).<br><br>Use student learning data, only, to close gaps.<br><br>Focus on "Bubble Kids." | Embrace whom they have as students and learn how to meet their needs, and ensure that *all* achieve.<br><br>Have all staff use demographic, perceptions, student learning, and school processes data to understand how to—<br>• meet the needs of students,<br>• understand what is working and what is not working,<br>• use what is working to serve *all* students, and<br>• predict and prevent failures, and optimize successes. |
| **Problem Solving** | Use problem solving in a reactive fashion. They tend to add fixes when problems occur. | Prepare staff to know how to problem solve together to get to and eliminate contributing causes, in a proactive fashion. |
| **Vision** | Focus only on achieving compliance and making Adequate Yearly Progress.<br><br>Add programs and interventions to what they are already doing when change is needed. | Have a vision about doing whatever it takes to improve teaching and learning.<br><br>Use data to inform the schoolwide vision that is created, embraced, and implemented by all staff members. The vision clarifies what teachers will teach, how teachers will teach and assess, and how everyone in the organization will treat each other, related to student learning standards. The vision provides the means for strategic, fast action-the scenarios have been played through. |
| **Planning** | Write school improvement plans to close gaps related to compliance. School goals are limited to improving test scores versus improving student learning. Reactive to compliance reports, these plans are usually about "fixing the kids" by prescribing add-on interventions. | Proactively write continuous school improvement plans to implement a vision that improves learning for *all* students and prepares them for college and careers. The plan interweaves the leadership structure, professional learning, and partnerships needed to implement the vision. |
| **Leadership** | Have top-down leadership that requires a focus on compliance and closing gaps. Areas of emphasis change as leaders change. | Create shared decision-making structures that support each other as they implement the vision, and improve learning for all students |
| **Professional Learning** | Use professional learning as a carrot and a stick. "If we are failing in this area, everyone has to go to this workshop."<br><br>Without new information, teachers do the same things over and over and hope for different results. | Understand that *collaboration* is required to improve teaching and learning. They build structures for all staff to collaborate and learn together. Time is dedicated for collaborative teams to review and make meaning of classroom and schoolwide data, and to discuss and apply options for improving student learning. |
| **Partnerships** | Have top-down leadership that requires a focus on compliance and closing gaps. Areas of emphasis change as leaders change. | Create shared decision-making structures that support each other as they implement the vision, and improve learning for all students |
| **Evaluation** | Use evaluation when required for external accountability. | Use data to continuously improve all aspects of the learning organization. |
| **Compliance** | Focus on what is being measured for compliance purposes only, and are expert at gap analysis.<br><br>Are content with the status quo as long as it meets compliance requirements.<br><br>Look for the easiest routes to becoming "adequate," as in making Adequate Yearly Progress. | Focus on creating and improving the learning organization to ensure learning for *all* students in all subject areas, so all students can be college and career ready. Accountability and compliance are a part of the process, but not the sole focus. |

## PURPOSE OF THIS BOOK

*Data Analysis for Continuous School Improvement,* Third Edition, is a call to action. It is about inspiring schools and districts to commit to a continuous school improvement framework that will result in improving teaching for every teacher, and improving learning for every student, in one year, through the comprehensive use of data. It is about providing a new definition of improvement, away from compliance, toward a commitment to excellence. This book provides the framework for continuous school improvement and guides staff through the work of moving the entire system forward with examples and tools. Any staff can start wherever they are, follow along, and commit to new levels of improvement, data literacy, and data use.

Used in this context, *data literacy* is the ability to collect, analyze, communicate, and use multiple measures of data to continuously improve all aspects of the learning organization, especially teaching and learning. *Data use* is the ability to transform data into information and then into action to improve all aspects of the learning organization.

To grow a data literate staff that uses data for continuous school improvement, multiple measures of data must be organized and accessible so staff can spend their time analyzing, making meaning of the results, and collaborating with one another to improve instruction. Data use will not happen on its own. Structures for gathering, analyzing, and reporting data, and structures for collaborating and learning together must be created, modeled, monitored, and encouraged. An organizational shift away from a singular focus on compliance, toward a true commitment to improvement through a shared vision is required.

## STRUCTURE OF THIS BOOK

*Data Analysis for Continuous School Improvement,* Third Edition, starts with the framework for continuous school improvement and comprehensive data analysis. This book describes each of the components of the framework, structures that lead to a commitment to improved teaching and learning, and provides examples and activities for schools to do the work on their own. After the components are described, with references to tools to support the work of the components, a timeline for doing all the work within one school year is presented. All tools described in this text are provided in the chapters or appendices.

*"Data literacy" is the ability to collect, analyze, communicate, and use multiple measures of data to continuously improve all aspects of the learning organization, especially teaching and learning. "Data use" is the ability to transform data into information and then into action to improve all aspects of the learning organization.*

*To grow a data literate staff that uses data for continuous school improvement, multiple measures of data must be organized and accessible so staff can spend their time analyzing, making meaning of the results, and collaborating with one another to improve instruction.*

*All tools described in this text are provided in the chapters or appendices.*

## The Framework for Continuous School Improvement

Chapter 2, *The Continuous School Improvement Framework,* describes the framework for continuous school improvement that provides a simple, logical structure for reviewing and using multiple measures of data, creating and implementing a shared vision, and for measuring the impact of the vision and the vision implementation strategies on student learning.

## Gathering the Data and Cleaning Up the System

Chapter 3, *Who We Are:* Demographic Data; Chapter 4, *How We Do Business:* Perceptions Data; Chapter 5, *How Are Our Students Doing:* Student Learning Data; Chapter 6, *What Are Our Processes:* School Processes Data, feature the data (demographics, perceptions, student learning, and school processes) that are important for understanding *Where are we now?* in the continuous school improvement framework and in improving learning for *all* students. Each chapter defines a data category, why each is important for continuous school improvement, what data need to be gathered, and how to analyze, report, and use the data.

## Engaging Staff in Reviewing and Using Schoolwide Data

Chapter 7, *How Did We Get To Where We Are:* Looking Across All of the Data, describes how to engage staff in analyzing all types of data for comprehensive data analysis that will support your continuous school improvement efforts. This comprehensive data analysis sets up your school for planning, visioning, and evaluating.

## Going Deeper in the Data to Understand How the School is Getting Its Results

Chapter 8, *What Is Working and What Is Not Working:* Delving Deeper Into the Data, goes deep into a school's data to understand how the school is getting its current results. These analyses help staff understand what is working, what is not working, what to do to get different results, and add urgency to do so.

*It is the shared vision that allows staff to integrate large concepts into a single structure that everyone on staff can understand in the same way.*

## Engaging Staff in Creating a Shared Vision

Chapter 9, *Where Do We Want to Go:* Creating a Shared Vision and Monitoring Its Implementation, shows how to create, implement, and monitor a schoolwide, shared vision. It is the shared vision that allows staff to integrate large concepts into a single structure that everyone on staff can understand in the same way. It is the vision that ensures that data get used.

## Creating Structures to Implement the Shared Vision

**Chapter 10,** *How Are We Going to Get to Where We Want to Be:* **Implementing the Shared Vision by Creating a Plan for Continuous School Improvement,** describes how to create a continuous school improvement plan for implementing the shared vision in a manner that will lead to improved teaching and ultimately, increased student learning for *all* students. The collaborative structures that help with the implementation of the vision and plan include leadership, professional learning, and partnerships.

*The collaborative structures that help with the implementation of the vision and plan include leadership, professional learning, and partnerships.*

## Collaborating to Use Data

**Chapter 11,** *Strategies for Teachers:* **Using Data to Implement the Vision Through the Continuous School Improvement Plan to Improve Teaching and Learning,** discusses meaningful strategies for helping teachers collaborate to use data to improve their teaching, and the learning for *all* students.

## Evaluating the Work

**Chapter 12,** *Is What We Are Doing Making a Difference:* **Evaluating Our Efforts,** provides structures for mere mortals to use to evaluate their continuous school improvement efforts, including evaluation of programs and processes, the continuous school improvement plan, goals, and vision.

## Making the Time for Continuous School Improvement

**Chapter 13,** *Continuous School Improvement Timeline:* **Making Time to Do the Work,** pulls all the work together into a timeline, with cross-references to components described in preceding chapters, tools provided in the appendices, and a description of the artifacts a school would produce using the tools and information gained from this book.

## Transforming a Complying School to a Learning Organization

**Chapter 14,** *The Transformation From a Complying School to a Learning Organization,* concludes the book by reviewing how committing to and implementing continuous school improvement creates learning organizations that improve teaching and learning on an ongoing basis.

Each chapter ends with a notice about time, **How Much Time Does It Take?,** which describes how much time it would take to do the work described in each chapter.

Also, at the end of each chapter, are **Reflection Questions** and **Application Opportunities.** Reflection questions ensure that readers/book study groups capture the main concepts of each chapter. You might want to review these questions before you read the chapter, as they also serve as learner outcomes. The application opportunities guide school staff through the work of comprehensive data analysis and continuous school improvement.

**Appendices.** The appendices house the activities and strategies referenced in the chapters and the timeline. A list of appendices is shown with the Table of Contents. Some readers might wonder why some of the appendices were not placed in the chapters. Appendices that have multiple uses are placed in the back for easy access and multiple reference and application. For example, instead of splitting up the data profile graphs and placing some in each data chapter, the graphs are shown in total as a complete data profile that models what we want schools to put together. At the same time, the data profile can be used as a case study. Readers can see what it looks like in complete form; teams can follow it to create their data profile; and a facilitator can use the whole data profile as a practice case study.

## UPDATES

This book updates *Data Analysis for Continuous School Improvement* (Second Edition, 2004; and First Edition, 1998). It shares new, evidence-based learnings about how to analyze, report, communicate, and use multiple measures data for continuous school improvement, and also provides new tools, timelines, and strategies to help schools use data to improve teaching and learning. This book provides an updated continuous school improvement framework, explains the components and structures for using schoolwide data for the purpose of continuous school improvement, and organizes the information for easy retrieval and application.

## INTENDED AUDIENCE

The intended audiences for this book are—

1. School and district administrators and teachers working to engage, lead, and encourage all staff members to commit to using data to continuously improve their learning organizations.

2. College professors and students learning about continuous school improvement and data analysis implementation in schools. I would highly recommend the creation, analysis, and use of a data profile as a thesis or culminating project.

3. School staff book study groups. This book can help staff start, troubleshoot, and evaluate their own efforts.

4. District administrator book study groups. This book can help district administrators think about continuous school improvement implementation from the perspective of the schools, help them provide data for the schools, and help them implement a framework in which all their schools can thrive.

5. Leadership Training Programs, especially Performance-Based Leadership Courses, that are teaching administrative candidates about the impact strong leadership and data can have on the implementation of continuous school improvement in schools. *Data Analysis for Continuous School Improvement*, Third Edition, can be used to engage candidates in the work of continuous school improvement and comprehensive data analysis while getting certificated.

**My heartfelt hope** is that this book will prove to be so valuable that readers will never want to part with it in their lifetimes. I would love this book to be one of those books that graduate students keep with them after they complete their Administrative Credentials, Masters or Doctoral Programs, and find helpful throughout their careers.

## HOW MUCH TIME DOES IT TAKE?

**It will take one school year for a school staff to do all the work described in this book. If parts of the work are already done, a staff might still want to spread out the work throughout the year.**

## REFLECTION QUESTIONS

1. What would it take to get student learning increases for every student in your school?

2. Where does your school stand with respect to Figure 1.1?

3. Why might you read this book independently, or as a staff, to learn about how to improve teaching and learning through continuous school improvement and comprehensive data analysis?

4. What might help to engage your staff to commit to continuous school improvement and following the application opportunities at the end of each chapter?

## APPLICATION OPPORTUNITIES

1. Take an honest look at your school's student achievement results. Are the results improving in every grade level, subject area, student group, and for every student? If the answer is "no," please commit to engaging in these continuous school improvement efforts.

2. Review Figure 1.1. On which side of the figure does your school fall most often? Discuss with staff.

3. Does your staff want and need support in determining how to continuously improve all aspects of your learning organization? Join us in this journey. We will guide you through the process.

# THE CONTINUOUS SCHOOL IMPROVEMENT FRAMEWORK

**CHAPTER 2**

*Schools engaged in continuous school improvement clarify whom
they have as students, understand where the learning organization
is right now on all measures, consider processes as well as results,
create visions that make a difference for whom they have
as students, help everyone get on the same page with
understanding how to achieve the vision, and know if what
the learning organization is doing is making a difference.*

*Education for the Future*

Schools need a framework that is true to the roots of traditional continuous improvement to help them advance their entire systems—a framework to improve teaching for all teachers and learning for all students.

*Schools need a framework that is true to the roots of traditional continuous improvement to help them advance their entire systems—a framework to improve teaching for all teachers and learning for all students.*

## TRADITIONAL CONTINUOUS IMPROVEMENT

Traditional continuous improvement, made common all over the world by W. Edwards Deming during the twentieth century, starting in 1950, is a four-step plan-do-check-act (PDCA) or plan-do-study-adjust (PDSA) cycle, also known as the Deming Cycle or Shewhart Cycle, that guides organizations through process improvement using the scientific method of hypothesis, experiment, and evaluation. This process improvement approach is credited for taking many organizations from the brink of extinction to high quality production. The PDSA cycle is used by the International Organization for Standardization (ISO) as an approach to developing and improving management systems. Examples are ISO 14000 standards for environmental management systems and ISO 9000 for quality management systems. These continuous improvement standards provide structured approaches to setting objectives, achieving them, and verifying that they have been achieved.

PLAN-DO-CHECK-ACT (PDCA) CYCLE          PLAN-DO-STUDY-ADJUST (PDSA) CYCLE

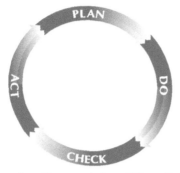

Reproduced by permission of Nancy R. Tague,
*The Quality Toolbox, Second Edition*
(Milwaukee: ASQ Quality Press, 2005).
To order this book, visit ASQ at:
*http://www.asq.org/quality-press.*

*Plan, Do, Check/Study, Act/Adjust* is defined as follows:

◆ **Plan:** Identify an opportunity and plan for change.

◆ **Do:** Implement the change.

◆ **Check/Study:** Use data to analyze the results of the change and determine whether the process made a difference. (Deming later changed *check* to *study* to deemphasize inspection and to emphasize analysis. PDSA.)

◆ **Act/Adjust:** If the change was successful, implement it on a wider scale and continuously assess the results. If the change was not successful, use what you learned, adjust, and begin the cycle again.

## CONTINUOUS SCHOOL IMPROVEMENT

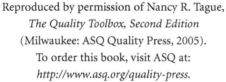

**Continuous School Improvement —**
- *Plan*
- *Implement*
- *Evaluate*
- *Improve*

Using the overall philosophy of continuous improvement, continuous school improvement is defined as the process of improving schools on an ongoing basis, as follows:

### Plan

◆ using data to understand where the school is now;

◆ understanding how the school is getting its current results;

◆ clarifying where the school wants to go, with respect to vision;

◆ determining how the school will get to where it wants to go;

### Implement

◆ implementing the processes and structures to take the school where it wants to go;

### Evaluate

♦ evaluating the parts and the whole on an ongoing basis to know if the parts are effective and aligned with where the school wants to go; and

### Improve

♦ improving the parts and the whole on an ongoing basis. Use what you learn, adjust, and begin the cycle again.

## THE CONTINUOUS SCHOOL IMPROVEMENT FRAMEWORK

Shifting from the historical to current times, *Education for the Future* created a framework using the concept of Plan-Implement-Evaluate-Improve, to move whole educational systems forward to continuous improvement. The continuous school improvement framework—

1. shows the big picture of continuous school improvement for whole staff understanding and commitment,

2. helps staff understand the components in the context of the conceptual framework, and

3. organizes the information in a way that makes it easy for staff to own, use, and apply.

> **The Continuous School Improvement Framework—**
>
> 1. *Shows the big picture of continuous school improvement for whole staff understanding and commitment,*
>
> 2. *Helps staff understand the components in the context of the conceptual framework, and*
>
> 3. *Organizes the information in a way that makes it easy for staff to own, use, and apply.*

Figure 2.1 displays the framework for continuous school improvement, helping schools create a learning organization that will make a difference for all students and all teachers. The framework consists of five simple, logical questions that incorporate continuous improvement principles: Plan, Implement, Evaluate, Improve.

♦ *Where are we now?*

♦ *How did we get to where we are?*

♦ *Where do we want to be?*

♦ *How are we going to get to where we want to be?*

♦ *Is what we are doing making a difference?*

These questions, or components of the framework, are presented in this chapter, along with why it is important to consider each question and the answers. The chapters and appendices that follow organize the information for easy application, show why each component is important, what it will look like when schools do this work, and how to engage staff members in the work.

Figure 2.1
CONTINUOUS SCHOOL IMPROVEMENT FRAMEWORK

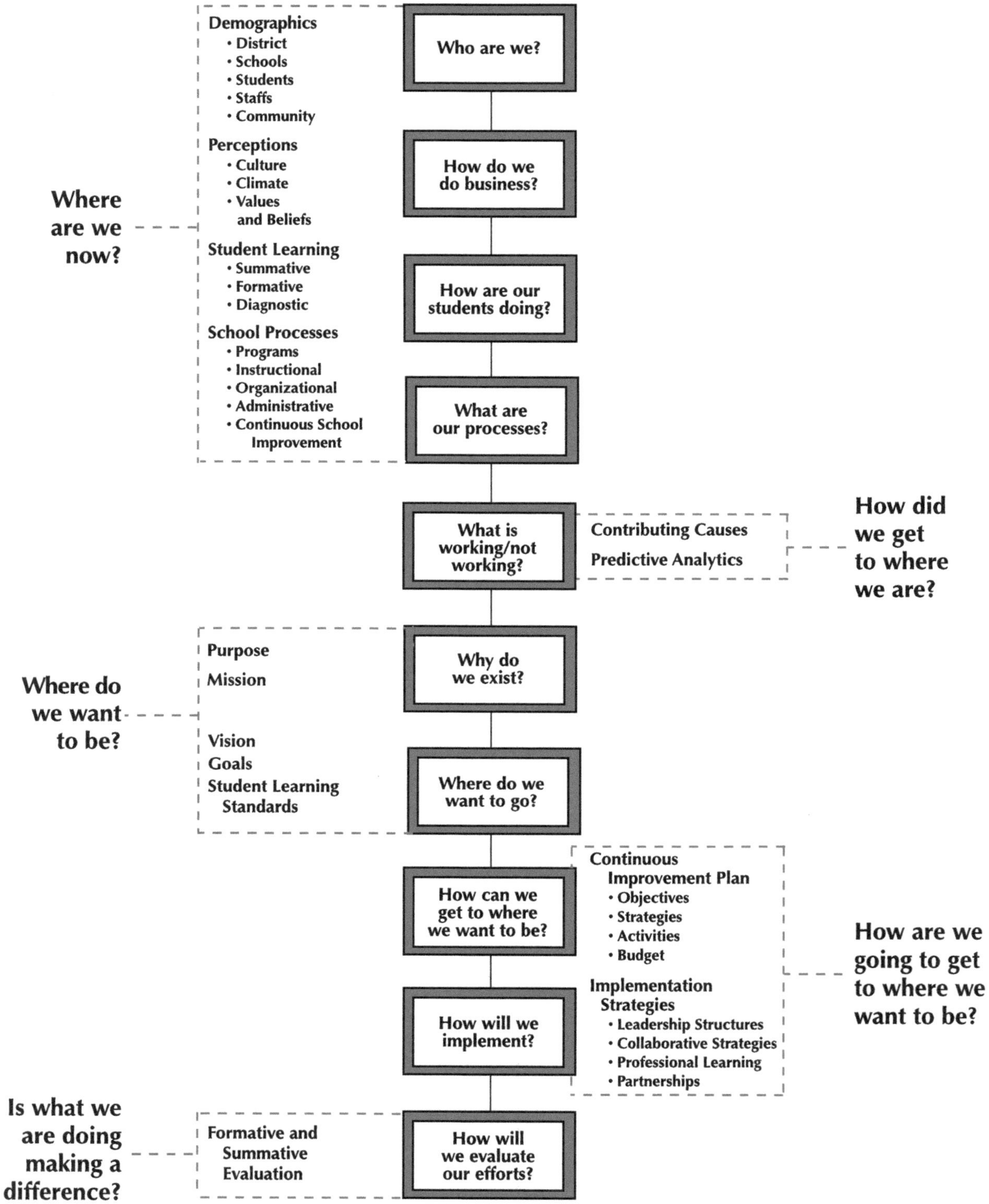

**Where are we now?**

Demographics
• District
• Schools
• Students
• Staffs
• Community

Perceptions
• Culture
• Climate
• Values and Beliefs

Student Learning
• Summative
• Formative
• Diagnostic

School Processes
• Programs
• Instructional
• Organizational
• Administrative
• Continuous School Improvement

**Who are we?**

**How do we do business?**

**How are our students doing?**

**What are our processes?**

**What is working/not working?**

Contributing Causes

Predictive Analytics

**How did we get to where we are?**

**Where do we want to be?**

Purpose

Mission

Vision

Goals

Student Learning Standards

**Why do we exist?**

**Where do we want to go?**

**How can we get to where we want to be?**

Continuous Improvement Plan
• Objectives
• Strategies
• Activities
• Budget

Implementation Strategies
• Leadership Structures
• Collaborative Strategies
• Professional Learning
• Partnerships

**How are we going to get to where we want to be?**

**How will we implement?**

**Is what we are doing making a difference?**

Formative and Summative Evaluation

**How will we evaluate our efforts?**

## Where Are We Now?

Knowing where a school is now is the part of planning for continuous school improvement that requires a comprehensive and honest look at *all* the school's data—not just student learning results. Looking at multiple measures of data can help staff answer the four sub-questions of ***Where are we now?***

- ◆ *Who are we?*
- ◆ *How do we do business?*
- ◆ *How are our students doing?* and
- ◆ *What are our processes?*

**Where are we now?**

> Who are we?

> How do we do business?

> How are our students doing?

> What are our processes?

*Knowing where a school is now is the part of planning for continuous school improvement that requires a comprehensive and honest look at all the school's data—not just student learning results.*

- ◆ *Who are we?* is answered through analysis of longitudinal demographic data. The current year's data can help staff see whom they have as students, and how the students are matched to whom they have as staff. The longitudinal analysis can help staff know how their populations have changed, and clarify what staff need to learn to meet the needs of whom they have as students. In demographic data, staff can see the system and leadership philosophies. Chapter 3 describes what demographic data are important, and how to report and analyze these data for continuous school improvement.

- ◆ *How do we do business?* is mostly answered through perceptions and organizational assessments which inform staff about how the learning environment is set up for student and teacher success. Culture and climate, which reflect how the learning organization does business, help create the results the school is getting. Looking over time, staff can see progress is being made when culture and climate are improved. Chapter 4 explains the importance and uses of perceptual data in continuous school improvement.

- ◆ *How are our students doing?* is answered through instruction-infused and formative and summative assessments, and helps staff know that students are learning what they are being taught. Over time, teachers can see individual student, teacher-classroom, grade, and school-level growth. Chapter 5 provides details for inventorying and analyzing student learning data for continuous school improvement.

- ◆ *What are our processes?* is answered through listing and analyzing programs and processes and shows what staff are doing to get the results they are getting. After listing the school's processes and programs, it is important to describe each process and program's purpose, outcomes,

*Answering the four sub-questions of **Where are we now?***

- • **Who are we?** *is answered through analysis of longitudinal demographic data.*

- • **How do we do business?** *is mostly answered through perceptions and organizational assessments.*

- • **How are our students doing?** *is answered through instruction-infused and formative and summative assessments.*

- • **What are our processes?** *is answered through listing and analyzing programs and processes.*

intended participants, how they are to be implemented, how implementation is being measured, and the results. If programs cannot be described and their implementation spelled out, faculties cannot implement them with *integrity* (i.e., the adherence to the intent and purpose) and *fidelity* (i.e., the delivery of content and instructional strategies in the way in which they were designed and intended to be delivered–accurately and consistently). Chapter 6 focuses on listing and measuring school processes.

*If you took all the data needed to answer the questions above, they would fall into four major categories of demographics, perceptions, student learning, and school processes.*

If you took all the data needed to answer the questions above, they would fall into four major categories of demographics, perceptions, student learning, and school processes. Figure 2.2 shows these four categories of data as overlapping circles. This figure illustrates the different types of information one can gain from each data type, with one year of data and over time, and the enhanced levels of analyses that can be gained from the intersections of the measures. Intersections of the four data categories are described in Chapter 8.

## How Did We Get to Where We Are?

*Looking across the four types of data allows schools to see what they are doing to get the results they are getting now, what is working, what is not working, and how data elements relate to each other to impact results.*

One measure, by itself, gives useful information. Looking across the four types of data allows schools to see what they are doing to get the results they are getting now, what is working, what is not working, and how data elements relate to each other to impact results. These analyses become comprehensive needs assessments, inform planning and visioning, and provide the data needed for evaluation. Chapter 7 details how school staff can analyze and use this comprehensive data analysis to inform a vision and create a plan for continuous school improvement. Chapter 8 shows how to go deeper into the data to understand contributing causes of undesirable results and how to predict and ensure success.

**How did we get to where we are?**

> **What is working/not working?**

It is particularly important to know how the school is getting its current results in all areas, so processes that are achieving the school's desired results are repeated, and those not making a difference can be eliminated.

## Where Do We Want to Be?

*Without a shared vision to which all staff members commit, a school's collective efforts have no target.*

A school defines its purpose through its mission, vision, goals, and objectives. The school's mission, vision, and goals must be created from the core values and beliefs of the staff. Creating a vision from core values and beliefs ensures a vision that all staff members can share and to which they can and will commit. Without a shared vision to which all staff members commit, a school's collective efforts have no

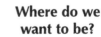

**Where do we want to be?**

> **Why do we exist?**

> **Where do we want to go?**

Figure 2.2
## MULTIPLE MEASURES OF DATA

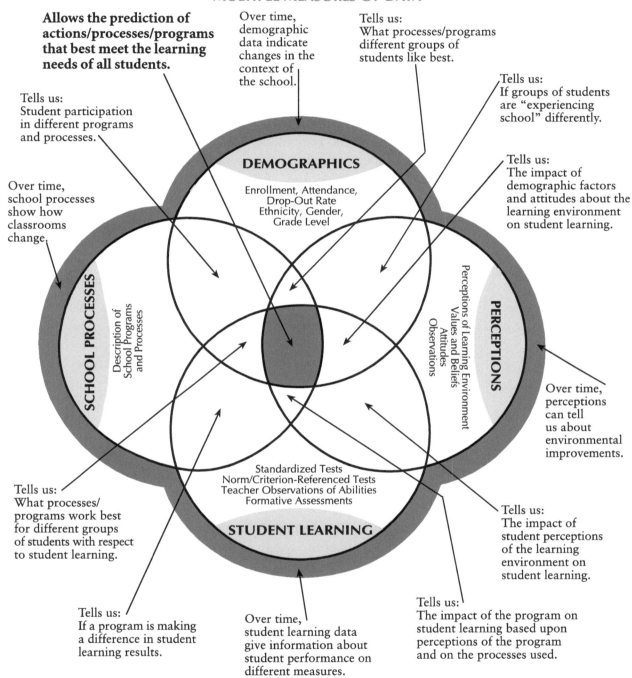

**Allows the prediction of actions/processes/programs that best meet the learning needs of all students.**

Over time, demographic data indicate changes in the context of the school.

Tells us: What processes/programs different groups of students like best.

Tells us: Student participation in different programs and processes.

Tells us: If groups of students are "experiencing school" differently.

Over time, school processes show how classrooms change.

Tells us: The impact of demographic factors and attitudes about the learning environment on student learning.

**DEMOGRAPHICS**
Enrollment, Attendance, Drop-Out Rate Ethnicity, Gender, Grade Level

**SCHOOL PROCESSES**
Description of School Programs and Processes

Perceptions of Learning Environment Values and Beliefs Attitudes Observations

**PERCEPTIONS**

Over time, perceptions can tell us about environmental improvements.

Standardized Tests
Norm/Criterion-Referenced Tests
Teacher Observations of Abilities
Formative Assessments

**STUDENT LEARNING**

Tells us: What processes/ programs work best for different groups of students with respect to student learning.

Tells us: The impact of student perceptions of the learning environment on student learning.

Tells us: If a program is making a difference in student learning results.

Over time, student learning data give information about student performance on different measures.

Tells us: The impact of the program on student learning based upon perceptions of the program and on the processes used.

*The answer to "How are we going to get to where we want to be?" is key to unlocking how the vision will be implemented and how results will be optimized.*

*Leadership structures, professional learning with structured collaboration to share data, and partnership involvement are key elements for ensuring staff commitment to the implementation of the shared vision.*

*Evaluation and reflective learning are required to assess the effectiveness of all school programs and processes, the alignment of all parts of the system to the vision, and to determine if what a school is doing is making a difference for students on an ongoing basis.*

target. A truly shared vision becomes the target for all that happens in the school. Chapter 9 specifies how to create and monitor the implementation of a shared vision.

## How Are We Going to Get to Where We Want to Be?

The answer to *How are we going to get to where we want to be?* is key to unlocking how the vision will be implemented and how results will be optimized. A continuous school improvement plan consisting of goals, objectives, strategies, activities, measurement of strategies and activities, person(s) responsible, due dates, timelines, and required resources, needs to be developed to implement and achieve the vision and goals, to eliminate the contributing causes of undesirable results, and to optimize results.

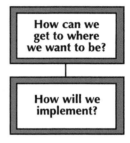

Leadership structures, professional learning with structured collaboration to share data, and partnership involvement are key elements for ensuring staff commitment to the implementation of the shared vision. Continuous school improvement plans must include how and when decisions will be made, identify professional learning and collaboration required to gain new skills and knowledge, and clarify how working with partners will help with achieving the vision. Chapter 10 describes how to create a continuous school improvement plan, complete with the leadership, professional learning, and partnership structures that will ensure the implementation of the vision and plan. Chapter 11 focuses on utilizing strategies to support educator collaboration for data use that will lead to improved teaching and learning.

## Is What We Are Doing Making a Difference?

Evaluation and reflective learning are required to assess the effectiveness of all school programs and processes, the alignment of all parts of the system to the vision, and to determine if what a school is doing is making a difference for students on an ongoing basis. Evaluations at the end of the year allow reflection on all the parts of the system, the alignment of the parts to the whole, and the appraisal of whether or not the school made the difference as expected. Chapter 12 reviews the different types of evaluation most needed in continuous school improvement, and how to best accomplish them.

**Is what we are doing making a difference?**

How will we evaluate our efforts?

## Continuous School Improvement Cycle

Figure 2.3 shows the continuous school improvement framework questions in the traditional PDSA cycle, with contemporary and school-focused terms, plan-implement-evaluate-improve, and vision located at the center. The questions fall into the cycle as follows:

With continuous school improvement, the vision is the target of everything that is done in the school. Schools PLAN to implement the vision by determining—

◆ *Where they are now,* through comprehensive data analysis;

◆ *How they got to where they are right now,* through deeper study of the results of current processes;

*With continuous school improvement, the vision is the target of everything that is done in the school.*

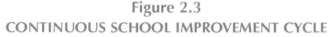

### Figure 2.3
### CONTINUOUS SCHOOL IMPROVEMENT CYCLE

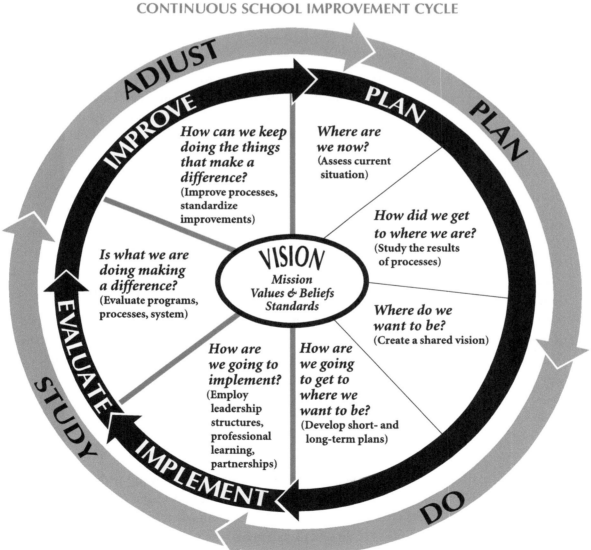

◆ *Where they want to be,* by creating or revisiting the vision and placing it at the center of everything they do; and

◆ *How they are going to get to the vision,* through short-term and long-term plans.

Note that the elements of Plan-Do-Study-Adjust (PDSA) are not equally distributed in reality. PLANNING takes up half of the cycle—more than the traditional cycle implies. There is a lot to do before implementation can begin.

Schools IMPLEMENT the vision using leadership structures, professional learning, and partnerships. They EVALUATE programs, processes, and the vision to know if what they are doing is making a difference. Then, they adjust and IMPROVE by continuing to do the things that are making a difference and stop doing the things that are not making a difference. And the cycle repeats.

## FROM COMPLIANCE TO CONTINUOUS SCHOOL IMPROVEMENT

The framework for continuous school improvement shown in Figure 2.1 sounds so simple and logical, most schools think they are already doing it. However, many schools skip the first three components of the continuous school improvement framework and begin their school improvement plans by looking at the gaps between where they are now and where they want to be with respect to summative student learning results, only. While these data provide valuable information, starting here does not give schools a complete picture. By starting and ending with the gaps, schools miss the opportunities to innovate, rethink, and improve their systems. By starting and ending with the summative testing gaps, schools tend to add interventions to "fix the kids." By starting with comprehensive data analysis, schools see how they are getting their current results. Then, with their vision, they can determine what *they* need to do to get different results for *all* students.

Figure 2.4 repeats the framework for continuous school improvement (previously seen in Figure 2.1), pointing out where schools too often begin and end their school improvement efforts. This is what complying to solely close gaps looks like.

## ASSESSING CONTINUOUS SCHOOL IMPROVEMENT WITH THE EDUCATION FOR THE FUTURE CONTINUOUS IMPROVEMENT CONTINUUMS

A tool we use to help schools reflect on where they are with continuous school improvement are the *Education for the Future Continuous Improvement Continuums* (CICs). Appearing in Appendix A, with complete instructions on how to use them, the *Continuums* help school staff know where their learning organizations are and what they need to do next with respect to continuous school improvement. The

*By starting and ending with the gaps, schools miss the opportunities to innovate, rethink, and improve their systems.*

*By starting with comprehensive data analysis, schools see how they are getting their current results.*

*The Education for the Future Continuous Improvement Continuums (CICs) appear in Appendix A with complete instructions on how to use them, and help school staff know where their learning organizations are and what they need to do next with respect to continuous school improvement.*

## Figure 2.4
## CONTINUOUS SCHOOL IMPROVEMENT FRAMEWORK—WITH FOCUS ON COMPLIANCE

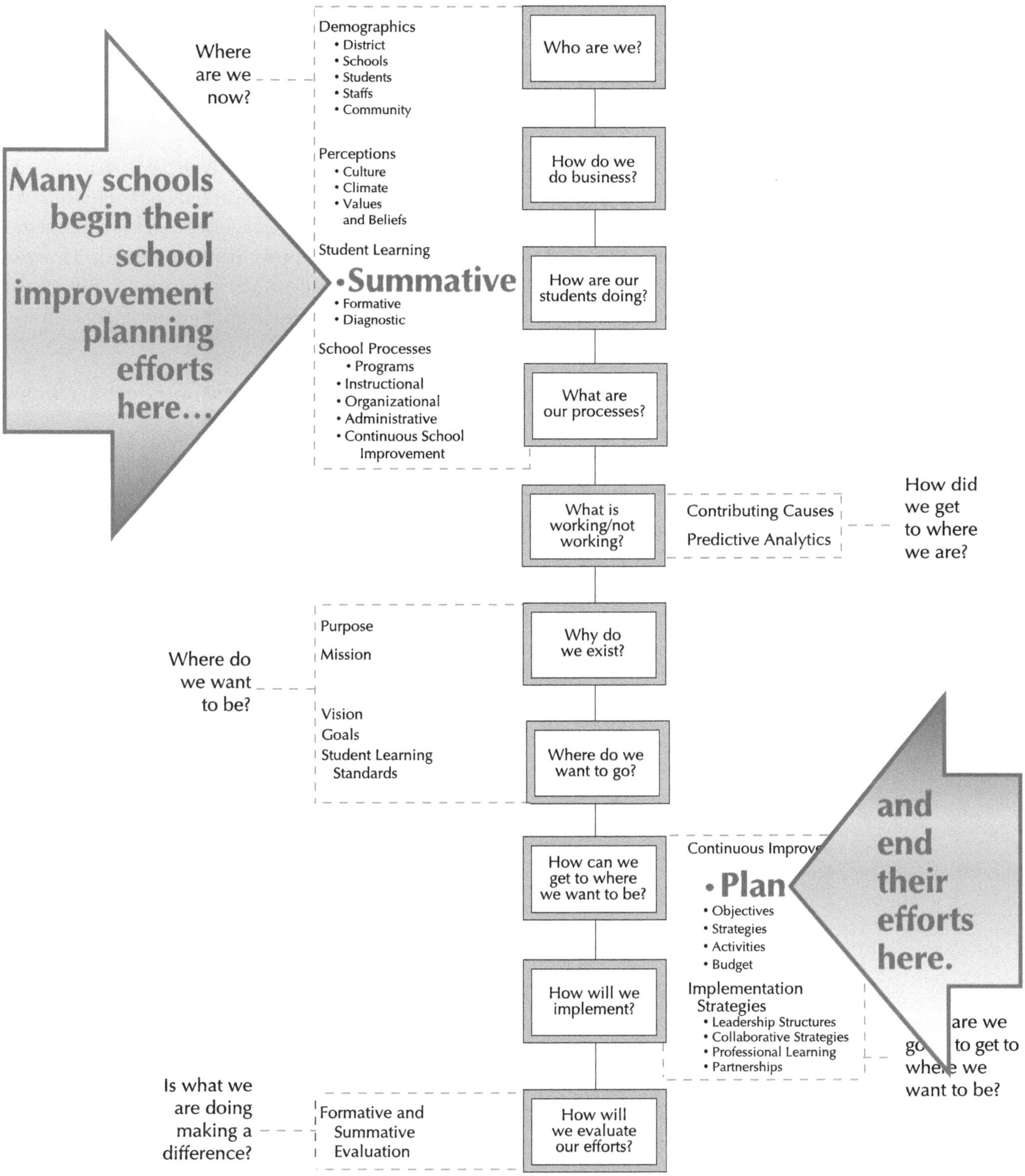

**Many schools begin their school improvement planning efforts here...**

Where are we now?

Demographics
- District
- Schools
- Students
- Staffs
- Community

Perceptions
- Culture
- Climate
- Values and Beliefs

Student Learning
- **Summative**
- Formative
- Diagnostic

School Processes
- Programs
- Instructional
- Organizational
- Administrative
- Continuous School Improvement

Who are we?

How do we do business?

How are our students doing?

What are our processes?

What is working/not working?

Contributing Causes

Predictive Analytics

How did we get to where we are?

Where do we want to be?

Purpose

Mission

Vision
Goals
Student Learning Standards

Why do we exist?

Where do we want to go?

How can we get to where we want to be?

Continuous Improve...

**Plan**
- Objectives
- Strategies
- Activities
- Budget

Implementation Strategies
- Leadership Structures
- Collaborative Strategies
- Professional Learning
- Partnerships

How will we implement?

**and end their efforts here.**

...are we go... to get to whe...e we want to be?

Is what we are doing making a difference?

Formative and Summative Evaluation

How will we evaluate our efforts?

*Continuous Improvement Continuums,* adapted from the *Malcolm Baldrige Award Program for Quality Business Management,* provide an authentic means for measuring schoolwide improvement and growth. Schools use these Continuums as a vehicle for ongoing self-assessment. They use the results of the assessment to acknowledge their accomplishments, to set goals for improvement, and to keep school districts and partners apprised of the progress they have made in their continuous school improvement efforts.

The *Continuous Improvement Continuums* are self-assessment tools that measure, on a one-to-five scale, where the school is with respect to its *approach, implementation,* and *outcome* for seven continuous improvement categories that are congruent with the components of the continuous school improvement framework. Those seven categories are Information and Analysis, Student Achievement, Quality Planning, Professional Learning, Leadership, Partnership Development, and Continuous Improvement and Evaluation.

Figure 2.5 shows the first in the series of seven, *Information and Analysis Continuum,* with descriptions of each of the five levels, summarized below.

◆ A "one" rating, located at the left of each *Continuum,* represents a school that has not yet begun to improve. Decisions are reactive.

> **The seven *Continuous Improvement Continuums* categories are—**
>
> · *Information and Analysis*
> · *Student Achievement*
> · *Quality Planning*
> · *Professional Learning*
> · *Leadership*
> · *Partnership Development*
> · *Continuous Improvement and Evaluation*

◆ A "two" rating implies that there are some good things going on in some places in the school, some of the time. Decisions are usually made on a problem-solving basis—when they are required.

◆ A "three" rating indicates that there is a system in place to do the work of the *Continuum.* There is also a system for making decisions.

◆ At a "four" level, schools have a system in place, everyone knows it, and it becomes the way business is done and decisions are made.

◆ "Five", located at the right of each *Continuum,* represents a school that is one step removed from "world class quality." The school knows how it gets its best results, which is optimized throughout the system. All decisions are proactive.

The elements from one to five describe how that *Continuum* is hypothesized to evolve in a continuously improving school. Each *Continuum* moves from a reactive mode to a proactive mode—from fire fighting to prevention. The five in Approach, Implementation, and Outcome in each *Continuum* is the target. Vertically, the Approach, Implementation, and Outcome statements, for any number one through five, are hypotheses. In other words, the implementation statement describes how

Figure 2.5

CONTINUOUS IMPROVEMENT CONTINUUMS FOR SCHOOLS ~ INFORMATION AND ANALYSIS

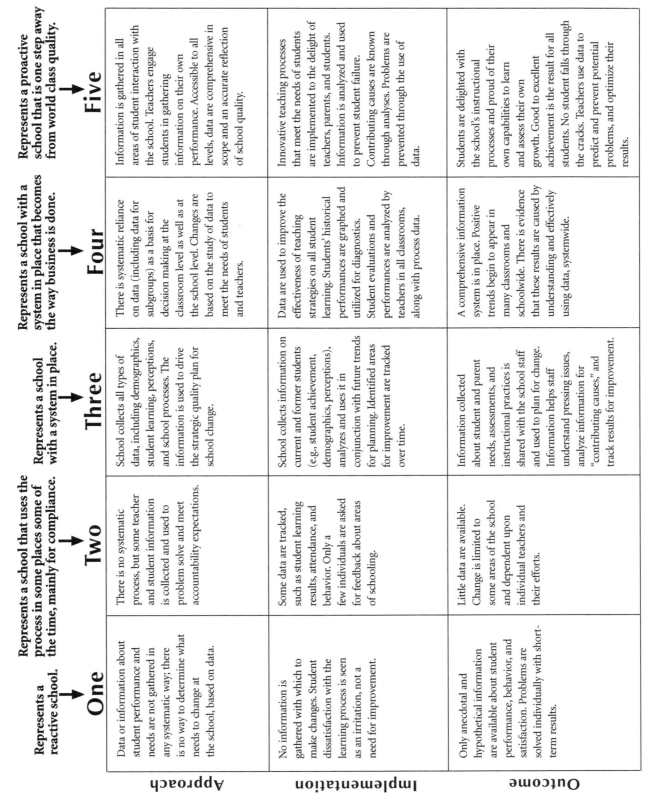

| | **One**<br>Represents a reactive school. | **Two**<br>Represents a school that uses the process in some places some of the time, mainly for compliance. | **Three**<br>Represents a school with a system in place. | **Four**<br>Represents a school with a system in place that becomes the way business is done. | **Five**<br>Represents a proactive school that is one step away from world class quality. |
|---|---|---|---|---|---|
| **Approach** | Data or information about student performance and needs are not gathered in any systematic way; there is no way to determine what needs to change at the school, based on data. | There is no systematic process, but some teacher and student information is collected and used to problem solve and meet accountability expectations. | School collects all types of data, including demographics, student learning, perceptions, and school processes. The information is used to drive the strategic quality plan for school change. | There is systematic reliance on data (including data for subgroups) as a basis for decision making at the classroom level as well as at the school level. Changes are based on the study of data to meet the needs of students and teachers. | Information is gathered in all areas of student interaction with the school. Teachers engage students in gathering information on their own performance. Accessible to all levels, data are comprehensive in scope and an accurate reflection of school quality. |
| **Implementation** | No information is gathered with which to make changes. Student dissatisfaction with the learning process is seen as an irritation, not a need for improvement. | Some data are tracked, such as student learning results, attendance, and behavior. Only a few individuals are asked for feedback about areas of schooling. | School collects information on current and former students (e.g., student achievement, demographics, perceptions), analyzes and uses it in conjunction with future trends for planning. Identified areas for improvement are tracked over time. | Data are used to improve the effectiveness of teaching strategies on all student learning. Students' historical performances are graphed and utilized for diagnostics. Student evaluations and performances are analyzed by teachers in all classrooms, along with process data. | Innovative teaching processes that meet the needs of students are implemented to the delight of teachers, parents, and students. Information is analyzed and used to prevent student failure. Contributing causes are known through analyses. Problems are prevented through the use of data. |
| **Outcome** | Only anecdotal and hypothetical information are available about student performance, behavior, and satisfaction. Problems are solved individually with short-term results. | Little data are available. Change is limited to some areas of the school and dependent upon individual teachers and their efforts. | Information collected about student and parent needs, assessments, and instructional practices is shared with the school staff and used to plan for change. Information helps staff understand pressing issues, analyze information for "contributing causes," and track results for improvement. | A comprehensive information system is in place. Positive trends begin to appear in many classrooms and schoolwide. There is evidence that these results are caused by understanding and effectively using data, systemwide. | Students are delighted with the school's instructional processes and proud of their own capabilities to learn and assess their own growth. Good to excellent achievement is the result for all students. No student falls through the cracks. Teachers use data to predict and prevent potential problems, and optimize their results. |

*Measuring a school's progress against identified criteria— such as the Education for the Future Continuous Improvement Continuums— provides a benchmark that schools can use to see if their actions have created the results they intended.*

the approach might look when implemented, and the outcome is the "pay-off" for implementing the approach. If the hypotheses are accurate, the outcome will not be realized until the approach is actually implemented.

Measuring a school's progress against identified criteria—such as the *Education for the Future Continuous Improvement Continuums*—provides a benchmark that schools can use to see if their actions have created the results they intended. These measures are supported by analyzing data gathered through questionnaires, performance measures, and observations of the learning environment. When these measures are used on a regular basis, the results clearly document trends and provide information that assists schools in determining next steps for improvement.

## ASSESSING ON THE CONTINUOUS IMPROVEMENT CONTINUUMS

In a whole-staff meeting, the facilitator (preferably not the principal, so she/he can participate in the discussion) introduces a *Continuum,* such as *Information and Analysis,* shown as Figure 2.5. Each staff member independently reads the *Continuum* from left to right, from a one and to a five, and identifies where she/he believes the school is right now, with respect to Approach, Implementation, and Outcome. Staff members place a colorful dot on the *Continuum* (enlarged and placed on the wall before staff arrived at the meeting) where they believe the *school* is with respect to Approach, Implementation, and Outcome. After everyone has placed her or his dot on the poster, staff discusses why they thought the school was a one, two, three, four, or five. After coming to consensus, staff members discuss what they need to do to move up in the *Continuum,* and the facilitator records next steps. They continue through the seven *Continuous Improvement Continuums.* By the time they have finished, it is clear to everyone in the school where they are as an organization and what they must do to improve.

Figure 2.6 shows the *Information and Analysis Continuum* completed by a staff in the Fall, on the left, and in the Spring, on the right. In the Fall, staff members felt they were somewhere between a two and a four most of the time—a school that has not been collaborating well. Some staff members believe data are only used when they have to, while others believe they use data all the time. The interesting part is to consider which dots represent the staff members who actually write the school improvement plan. Yes; they are the fours. They wonder why their plans are not implemented! After clarifying what they have for data and how they really do use data, they discuss next steps, and implement them.

Staff assessed again in the Spring. This time, as the picture on the right shows, they moved almost all the twos to at least threes. In other words, they picked up a portion of their staff and got them on the same page. With clarity of what they are really doing and what they need to do, the whole school can move ahead.

## Figure 2.6
## EXAMPLE OF CONTINUOUS IMPROVEMENT CONTINUUM ASSESSMENT, FALL AND SPRING

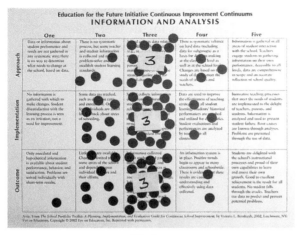

FALL                    SPRING

Assessing on the *Continuous Improvement Continuums* is a powerful way to find out what staff are believing, and therefore, acting on, with respect to the components of continuous school improvement. This assessment will show clearly why the school is getting its current results. By understanding staff preconceptions, we have a way to engage staff members, and bring them forward together. The discussion will automatically lead staff to what they need to do to get different results. Schools need only to assess once a year, although many schools choose to assess twice the first year.

Schools use these *Continuums* annually as a vehicle for ongoing self-assessment. School staffs use the assessments to renew staff commitment to continuous school improvement. They use the results of the assessments to—

◆ find out where they really are, as a staff;

◆ acknowledge their accomplishments;

◆ get all staff on the same page;

◆ set goals for improvement; and

◆ keep school districts and partners apprised of the progress they have made in their continuous school improvement efforts.

*Assessing on the Continuous Improvement Continuums is a powerful way to find out what staff are believing, and therefore, acting upon, with respect to the components of continuous school improvement.*

## HOW MUCH TIME DOES IT TAKE?

**Providing staff with an overview of the continuous school improvement framework, assessing on the *Education for the Future Continuous Improvement Continuums,* and discussing next steps will take about three hours.**

## REFLECTION QUESTIONS

1. What is continuous school improvement?

2. Why is it important to have a framework for continuous school improvement?

3. What are the five essential questions of continuous school improvement?

## APPLICATION OPPORTUNITIES

1. Provide an overview of the *Continuous School Improvement Framework* for staff.

2. As you review the *Continuous School Improvement Framework* (Figure 2.1), determine which components are missing from your school's continuous school improvement efforts.

3. Conduct an assessment on the *Continuous Improvement Continuums* (Appendix A) to find out where staff believe your school is right now and to determine what has to happen next to improve.

**CHAPTER 3**

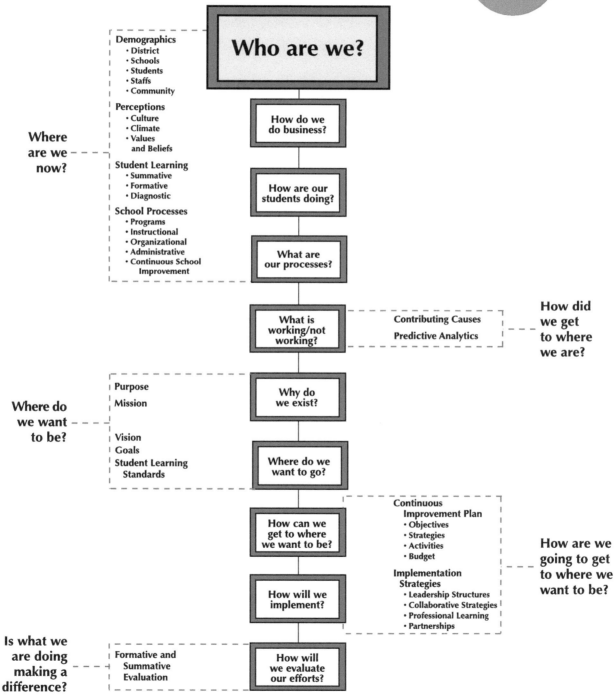

**Where are we now?**

Demographics
- District
- Schools
- Students
- Staffs
- Community

Perceptions
- Culture
- Climate
- Values and Beliefs

Student Learning
- Summative
- Formative
- Diagnostic

School Processes
- Programs
- Instructional
- Organizational
- Administrative
- Continuous School Improvement

**Who are we?**

**How do we do business?**

**How are our students doing?**

**What are our processes?**

**What is working/not working?**

Contributing Causes

Predictive Analytics

**How did we get to where we are?**

**Where do we want to be?**

Purpose
Mission

Vision
Goals
Student Learning Standards

**Why do we exist?**

**Where do we want to go?**

**How can we get to where we want to be?**

Continuous Improvement Plan
- Objectives
- Strategies
- Activities
- Budget

Implementation Strategies
- Leadership Structures
- Collaborative Strategies
- Professional Learning
- Partnerships

**How are we going to get to where we want to be?**

**How will we implement?**

**Is what we are doing making a difference?**

Formative and Summative Evaluation

**How will we evaluate our efforts?**

*Demographic data are extremely important for continuous school improvement. Demographics establish the current context of the school and describe trends. Trends help staffs predict and plan for the future, as well as understand all other data with which they work in their continuous school improvement efforts. Comprehensive demographic data inform about the structure of the school—the system—as well as leadership.*

*Education for the Future*

An excellent place to begin comprehensive data analysis is with the study of demographic data. Demographic data set the context for the school, describe those who are teaching and learning in the school, and help us understand all other numbers.

## DEMOGRAPHIC DATA: WHAT THEY ARE AND WHY THEY ARE IMPORTANT TO CONTINUOUS SCHOOL IMPROVEMENT

*Demographic data answer the continuous school improvement question, "Who are we?" Demographics establish the current context of the school and describe trends.*

Demographic data answer the continuous school improvement question, *Who are we?* Demographics establish the current context of the school and describe trends. Trends help staff predict and plan for the future, as well as understand all other measures with which they work in their continuous school improvement efforts. Comprehensive demographic data inform staff about the structure of the school— the system—as well as leadership.

### Demographics Describe Human Population Characteristics

Demographics are typically known as the statistical characteristics of human populations (such as age or ethnicity). In education, demographic data translate to items such as—

- ◆ number of students in the school,
- ◆ number of students with special needs,
- ◆ number of ESL students,
- ◆ age or grade of students in each cohort,
- ◆ socio-economical level of student population,
- ◆ teacher and student attendance,
- ◆ ethnicities/races/religious beliefs of the students and teachers in the school,
- ◆ number of graduates,

- number of students who drop out of school each year, and
- number of teachers by years of experience, and teaching assignments.

Through the study of demographic trends, we can predict with some accuracy such things as the number of students and the ethnic diversity with which the school can expect to work in the future. From an historical perspective, a school can use demographic data in its analyses of how well it has served its past and current populations and identify professional learning and changes needed to meet the needs of its future clients. It is very important for teachers to understand how the student population learns best, and to provide instruction to help all students learn. Most demographic factors can be mitigated with proper interventions.

## Demographics Describe the System

Demographic data do so much more than just inform us of human characteristics. Demographics also tell us about the system: how the parts relate and fit together to create the whole. For example, how a school staff disciplines students, what teachers and administrators do when students are absent, and how students are placed in different programs create the system that generates the school's results. Class sizes, number of years of teacher experience by grade level, number of students in special education programs, by gender and ethnicity, and the subgroups of students enrolled in different programs, such as advanced placement, or honors, are all part of demographics that make up the system.

Demographic data are not static data. Demographic data show the philosophy of the school, through indicators of which and how students are disciplined, identified for special education, advanced placement, gifted programs, etc. When reviewing demographic data such as behavior and program enrollment, staff need to think about what they would like these data to look like, and what they need to do to get there.

All staff should know the school's demographic data. These contextual variables are critical and required for understanding all other information gathered about the school, and to know how to change processes.

## WHAT DEMOGRAPHIC DATA ARE IMPORTANT
## FOR THE LEARNING ORGANIZATION

Schools have lots of demographic data. Most schools have student information systems that house their demographic data, gathered on an ongoing basis. Figure 3.1 shows typical demographic data that staffs should know about their school. This figure appears in Appendix B1 as a *Demographic Data Inventory* to assist your school in organizing its demographic data.

*From an historical perspective, a school can use demographic data in its analyses of how well it has served its past and current populations and identify professional learning and changes needed to meet the needs of its future clients.*

*Demographic data show the philosophy of the school, through indicators of which and how students are disciplined, identified for special education, advanced placement, gifted programs, etc.*

Figure 3.1
TYPICAL DEMOGRAPHIC DATA TO GATHER

| Community (Descriptive) | Students, Over Time, and by Grade Level *(Continued)* |
|---|---|
| • Location and history<br>• Economic base, population trends, and community resources (*www.census.gov* is a great resource for getting information about the community, as is your local chamber of commerce)<br>• Community involvement<br>• Business partnership | • Special Education by disability, gender, ethnicity, language fluency, free/reduced lunch<br>• Attendance/tardies<br>• Mobility (where students go/come from)<br>• Retention rates by gender, ethnicity, language fluency, free/reduced lunch<br>• Dropout rates by gender, ethnicity, free/reduced lunch, migrant, and special education (where students go/what they do) |
| **School District (Descriptive)** | • Number of students leaving middle school overall for grade, by gender, ethnicity, language fluency, free/reduced lunch |
| • Description and history<br>• Number of schools, administrators, students and teachers over time, and by grade level | • Extracurricular activity participation/clubs/service learning by gender, ethnicity, language fluency, free/reduced lunch |
| **School (Descriptive)** | • Number and types of participants in programs, such as AP, IB, Honors, Upward Bound, Gear-up, college-prep, vocational |
| • Description and history, attendance area, location<br>• Type of school, e.g., magnet, alternative, charter, private, private management<br>• Number of administrators, students and teachers over time, and by grade level<br>• Number of students electing to come to the school from out of the attendance area<br>• Grants and awards received<br>• Title 1/Schoolwide<br>• Safety/crime data<br>• State designation as a dangerous school<br>• Class sizes<br>• Extracurricular activities<br>• After-school programs/summer school<br>• Tutoring/peer mentoring<br>• Community support-services coordinated<br>• Counseling opportunities<br>• Facilities: equipped for networked computers and handicapped<br>• Facilities: age, capacity, maintenance<br>• Availability of supplies and necessities<br>• Uniqueness and strengths | • Number and types of participants in any programs<br>• Number of home schoolers associated with school<br>• Number of students electing to come to the school from out-of-attendance area<br>• Number of bus riders<br>• Student employment<br>• Discipline indicators (e.g., suspensions, referrals, types of incidences, number of students carrying weapons on school property, who, what, when, where)<br>• Number of drugs on school property (offered, sold, or given drugs)<br>• Graduation rates by gender, ethnicity, language proficiency, free/reduced lunch, migrant, and special education (where students go/what they do)<br>• Dropout rates, by gender, ethnicity, language proficiency, free/reduced lunch, migrant, and special education (where students go/what they do/how many come back to finish)<br>• Number of students concurrently enrolled in college courses |
| **Students, Over Time, and by Grade Level** | • Number of students meeting college course entrance requirements, by gender, ethnicity, language fluency, free/reduced lunch |
| • Living situation/family structure/family size/homeless<br>• Preschool/Head Start/Even Start<br>• Preschool attendance<br>• Gender of students<br>• Race/ethnicity, numbers and percentages<br>• Free/reduced lunch, numbers and percentages<br>• Language fluency by language<br>• Migrant/immigrants, by country, home languages | • Number of scholarships, by gender, ethnicity, language fluency, free/reduced lunch<br>• Number of students completing GEDs<br>• Adult education program<br>• Number and percentage of students going on to college; postgraduate training; and/or employment<br>• Grade-point average in college<br>• Number of graduates enrolled in college remedial classes |

**Figure 3.1** *(Continued)*
## TYPICAL DEMOGRAPHIC DATA TO GATHER

### Staff, Over Time

- Number of teachers, administrators, instructional specialists, support staff by assignments
- Grade/subjects teachers are teaching
- Years of experience, by grade level and/or role, in this school/in teaching
- Ethnicity, gender, languages spoken
- Retirement projections
- Types of certifications/licenses/teacher qualifications/ percentage of time teaching in certified area(s)
- National Board for Professional Teaching Standards (NBPTS) teachers
- Degrees
- Educational training of paraprofessionals
- Teacher-student ratios by grade level
- Teacher turnover rates
- Attendance rates
- Teacher involvement in extracurricular activities, program participation
- Number of teachers receiving high-quality professional development that impact classroom performance

### Parents

- Educational levels, home language, employment, socioeconomic status
- Involvement with their child's learning
- Involvement in school activities
- Incarceration

### Other Demographic Data

## SEEING THE SYSTEM AND LEADERSHIP IN DEMOGRAPHIC DATA

After reviewing the list of demographic data, consider this question: "What demographic data elements can change when leadership changes?"

If you really think about it, you might be surprised to know that demographic data that we often consider *givens,* actually change when the leader changes. What the changes show are philosophies of how the adults treat students and other adults, and how the students treat other students and adults. Items that most obviously show change when leaders change include, discipline, attendance, who is assigned to Special Education (by gender and ethnicity), who is allowed to be Gifted or placed in Advanced Placement classes, and dropout and graduation rates. These philosophies often come with the leader. A strong staff, through shared visioning and intentional programming, can create a philosophy that can outlast a leader. Study your demographic data to make sure the data are relaying the philosophy you want your school to show. If not, change it.

*A strong staff, through shared visioning and intentional programming, can create a philosophy that can outlast a leader.*

## TELLING YOUR STORY BY RECORDING DEMOGRAPHIC INFORMATION IN A DATA PROFILE

School staff must organize, analyze, and use comprehensive data that include demographic data, for the continuous improvement of the whole school. Educators need to understand whom they are serving, and determine how well they are meeting the needs of the students they are serving. Staff need to see the interconnections of the data elements that lead to different results. A school data profile organizes and houses the school's demographic, perceptions, student learning, and school processes data in an easy to access fashion.

*A school data profile organizes and houses the school's demographic, perceptions, student learning, and school processes data in an easy to access fashion.*

A data profile systematically displays data from the general to the specific. To be most useful for staff review, we need to pick a point in time (census) to gather demographic data elements and then include at least three years of information to show a trend. Five years give an even better idea of how your school's population is changing, and will assist with the prediction of how your population might change in the future. Make sure the point in time used to describe your demographics is both noted and typical of what your state or province uses, so all school reports can have the same information. Most states and provinces have a date in the fall and/or spring for official school census information.

*A school data profile begins with comprehensive demographic data to describe the context of the school in chart and table formats.*

A school data profile begins with comprehensive demographic data to describe the context of the school in chart and table formats. The beginning pages of an example demographic profile are shown in Figure 3.3. The complete data profile is shown in the Appendix F, Case Study. Use the case study to guide your creation of a data profile. (*Note: Using Data to Improve Student Learning in Elementary Schools; Middle Schools; High Schools;* and *School Districts* [Bernhardt, 2003, 2004, 2005, 2006], provide *graphing templates and examples on accompanying CDs for doing this work.*

*Response to Intervention (RtI) and Continuous School Improvement (CSI): Using Data, Vision, and Leadership to Design, Implement, and Evaluate a Schoolwide Prevention System* [Bernhardt and Hébert, 2011] shows another complete data profile.)

The data profile tells the story of the school. If you do not like the story of your school, you can change it. You just have to know what it is. If you are not looking at all your data, you do not know the whole story of your school.

*The data profile tells the story of the school. If you do not like the story of your school, you can change it.*

Figure 3.3
SOMEWHERE ELEMENTARY SCHOOL PROFILE

### DEMOGRAPHICS

Somewhere Elementary is a kindergarten through grade five school located in Somewhere Valley. Somewhere Elementary School is part of the Somewhere Valley School District, which in 2012-13, served 13,225 students in 19 schools: 9 elementary (K-5), 2 K-8 schools, 3 middle (6-8), 2 comprehensive high (9-12), and 3 alternative schools. In 2003-04, the district served 13,935 students. This decrease (after a few years of increases) in overall district enrollment is shown in Figure F-1.

**Look Fors:** Increasing, steady, or decreasing enrollment.

**Planning Implications:** Is there a need to expand or decrease district/school facilities, services, and/or staff? Are enrollment changes congruent with community population changes?

Figure F-1

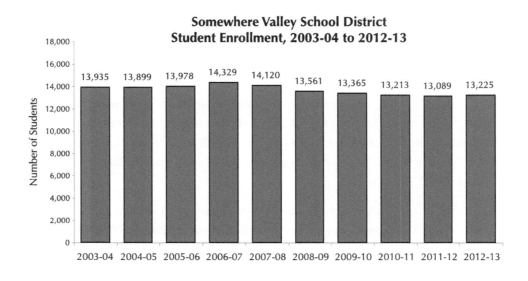

34

## Figure 3.3
### SOMEWHERE ELEMENTARY SCHOOL PROFILE *(Continued)*

Somewhere Elementary School served 458 students in 2012-13, down 18 students from the previous year (Figure F-2). The lowest enrollment was 445 students in 2004-05; the highest was 529 in 2007-08.

*Look Fors:*   **Increasing, steady, or decreasing enrollment.**

*Planning*   **Is there a need to expand or decrease facilities, services, and/or staff?**
*Implications:*   **Why is enrollment increasing or decreasing?**

### Figure F-2

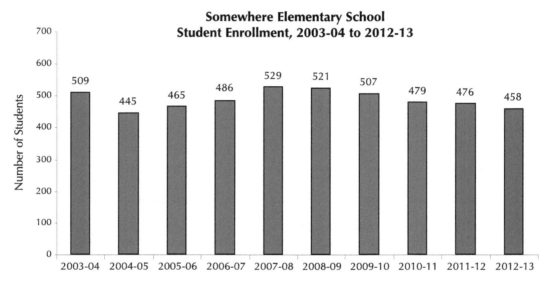

**Somewhere Elementary School
Student Enrollment, 2003-04 to 2012-13**

The district student enrollment is shown in Figure F-3 by percent ethnicity. Figure F-4 shows the enrollment by percent ethnicity for the elementary schools in Somewhere Valley School District (excluding Somewhere School). Figure F-5 shows enrollment by percent ethnicity for Somewhere Elementary. In 2012-13, 59% of the district population was Caucasian ($n$=7,803), and 26% was Hispanic ($n$=3,439). The remaining student population was made up of 6% Asian ($n$=794), 3.0% African-American ($n$=397), 3% Filipino ($n$=397), 0.5% Pacific Islander ($n$=66), 0.5% American Indian ($n$=66), and 2% Multiple/Other ($n$=265) ethnicities. In 2012-13, elementary schools (Figure F-4), excluding Somewhere School, had 53.3% of the student population Caucasian ($n$=2,977), 29.4% Hispanic/Latino ($n$=1,1,641), 6.4% Asian ($n$=356), 2.8% African-American ($n$=154), 3.1% Filipino ($n$=174), 0.6% Pacific Islander ($n$=33), 0.5% American Indian ($n$=28,) and 4.0% Multiple/Other ($n$=223) ethnicities.

In 2012-13, 75.3% of Somewhere School students were Hispanic ($n$=345) and 15.9% of students were Caucasian ($n$=72). The remaining student population was made up of 0.9% Asian ($n$=4), 1.5% (African-American ($n$=7), 3.1% Filipino ($n$=14), 0.2% American Indian ($n$=1), and 3.3% Multiple/Other ($n$=15).

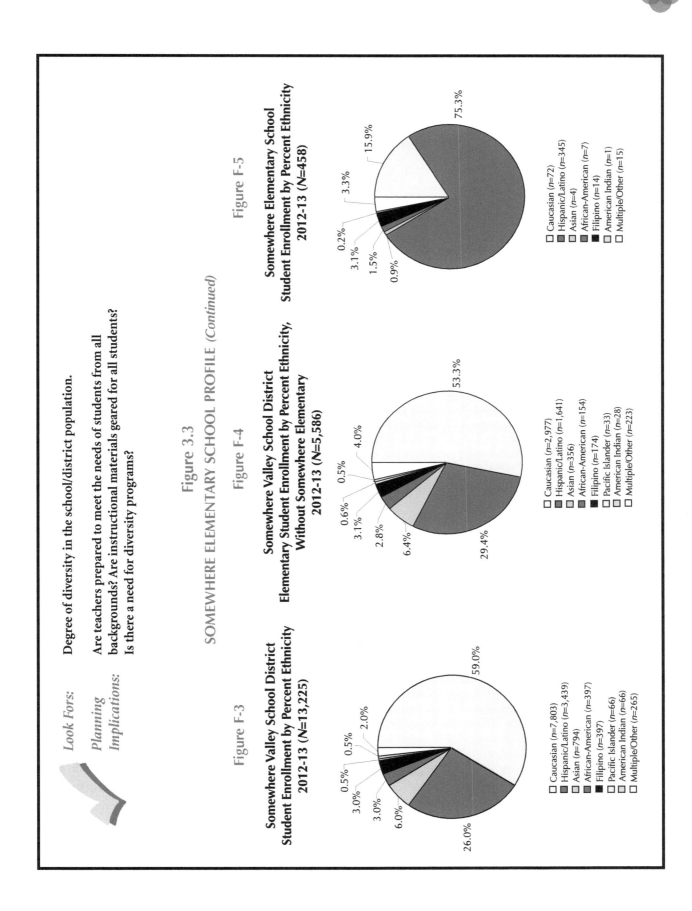

*Look Fors:* **Degree of diversity in the school/district population.**

*Planning Implications:* **Are teachers prepared to meet the needs of students from all backgrounds? Are instructional materials geared for all students? Is there a need for diversity programs?**

Figure 3.3
SOMEWHERE ELEMENTARY SCHOOL PROFILE *(Continued)*

Figure F-3

**Somewhere Valley School District Student Enrollment by Percent Ethnicity 2012-13 (N=13,225)**

- Caucasian (n=7,803)
- Hispanic/Latino (n=3,439)
- Asian (n=794)
- African-American (n=397)
- Filipino (n=397)
- Pacific Islander (n=66)
- American Indian (n=66)
- Multiple/Other (n=265)

Figure F-4

**Somewhere Valley School District Elementary Student Enrollment by Percent Ethnicity, Without Somewhere Elementary 2012-13 (N=5,586)**

- Caucasian (n=2,977)
- Hispanic/Latino (n=1,641)
- Asian (n=356)
- African-American (n=154)
- Filipino (n=174)
- Pacific Islander (n=33)
- American Indian (n=28)
- Multiple/Other (n=223)

Figure F-5

**Somewhere Elementary School Student Enrollment by Percent Ethnicity 2012-13 (N=458)**

- Caucasian (n=72)
- Hispanic/Latino (n=345)
- Asian (n=4)
- African-American (n=7)
- Filipino (n=14)
- American Indian (n=1)
- Multiple/Other (n=15)

## ANALYZING DEMOGRAPHIC INFORMATION IN A DATA PROFILE

We recommend pulling all your school's data together before analyzing your demographic data. Chapter 7 and Appendix H, *Analyzing Data for Continuous School Improvement Planning*, guide you through the steps in the process. To summarize:

Step 1.  **Independent Review.** After creating a data profile that includes each type of data, demographics, perceptions, student learning, and school processes, described in the following chapters, have each member of your staff independently analyze the data for strengths, challenges, implications for the continuous school improvement plan, and identify other data they wished they had. These should be the first ideas that come to mind, as opposed to reviewing the data and then making notes. The analysis will be much richer. (A template for documenting strengths, challenges, implications for the school improvement plan, and other data is included in Appendix H.) Note that each figure in the data profile has "Look Fors" and "Planning Implications" to help guide the analysis.

Step 2.  **Small group review.** In small groups, have staff members share what they saw for strengths, challenges, implications for the continuous school improvement plan, and other data they wished they had, for each type of data, recording commonalities on chart paper.

- ◆ **Strengths** are positive elements one can see in the data. These are ideas for which the school wants to keep track, and keep doing. Strengths can be used as leverage for improving a challenge. An example strength: "This school has an excellent student teacher ratio."

- ◆ **Challenges** found in data imply something might need attention, is out of a school's control, or a potential undesirable result. An example challenge: "The number of students living in poverty in this school has tripled in the past five years."

- ◆ **Implications for the continuous school improvement plan** are ideas that the reviewer jots down while reviewing the data. Implications are placeholders until all the data are analyzed. Implications most often are constructive responses to challenges. An example implication derived from the challenge example above might be: "Do all staff have the professional learning they need to meet the needs of the students who live in poverty?"

---

### ANALYZING DEMOGRAPHIC DATA

**Step 1.  Independent review.** *After creating a data profile, have each member of your staff independently analyze the data for strengths, challenges, implications for the continuous school improvement plan, and identify other data they wished they had.*

**Step 2.  Small group review.** *In small groups, have staff members share what they saw for strengths, challenges, implications for the continuous school improvement plan, and other data they wished they had, for each type of data, recording commonalities on chart paper.*

**Step 3.  Large group consensus.** *Combine the small group results to get a comprehensive set of strengths, challenges, implications for the continuous school improvement plan, and other data they wished they had.*

**Step 4.  Implication commonalities.** *Line up the consolidated implications for demographics, perceptions, student learning, and school processes.*

**Step 5.  Aggregation of commonalities.** *Aggregate, or consider as a whole, those highlighted commonalities.*

◆ **Other data we wished the school had.** When school staff review the school's data, effectively, they always uncover other data they wish they had available. The examination of the data will highlight issues in data collection, storage, and reporting, as well. It is important to make note of these issues so data can be gathered appropriately. An example: "We need to do a more comprehensive job of identifying who, what, where, and when behavior issues take place at the school site." Staff would need to clarify what data they need to gather, how each staff member will gather and report the data, and how and when they will review the data, and then do something about the results.

## DEMOGRAPHIC DATA

| 1. What are Somewhere School's demographic *strengths* and *challenges?* | |
| --- | --- |
| *Strengths* | *Challenges* |
| | |

| 2. What are some *implications* for the Somewhere continuous school improvement plan? |
| --- |
| |

| 3. Looking at the data presented, what other demographic data would you want to answer the question *Who are we?* for Somewhere Elementary School? |
| --- |
| |

Step 3. **Large group consensus.** Combine the small group results to get a comprehensive set of strengths, challenges, implications for the continuous school improvement plan, and other data they wished they had. This becomes a set of information with which everyone agrees.

Step 4. **Implication commonalities.** Line up the consolidated implications for demographics, perceptions, student learning, and school processes. Look across the implications and highlight the commonalities. Staff members will be amazed to see that there are many things which need to change in demographics, perceptions, and school processes if they want student learning increases.

Step 5. **Aggregation of commonalities.** Aggregate, or consider as a whole, those highlighted commonalities. Make a list of the items that must be addressed in the continuous school improvement plan, based on data. Those aggregated commonalities most often include professional learning for all staff, need for a vision, need for consistency in how students are treated (behavior), support and modeling for implementing learning standards and using data, strategies to welcome students to school, and so on.

Appendix G shows what we saw in the case study data, and how we got to aggregated implications for the continuous school improvement plan. The implication commonalities provide powerful information for a school's continuous school improvement efforts.

## Dynamic Demographic Data

*Most schools have student information systems that gather and store demographic data daily.*

The data profile uses mostly static—based on a point in time—data to provide a method to help staff review demographic data in the context of other data. Most schools have student information systems that gather and store demographic data daily. Within the demographic data profile, there are some data, such as attendance and behavior, that require staff to look across months and weeks to understand them. It becomes overwhelming to try to display these data without appropriate tools; however, with business intelligence systems to produce and disseminate graphs, tables, and reports, and a purpose for looking at dynamic data, one can truly understand how and when things happen, and relationships of variables. This will be discussed more in Chapter 8.

## DISAGGREGATION

*The separation of results into different subgroups that make up the population is called "disaggregation."*

The separation of results into different subgroups that make up the population is called "disaggregation." Demographics play an important role in the disaggregation of data. Demographic subgroupings of achievement or perceptions measures allow us to isolate variations among different student groups to understand if all students are achieving or experiencing school in the same way, and to know if there is something the adults need to learn about particular student groups to better meet their needs.

*Disaggregation helps us find student groups that are not responding to our processes in the way others are—enabling us to understand why and to search for new processes so all students do learn.*

Disaggregation helps us understand if we are truly meeting the purpose and mission of our school. If we are acting on the belief *all* students can achieve, any breakdown of subgroups of students should show few differences. Disaggregation helps us find student groups that are not responding to our processes in the way others are—enabling us to understand why and to search for new processes so *all* students do learn.

Disaggregation provides powerful information in the analysis of school variables, test scores, and questionnaire results. Schools need to disaggregate their important student achievement, perceptions, and school process data by demographic variables that impact student learning to understand all aspects of the population of the school and look for problems and contributing causes.

It is best to disaggregate for few rather than many subpopulations at a time. When too many subpopulations are used (e.g., gender, ethnicity, *and* English as a Second Language), group sizes may become so small that individuals can easily be identified, and the reliability of the results diminish. In fact, most states use 40 as a minimal group size they believe will lead to reliable results. Please note that this minimal group size is for looking at the data from the outside in. When you are looking at your data and reporting the data in-house, you want to be able to identify students for individualized planning, so the 40 rule will not apply.

*When too many subpopulations are used (e.g., gender, ethnicity, AND English as a Second Language), group sizes may become so small that individuals can easily be identified, and the reliability of the results diminish.*

## HOW MUCH TIME DOES IT TAKE?

Most schools already gather demographic data in their student information systems. Organizing the data into a school data profile might take one person two or three days, up to two to three weeks, depending upon how much graphing needs to be done. With an automated tool like the *School Portfolio* Application offered through *Education for the Future* (See *http://eff.csuchico.edu),* the data are uploaded and the data profile, complete with look fors and planning implications, is created in minutes.

## REFLECTION QUESTIONS

1. What are demographic data?

2. Why are demographic data important to continuous school improvement?

3. Are your demographic data reliable; if not, what needs to be fixed?

4. Do you have access to the data in a relatively simple manner? Do you have the technology and the technical support to easily generate typical comprehensive reports? At what frequency?

5. Why is a school data profile important?

6. Who should know the demographic data of a school?

7. What does it mean to disaggregate data, and why is it important to do?

## APPLICATION OPPORTUNITIES

1. Use the *Demographic Data Inventory* (Appendix B1) to organize your demographic data.

2. Graph your demographic data into a data profile so staff can analyze and use the results. Use Appendix F as an example.

3. See Chapter 7 for more on engaging staff in analyzing demographic data, along with perceptions, student learning, and school processes data.

# HOW WE DO BUSINESS:
## PERCEPTIONS DATA

**4**

**CHAPTER**

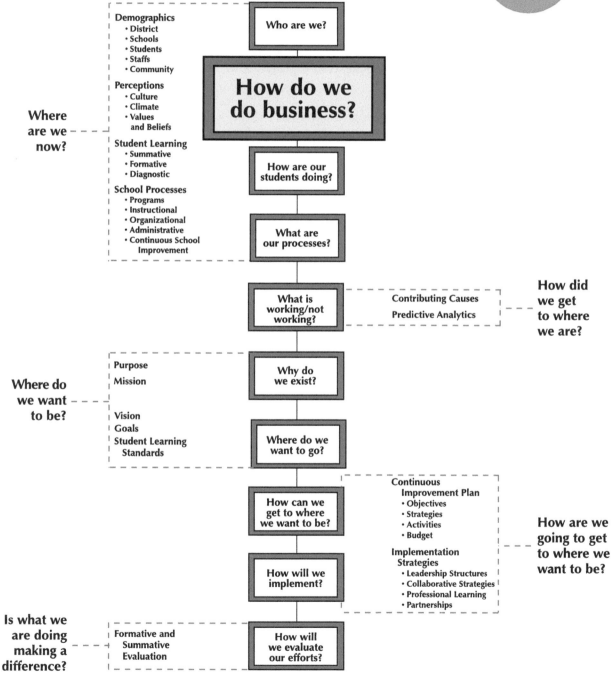

**Where are we now?**

- **Demographics**
  - District
  - Schools
  - Students
  - Staffs
  - Community
- **Perceptions**
  - Culture
  - Climate
  - Values and Beliefs
- **Student Learning**
  - Summative
  - Formative
  - Diagnostic
- **School Processes**
  - Programs
  - Instructional
  - Organizational
  - Administrative
  - Continuous School Improvement

Who are we?

**How do we do business?**

How are our students doing?

What are our processes?

What is working/not working?

**How did we get to where we are?**

Contributing Causes

Predictive Analytics

**Where do we want to be?**

- Purpose
- Mission

- Vision
- Goals
- Student Learning Standards

Why do we exist?

Where do we want to go?

How can we get to where we want to be?

How will we implement?

**How are we going to get to where we want to be?**

- **Continuous Improvement Plan**
  - Objectives
  - Strategies
  - Activities
  - Budget
- **Implementation Strategies**
  - Leadership Structures
  - Collaborative Strategies
  - Professional Learning
  - Partnerships

**Is what we are doing making a difference?**

- Formative and Summative Evaluation

How will we evaluate our efforts?

*Not to understand another person's way of
thinking does not make that person confused.*

Michael Quinn Patton

*We do not act
differently from
what we value,
believe, or perceive.*

All of us have perceptions of the way the world operates. We act upon these perceptions everyday as if they are reality. Basically, we do not act differently from what we value, believe, or perceive. If we want to know what students, staff, and parents perceive about the learning environment, we need to ask them.

The definitions of *perception* and its synonyms provide almost enough information to understand why it is important to know the perceptions of our students, teachers, administrators, parents, and members of our communities. The word perception leads us to such words as "observation" and "opinion," with definitions that include—

*If we want to know
what students, staff,
and parents perceive
about the learning
environment, we
need to ask them.*

◆ a view, judgment, or appraisal formed in the mind about a particular matter

◆ a belief stronger than impression and less strong than positive knowledge

◆ a generally held view

◆ a formal expression of judgment or advice

◆ a judgment one holds as true

Synonyms include opinion, view, belief, conviction, persuasion, and sentiment.

◆ *Opinion* implies a conclusion thought out yet open to dispute.

◆ *View* suggests a subjective opinion.

◆ *Belief* implies often deliberate acceptance and intellectual assent.

◆ *Conviction* applies to a firmly and seriously held belief.

◆ *Persuasion* suggests a belief grounded on assurance (as by evidence) of its truth.

◆ *Sentiment* suggests a settled opinion reflective of one's feelings.

*Perceptions data
are important to
continuous school
improvement because
they can tell us what
students, staff, and
parents are thinking
about the learning
organization, and
answer the continuous
school improvement
question, "How do
we do business?"*

## PERCEPTIONS DATA: WHAT THEY ARE AND WHY THEY ARE IMPORTANT TO CONTINUOUS SCHOOL IMPROVEMENT

Perceptions data are important to continuous school improvement because they can tell us what students, staff, and parents are thinking about the learning organization, and answer the continuous school improvement question, *How do we do business?* This question is answered through assessing the school's culture, climate, and organizational processes.

Staff values and beliefs, most often assessed through a questionnaire, tell a staff if a vision needs to be created or revisited, if team building or specific professional learning is necessary, and if there is enough cohesiveness to implement change. Perceptions can also show where the deep changes are happening in the school with respect to staff values and beliefs.

Student and parent questionnaires can add different perspectives to the information generated from staff data. Students can report what it takes for them to learn, their interests, and how they are being taught and treated. Parent perceptions can help staff know what parents need to become more involved in their child's learning.

## ASSESSING PERCEPTIONS

Common approaches to understanding perceptions in schools include the use of interviews, focus groups, questionnaires, and self-assessment tools, similar to the *Education for the Future Continuous Improvement Continuums,* described in Chapter 2, and shown with the activity that describes the process for doing the assessments with staff (Appendix A). A schoolwide self-assessment, such as the *Continuous Improvement Continuums,* can provide an overview of where the staff believes the school is on the measures that make a difference for continuous school improvement. These assessments often surprise administrators who may think all staff members are thinking about school, and ultimately "doing" school, in the same way. If a planning team does not know how the school staff does business in reality, it could be creating plans and structures that might never be implemented or might not lead to the desired outcomes.

*A schoolwide self-assessment, such as the Continuous Improvement Continuums, can provide an overview of where the staff believes the school is on the measures that make a difference for continuous school improvement.*

Interviews with individuals allow for in-depth understandings of topics and content. Interviews can be done in person, on the telephone, or through electronic methods like the Internet. To be able to merge interview results, specific questions should be agreed upon and used for each interview. If more than one person is conducting the interviews, standardized questions need to be created. Follow the procedures for designing good questionnaire questions.

Focus groups are small groups of representative people who are asked their opinions. Focus groups of students are often used to understand what the larger group of students is thinking or why they respond in a certain way. To understand what the student body is thinking about something in particular, one could organize groups of representative students (e.g., girls/boys, grade levels, ethnicities), randomly selected, to discuss a topic. While it might seem logical to put highly diverse people in the room, it really is not a good way to hear from all participants. You will get more information from homogeneous groupings, or groups with similar backgrounds. For example, instead of putting students from Grades 9 through 12 together, one should organize students by grade levels. This is because people tend to censor their ideas in the presence of people with different status and

*Focus groups are small groups of representative people who are asked their opinions.*

44

*Questionnaires are an excellent way to assess perceptions because they can be completed anonymously and re-administered to assess the changes in perceptions over time.*

*No matter what the reason for administering a questionnaire, or interview, the steps in the process are pretty much the same— you need to start with a purpose; adopt, adapt, or create an instrument complete with questions to get to what it is you want to know.*

*To put together a valid (the "right" content), understandable questionnaire that is easy to complete and analyze, it is critical to think about and agree upon what you want to know or learn by administering the questionnaire, and how the results are going to be used.*

power. (See *Focus Group Fundamentals: A Methodology Brief,* 2004.) Multiple sessions of ten to twelve participants in a group is best. Focus groups could also benefit from the steps outlined for creating questionnaire questions.

Questionnaires are an excellent way to assess perceptions because they can be completed anonymously and re-administered to assess the changes in perceptions over time. Questionnaire results appear with the other data in the school data profile. Appendix C, *Getting to Perceptions through Questionnaires,* has five parts that will help you design, administer, analyze, present, and use questionnaire data. Visit the *Education for the Future* website *(http://eff.csuchico.edu)* for questionnaire resources, including student, staff, and parent questionnaires. For more details on questionnaire design, administration, analysis, and use, see From *Questions to Actions: Using Questionnaire Data for Continuous School Improvement* (Bernhardt, V.L. & Geise, B.J., 2009).

## OVERVIEW OF THE QUESTIONNAIRE PROCESS

No matter what the reason for administering a questionnaire, or interview, the steps in the process are pretty much the same—you need to start with a purpose; adopt, adapt, or create an instrument complete with questions to get to what it is you want to know. You also need the right people to take the questionnaire; a system to administer the questionnaire; a method for analyzing the results; and strategies for displaying, sharing, and using the results.

Figure 4.1 shows the major steps in the questionnaire process, which are described below.

### Determine the Purpose and Uses for the Questionnaire

To put together a valid (the "right" content), understandable questionnaire that is easy to complete and analyze, it is critical to think about and agree upon what you want to know or learn by administering the questionnaire, and how the results are going to be used.

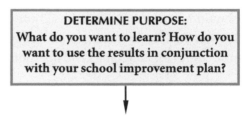

**DETERMINE PURPOSE:**
**What do you want to learn? How do you want to use the results in conjunction with your school improvement plan?**

*What do you really want to know? Why are you administering a questionnaire? To what end are you asking these questions? How do you plan to use the information? How will this information be used with your school improvement plan? Who is going to do the work?* You might want to know perceptions of parents, students, teachers, and administrators with respect to a shared vision or what each constituency values and believes about school, education, teaching, and learning. These might be questions that you want to continue to ask over time to watch the responses change as new ideas and innovations are implemented. One might also want to know the degree to which standards are being implemented in classrooms. The use of this questionnaire would be to understand what would help teachers implement the standards.

## Determine Content and From Whom You Will Gather the Information

Once the questionnaire committee has been established and has agreed upon the purpose of the questionnaire and how the results will be used, the next step is to brainstorm concepts to measure and to determine who will be able to give you the most information about those concepts. You might need to do a literature search to learn more about the specific concepts you want to study. Appendix C1, *Designing Questionnaires,* will guide you through these steps.

> **DETERMINE PURPOSE:**
> What do you want to learn? How do you want to use the results in conjunction with your school improvement plan?
>
> **DETERMINE CONTENT:**
> What content is desired and from whom?

*Identify whom you want to survey.* As you think through the purpose for administering the questionnaire, determine the logical sources of information to answer the questions. When possible, you want to go directly to the source; i.e., if you want to know what parents are thinking, you need to survey parents. (A focus group or interviews would work as well.) Consider whether the questionnaires will be given anonymously, if you will connect individual responses to data in other databases, or if you will ask for respondents' names or identification numbers. If you want honest, non-threatened responses, you might consider not asking for names or information that could identify the respondents. This depends on the purpose and uses of the questionnaire.

*Check for existing tools.* There just might be questionnaires already created that could be used, as is, or adapted for your purposes and uses. Always start with something existing, if it meets your purpose. Creating a questionnaire from scratch is difficult and time consuming to do well.

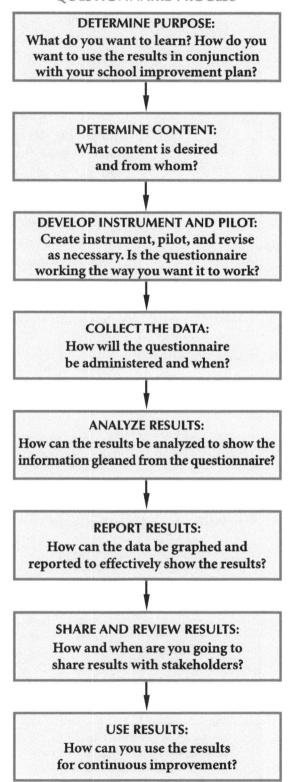

**Figure 4.1**
**QUESTIONNAIRE PROCESS**

**DETERMINE PURPOSE:**
What do you want to learn? How do you want to use the results in conjunction with your school improvement plan?

**DETERMINE CONTENT:**
What content is desired and from whom?

**DEVELOP INSTRUMENT AND PILOT:**
Create instrument, pilot, and revise as necessary. Is the questionnaire working the way you want it to work?

**COLLECT THE DATA:**
How will the questionnaire be administered and when?

**ANALYZE RESULTS:**
How can the results be analyzed to show the information gleaned from the questionnaire?

**REPORT RESULTS:**
How can the data be graphed and reported to effectively show the results?

**SHARE AND REVIEW RESULTS:**
How and when are you going to share results with stakeholders?

**USE RESULTS:**
How can you use the results for continuous improvement?

## Develop the Instrument and Pilot

*It is imperative that you pilot the questionnaire and analyze the pilot data to ensure that you are asking questions that respondents understand.*

Creating the questionnaire can be a challenging task. Many people who want to design a questionnaire often stop when they begin formulating the questions because the job becomes too difficult. Writing the questions looks easier than it actually is. Writing good questions is labor intensive, but having good questions is the best way to get to the true perceptions of respondents.

> **DETERMINE PURPOSE:**
> What do you want to learn? How do you want to use the results in conjunction with your school improvement plan?

> **DETERMINE CONTENT:**
> What content is desired and from whom?

> **DEVELOP INSTRUMENT AND PILOT:**
> **Create instrument, pilot, and revise as necessary. Is the questionnaire working the way you want it to work?**

*Pilot the questionnaire.* No matter how many times you go over an individual question, no matter how many times you look at the questions collectively, you won't know how the questions will actually be interpreted until you administer them to a sample of respondents in your target group. It is imperative that you pilot the questionnaire and analyze the pilot data to ensure that you are asking questions that respondents understand.

*After you study the responses from the pilot group, revise the questionnaire to reflect what you have learned.*

*Review pilot results.* After the pilot responses come in, look over those responses very carefully. Consider each of the responses to the questions to see if each item was understandable. If you are including open-ended questions, look at the open-ended responses for clues to multiple choice responses you felt were not logical. Ask respondents, if they are available, to tell you why particular questions were hard to understand.

> **DETERMINE PURPOSE:**
> What do you want to learn? How do you want to use the results in conjunction with your school improvement plan?

> **DETERMINE CONTENT:**
> What content is desired and from whom?

> **DEVELOP INSTRUMENT AND PILOT:**
> Create instrument, pilot, and revise as necessary. Is the questionnaire working the way you want it to work?

> **COLLECT THE DATA:**
> **How will the questionnaire be administered and when?**

> **ANALYZE RESULTS:**
> **How can the results be analyzed to show the information gleaned from the questionnaire?**

*Revise, review again, and finalize.* After you study the responses from the pilot group, revise the questionnaire to reflect what you have learned. Have several people review the questionnaire once it has been put into its final form to ensure there are no typographical errors and to ensure that the content flow is as you intend. You are then ready to finalize the questionnaire.

Appendix C1 provides the details for creating questionnaires.

## Collect the Data

In data collection, we address two main issues—how will the questionnaire be administered and when. If you are able to use technology to collect questionnaire responses, it is recommended that you do so. Technology provides an effective and efficient approach to gathering data. When to administer questionnaires within schools and districts depends on the school calendar. Data collection is discussed in detail in Appendix C2, *Administering Questionnaires.*

## Analyze Results

For questionnaires to be useful to the intended audience, the analysis must allow the audience to take action on the results. How the results are displayed affects the use and usefulness of the results. Appendices C3, *Analyzing Questionnaire Results,* and C4, *Analyzing Open-Ended Responses,* describe and show effective data analysis approaches for questionnaires, and Appendix C5, *Presenting and Using Questionnaire Results,* describes and shows effective presentation approaches for questionnaires.

## Report Results

For questionnaire results to be used for improvement, it is necessary to present results effectively, in a timely fashion, and to provide avenues for the use of results. The primary goal for the entire process must be to move the analysis of perceptions data into reports that can be easily interpreted, and to get the results into the hands of the people that need them the most in time for them to use the results.

Pages of complex disaggregated results should be reduced to individual and easy to read graphs. Our goal is the immediate and easy interpretation of results. Appendix C5, *Presenting and Using Questionnaire Results,* addresses this issue, and Figure 4.2 shows the results of a disaggregated student questionnaire displayed in a way that staff like to read.

## Share and Review Results

For the results to be used, the findings must be shared with and analyzed by staff and stakeholders. Different approaches to using the results with different stakeholders are described in Appendix C5, *Presenting and Using Questionnaire Results.*

*Note:* As you review questionnaire results over time, you might notice that your school is getting the same results each year. This could be an indication that staff are not using their results and that nothing is changing in the school with respect to school improvement.

## CHANGING PERCEPTIONS

Is it possible to change perceptions? Absolutely. How do we get perceptions to change? The most effective approach is through behavior changes. That means if parents, educational partners, or the school community do not believe in an approach we are taking in the

*For questionnaire results to be used for improvement, it is necessary to present results effectively, in a timely fashion, and to provide avenues for the use of results.*

DETERMINE PURPOSE:
What do you want to learn? How do you want to use the results in conjunction with your school improvement plan?

DETERMINE CONTENT:
What content is desired and from whom?

DEVELOP INSTRUMENT AND PILOT:
Create instrument, pilot, and revise as necessary. Is the questionnaire working the way you want it to work?

COLLECT THE DATA:
How will the questionnaire be administered and when?

ANALYZE RESULTS:
How can the results be analyzed to show the information gleaned from the questionnaire?

REPORT RESULTS:
How can the data be graphed and reported to effectively show the results?

SHARE AND REVIEW RESULTS:
How and when are you going to share results with stakeholders?

## Figure 4.2
## EXAMPLE STUDENT QUESTIONNAIRE GRAPH BY ETHNICITY

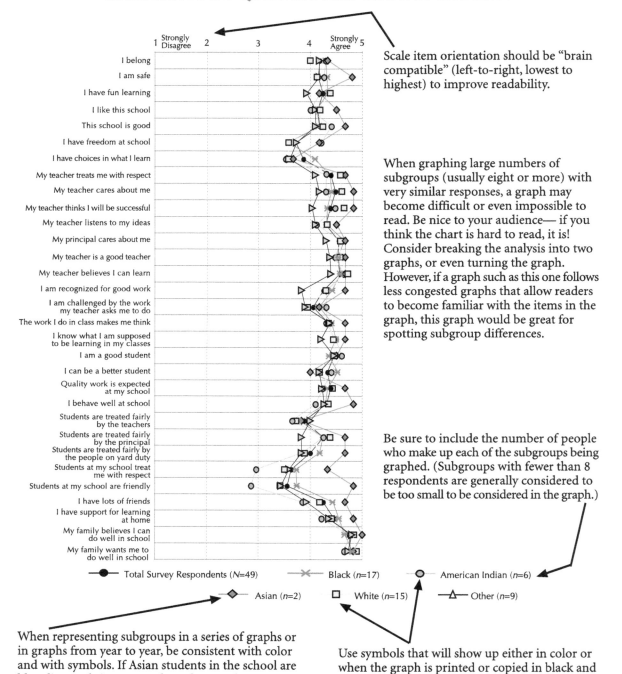

Scale item orientation should be "brain compatible" (left-to-right, lowest to highest) to improve readability.

When graphing large numbers of subgroups (usually eight or more) with very similar responses, a graph may become difficult or even impossible to read. Be nice to your audience— if you think the chart is hard to read, it is! Consider breaking the analysis into two graphs, or even turning the graph. However, if a graph such as this one follows less congested graphs that allow readers to become familiar with the items in the graph, this graph would be great for spotting subgroup differences.

Be sure to include the number of people who make up each of the subgroups being graphed. (Subgroups with fewer than 8 respondents are generally considered to be too small to be considered in the graph.)

When representing subgroups in a series of graphs or in graphs from year to year, be consistent with color and with symbols. If Asian students in the school are blue diamonds in one graph, make sure they are presented as blue diamonds in subsequent graphs, so that comparisons can be made easily.

Use symbols that will show up either in color or when the graph is printed or copied in black and white. Each of the subgroups are represented here with different colors and different symbols.

*Note:* When disaggregating by subgroups, numbers do not always add up to the total number of respondents because some respondents do not identify themselves by the demographic, or they may have the option of indicating more than one subgroup in the demographic. Total will show all the responses. Subgroups show responses of those who identified themselves as a subgroup.

classroom, one way to change the constituency's collective minds is to increase their understanding of the approach and give them an opportunity to experience it. Awareness and experience can lead to basic shifts in opinions first, and then changes in attitudes and beliefs. Giving parents an opportunity to understand and experience a new approach helps them understand a different perspective, which could make them more supportive of new programs. Giving teachers a safe opportunity to try out new approaches will often cause their opinions of a process or program to change.

Another way to change perceptions is through cognitive dissonance. *Cognitive dissonance* is the discomfort one feels when holding two thoughts, opinions, or ideas that are inconsistent. Cognitive dissonance creates perception changes when people experience a conflict between what they believe and what they, or trusted sources, experience.

*Cognitive dissonance creates perception changes when people experience a conflict between what they believe and what they, or trusted sources, experience.*

Communicating transparent information could also help in changing perceptions. Faced with an absence of reliable and transparent information, people will fill the void from disparate events and facts. This could lead to biased perceptions.

In order to change the way business is done, schools must establish guiding principles which include the mission and vision of the school. These principles grow out of the values and beliefs of the individuals who make up the school community. Sometimes school communities adopt guiding principles they want and hope to believe in, as opposed to those they do believe in. The idea is those who try out behaviors that are consistent with these principles will see a positive impact, leading to change in their internal thinking and belief in those principles. This is okay. Changed attitudes represent change at the deepest level of an organization's culture.

*In order to change the way business is done, schools must establish guiding principles which include the mission and vision of the school.*

Too often, schools think of their guiding principles as being sacred and static. They might be sacred, but they should never be static. Even if a school keeps its guiding principles intact, their meanings evolve as people reflect and talk about them and as the principles are applied to guide decisions and actions.

## HOW MUCH TIME DOES IT TAKE TO ASSESS PERCEPTIONS WITH QUESTIONNAIRES?

Designing your own questionnaires could take an entire year! It is best to find questionnaires that already exist to meet your needs.

Using the *Education for the Future* School Improvement Questionnaires, and having *Education for the Future* do your online setup, you would need to focus only on administering the questionnaires to your students, staff, and parents. Each type of questionnaire should take no more than thirty minutes for any respondent to complete.

## HOW MUCH TIME DOES IT TAKE TO ASSESS PERCEPTIONS THROUGH INTERVIEWS AND FOCUS GROUPS?

**Determining and agreeing on the questions to ask during interviews and focus groups depends upon how long the interviews or focus groups are expected to be.**

**Questions agreement might take anywhere from one hour to weeks, depending upon the stakes involved and length of time for the interviewing.**

**Interviews should be short—less than 15 minutes. Focus groups might take an hour per group.**

## REFLECTION QUESTIONS

1. What are perceptions data?

2. Why are perceptions data important for continuous school improvement?

3. Who knows now, and who should know, your perceptions data results?

4. Can you change perceptions? If yes, how?

## APPLICATION OPPORTUNITIES

1. Using the *Perceptions Data Inventory* in Appendix B2, list the different perceptions data being administered in your school, their purposes, and when the data are gathered. Determine what perceptions data need to be eliminated, and other perceptions data needed to be gathered.

2. Read Appendix C about designing, administering, analyzing, and presenting/using questionnaire results, and make sure the interviews, focus groups, and questionnaires you are administering are asking the appropriate questions for the purposes you want, you are getting the proper amount of participant returns, and the results are displayed in such a way that they will be used.

3. Commit to administering, analyzing, and using questionnaires, and or to interview or hold focus groups to help you and your staff understand *Where are we now* with *How we do business.* Visit the *Education for the Future* website (*http://eff.csuchico.edu*) for questionnaire resources, including student, staff, and parent questionnaires.

# HOW ARE OUR STUDENTS DOING:
## STUDENT LEARNING DATA

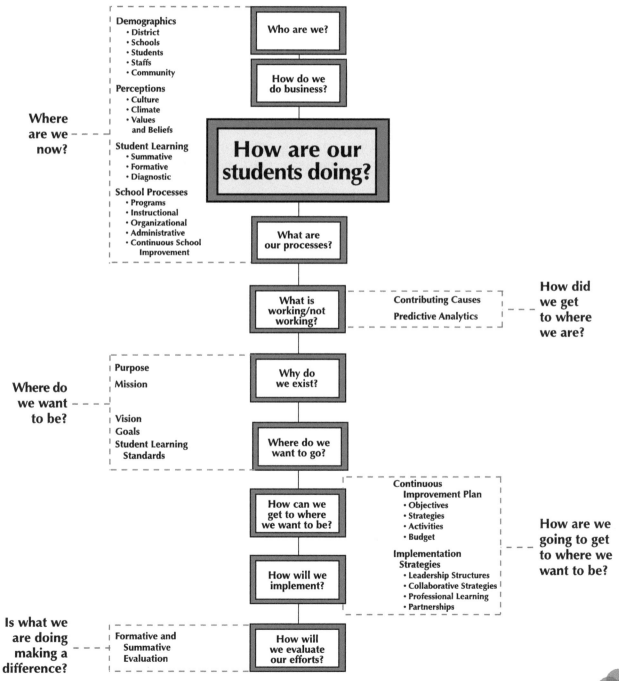

**Where are we now?**

**Demographics**
- District
- Schools
- Students
- Staffs
- Community

**Perceptions**
- Culture
- Climate
- Values and Beliefs

**Student Learning**
- Summative
- Formative
- Diagnostic

**School Processes**
- Programs
- Instructional
- Organizational
- Administrative
- Continuous School Improvement

Who are we?

How do we do business?

**How are our students doing?**

What are our processes?

What is working/not working?

**How did we get to where we are?**

Contributing Causes

Predictive Analytics

**Where do we want to be?**

Purpose

Mission

Vision

Goals

Student Learning Standards

Why do we exist?

Where do we want to go?

**How are we going to get to where we want to be?**

**Continuous Improvement Plan**
- Objectives
- Strategies
- Activities
- Budget

**Implementation Strategies**
- Leadership Structures
- Collaborative Strategies
- Professional Learning
- Partnerships

How can we get to where we want to be?

How will we implement?

**Is what we are doing making a difference?**

Formative and Summative Evaluation

How will we evaluate our efforts?

*Learning does not take place in isolation.*
*Students bring to the learning setting what they*
*have experienced and the values they have been*
*taught at home and in their neighborhoods.*
*This effects how they respond.*

**National Center for Education Statistics**

*Schools committed to continuous school improvement use multiple and ongoing measures of data to understand what students know as a result of instruction, what teachers are teaching, and which students need extra help and on what.*

*Student learning data show if schools are meeting the needs of all students and uncover strengths in learning and areas for improvement.*

When schools focus on compliance, they typically use only summative measures to judge their progress. Schools committed to continuous school improvement use multiple and ongoing measures of data to understand what students know as a result of instruction, what teachers are teaching, and which students need extra help and on what. These schools use student learning measures to provide valuable information for adjusting instruction to meet the needs of *all* students.

## STUDENT LEARNING DATA: WHAT THEY ARE AND WHY THEY ARE IMPORTANT TO CONTINUOUS SCHOOL IMPROVEMENT

*How are our students doing?*, a sub-question within the continuous school improvement framework question, *Where are we now?*, requires a synthesis of student learning data in all subject areas, disaggregated by student demographic groups, by teachers, by grade levels, by following the same groups of students (cohorts) over time, as well as looking at individual student growth. Student learning data show if schools are meeting the needs of all students and uncover strengths in learning and areas for improvement. If students are not proficient, teachers need to know what the students know and what they do not know. If students are not proficient, teachers need to know how many are not proficient, and by how much students must improve to become proficient. Looking at student learning data within grade levels, and looking at student learning across grade levels show if a school has instructional coherence, the alignment of curriculum, instruction, and assessment within grade levels, and across grade levels to create a continuum of learning for students.

## MEASURES OF STUDENT LEARNING

Assessment plays a major role in how students learn, their motivation to learn, and how teachers teach. Assessment is used for three main purposes, as succinctly described in this Manitoba Education website: *http://www.edu.gov.mb.ca/k12/assess/wncp/rethinking_assess_mb.pdf.*

---

### The Role of Assessment in Learning

- *Assessment* FOR *learning:* where assessment helps teachers gain insight into what students understand in order to plan and guide instruction, and provide helpful feedback to students.
- *Assessment* AS *learning:* where students develop an awareness of how they learn and use that awareness to adjust and advance their learning, taking an increased responsibility for their learning. (*Note:* This is essential for successful Common Core State Standards implementation.)
- *Assessment* OF *learning:* where assessment informs students, teachers and parents, as well as the broader educational community, of achievement at a certain point in time in order to celebrate success, plan interventions, and support continued progress.

Assessment must be planned with its purpose in mind. Assessment FOR, AS, and OF learning all have a role to play in supporting and improving student learning, and must be appropriately balanced. The most important part of assessment is the interpretation and use of the information that is gleaned for its intended purpose.

Assessment is embedded in the learning process. It is tightly interconnected with curriculum and instruction. As teachers and students work toward the achievement of curriculum outcomes, assessment plays a constant role in informing instruction, guiding the student's next steps, and checking progress and achievement. Teachers use many different processes and strategies for classroom assessment, and adapt them to suit the assessment purpose and needs of individual students.

Research and experience show that student learning is best supported when—

- Instruction and assessment are based on clear learning goals.
- Instruction and assessment strategies are differentiated according to student learning needs.
- Students are involved in the learning process (they understand the learning goal and the criteria for quality work, receive and use descriptive feedback, and take steps to adjust their performance) and learn to self-regulate.
- Assessment information is used to make decisions that support further learning.
- Parents are well informed about their child's learning, and work with the school to help plan and provide support.
- Students, families, and the general public have confidence in the system.

Reproduced from Manitoba Education. "The Role of Assessment in Learning." *Assessment and Evaluation.* *www.edu.gov.mb.ca/k12/assess/role.html* (January 2013).

---

## WAYS TO MEASURE STUDENT LEARNING

Comparing results on different measures gives teachers insight into what teaching strategies, as well as testing strategies, work best with different students. Teachers can also determine which formative assessments best prepare students for summative tests. Appendix B3, the *Student Learning Data Inventory,* helps schools organize their assessments within and across grade levels and subject areas, by assessment type. Typical assessment terms, organized by assessments for, as, and of learning, are defined in Figure 5.1.

*Comparing results on different measures gives teachers insight into what teaching strategies, as well as testing strategies, work best with different students.*

## Figure 5.1
### ASSESSMENT DEFINITIONS AND USES

*Assessments* **FOR** *Learning* are in-class measures, usually given frequently, to determine student success with the curriculum and for teachers to determine what additional or modified instruction is needed. (Stiggins, R. J. (1999). Teams. *Journal of Staff Development, 20*(3), 17-21).

| Definitions | Cautions |
|---|---|
| **Classroom assessment.** An assessment developed, administered, and scored by a teacher or set of teachers with the purpose of evaluating individual or classroom student performance on a topic. Classroom assessments may be aligned into an assessment system that includes alternative assessments and norm-referenced and/or criterion-referenced assessments. (Center for Research on Evaluation, Standards, and Student Testing [CRESST], retrieved 08/26/12) | Ideally, the results of a classroom assessment are used to inform and influence instruction that helps students reach high standards. |
| **Diagnostic tests,** usually standardized and normed, are given before instruction begins to help the instructor(s) understand student learning needs. | Diagnostic tests can help teachers know the nature of students' difficulties, through sub-domain performance. Many different score and question types are used with diagnostic tests. |
| **Formative assessment** is a range of formal and informal assessment procedures employed by teachers during the learning process in order to modify teaching and learning activities to improve student attainment. | When incorporated into classroom practice, formative assessments provide the information needed to adjust teaching and learning while they are happening. In this sense, formative assessments inform both teachers and students about student understanding at a point when timely adjustments can be made. These adjustments help to ensure students achieve targeted, standards-based learning goals within a set time frame. |
| **Progress monitoring assessments** are used to assess students' academic performance, to quantify a student rate of improvement or responsiveness to instruction, and to evaluate the effectiveness of instruction. Progress monitoring can be implemented with individual students or an entire class. (Retrieved from www.rti4success.org/pdf/glossry_of_terms, 11/06/12) | Progress monitoring assessments allow a teacher to track students in a specific skill area, or they could be more general tests of grade level curricula. Progress monitoring is conducted at least monthly, but often more frequently, to (a) estimate rates of improvement, (b) identify students who are not demonstrating adequate progress, and/or (c) compare the efficacy of different forms of instruction to design more effective, individualized instruction. |
| **Screeners** involve brief assessments that are valid, reliable, and evidence-based. They are typically applied three times per year. | Screeners are conducted with all students or targeted groups of students to identify students who are at risk of academic failure and, therefore, likely to need additional or alternative forms of instruction to supplement the conventional general education approach. |

**Figure 5.1** *(Continued)*
## ASSESSMENT DEFINITIONS AND USES

*Assessments* **AS** *Learning* are in-class measures, usually given frequently, to determine student success with the curriculum and for teachers to determine what additional or modified instruction is needed. (Stiggins, R. J. (1999). Teams. *Journal of Staff Development*, 20(3), 17-21).

| Definitions | Cautions |
|---|---|
| **Alternative assessments (AKA authentic assessment, performance assessment)** are assessments that require students to generate a response to a question rather than choose from a set of responses provided to them. Exhibitions, investigations, demonstrations, written or oral responses, journals, and portfolios are examples of the assessment alternatives we think of when we use the term "alternative assessment." Alternative assessments are usually one element of an assessment system. (CRESST, retrieved 08/26/12) | Ideally, alternative assessments require students to actively accomplish complex and significant tasks, while bringing to bear prior knowledge, recent learning, and relevant skills to solve realistic or authentic problems. |
| **Performance assessments** refer to assessments that measure skills, knowledge, and ability directly-such as through performance. In other words, if you want students to learn to write, you assess their ability on a writing activity. | One must find a way to score these results and make sense for individual students and groups of students. |
| A **rubric** is a scoring tool that judges work against a set of criteria. A rubric divides, on a descriptive scale, the assigned work into component parts and provides clear descriptions of the characteristics of the work associated with each component, at varying levels of mastery. | Rubrics can be used for a wide array of assignments: papers, projects, oral presentations, artistic performances, group projects, etc. Rubrics can be used as scoring or grading guides, to provide formative feedback to support and guide ongoing learning efforts, or both. |
| **Standardized tests** are assessments that have uniformity in content, administration, and scoring. | Standardized tests can be used for comparing results across students, classrooms, schools, school districts, and states. Norm-referenced, criterion-referenced, and diagnostic tests are the most commonly used standardized tests. Psychometric and edumetric standardized tests are often used to identify children with special needs. |

**Figure 5.1** *(Continued)*
## ASSESSMENT DEFINITIONS AND USES

*Assessments* **OF** *Learning* inform students, teachers, and parents, as well as the broader educational community, of achievement at a certain point in time in order to celebrate success, plan interventions, and support continued progress.

| Definitions | Cautions |
|---|---|
| **Benchmark.** A detailed description of a specific level of performance expected of students at particular ages, grades, or development levels. Benchmarks are often represented by scoring rubrics and exemplars of student work. (CRESST, retrieved 08/26/12) | A set of benchmarks can be used as "checkpoints" to monitor progress toward meeting performance goals within and across grade levels, i.e., benchmarks for expected mathematics capabilities at Grades 3, 7, 10, graduation. |
| **Criterion-referenced** measures compare an individual's performance to a specific learning objective or performance standard and not to the performance of other test takers. Criterion-referenced assessments tell us how well students are performing on specific criteria, goals, or standards. (CRESST, retrieved 08/26/12) | For school level analyses, criterion-referenced tests are usually scored on descriptive scales in terms of the number or percentage of students meeting the standard or criterion, or the number or percentage of students falling in typical descriptive categories, such as far below basic, below basic, basic, proficient, and advanced. Criterion-referenced tests can be standardized or not, and they can also have norming groups. |
| **End-of-Course Exams, Including Certification Exams** End-of-Course Exams are criterion-referenced tests given at the completion of a course of study. | End-of-course exams are given to determine whether a student demonstrates attainment of the knowledge and skills necessary for mastery of that subject. |
| **Norm-referenced tests** are standardized tests. Norm-referenced test scores create meaning through comparing the test performance of a school, group, or individual, with the performance of a norming group. A norming group is a representative group of students whose results on a norm-referenced test help create the scoring scales with which others compare their performance. Norming groups' results are professed to look like the normal curve, shown in Figure 5.2. | Norm-referenced test results are used to understand how your students scored in comparison to the norming group. |
| **Outcome assessments** are given at the end of the school year. Outcome tests are frequently group-administered tests of important outcomes. | Outcome assessments are often used for district, state, and provincial reporting purposes. These tests are important because they give school leaders and teachers feedback about the overall effectiveness of their instructional program. As part of an effective assessment plan, outcome assessments should be administered at the end of every year. |
| **Provincial assessments** are mostly outcome assessments that vary by province. | Provincial assessments are used to tell schools and boards how students are performing with respect to specific subjects. |
| **Standards-based assessments** assess student achievement on the basis of outcomes or standards performance. They are usually criterion-referenced. | Standards-based assessments use cut scores to know if standards have been met. Most common uses are to know the number or percentage of students meeting or exceeding a standard. |

**Figure 5.1** *(Continued)*
## ASSESSMENT DEFINITIONS AND USES

| Definitions | Cautions |
|---|---|
| **Standards-based assessments** assess student achievement on the basis of outcomes or standards performance. They are usually criterion-referenced. | Standards-based assessments use cut scores to know if standards have been met. Most common uses are to know the number or percentage of students meeting or exceeding a standard. |
| **Standardized tests** are assessments that have uniformity in content, administration, and scoring. | Standardized tests can be used for comparing results across students, classrooms, schools, school districts, and states. Norm-referenced, criterion-referenced, and diagnostic tests are the most commonly used standardized tests. Psychometric and edumetric standardized tests are often used to identify children with special needs. |
| **Summative assessments** provide a bottom line of learning as related to established grade-level standards and norms. Most summative assessments are given yearly or pre-and post during a year. | Summative assessments are developed and scored in ways that ensure reliability and validity, and may be norm or criterion referenced. Summative or outcome assessments are used for student screening, accountability, or pre-post measures of the efficacy of programs. |
| **Teacher-assigned grades.** Teachers use number or letter grades to judge the quality of a student's performance on a task, unit, or during a period of time. Grades are most often given as A, B, C, D, F, (or R, 1, 2, 3, 4), with pluses and minuses given by some teachers for the first four to distinguish among students. | Grades are mostly used to tell students and parents how well the students did on a task, or during a period of time. Grades mean different things to different teachers. Needless to say, grades can be subjective. |

Student learning data come from screening assessments, diagnostic assessments, classroom assessments, classroom assignments and activities, formative assessments, state/provincial assessments, performance and standards assessments, and grades. In a perfect scenario, teachers are clear and agree on what they want students to know and be able to do by the end of the year, course, or lesson, also referred to as student learning standards. Short screening assessments, or screeners, administered to all students help teachers know if students are at risk of failure. For students who did not perform well on the screeners, teachers use longer diagnostic assessments to understand what the students do and do not know, and consider how they can help each student with her/his learning needs. Teachers plan for instruction for all students with this information. On a regular basis, teachers assess to understand what students are learning and which students need extra support, and adjust instruction to meet all student needs. Teachers then assess to know if the students learned what they were expected to learn.

*Student learning data come from screening assessments, diagnostic assessments, classroom assessments, classroom assignments and activities, formative assessments, state/provincial assessments, performance and standards assessments, and grades.*

*Analyses of all types of student learning measures used in the school can help one know if all students are learning, and if true learning can be detected better with one measure than another.*

*In a normal distribution, the measures are distributed symmetrically about the mean, or average score.*

Analyses of all types of student learning measures used in the school can help one know if all students are learning, and if true learning can be detected better with one measure than another. Looking across measures, teachers can determine how the different measures compare in performance and if students perform differently on one type of test versus another.

## THE NORMAL CURVE AND RELATED SCORE TYPES

A text on data analysis would not be complete if it did not include a section on the normal curve, and the scores associated with it. The normal curve (Figure 5.2) is a distribution of scores or other measures that in graphic form has a distinctive bell-shaped appearance. In a normal distribution, the measures are distributed symmetrically about the mean, or average score. Most results are near the mean and decrease in frequency the farther one departs from the mean. Stated another way—the theory of the normal curve basically says that when a test is given to a representative sample of students, most students score around the mean with few students scoring very high or very low. Using this theory, test publishers are able to create scales that are useful for schools to compare their scores with the norming group.

### Figure 5.2
### THE NORMAL CURVE AND SCORES

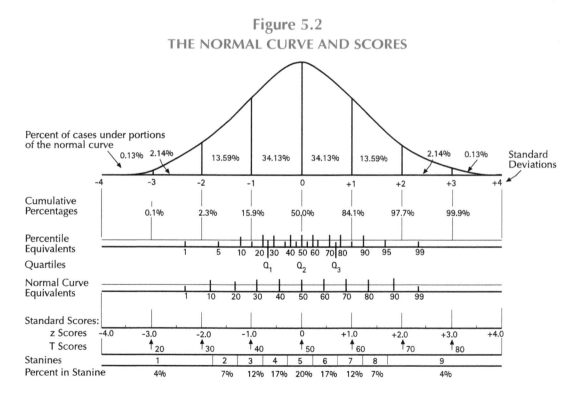

Stanford Achievement Test: Eighth Edition. Copyright © 1989 by
The Psychological Corporation. Reproduced by permission. All rights reserved.

*National Percentile Ranks (NPR).* The two most commonly used and useful normed scales, or score types, are national percentile ranks and normal curve equivalents. The national percentile rank, also known as the national percentile equivalent, ranges from 1 to 99, with a midscore of 50. The NPR is one of the most used scales; it is also misused the most. The misuse of this scale stems from the fact that it is an unequal interval scale, which prohibits adding, subtracting, multiplying, and dividing the scores. *One should not look at gains, losses, or averages with percentile ranks* because of the unequal interval scale, and because the scores are dependent on how the norming group performed. If a student performed at the 70th percentile last year and 75th percentile this year—that is how the performance is described. You can see on the normal curve (Figure 5.2) how her/his performance has changed with respect to the norming group. Median scores, or the middle scores, are the most appropriate means of describing a whole school's typical performance.

*Normal Curve Equivalent Scores (NCE).* Normal curve equivalent (NCE) scores were created by educational researchers to alleviate the problem of unequal interval scales. This equal interval scale has a mean of 50, and range of 1 to 99, just like the NPR. A standard deviation of 21.06 is used to ensure that NCE and percentile ranks have equivalent scores at the 1st, 50th, and 99th percentiles. NCEs have the same meaning across students, subtests, grade levels, classrooms, schools, and school districts. Fifty (50) is what one would expect for an average year's growth; put another way, 50 is grade level—always the national average for the grade and month the test is taken. You can look at how close your scores are to expected performance, averages, gains, losses, highest, and lowest scores. NCEs are excellent for looking at scores over time.

Convert percentile ranks to NCEs so you can compare scores over time, or NCEs to percentiles to understand how your students did in relationship to other similar students, using the tables in Figures 5.3 and 5.4. Note how the conversion can be more exact going from NCE scores to percentiles. A conversion in the opposite direction uses an average NCE.

*The two most commonly used and useful normed scales, or score types, are national percentile ranks and normal curve equivalents.*

*The national percentile rank, also known as the national percentile equivalent, ranges from 1 to 99, with a midscore of 50.*

*Normal curve equivalent (NCE) scores were created by educational researchers to alleviate the problem of unequal interval scales.*

## Figure 5.3
### NCE TO PERCENTILE CONVERSION TABLE

| NCE Range | Percentile Rank | NCE Range | Percentile Rank | NCE Range | Percentile Rank | NCE Range | Percentile Rank |
|---|---|---|---|---|---|---|---|
| 1.0 – 4.0 | 1 | 36.1–36.7 | 26 | 50.3–50.7 | 51 | 64.6–65.1 | 76 |
| 4.1 – 8.5 | 2 | 36.8–37.3 | 27 | 50.8–51.2 | 52 | 65.2–65.8 | 77 |
| 8.6–11.7 | 3 | 37.4–38.0 | 28 | 51.3–51.8 | 53 | 65.9–66.5 | 78 |
| 11.8–14.1 | 4 | 38.1–38.6 | 29 | 51.9–52.3 | 54 | 66.6–67.3 | 79 |
| 14.2–16.2 | 5 | 38.7–39.2 | 30 | 52.4–52.8 | 55 | 67.4–68.0 | 80 |
| 16.3–18.0 | 6 | 39.3–39.8 | 31 | 52.9–53.4 | 56 | 68.1–68.6 | 81 |
| 18.1–19.6 | 7 | 39.9–40.4 | 32 | 53.5–53.9 | 57 | 68.7–69.6 | 82 |
| 19.7–21.0 | 8 | 40.5–40.9 | 33 | 54.0–54.4 | 58 | 69.7–70.4 | 83 |
| 21.1–22.3 | 9 | 41.0–41.5 | 34 | 54.5–55.0 | 59 | 70.5–71.3 | 84 |
| 22.4–23.5 | 10 | 41.6–42.1 | 35 | 55.1–55.5 | 60 | 71.4–72.2 | 85 |
| 23.6–24.6 | 11 | 42.2–42.7 | 36 | 55.6–56.1 | 61 | 72.3–73.1 | 86 |
| 24.7–25.7 | 12 | 42.8–43.2 | 37 | 56.2–56.6 | 62 | 73.2–74.1 | 87 |
| 25.8–26.7 | 13 | 43.3–43.8 | 38 | 56.7–57.2 | 63 | 74.2–75.2 | 88 |
| 26.8–27.6 | 14 | 43.9–44.3 | 39 | 57.3–57.8 | 64 | 75.3–76.3 | 89 |
| 27.7–28.5 | 15 | 44.4–44.9 | 40 | 57.9–58.3 | 65 | 76.4–77.5 | 90 |
| 28.6–29.4 | 16 | 45.0–45.4 | 41 | 58.4–58.9 | 66 | 77.6–78.8 | 91 |
| 29.5–30.2 | 17 | 45.5–45.9 | 42 | 59.0–59.5 | 67 | 78.9–80.2 | 92 |
| 30.3–31.0 | 18 | 46.0–46.5 | 43 | 59.6–60.1 | 68 | 80.3–81.7 | 93 |
| 31.1–31.8 | 19 | 46.6–47.0 | 44 | 60.2–60.7 | 69 | 81.8–83.5 | 94 |
| 31.9–32.6 | 20 | 47.1–47.5 | 45 | 60.8–61.3 | 70 | 83.6–85.5 | 95 |
| 32.7–33.3 | 21 | 47.6–48.1 | 46 | 61.4–61.9 | 71 | 85.6–88.0 | 96 |
| 33.4–34.0 | 22 | 48.2–48.6 | 47 | 62.0–62.5 | 72 | 88.1–91.0 | 97 |
| 34.1–34.7 | 23 | 48.7–49.1 | 48 | 62.6–63.1 | 73 | 91.1–96.4 | 98 |
| 34.8–35.4 | 24 | 49.2–49.6 | 49 | 63.2–63.8 | 74 | 96.5–99.0 | 99 |
| 35.5–36.0 | 25 | 49.7–50.2 | 50 | 63.9–64.5 | 75 | | |

## Figure 5.4
## PERCENTILE TO NCE CONVERSION TABLE

| Percentile Rank | NCE | Percentile Rank | NCE | Percentile Rank | NCE | Percentile Rank | NCE |
|---|---|---|---|---|---|---|---|
| 1 | 1.0 | 26 | 36.5 | 51 | 50.5 | 76 | 64.9 |
| 2 | 6.7 | 27 | 37.1 | 52 | 51.1 | 77 | 65.6 |
| 3 | 10.4 | 28 | 37.7 | 53 | 51.6 | 78 | 66.3 |
| 4 | 13.1 | 29 | 38.3 | 54 | 52.1 | 79 | 67.0 |
| 5 | 15.4 | 30 | 39.0 | 55 | 52.6 | 80 | 67.7 |
| 6 | 17.3 | 31 | 39.6 | 56 | 53.2 | 81 | 68.5 |
| 7 | 18.9 | 32 | 40.1 | 57 | 53.7 | 82 | 69.3 |
| 8 | 20.4 | 33 | 40.7 | 58 | 54.2 | 83 | 70.1 |
| 9 | 21.8 | 34 | 41.3 | 59 | 54.8 | 84 | 70.9 |
| 10 | 23.0 | 35 | 41.9 | 60 | 55.3 | 85 | 71.8 |
| 11 | 24.2 | 36 | 42.5 | 61 | 55.9 | 86 | 72.8 |
| 12 | 25.3 | 37 | 43.0 | 62 | 56.4 | 87 | 73.7 |
| 13 | 26.3 | 38 | 43.6 | 63 | 57.0 | 88 | 74.7 |
| 14 | 27.2 | 39 | 44.1 | 64 | 57.5 | 89 | 75.8 |
| 15 | 28.2 | 40 | 44.7 | 65 | 58.1 | 90 | 77.0 |
| 16 | 29.1 | 41 | 45.2 | 66 | 58.7 | 91 | 78.2 |
| 17 | 29.9 | 42 | 45.8 | 67 | 59.3 | 92 | 79.6 |
| 18 | 30.7 | 43 | 46.3 | 68 | 59.9 | 93 | 81.1 |
| 19 | 31.5 | 44 | 46.8 | 69 | 60.4 | 94 | 82.7 |
| 20 | 32.3 | 45 | 47.4 | 70 | 61.0 | 95 | 84.6 |
| 21 | 33.0 | 46 | 47.9 | 71 | 61.7 | 96 | 86.9 |
| 22 | 33.7 | 47 | 48.4 | 72 | 62.3 | 97 | 89.6 |
| 23 | 34.4 | 48 | 48.9 | 73 | 62.9 | 98 | 93.3 |
| 24 | 35.1 | 49 | 49.5 | 74 | 63.5 | 99 | 99.0 |
| 25 | 35.8 | 50 | 50.0 | 75 | 64.2 | | |

*Stanford Achievement Test: Eighth Edition.* Copyright © 1989 by The Psychological Corporation.
Reproduced by permission. All rights reserved.

When displaying NCE results, many schools show results for grade levels over time as shown in Figure 5.5. One can make few comparisons within grade levels over time because the students are not the same. However, one usually can see the scores are fairly stable, unless something very different happens, such as using new teaching strategies or adding new teachers. Grades three and four illustrate the type of increases we would like to see every year.

NCE scores can be used for comparisons because they—

- have equal intervals;
- can be aggregated, disaggregated, and averaged;
- have a derived average of 50 and a standard deviation of 21.06;
- can be compared from one grade to another;
- can be used to calculate gain scores;
- match percentiles of 1 to 99;
- can be converted to percentiles after analysis.

## Figure 5.5
### EXAMPLE GRAPH: NCE RESULTS BY GRADE LEVEL
**2008-09 to 2011-12**

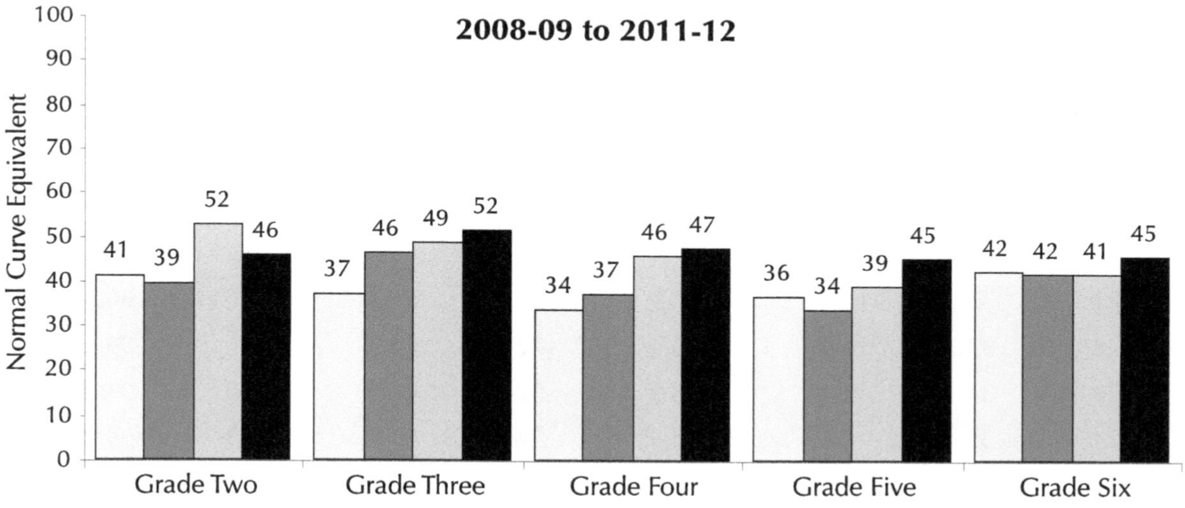

Figure 5.6 shows how to reorganize a grade level over time graph to follow the same group of students. This type of graph is called a "cohort graph." The cohorts can be matched (following the same students over time), or unmatched (following the same groups over time).

**Figure 5.6**
**EXAMPLE GRAPH: MATCHED NCE MATH SCORES BY CLASS**

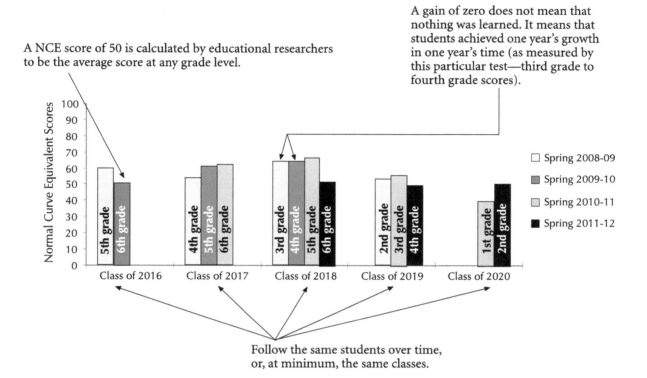

A NCE score of 50 is calculated by educational researchers to be the average score at any grade level.

A gain of zero does not mean that nothing was learned. It means that students achieved one year's growth in one year's time (as measured by this particular test—third grade to fourth grade scores).

Follow the same students over time, or, at minimum, the same classes.

## THE MEANING OF THE BLOOM QUOTE

*The normal curve is a distribution most appropriate to chance and random activity. Education is a purposeful activity and we seek to have students learn what we would teach. Therefore, if we are effective, the distribution of grades will be anything but a normal curve. In fact, a normal curve is evidence of our failure to teach.*

Benjamin Bloom

*The normal curve serves the purpose of showing us how our students score in relationship to norming groups.*

The normal curve serves the purpose of showing us how our students score in relationship to norming groups. It says that when we give a test to many students, few will score very low, few will score very high, and most will score around the average score.

"*. . . A normal curve is evidence of our failure to teach.*" What this means is that as teachers, we have the challenge to instruct and to ensure that students achieve what we want them to know and be able to do. Our objective with teaching should be to make sure that the normal curve does not exist in our classroom. We want all students to learn the information.

*Our objective with teaching should be to make sure that the normal curve does not exist in our classroom.*

### Standardized Test Score Terms

Standardized assessments have uniformity in content, administration, and scoring. Standardized test score terms are defined in Figure 5.7, along with a description of most effective uses and cautions for use.

Figure 5.7
STANDARDIZED TEST SCORE TERMS, THEIR MOST EFFECTIVE USES,
AND CAUTIONS FOR THEIR USES

| Score | Definition | Most Effective Uses | Cautions |
|---|---|---|---|
| *Anticipated Achievement Scores* | A student's anticipated achievement score is an estimate of the average score for students of similar ages, grade levels, and academic aptitude. It is an estimate of what we would expect the student to score on an achievement test. | Anticipated achievement scores can be used to see if a student is scoring "above" or "below" an expected score, indicating whether or not she/he is being challenged enough, or if her/his needs are being met. | It is easy to think of these scores as "IQ" scores. They are just achievement indicators on a standardized test. |
| *Cognitive Abilities or Skills Index* | The cognitive skills index is an age-dependent normalized standard score based on a student's performance on a cognitive skills test with a mean of 100 and standard deviation of 16. The score indicates a student's overall cognitive ability or academic aptitude relative to students of similar age, without regard to grade level. | Cognitive skills index scores can be used to see if a student is scoring "above" or "below" an expected score, indicating whether or not she/he is being challenged enough, or if her/his needs are being met. | It is easy to think of these scores as "IQ" scores. They are just achievement indicators on a standardized test. |
| *Criterion-Referenced Tests* | Tests that judge how well a test-taker does on an explicit objective relative to a predetermined performance level. | Tell us how well students are performing on specific criteria, goals, or standards. | CRTs test only what was taught, or planned to be taught. CRTs can not give a broad estimate of knowledge. |
| *Deciles* | Deciles divide a distribution into ten equal parts: 1–10; 11–20; 21–30; 31–40; 41–50; 51–60; 61–70; 71–80; 81–90; 91–99. Just about any scale can be used to show deciles. | Deciles allow schools to show how all students scored throughout the distribution. One would expect a school's distribution to resemble a normal curve. Watching the distribution move to the right, over time, could imply that all students in the distribution are making progress. | One must dig deeper to understand if all students and all groups of students are moving forward. |
| *Diagnostic Tests* | Diagnostic tests, usually standardized and normed, are given before instruction begins to help the instructor(s) understand student learning needs. Many different score types are used with diagnostic tests. | Help teachers know the nature of students' difficulties, but not the cause of the difficulty. | Make sure the diagnostic test is measuring what you want it to measure and that it can be compared to formative and summative assessments used. |

**Figure 5.7** *(Continued)*
## STANDARDIZED TEST SCORE TERMS, THEIR MOST EFFECTIVE USES, AND CAUTIONS FOR THEIR USES

| Score | Definition | Most Effective Uses | Cautions |
|---|---|---|---|
| **Grade-Level Equivalents** | Grade-level equivalents indicate the grade and month of the school year for which a given score is the actual or estimated average. Based on a ten-month school year, scores would be noted as 3.1 for third grade, first month, or 5.10 for fifth grade, tenth month. | Grade-level equivalents are most effectively used as a snapshot in time. Scores are comparable across subtests. | These scores should not be taken literally. If a third grader scored a 5.8 on a subtest, that does not mean that she/he should be doing fifth grade, eighth-month work. It only means that the student obtained the same score that one would expect average fifth-grade students in their eighth month of school to score if they took the third-grade test. |
| **Latent-Trait Scale** | A latent-trait scale is a scaled score obtained through one of several mathematical approaches collectively known as Latent-Trait Procedures or Item Response Theory. The particular numerical values used in the scale are arbitrary, but higher scores indicate more knowledgeable students or more difficult items. | Latent-trait scales have equal intervals allowing comparisons over time. | These are scores set up by testing professionals. Laypeople typically have difficulty understanding their meaning. |
| **NCE (National or Local)** | Normal Curve Equivalent (NCE) scores are standard scores with a mean of 50, a standard deviation of 21.06, and a range of 1 to 99. The term National would indicate that the norming group was national; local usually implies a state or district norming group. | NCEs have equal intervals so they can be used to study gains over time. The scores have the same meaning across subtests, grade levels, and years. A 50 is what one would expect in an average year's growth. | This score, just like all scores related to norm-referenced tests, cannot be taken literally. The score simply shows relative performance of a student group or of students to a norming group. |
| **Norm-Referenced Tests** | A norm-referenced test is a type of standardized test, assessment, or evaluation which yields an estimate of the position of the tested individual in a predefined population, with respect to the trait being measured. | Norm-referenced tests create meaning through comparing the test performance of a school, group, or individual with the performance of a norming group. The tests allow us to compare a student's skills to others in her/his age group. | Some norm-referenced score types are unequal interval scales, and should not be added, subtracted, or averaged. |
| **Percent Passing** | Percent passing is a calculated score implying the percentage of the student group meeting and exceeding some number, usually a cut score, proficiency/mastery level, or a standard. | With standards-based accountability, it is beneficial to know the percentage of the population meeting and exceeding a standard and to compare a year's percentages with the previous year(s) to understand progress being made. | This is a very simple statistic, and its interpretation should be simple as well. Total numbers (n=) of students included in the percentage must always be noted with the percentage to assist with the understanding. |

**Figure 5.7** *(Continued)*
STANDARDIZED TEST SCORE TERMS, THEIR MOST EFFECTIVE USES,
AND CAUTIONS FOR THEIR USES

| Score | Definition | Most Effective Uses | Cautions |
|---|---|---|---|
| *Percentile / Percentile Rank (PR) (National or Local)* | Percentile ranks indicate the percentage of students in a norm group (e.g., national or local) whose scores fall below a given score. The range is from 1 to 99. 50th percentile ranking would mean that 50 percent of the scores in the norming group fall below a specific score. The term National would indicate that the norming group was national; local usually implies a state or district norming group. | One-year comparison to the norming group. Schools can see the relative standing of a student or group in the same grade to the norm group who took the test at a comparable time. | Percentile rank is not a score to use over time to look for gains because of unequal intervals, unless the calculations are made with equal interval scores and then converted to percentile ranks. One cannot calculate averages using NPR because of the unequal intervals. Medians are the most appropriate statistic to use. |
| *Proficiency / Performance Levels* | Proficiency or performance levels describe student achievement results, related to ranges of scores on an assessment, usually as *below basic, basic, proficiency, advanced.* | Proficiency levels show the numbers and percentages of students scoring proficient and above, and the numbers and percentages of students scoring below proficiency -- with an indication of how far below – close/basic or not so close/below basic. Proficiency levels are good for displaying the distributions of results for a group and its subgroups. | Without the scores, proficiency levels do not provide an idea of where individual students scored within the proficiency ranges. Cannot calculate proficiency levels. Proficiency levels change by test. |
| *Quartiles* | There are three quartiles— Q1, Q2, Q3 — that divide a distribution into four equal groups: Q1=25th percentile Q2=50th percentile (Median) Q3=75th percentile | Quartiles allow schools to see the distribution of scores for any grade level, for instance. Over time, schools trying to increase student achievement would want to monitor the distribution to ensure that all students are making progress. | With quartiles, one cannot tell if the scores are at the top of a quartile or the bottom. There could be "real" changes taking place within a quartile that would not be evident. |
| *Raw Scores* | Raw scores are the number of questions answered correctly on a test or subtest. A raw score is simply calculated by adding the number of questions answered correctly. The raw score is a person's observed score. | The raw score provides information about the number of questions answered correctly. To get a perspective on performance, raw scores must be used with the average score for the group and/or the total number of questions. Alone, it has no meaning. | Raw scores do not provide information related to other students taking the test or to other subtests. One needs to keep perspective by knowing the total number possible. Raw scores should never be used to make comparisons between performances on different tests unless other information about the characteristics of the tests are known and identical. |

**Figure 5.7** *(Continued)*
STANDARDIZED TEST SCORE TERMS, THEIR MOST EFFECTIVE USES,
AND CAUTIONS FOR THEIR USES

| Score | Definition | Most Effective Uses | Cautions |
|---|---|---|---|
| *RIT Scale Scores* | RIT scores, named for George Rasch who developed the theory of this type of measurement, are scaled scores that come from a series of tests created by the Northwest Evaluation Association (NWEA). The tests, which draw from an item bank, are aligned with local curriculum and state/local standards. | RIT scores provide ongoing measurement of curriculum standards and a way for students to see progress in their knowledge. The scores can also be shown as percentiles to know performance related to other students of similar ages and/or grades. You will most probably see gains each time a measurement is taken with a group of students. | RIT scores are great as long as the test was carefully designed to measure standards. |
| *Scaled Scores* | A scaled score is a mathematical transformation of a raw score. | The best uses of scaled scores are averages and averages calculated over time allowing for the study of change.<br><br>These scores are good to use for calculations because of equal intervals.<br><br>The scores can be applied across subtests on most tests.<br><br>Scaled scores facilitate conversions to other score types. | Ranges vary, depending upon the test. Watch for the minimum and maximum values.<br><br>It is sometimes hard for laypeople to create meaning from these scores. The normal curve is needed to interpret the results with respect to other scores and people. |
| *Standard Scores* | Standard score is a general term referring to scores that have been "transformed" for reasons of convenience, comparability, ease of interpretation, etc. z-scores and T-scores are standard scores. | The best uses of standard scores are averages and averages calculated over time, allowing for the study of change.<br><br>These scores are good to use for calculations because of equal intervals.<br><br>The scores can be applied across subtests on most tests.<br><br>Scaled scores facilitate conversions to other score types. | Ranges vary, depending upon the test. Watch for the minimum and maximum values.<br><br>It is sometimes hard for laypeople to create meaning from these scores. The normal curve is needed to interpret results with respect to other scores and people. |
| *Standards-Based Assessments* | Standards-based assessments measure students' progress toward mastering local, state, and/or national content standards. | The way standards-based assessments are analyzed depends upon the scales used. The most effective uses are in revealing the percentage of students achieving a standard. | One has to adhere to the cautions of whatever test or score type used.<br><br>It is important to know how far from mastering the standard the students were when they did not meet the standard. |

**Figure 5.7** *(Continued)*
## STANDARDIZED TEST SCORE TERMS, THEIR MOST EFFECTIVE USES, AND CAUTIONS FOR THEIR USES

| Score | Definition | Most Effective Uses | Cautions |
|---|---|---|---|
| *Stanines* | Stanines are a nine-point standard score scale. Stanines divide the normal curve into nine equal points: 1 to 9. | Stanines, like quartiles, allow schools to see the distribution of scores for any grade level, for instance. Over time, schools trying to increase student achievement would want to monitor the distribution to ensure that all student scores are improving. | Often, the first three stanines are interpreted as "below average," the next three as "average," and the top three as "above average." This can be misleading. As with quartiles, one cannot tell if the scores are at the top of a stanine or the bottom. There could be "real" changes taking place within a stanine that would not be evident. |
| *T-scores* | A T-score is a standard score with a mean of 50 and a standard deviation of 10. T-scores are obtained by the following formula: $$T = 10z + 50$$ | The most effective uses of T-scores are averages and averages calculated over time. T-scores are good to use for calculations because of their equal intervals. T-scores can be applied across subtests on most tests because of the forced mean and standard deviation. | T-scores are rarely used because of the lack of understanding on the part of most test users. |
| *z-scores* | A z-score is a standard score with a mean of zero and a standard deviation of one. z-scores are obtained by the following formula: $$z = \frac{\text{raw score } (x) - \text{mean}}{\text{standard deviation (sd)}}$$ | z-scores can tell one how many standard deviations a score is away from the mean. z-scores are most useful, perhaps, as the first step in computing other types of standard scores. | z-scores are rarely used by the lay public because of the difficulty in understanding the score. |

## MEASURING COMMON CORE STATE STANDARDS

With the adoption of the Common Core State Standards, most states in the United States will be changing the way they assess student achievement. Two consortia are tasked with creating student assessment systems aligned to a common core of academic content standards that:

- balance summative, interim, and formative testing through an integrated system of standards, curriculum, assessment, and instruction;

- effectively gauge college and career readiness; and

- support quick turnaround of results.

As of the writing of this book, example assessments have not been released to allow us to describe how best to analyze and use the results. Watch for articles and addenda on the *Education for the Future* website: *http://eff.csuchico.edu.*

## ANALYZING THE RESULTS, DESCRIPTIVELY

Descriptive statistics (i.e., mean, median, percent correct) can give schools very powerful information. It is imperative that the appropriate analyses be used for the specific score type. Figure 5.8 summarizes terms of analyses, their definitions, their most effective uses, and cautions for their uses in analyzing student achievement scores descriptively.

Descriptive statistics summarize the basic characteristics of a particular distribution, without making any inferences about population parameters. Graphing the information can also be considered descriptive.

*With the adoption of the Common Core State Standards, most states in the United States will be changing the way they assess student achievement.*

*It is imperative that the appropriate analyses be used for the specific score type.*

*Descriptive statistics summarize the basic characteristics of a particular distribution, without making any inferences about population parameters.*

## Figure 5.8
### TERMS RELATED TO ANALYZING STUDENT ACHIEVEMENT RESULTS, DESCRIPTIVELY, THEIR MOST EFFECTIVE USES, AND CAUTIONS FOR THEIR USES

| Term | Definition | Most Effective Uses | Cautions |
|---|---|---|---|
| *Disaggregate* | Disaggregation is breaking a total score into groups for purposes of seeing how subgroups performed. One disaggregates data to make sure all subgroups of students are learning. | Disaggregating student achievement scores by gender, ethnicity, backgrounds, etc., can show how different subgroups performed. | Disaggregations are for helping schools understand how to meet the needs of all students, not to say, "This group always does worse than the other group and always will." We must exercise caution in reporting disaggregations with small numbers in a subgroup. |
| *Gain* | Gain scores are the change or difference between two administrations of the same test. Gain scores are calculated by subtracting the previous score from the most recent score. One can have negative gains, which are actually losses. | One calculates gains to understand improvements in learning for groups of students and for individual students. | Gain scores should not be calculated using unequal interval scores, such as percentiles. The quality of gain score results is dependent upon the quality of the assessment instrument; the less reliable the assessment tool, the less meaningful the results. One needs to make sure the comparisons are appropriate, e.g., same students, same score types. |
| *Item Analysis* | Item analysis refers to the statistics surrounding students' performance on items on a test. Those statistics include item difficulty, discrimination, reliability, and distractor levels. | Item analysis is important for teachers to understand how students performed on each item, which response options received the most responses from students to reteach misconceived concepts. | Some of the statistics are hard for teachers to take the time to understand. It is important for teachers to know why students missed items. |
| *Maximum* | A maximum is the highest score achieved, or the highest possible score on a test. | Maximum possible scores and highest received scores are important for understanding the relative performance of any group or individual, especially when using scaled or standard scores. | A maximum can tell either the highest score possible or the highest score received by a test-taker. One needs to understand which maximum is being used in the analysis. It is best to use both. |
| *Mean* | A mean is the average score in a set of scores. One calculates the mean, or average, by summing all the scores and dividing by the total number of scores. | A mean can be calculated to provide an overall average for the group, and/or student, taking a specific test. One can use any equal interval score to get a mean. | Means should not be used with unequal interval scores, such as percentile ranks. Means are more sensitive to extreme results when the size of the group is small. |
| *Median* | A median is the score that splits a distribution in half: 50 percent of the scores fall above and 50 percent of the scores fall below the median. If the number of scores is odd, the median is the middle score. If the number of scores is even, one must add the two middle scores and divide by two to calculate the median. | Medians are the way to get a midpoint for scores with unequal intervals, such as percentile ranks. The median splits all scores into two equal parts. Medians are not sensitive to outliers, like means are. | Medians are relative. Medians are most effectively interpreted when reported with the possible and actual maximum and minimum. |

**Figure 5.8** *(Continued)*
## TERMS RELATED TO ANALYZING STUDENT ACHIEVEMENT RESULTS, DESCRIPTIVELY, THEIR MOST EFFECTIVE USES, AND CAUTIONS FOR THEIR USES

| Term | Definition | Most Effective Uses | Cautions |
|---|---|---|---|
| **Minimum** | A minimum is the lowest score achieved, or the lowest possible score on the test. | Minimum possible scores and lowest received scores are important for understanding the relative performance of any group or individual. | A minimum tells either the lowest score possible or the lowest score received by a test-taker. One needs to understand which minimum is being used. It is best to use both. |
| **Mode** | The mode is the score that occurs most frequently in a scoring distribution. | The mode basically tells which score or scores appear most often. | There may be more than one mode. The mode ignores other scores. |
| **Percent Correct** | Percent correct is a calculated score implying the percentage of students meeting and exceeding some number, usually a cut score, or a standard. | This calculated score can quickly tell educators how well the students are doing with respect to a specific set of items. It can also tell educators how many students need additional work to become proficient. | Percent correct is a calculated statistic, based on the number of items given. When the number of items given is small, the percent correct can be deceptively high or low. |
| **Percent Proficient** **Percent Passing** **Percent Mastery** | Percent proficient, passing, or mastery represent the percentage of students who passed a particular test at a "proficient," "passing," or "mastery" level, as defined by the test creators or the test interpreters. | With standards-based accountability, it is beneficial to know the percentage of the population meeting and exceeding the standard and to compare a year's percentage with the previous year(s) to understand progress being made. | This is a very simple statistic, and its interpretation should be simple as well. Total numbers (N=) of students included in the percentage must always be noted with the percentage to assist in understanding the results. Ninety percent passing means something very different for 10 or 100 test-takers. |
| **Range** | Range is a measure of the spread between the lowest and the highest scores in a distribution. Calculate the range of scores by subtracting the lowest score from the highest score. Range is often described as end points also, such as the range of percentile ranks is 1 and 99. | Ranges tell us the width of the distribution of scores. Educators working on continuous improvement will want to watch the range, of actual scores, decrease over time. | If there are outliers present, the range can give a misleading impression of dispersion. |
| **Raw Scores** | Raw scores refer to the number of questions answered correctly on a test or subtest. A raw score is simply calculated by adding the number of questions answered correctly. The raw score is a person's observed score. | The raw score provides information only about the number of questions answered correctly. To get a perspective on performance, raw scores must be used with the average score for the group and the total number of questions. Alone, raw scores have little meaning. | Raw scores do not provide information related to other students taking the test or to other subtests or scores. One needs to keep perspective by knowing the total number possible. Raw scores should never be used to make comparisons between performances on different tests unless other information about the characteristics of the tests are known and identical. |

**Figure 5.8** *(Continued)*
TERMS RELATED TO ANALYZING STUDENT ACHIEVEMENT RESULTS, DESCRIPTIVELY,
THEIR MOST EFFECTIVE USES, AND CAUTIONS FOR THEIR USES

| Term | Definition | Most Effective Uses | Cautions |
|---|---|---|---|
| *Relationships* | Relationships refer to looking at two or more sets of analyses to understand what they mean to each other without using extensive statistical techniques. | Descriptive statistics lend themselves to looking at the relationships of different analyses to each other; for instance, student learning results disaggregated by ethnicity, compared to student questionnaire results disaggregated by ethnicity. | This type of analysis is general and the results should be considered general as well. This is not a "correlation." |
| *Standard Deviation* | The standard deviation is a measure of variability in a set of scores. The standard deviation indicates how far away scores are from the mean. The standard deviation is the square root of the variance. Unlike the variance, the standard deviation is stated in the original units of the variable. Approximately 68 percent of the scores in a normal distribution lie between plus one and minus one standard deviation of the mean. The more scores cluster around the mean, the smaller the variance. | Tells us about the variability of scores. Standard deviations indicate how spread-out the scores are without looking at the entire distribution. A low standard deviation would indicate that the scores of a group are close together. A high standard deviation would imply that the range of scores is wide. | Often this is a confusing statistic for laypeople to understand. There are more descriptive ways to describe and show the variability of student scores, such as with a decile graph. Standard deviations only make sense with scores that are distributed normally. |
| *Triangulation* | Triangulation is a term used for combining three or more measures to get a more complete picture of student achievement. | If students are to be retained based on standards proficiency, educators must have more than one way of knowing if the students are proficient or not. Some students perform well on standardized measures and not on other measures, while others do not do well with standardized measures. Triangulation allows students to display what they know on three different measures. | It is sometimes very complicated to combine different measures to understand proficiency. When proficiency standards change, triangulation calculations will need to be revised. Therefore, all the calculations must be documented so they can be recalculated when necessary. |

## ANALYZING THE RESULTS, INFERENTIALLY

Many school administrators and teachers have taken statistics courses that taught them it is important to have control groups, experimental designs, and to test for significant differences. These terms fall in the category of inferential statistics. Inferential statistics are concerned with measuring a sample from a population, and then making estimates, or inferences, about the population from which the sample was taken. Inferential statistics help generalize the results of data analysis when one is not using the entire population in the analysis.

Descriptive analyses provide helpful and useful information and can be understood by a majority of people. When using the entire school population in your analyses, there is no need to generalize to a larger population—you have the whole population. There is little need for inferential statistics when doing basic data analysis work.

Inferential statistical methods, such as analyses of variance, correlations, and regression analyses are complex and require someone who knows statistics to meet the conditions and verify the conformity to the assumptions (postulates) of the analyses. Since there are times when a statistician is available to perform inferential statistics, some of the terms the statistician might use with tests include those listed in Figure 5.9.

*Inferential statistics are concerned with measuring a sample from a population, and then making estimates, or inferences, about the population from which the sample was taken.*

*Inferential statistical methods, such as analyses of variance, correlations, and regression analyses are complex and require someone who knows statistics to meet the conditions and verify the conformity to the assumptions (postulates) of the analyses.*

## Figure 5.9
### TERMS RELATED TO ANALYZING STUDENT ACHIEVEMENT RESULTS, INFERENTIALLY, THEIR MOST EFFECTIVE USES, AND CAUTIONS FOR THEIR USES

| Term | Definition | Most Effective Uses | Cautions |
|------|-----------|--------------------|----------|
| *Analysis of Variance (ANOVA)* | Analysis of variance is a general term applied to the study of differences in the application of approaches, as opposed to the relationship of different levels of approaches to the result. With ANOVAs, we are testing the differences of the means of at least two different distributions. | ANOVAs can be used to determine if there is a difference in student achievement scores between one school and another, keeping all other variables equal. It cannot tell you what the differences are, per se, but one can compute confidence intervals to estimate these differences. | Very seldom are the conditions available to study differences in education in this manner. Too many complex variables get in the way, and ethics may be involved. There are well-defined procedures for conducting ANOVAs to which we must adhere. |
| *Correlation Analyses* | Correlation is a statistical analysis that helps one understand the relationship of scores in one distribution to scores in another distribution. Correlations show magnitude and direction. Magnitude indicates the degree of the relationship. Correlation coefficients have a range of -1.0 to +1.0. A correlation of around zero would indicate little relationship. Correlations of .8 and higher, or -.8 and lower would indicate a strong relationship. When the high scores in one distribution are also high in the comparing distribution, the direction is positive. When the high scores in one distribution are related to the low scores in the other distribution, the result is a negative correlational direction. | Correlations can be used to understand the relationship of different variables to each other, e.g., attendance and performance on a standardized test; .40 to .70 are considered moderate correlations. Above .70 is considered to be high correlations. | It is wise to plot the scores to understand if the relationship is linear or not. One could misinterpret results if the scores are not linear. Pearson correlation coefficient requires linear relationships. Also, a few outliers could skew the results and oppositely skewed distributions can limit how high a Pearson coefficient can be. Also, one must remember that correlation does not suggest causation. |
| *Regression Analyses* | Regression analysis results in an equation that describes the nature of the relationship between variables. Simple regression predicts an object's value on a response variable when given its value on one predictor variable. Multiple regression predicts an object's value on a response variable when given its value on each of several predictor variables. Correlation tells you strength and direction of relationship. Regression goes one step further and allows you to predict. | A regression equation can be used to predict student achievement results, for example. Regression can determine if there is a relationship between two or more variables (such as attendance and student background) and the nature of those relation-ships. This analysis helps predict and prevent student failure, and predict and ensure student successes. | One needs to truly understand the statistical assumptions that need to be in place in order to perform a regression analysis. This is not an analysis to perform through trial and error. |

**Figure 5.9** *(Continued)*
## TERMS RELATED TO ANALYZING STUDENT ACHIEVEMENT RESULTS, INFERENTIALLY, THEIR MOST EFFECTIVE USES, AND CAUTIONS FOR THEIR USES

| Term | Definition | Most Effective Uses | Cautions |
|---|---|---|---|
| *Control Groups* | During an experiment, the control group is studied the same as the experimental group, except that it does not receive the treatment of interest. | Control groups serve as a baseline in making comparisons with treatment groups. Control groups are necessary when the general effectiveness of a treatment is unknown. | It may not be ethical to hold back from students some method of learning that we believe would be useful. |
| *Experimental Design* | Experimental design is the detailed planning of an experiment, made beforehand, to ensure that the data collected are appropriate and obtained in a way that will lead to an objective analysis, with valid inferences. | Experimental designs can maximize the amount of information gained, given the amount of effort expended. | Sometimes it takes statistical expertise to establish an experimental design properly. |
| *Experimental Group* | An experimental group is a group of individuals who are part of a clinical study or experiment who are exposed to the treatments of the experiment, while another group, the control group, is not. | Experimental groups are most effectively used in education when win-win situations are created. In other words, the control group will not be at a disadvantaged because they did not receive the treatment. | We do not always need experimental groups to test theories of what is working and what is not working. We can study results with all students. |
| *Tests of Significance* | Tests of significance use samples to test claims about population parameters. | Tests of significance can estimate a population parameter, with a certain amount of confidence, from a sample. | Often lay people do not know what *statistically significant* really means. |

## MEASUREMENT ERROR

All measurement, by definition, contains some error. However, that error can be measured.

We often hear people talk about sample sizes being too small to make any conclusions. Typically, what this means is that the larger the number of students in a sample, the more confidence we have that the score is an accurate reflection of that sample group's abilities. We also want to know if the increases showing up in a testing program in any year are because of "true" increases in learning. In order to understand a "true" gain resulting from an instructional program, we construct confidence bands or intervals that give each score a range as opposed to a single number. This range provides flexibility in understanding what the score would be if there were "errors" in the test. The table in Figure 5.10 gives the calculated standard error of measure for normal NCEs.

*The larger the number of students in a sample, the more confidence we have that the score is an accurate reflection of that sample group's abilities.*

**Figure 5.10**
GIVE AND TAKE TABLE

| Number of Students | Error (NCEs) | Number of Students | Error (NCEs) |
|---|---|---|---|
| 1 | 10.1 | 20 | 2.3 |
| 2 | 7.1 | 25 | 2.0 |
| 3 | 5.8 | 30 | 1.8 |
| 4 | 5.1 | 35 | 1.7 |
| 5 | 4.5 | 40 | 1.6 |
| 6 | 4.1 | 45 | 1.5 |
| 7 | 3.8 | 50 | 1.4 |
| 8 | 3.6 | 75 | 1.2 |
| 9 | 3.4 | 100 | 1.0 |
| 10 | 3.2 | 200 | 0.7 |
| 15 | 2.6 | 300 | 0.6 |

*Stanford Achievement Test: Eighth Edition.* Copyright © 1989 by The Psychological Corporation. Reproduced by permission. All rights reserved.

To construct a confidence band, consider that a group of five students had an average score of 40 on a reading test. We need to look at Figure 5.10, the *Give and Take Table,* to see that the error of measurement associated with the five students in this group is 4.5—the smaller the number of students, the more likely it is that the average represents a chance occurrence or error. The confidence band would then be formed from 35.5 to 44.5 (i.e., 40 - 4.5 = 35.5; 40 + 4.5 = 44.5). The interpretation: We can feel confident (68% of the time—one standard deviation) that the average true score of these students would be somewhere between 35.5 and 44.5. We can feel 95 percent confident that the average true score would be between 31 and 49 (double the size of the band, or two standard deviations, 2 x 4.5 = 9) (i.e., 40 - 9 = 31; 40 + 9 = 49).

## VALIDITY AND RELIABILITY OF ASSESSMENTS

Other important terms associated with testing are defined below. Please see the *References and Resources* section at the end of this book for further information about these terms.

## VALIDITY

The validity of a test or assessment refers to whether it provides the type of information desired. Validity can be enhanced by asking appropriate questions that get to what you want to know.

Ways to document and demonstrate validity include the following:

◆ Content validity relates to the appropriateness of the items with respect to the content, instruction, or the curriculum being measured.

◆ Predictive validity refers to a test's ability to predict future performance in the area that the instrument is measuring.

◆ Face validity relates to the appearance that the test (or the items on the test) measures what it claims to measure.

◆ Construct validity refers to the degree to which the test actually measures the particular construct (trait or aptitude) in question.

◆ Concurrent validity refers to the scores on a test being related to currently existing measures of the same content or behavior.

◆ Differential validity refers to the degree to which a test does not have a bias that would favor a particular sub-group of individuals (boys versus girls).

◆ Consequential validity refers to the wanted and unwanted implications resulting from the use of a test.

*The validity of a test or assessment refers to whether it provides the type of information desired.*

## RELIABILITY

The reliability of a test or assessment relates to the consistency with which knowledge is measured. Reliability tells us that if students were to take the test more than once, they would get the same (or nearly the same) score.

Reliability is impacted, among other things, by—

◆ the range of individual differences (a test administered to a heterogeneous group will increase the reliability of the results);

◆ the length of the test in terms of number of items (reliability increases with length);

◆ the time limit (if the test is too long and students cannot complete all the questions, the answers at the end, the ones not completed, will show high correlation because the scores are usually 0. That will artificially show an undue increase in reliability);

◆ the range of item difficulty (very easy tests or very difficult tests will have a lower reliability);

◆ the unidimensionality (all items should measure the same dimension, trait, or construct); and

*The reliability of a test or assessment relates to the consistency with which knowledge is measured.*

◆ the consistency of the testing environment and the testing material (booklets) among test sites and in time. Reliability increases when sources of errors are limited and controlled.

*A test may be reliable without being valid, but it cannot be valid without being reliable.*

A test may be reliable without being valid, but it cannot be valid without being reliable. As an example, a tape measure is an extremely "reliable" tool when measuring the length of a wall. However, it would be a non-"valid" measuring tool when preparing the mix for a cake. Also, a kitchen scale is a "valid" tool to measure the weight, but would be non-reliable and non-"valid" at measuring an adult's body weight.

## HOW MUCH TIME DOES IT TAKE?

**Most schools have summative student learning data available through their state or provincial offices of education. The Data Team might want to spend a couple of hours reorganizing the data for the data profile.**

**Organizing multiple measures of student learning data will take a little longer, starting with identifying what is being used in all grade levels and subject areas.**

## REFLECTION QUESTIONS

1. What are student learning data?

2. Why are student learning data important for continuous school improvement?

3. How is your school assessing student learning, and why? Are these approaches appropriate?

4. Who should know the student learning data of a school?

## APPLICATION OPPORTUNITIES

1. Use the student learning data inventory (Appendix B3) to list how your school assesses student learning. Note gaps in assessments and uses of assessments. Make sure your assessments are appropriate for the intended uses and information.

2. Graph your schoolwide student achievement data, disaggregated in the ways mentioned in the chapter and as shown in Appendix F.

**6**

CHAPTER

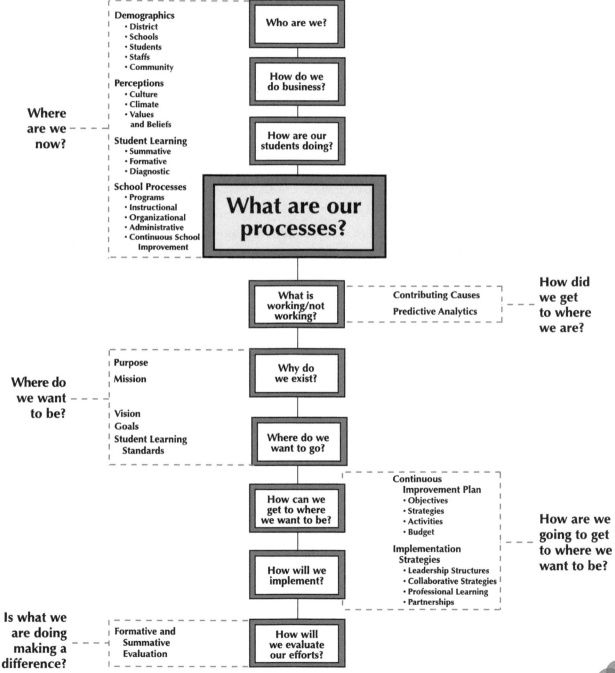

**Where are we now?**

Demographics
- District
- Schools
- Students
- Staffs
- Community

Perceptions
- Culture
- Climate
- Values and Beliefs

Student Learning
- Summative
- Formative
- Diagnostic

School Processes
- Programs
- Instructional
- Organizational
- Administrative
- Continuous School Improvement

Who are we?

How do we do business?

How are our students doing?

**What are our processes?**

What is working/not working?

**How did we get to where we are?**

Contributing Causes

Predictive Analytics

**Where do we want to be?**

Purpose

Mission

Vision

Goals

Student Learning Standards

Why do we exist?

Where do we want to go?

How can we get to where we want to be?

**How are we going to get to where we want to be?**

Continuous Improvement Plan
- Objectives
- Strategies
- Activities
- Budget

Implementation Strategies
- Leadership Structures
- Collaborative Strategies
- Professional Learning
- Partnerships

How will we implement?

**Is what we are doing making a difference?**

Formative and Summative Evaluation

How will we evaluate our efforts?

*"Schools" are perfectly designed to get the results they are getting now. If "schools" want different results, they must measure and then change their processes to get the results they really want.*

Adapted from W. Edwards Deming
Continuous Improvement Guru

*School processes are the only measures over which we have almost complete control in the education setting.*

School processes are the only measures over which we have almost complete control in the education setting. Public schools cannot control who the students are, where they come from, or why they think the way they do when they come to us. However, schools can control a portion of the student learning results—through their processes (i.e., curriculum, instructional strategies, assessment practices, programs, environment).

## SCHOOL PROCESSES DATA: WHAT THEY ARE AND WHY THEY ARE IMPORTANT TO CONTINUOUS SCHOOL IMPROVEMENT

*School processes are actions administrators and teachers take to achieve the purpose of the school— the vision.*

School processes are actions administrators and teachers take to achieve the purpose of the school—the vision. School processes are those things that teachers do by habit, by custom, or inadvertently, and those things that may help or hinder progress. School processes also include those elements that help your school improve.

School processes data are important because they tell us about the way we work, about how we get the results we are getting, set us up to know what is working and what is not working, and answer the continuous school improvement question, *What are our processes?* School processes are important to continuous school improvement because they are what produce school and classroom results.

*School processes are important to continuous school improvement because they are what produce school and classroom results.*

There are different types of school processes that we need to study and improve. Categories were established to help us think about all the processes that create the results we are getting in schools. Examples of each type of school process are shown below for—

◆ *Instructional processes*—the techniques and strategies that teachers use in the learning environment.

◆ *Organizational processes*—those structures the school puts in place to implement the vision.

◆ *Administrative processes*—elements about schooling that we count, such as class sizes.

◆ *Continuous school improvement processes*—the structures and elements that help schools continuously improve their systems.

Some data collected as demographics imply processes behind the terms, such as administrative processes. Programs are school processes too. Programs are planned series of activities and processes, with specific goals. See the lists of example processes and programs in Figure 6.1.

Understanding the schools' processes and programs is the first step in clarifying how a school is achieving its goals and getting its results, and determining if instructional congruence exists. Understanding the cumulative effect of the entire system, including classroom processes, is necessary for determining what needs to change to ensure learning for *all* students, and what and how we want to staff to implement certain processes. While all of the elements listed in Figure 6.1 are part of the processes that tell us how we are fulfilling the vision of our school, it may be the instructional strategies and assessments occurring every day in our classrooms that deserve the first analysis.

*Understanding the schools' processes and programs is the first step in clarifying how a school is achieving its goals and getting its results, and determining if instructional congruence exists.*

## HOW TO ANALYZE SCHOOL PROCESSES DATA

The evidence of what we do and how we do it is data. Four steps will support your analysis of school processes data:

Step 1.  *List the programs and processes being used in your school.* Use the school processes inventory (Appendix B4) or something similar. It is important to be as comprehensive as possible. To understand how we got our results and to get even better results, staff must be clear about what is being implemented to get these results.

Step 2.  *Analyze the lists of programs and processes.* As a staff, determine which programs and processes need to be deleted, added, and implemented by everyone. Keep the school vision, purpose, and goals at the forefront as you review.

Step 3.  *Analyze the programs and processes using the Measuring Programs and Processes Table.* The complete *Measuring a Program or Process* activity is found in Appendix D. This powerful table helps staff spell out the important concepts for developing, implementing, and evaluating a program or process with fidelity and integrity. The questions in the table are:

- ◆ What is the purpose of the program or process?

- ◆ How will you know the purpose is being met? Or what are the outcomes?

> **HOW TO ANALYZE SCHOOL PROCESSES DATA**
>
> Step 1.  *List the programs and processes being used in your school.*
> Step 2.  *Analyze the lists of programs and processes.*
> Step 3.  *Analyze the programs and processes using the Measuring Programs and Processes Table.*
> Step 4.  *Use flowcharts to describe and visualize how a program or process is to be implemented.*

Figure 6.1
SCHOOL PROCESSES EXAMPLES

| Instructional Processes | Organizational Processes | Administrative Processes | Continuous School Improvement Processes | Programs |
|---|---|---|---|---|
| • Curriculum (what we teach)<br>• Instructional Strategies (how we teach)<br>• Assessments (how we know students are learning what we teach)<br>• Differentiated Instruction<br>• Direct Instruction<br>• Flipped Classrooms<br>• Grading<br>• Homework<br>• Immersion<br>• Academic conversations with students<br>• Classroom discussions (teacher talk, student-to student talk, student-to teacher talk)<br>• Classroom assignments (types of tasks, choices, projects, collaboration)<br>• Inquiry process<br>• Student reflection and self-assessment<br>• Standards Implementation<br>• Technology Integration<br>• Tutoring | • Teacher Collaboration<br>• Data Teams<br>• Data Use<br>• Leadership Structure (Leadership Teams)<br>• Professional Learning Communities<br>• Response to Intervention (RtI)<br>• Mentoring<br>• Instructional Coaching<br>• Referral Process<br>• Policies and Procedures<br>• Parent Involvement<br>• Teacher Hiring<br>• Teaching Assignments<br>• Teacher renewal (professional learning)<br>• Professional reflection<br>• Teacher evaluation<br>• Inquiry process<br>• Problem-solving<br>• Professional discussions and support<br>• Teacher observations<br>• Mission<br>• Vision | • Scheduling of classes<br>• Class sizes<br>• Discipline strategies<br>• Student groupings<br>• Policies and procedures<br>• Enrollment in different courses/programs/program offerings<br>• Retentions<br>• Attendance Program<br>• Dropout rates<br>• Graduation rates<br>• Teacher hiring<br>• Teacher assignments<br>• Teacher certification<br>• Teacher turnover rates<br>• Leadership turnover rates<br>• Number of support personnel<br>• Data collection | • Data analysis and use<br>• Contributing cause analysis<br>• Vision<br>• Mission<br>• Continuous school improvement planning<br>• Leadership<br>• Professional learning<br>• Partnership<br>• Evaluation<br>• Self-assessment | • AVID<br>• A+<br>• Accelerated Reader/Math<br>• Advanced Placement<br>• After School<br>• Advanced Placement<br>• At-Risk<br>• Bilingual<br>• Dropout Prevention<br>• Gifted and Talented<br>• International Baccalaureate<br>• Interventions<br>• 9th Grade Academy<br>• Science Fairs<br>• Service Learning<br>• Special Education |

◆ Who is the program/process intended to serve? Who is being served/who is not being served?

◆ What would it look like when the program/process is fully implemented?

◆ How is implementation being measured? (Should it be measured differently?)

◆ To what degree is the program/process being implemented?

◆ What are the results (in the short term and in the long term)?

An example of *The Measuring Programs and Processes Table* is shown as Figure 6.2. This example was created by Somewhere School staff members as they were starting to implement the *Common Core State Standards*. The work described in the table helps all teachers keep the purpose for doing the work at the forefront of their efforts. It shows them what it will look like when they are implementing the standards, and it sets up the monitoring and evaluation of the implementation. As their work progresses, they will add more details. (Other examples appear as Figure 12.3, and in Appendix D.)

Figure 6.2

MEASURING PROCESSES: IMPLEMENTATION OF THE COMMON CORE STATE STANDARDS

| PURPOSE | | PARTICIPANTS | IMPLEMENTATION | | RESULTS |
|---|---|---|---|---|---|
| *What is the purpose of the program or process?* | *How will you know the purpose is being met? (What are the outcomes?)* | *Who is the program/process intended to serve? Who is being served/not being served?* | *What would it look like when the program/process is fully implemented?* | *How is implementation being measured?* | *To what degree is the program being implemented?* |
| *The intent in implementing the CCSS is to do the following.*<br>• Ensure that all students are college and career ready by graduation for a "21st Century, globally competitive society."ii<br>• Provide a focused and coherent CCSS curriculum that is results-oriented and supported by aligned instructional resources.<br>• Use consistently CCSS based instructional strategies that are research-based, differentiated, culturally relevant and responsive, and implemented with fidelity.<br>• Define how implementation of the CCSS supports the belief that *all students can learn* and define the implementation roles and responsibilities for each segment of the school community: students, staff, parents, and community members. | *When an effective CCSS Continuous School Improvement (CSI) and Response to Intervention (RtI) model is implemented by all school staff with fidelity, analyses of qualitative and quantitative data will reveal the following outcomes.*<br>• *All* students are meeting grade level CCSS proficiency standards and are on a trajectory for graduating from high school prepared for success in college and career in the 21st Century globally competitive world.<br>• *All* teachers are implementing the school's Continuous School Improvement (CSI) and Response to Intervention (RtI) models with fidelity, resulting in yearly increases in students attaining CCSS proficiency and the consistent reduction of the student failure rate.<br>• *All* students receive a focused and coherent CCSS curriculum that is built upon a progression of learning that is implemented with fidelity, using aligned resources and evidence based, monitoring tools, differentiated, culturally relevant and responsive instructional strategies.<br>• *All teachers'* classroom instruction, as well as their professional growth endeavors and collaborative faculty work, reflect the core intent of the CCSS and main principle of the CSI Model—the belief that *all students can learn to rigorous standards (CCSS focus on accessibility).* | *The CSI and RtI programs supporting the implementation of the CCSS are intended to serve—*<br>• *All Students*<br><br>*Those not being served by the CSI and RtI programs designed to implement the CCSS include—*<br>• *Students who are not attaining proficiency on CCSS annually as shown by results on the SBAC or PARCC.iv* | (Description below. Also see attached flowchart.)<br>*When implementation of the CCSS is fully in place, the following will occur.*<br>All consistencies of the school community are fulfilling their defined roles in implementing the CCSS as is evidenced in the following ways.<br>• Students are actively engaged in problem-solving and innovative work, assuming responsibility for their own learning, participating in and leading quality classroom discussions, demonstrating collaborative skills in group work, using technology effectively and efficiently, attaining proficiency on yearly summative assessments, staying in school with high attendance rates and few tardies, and, in high school, graduating on schedule and being accepted into an accredited college or university by end of the senior year.<br>• *All teachers* are implementing a focused and coherent curriculum, using technology and aligned instructional resources and evidenced-based, differentiated instructional strategies with the fidelity that results in *all* students achieving proficiency on the grade level CCSS. (CSI Program Goal by Year 5). | **Continuous School Improvement Model**<br>**Perceptions**<br>Surveys, inventories, self-assessments related to culture, climate, values, and beliefs of various populations including—<br>• Students<br>• All staff serving the school<br>• Parents<br>• Community members<br><br>**Demographics**<br>District and school data and analysis of demographic data (by subgroups)—<br>• District<br>• School<br>• Staff<br>• Students<br>• Community<br><br>**Student Learning**<br>Data from a variety of sources that include:<br>*Formative Assessments*<br>• Diagnostic assessment tools.<br>• Instructionally embedded assessments.<br>• Observations.<br>• Teacher, peer, and self-evaluations of student work. | **CCSS Implementation**<br>*Staff is at the starting point having done the following.*<br>• Participated in several webinars.<br>• Read the CCSS for their content area and literacy across History, Social Studies, Science, and Technical Subjects.<br>• Determined that they are at the *novice* level of CCSS knowledge and so have made the CCSS the staff's top priority for the upcoming year.<br><br>*The staff plan for the upcoming year includes the following—*<br>• Conduct a CCSS Standards Study in the CoPP (PD).<br>• Conduct an alignment of instructional resources.<br>• Identify and fill gaps.<br>• Write new CSI and RtI plans aligned to the CCSS.<br>• Lay out an instructional sequence plan for teaching the CCSS by grade level.<br>• Create materials to share with parents and community to involve them in the CCSS conversation and start a dialogue about what the CCSS will mean for students. |

*CCSS Example developed by: Cheryl Z.Tibbals ~ cztibbalsconsulting@gmail.com ~ (Office) 925-385-9097 ~ (Cell) 415-602-9097*
*Senior Advisor to Evans Newton Incorporated (ENI) ~ Scottsdale, AZ ~ (Home Office) 480-998-2777*

Figure 6.2 (Continued)

MEASURING PROCESSES: IMPLEMENTATION OF THE COMMON CORE STATE STANDARDS

| PURPOSE | | PARTICIPANTS | IMPLEMENTATION | | RESULTS |
|---|---|---|---|---|---|
| *What is the purpose of the program or process?* | *How will you know the purpose is being met?* (*What are the outcomes?*) | *Who is the program/process intended to serve? Who is being served/not being served?* | *What would it look like when the program/process is fully implemented?* | *How is implementation being measured?* | *To what degree is the program being implemented?* |
| • Support *all* students' effective CCSS transition through the school's Continuous School Improvement (CSI) and Response to Intervention (RtI) Models to prevent school failure.<br>• Provide curriculum and instruction that result in *all* students achieving *proficiency in* English Language Arts, Mathematics, and Literacy in History/Social Studies, Science, and Technical Subjects.<br>• Provide *all* students with continuous and timely feedback as a result of instruction that embeds formative assessment in all lessons, providing feedback in the form of teacher comments, peer feedback, and student self evaluation of work (metacognition). | • *All students are consistently engaged in* authentic work and instruction is evidence-based, embedding formative assessment, and targeted differentiation to address the needs of all students (those above, at, and below proficiency, special education, students with disabilities, and students transitioning from another language).<br>• *All teachers consistently embed a range of appropriate formative assessment strategies in* their daily instruction, gathering data that provides *timely* feedback and re-teaching, improving future instruction and student results.<br>• Evidence indicates that the CSI Model is being successfully supported by effective professional development, that this includes teacher collaboration on standards study, lesson study, instructional alignment, and filling instructional resource gaps.<br>• Coaching is aligned to CCSS and is continually improving instructional design and delivery.<br>• All students produce work consistently that represents grade level mastery of the CCSS, including use of critical thinking skills;[iii] proficiency in problem-solving; ability to read complex text critically and take a stance, write and speak to a variety of audiences and for a variety of purposes across content areas, apply 21st Century skills, collaborate and work effectively on teams, conduct research using a variety of technical and other resources, use feedback to improve work (teacher, peer, metacognitive), demonstrate creativity and innovation, and develop habits of mind that result in students who think like mathematicians, scientists, writers, etc. | | • Students in *all* teachers' classrooms are realizing at least one year's academic growth on summative CCSS assessments (SBAC or PARCC), while the remainder of the students are attaining more than one year's growth on the CCSS. (Program Goals for Years 1–4.)<br>• CCSS implementation is the number one agenda item at all faculty meetings, and the focus of work in the school's community of professional practice (CoPP). *All staff members are active participants in the CoPP.*<br>• Coaching, student counseling, and afterschool learning programs are aligned to the CCSS and evaluation indicates that these strategies and programs are resulting in consistent increases in student achievement and attendance, while reducing tardies and drop-outs.<br>• School leadership goals and practices are evidence-based, aligned to the staff's identified intent for the implementation of the CCSS.<br>• Ongoing *formative* assessment of the school's CSI and RtI Models involves all staff and is providing for timely corrections and adjustments during the school year, while summative assessments provide for annual re-examination of the entire CSI and RtI programs, providing an opportunity to make more major and substantive data-based changes and additions. | • Inventories and surveys<br>• Staff created formative assessments that accompany lessons/units.<br><br>**Summative CCSS Assessments**<br>• End-of-course or end-of-unit assessments.<br>• School or district Periodic, Interim, or Benchmark Assessments (can be used as formative, summative, or both).<br>• Accountability Assessments<br>　* Partnership for Assessment and Readiness for College and Careers (PARCC) and SMARTER Balanced Assessment Consortium (SBAC).<br><br>**College Entrance and Placement Examinations**<br>• College Entrance and Examinations (e.g., Entrance Exams–ACT, SAT).<br>• College Placement Examinations (e.g., the University of California Analytical Writing Placement Examination, Yale Mathematics Placement Exam). | • Become familiar with the content and item specifications of the assessment Consortium (SBAC or PARCC) that will be providing their state accountability assessments.<br>• Develop a three-year CCSS implementation plan as part of the school's new CSI plan.<br>• Develop a *formative* assessment plan to inform and guide the development of the new CSI plan and to monitor progress.<br>• Conduct a summative evaluation of the work complete and the processes in place to inform the next year's CCSS implementation work. |

CCSS Example developed by: Cheryl Z. Tibbals -- cztibbalsconsulting@gmail.com ~ (Office) 925-385-9097 ~ (Cell) 415-602-9097
Senior Advisor to Evans Newton Incorporated (ENI) ~ Scottsdale, AZ ~ (Home Office) 480-998-2777

Figure 6.2 *(Continued)*

## MEASURING PROCESSES: IMPLEMENTATION OF THE COMMON CORE STATE STANDARDS

| PURPOSE | | PARTICIPANTS | IMPLEMENTATION | | RESULTS |
|---|---|---|---|---|---|
| *What is the purpose of the program or process?* | *How will you know the purpose is being met? (What are the outcomes?)* | *Who is the program/process intended to serve? Who is being served/ not being served?* | *What would it look like when the program/process is fully implemented?* | *How is implementation being measured?* | *To what degree is the program being implemented?* |
| • Provide instruction that is designed to *engage all students* in complex, authentic tasks that require them to: <br> * Apply critical thinking skills (problem-solving, problem-creation); <br> * Read complex literary and informational texts critically for a variety of purposes and across content areas; <br> * Write for a variety of audiences and purposes across disciplines; <br> * Speak and write clearly, identify crucial points in speeches and text, use reasoning supported by evidence, take a critical stance in reading, writing and speaking; <br> * Establish and defend an *argument* rationally in oral and written work; <br> * Solve problems with more than one right answer or no apparent right answer; <br> * Justify mathematical solutions; <br> * Connect mathematical content and practices in solving problems efficiently and effectively; <br> * Conduct research, collecting, synthesizing, and evaluating information critically, using a variety of resources including media and technology. <br> * Construct/produce knowledge; <br> * Revise, edit, and improve work. <br> * Demonstrate creativity, innovation, and habits of mind. | | | • Parents are continually articulating the goals and importance of the CCSS to their children, providing support for homework, communicating regularly with teachers about student progress, and participating in CCSS meetings and virtual parent education. <br> • Community members are supporting CCSS implementation through local informational campaigns, rallies, and online Community CCSS parent chat groups. | **School Processes** <br> • Analyses of data that show how well each student population is being served including how many Level 2 students move into Level 1 or Level 3 or stay in Level 2, percent (by subgroup) of students identified for Special Education after receiving Level 2 and 3 assistance, etc. <br> • Analyses of data specific to problem areas in curriculum, assessment, and instruction (where is the curriculum, assessment, instruction failing the students–which students? <br> • Analyses of implementation data to identify effective and ineffective implementation strategies, or implementation strategies not being implemented with fidelity. <br> • Analyses of data to identify needed revisions to the Action Plan. <br> • Re-examination of alignment of resources using student assessment data to pinpoint resources not fully in alignment with the CCSS. | |

*Page 3 of 3*

CCSS Example developed by: Cheryl Z. Tibbals ~ cztibbalsconsulting@gmail.com ~ (Office) 925-385-9097 ~ (Cell) 415-602-9097
Senior Advisor to Evans Newton Incorporated (ENI) ~ Scottsdale, AZ ~ (Home Office) 480-998-2777

*i* Step 1 of this CCSS Implementation Model addresses the content areas of English Language Arts and Mathematics. It touches on *Literacy in History/Social Studies, Science, and Technical Subjects*, but does not represent a full implementation plan in the cross content areas during year one. The assumption is that the ELA teachers will need the first year to master their own CCSS standards before working with teachers across content areas on the *Literacy* skills that they will be incorporating in their instructional programs. A school that feels ready to take the *Literacy* standards as well during the first year could easily modify this plan to accommodate implementation of all CCSS in year one.

*ii* *Common Core State Standards for English Language Arts & History/Social Studies, Science, and Technical Subjects*, Introduction, page 3 found at: *http://www.corestandards.org/assets/CCSSI_ELA%20Standards.pdf*

*iii* Hess, Carlock, Jones, & Walkup. A "*Snapshot*" *of the Cognitive Rigor Matrix.* 2009. NCIEA.

*iv* SBAC = SMARTER Balanced Assessment Consortium. PARCC = Partnership for Assessment of Readiness for College and Careers.

Step 4.  *Use flowcharts to describe and visualize how a program or
process is to be implemented.* A flowchart allows everyone to
see and to agree upon the major steps, in sequence, in the same
way. Flowcharts help with the design, implementation, and
evaluation of programs, processes, and procedures. (See
Appendix E for *Flowcharting a School Process* and more
examples.) The typical symbols used in flowcharting
educational processes include:

Figure 6.3 shows the flowchart for Somewhere School's implementation of the
Common Core State Standards. This specific flowchart shows their agreements for
how they will start with the standards and assessments, what they will do when
students know the information, and what they will do when students do not know
the information taught. The flowchart provides staff members with a clear message
of what is expected of them in their classrooms. The flowchart also provides the
details needed for monitoring implementation, and for evaluating the impact of the
approach.

Figure 6.4 shows a big picture flowchart for how Somewhere School will implement
the Common Core State Standards.

*Use flowcharts to
describe and visualize
how a program or
process is to be
implemented. A
flowchart allows
everyone to see and to
agree to the major steps,
in sequence,
in the same way.*

*Flowcharts help
with the design,
implementation,
and evaluation of
programs, processes,
and procedures.*

### Figure 6.3
## SOMEWHERE SCHOOL PREVENTION SYSTEM FLOWCHART (Part 1)

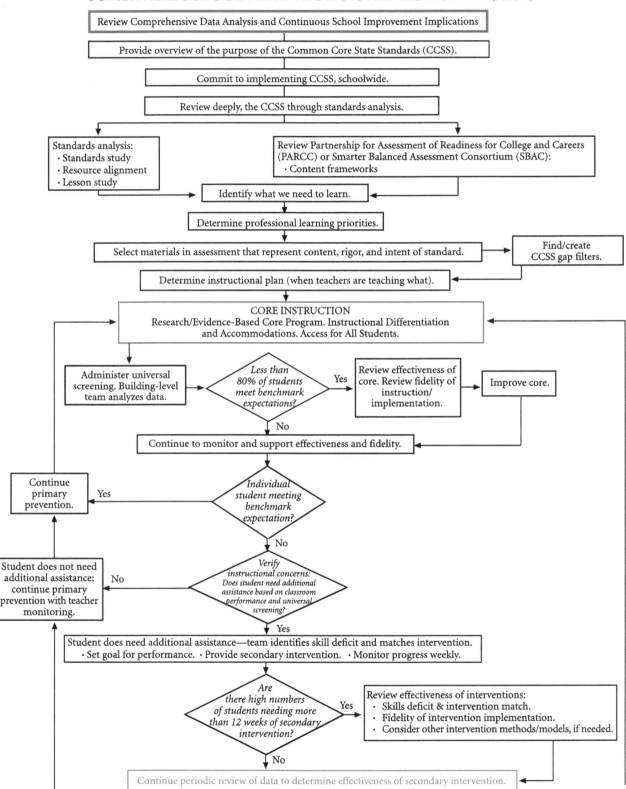

**Figure 6.3**
**SOMEWHERE SCHOOL PREVENTION SYSTEM FLOWCHART (Part 2)**

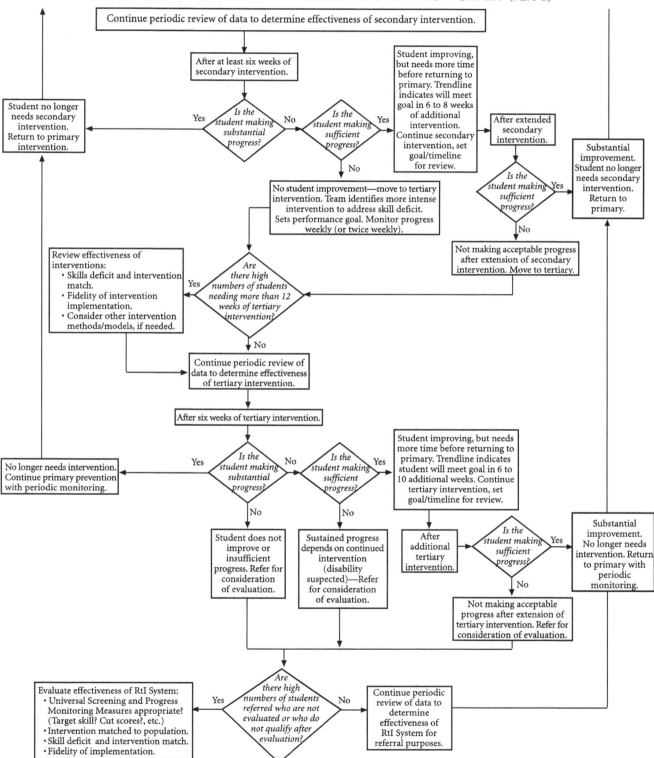

Figure 6.4
COMMON CORE STATE STANDARDS FLOWCHART

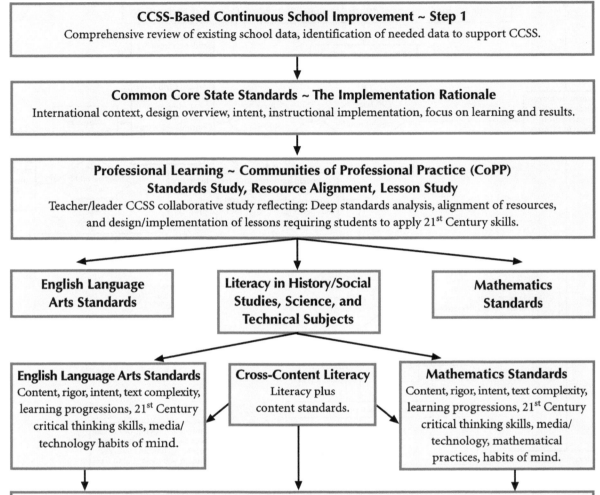

**CCSS-Based Continuous School Improvement ~ Step 1**
Comprehensive review of existing school data, identification of needed data to support CCSS.

**Common Core State Standards ~ The Implementation Rationale**
International context, design overview, intent, instructional implementation, focus on learning and results.

**Professional Learning ~ Communities of Professional Practice (CoPP)**
**Standards Study, Resource Alignment, Lesson Study**
Teacher/leader CCSS collaborative study reflecting: Deep standards analysis, alignment of resources, and design/implementation of lessons requiring students to apply 21st Century skills.

**English Language Arts Standards**

**Literacy in History/Social Studies, Science, and Technical Subjects**

**Mathematics Standards**

**English Language Arts Standards**
Content, rigor, intent, text complexity, learning progressions, 21st Century critical thinking skills, media/technology habits of mind.

**Cross-Content Literacy**
Literacy plus content standards.

**Mathematics Standards**
Content, rigor, intent, text complexity, learning progressions, 21st Century critical thinking skills, media/technology, mathematical practices, habits of mind.

**Standards Study, Lesson Study, Formative Assessment**
What is different about the CCSS? What are the instructional implications of these differences (e.g., use of evidence-based strategies, formative assessment, student engagement, problem-solving tasks, etc.)? What aligned instructional resources do we have? What are the gaps? How will roles of students and staff change in the CCSS world? What should CCSS lessons look like? What are the elements of effective CCSS lessons? How can Lesson Study help?

**Continuous School Improvement (CSI) and Response to Intervention (RtI)**
How will our step 1 professional learning plan help us implement the CCSS successfully? How will we reconstruct the school's CSI Plan so that the CCSS is the core of the program? Will our existing RtI System provide the multi-level prevention system we will need in the CCSS world? If not, what do we need to rethink or change? What is the next step for our continuous CCSS professional learning.

Developed by: Cheryl Z. Tibbals ~ *cztibbalsconsulting@gmail.com* ~(Office) 925-385-9097 ~ (Cell) 415-602-9097
Senior Advisor to Evans Newton Incorporated (ENI) ~ Scottsdale, AZ ~ (Home Office) 480-998-2777

## MEASUREMENT OF SYSTEM-LEVEL PROCESSES

Continuous school improvement is a major process that can be analyzed by using the *Continuous Improvement Continuums* that are described in Chapter 2 and Appendix A. It is important to do the self-analysis with the *Continuous Improvement Continuums.* The main reason is to discover where staff perceive the school is right now on major areas of continuous school improvement, which shows everyone where the school is right now. Knowing where they are right now makes it easy to know what needs to happen to move everyone forward together. The second main reason it is important to do the self-assessment with the *Continuous Improvement Continuums* is that it keeps staff working together and moving forward on continuous school improvement. If school staff do not know where they are in the process and if they do not know they are making progress, they tend to end their school improvement processes within two years.

When schools commit to continuous school improvement, they understand processes must be studied and improved. Analyzing processes is a must as schools move from compliance to commitment to continuous school improvement.

*If school staff do not know where they are in the process and if they do not know they are making progress, they tend to end their school improvement processes within two years.*

*Analyzing processes is a must as schools move from compliance to commitment to continuous school improvement.*

## HOW MUCH TIME DOES IT TAKE?

It will probably take about a couple of hours for staff to list major programs and processes operating in the school, and maybe another half hour to discuss which programs and processes all staff members should be using, and which programs and processes should be eliminated.

It will take about an hour to describe each program in the *Measuring Programs and Processes Table,* and another hour to flowchart what it would look like when the program or process is implemented with full integrity and fidelity.

## REFLECTION QUESTIONS

1. What are school process data?

2. Why are school process data important for continuous school improvement?

3. Do you know what programs and processes are being implemented in your school?

## APPLICATION OPPORTUNITIES

1. Use the school processes inventory (Appendix B4) to list the programs and processes that your teachers are using.

2. Determine which programs or processes need to be dropped, added, and those that need to be implemented by everyone on staff.

3. Use the *Measuring Programs and Processes Table* (Appendix D) to set up your programs/processes for consistent implementation and for evaluation.

4. Use flowcharting tools (Appendix E) to show what your major programs will look like when they are implemented as intended.

# *HOW DID WE GET TO WHERE WE ARE:*
## LOOKING ACROSS ALL THE DATA

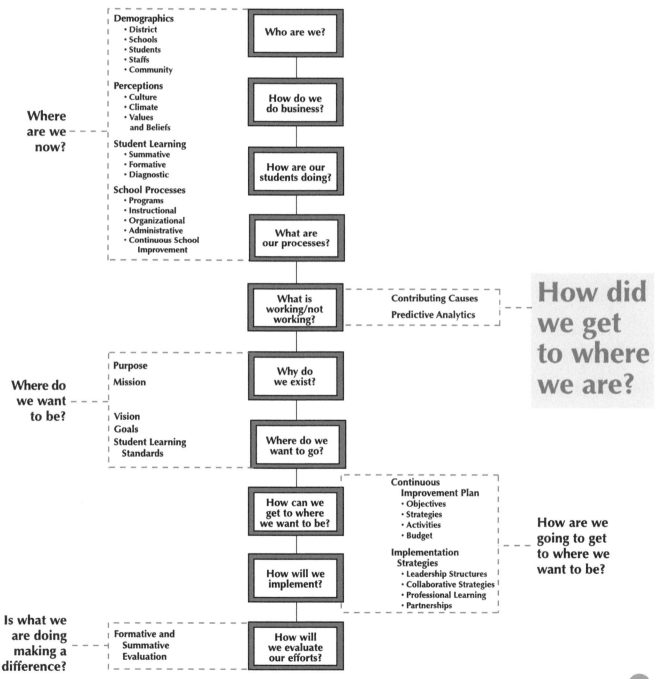

**Where are we now?**

**Demographics**
- District
- Schools
- Students
- Staffs
- Community

**Perceptions**
- Culture
- Climate
- Values and Beliefs

**Student Learning**
- Summative
- Formative
- Diagnostic

**School Processes**
- Programs
- Instructional
- Organizational
- Administrative
- Continuous School Improvement

Who are we?

How do we do business?

How are our students doing?

What are our processes?

What is working/not working?

Contributing Causes

Predictive Analytics

**How did we get to where we are?**

**Where do we want to be?**

Purpose
Mission

Vision
Goals
Student Learning Standards

Why do we exist?

Where do we want to go?

How can we get to where we want to be?

How will we implement?

**Continuous Improvement Plan**
- Objectives
- Strategies
- Activities
- Budget

**Implementation Strategies**
- Leadership Structures
- Collaborative Strategies
- Professional Learning
- Partnerships

**How are we going to get to where we want to be?**

**Is what we are doing making a difference?**

Formative and Summative Evaluation

How will we evaluate our efforts?

*Learning takes place neither in isolation,
nor only at school. Multiple measures must be considered
and used to understand the multifaceted world of learning from
the perspective of everyone involved. If staff want to know if the
school is achieving its purpose and how to continually improve all
aspects of the school, multiple measures—gathered from
varying points of view—must be used.*

*Education for the Future*

*Bringing all the data together with a process that engages staff to identify strengths, challenges, and implications for the continuous school improvement plan is what makes the data profile so powerful.*

*The data profile allows staff members to look across the different types of data and see how they can move the whole system as easily as focusing on one gap.*

By starting with an in-depth appraisal of where your school is on the four types of data described in Chapters 3, 4, 5, and *6—demographics, perceptions, student learning,* and *school processes*—and organizing them into a comprehensive school data profile, your school staff will have the story of the school, showing the results they are getting with the processes they are currently implementing. Independently, each area of data is informative and important. Bringing all the data together with a process that engages staff to identify strengths, challenges, and implications for the continuous school improvement plan is what makes the data profile so powerful.

The data profile allows staff members to look across the different types of data and see how they can move the whole system as easily as focusing on one gap. They see how changes in elements in demographics, perceptions, and school processes can improve student learning. The data profile is a needs assessment as well as a beginning of the evaluation of the system. Schools need to gather the data once and use it many ways. Appendix F shows a data profile that includes demographic data, perceptions data examples, summative student learning results, and some school processes examples.

## WHY IT IS IMPORTANT FOR CONTINUOUS SCHOOL IMPROVEMENT TO LOOK ACROSS ALL TYPES OF DATA?

*Looking across all types of data is important for seeing how elements of the learning organization relate to each other, as well as the linkages in the data results.*

Looking across all types of data is important for seeing how elements of the learning organization relate to each other, as well as the linkages in the data results. It is guaranteed that issues will show up in demographics, perceptions, and school processes that can help explain how a school is getting the results it is getting in student learning. Consequently, that information is useful for positively impacting student learning results. It is also guaranteed that a school will not see the same issues if only summative student learning data are reviewed. Looking across all data can help schools work efficiently to improve all content areas at the same time, not just the lowest performing area.

There is no doubt that continuous school improvement plans based on multiple measures of data look very different from school improvement plans that are focused only on student learning data. School improvement plans based only on summative student learning results add interventions to "fix" the students, or to get their scores up, to meet compliance. Continuous school improvement plans based on all types of data are able to move the entire system forward more efficiently and effectively, partly because they have engaged all staff in seeing the linkages of all data, and can swiftly move together. Staff members creating continuous school improvement plans, based on multiple measures of data, see that teaching and student learning results can improve by improving instructional processes focused on learning standards, improving behavior with schoolwide consistency, engaging interests of student groups, giving students a reason to attend school, and improving attitudes by listening to students, staffs, and parents, for example.

*Continuous school improvement plans based on all types of data are able to move the entire system forward more efficiently and effectively, partly because they have engaged all staff in seeing the linkages of all data, and can swiftly move together.*

## HOW TO LOOK ACROSS ALL TYPES OF DATA: ANALYZING YOUR SCHOOL'S DATA PROFILE

We recommend that all staff get involved in analyzing your school's four types of data. (*The Analyzing Data for Continuous School Improvement Planning* activity that appears in Appendix H will guide the process.) A summary of the process for synthesizing findings across the school follows.

## DEMOGRAPHIC DATA

| 1. What are Somewhere Elementary School's demographic *strengths* and *challenges?* ||
|---|---|
| **Strengths** | **Challenges** |
|  |  |
| 2. What are some *implications* for the Somewhere School continuous school improvement plan? ||
|  ||
| 3. Looking at the data presented, what other Somewhere School demographic data would you want to answer the question *Who are we?* ||
|  ||

After creating a data profile for each type of data as described in the preceding chapters, complete the following:

Step 1. **Independent Review.** Have each member of your staff independently analyze each type of data—demographics, perceptions, student learning, and school processes—(one type at a time) for strengths, challenges, implications for the continuous school improvement plan, and identify other data they wished they had. These should be the first ideas that come to mind, as opposed to reviewing the data and then making notes. The analysis will be much richer. (A template for documenting strengths, challenges, implications for the school improvement plan, and other data is included in Appendix H.)

> ## ANALYZING YOUR SCHOOL'S DATA PROFILE
>
> - *Strengths*
> - *Challenges*
> - *Implications*
> - *Other data*

**Strengths** are positive elements one can see in the data. These are ideas for which the school wants to keep track, and keep doing. Strengths can be used as leverage for improving a challenge. An example strength: "This school has an excellent student teacher ratio."

**Challenges** found in data imply something might need attention, is out of a school's control, or a potential undesirable result. An example challenge: "The number of students living in poverty in this school has tripled in the past five years."

**Implications for the continuous school improvement plan** are ideas that the reviewer jots down while reviewing the data. Implications are placeholders until all the data are analyzed. Implications most often are constructive responses to challenges. An example implication derived from the challenge example above might be: "Do all staff have the professional learning they need to meet the needs of the students who live in poverty?"

**Other data we wished the school had.** When school staff review the school's data effectively, they always uncover other data they wish they had available. The examination of the data will highlight issues in data collection, storage, and reporting, as well. It is important to make note of these issues so data can be gathered appropriately. An example: "We need to do a more comprehensive job of identifying who, what, where, and when behavior issues take place at the school site." Staff would need to clarify what data they need to gather, how each staff member will gather and report the data, and then how and when they will review the data, and do something about the results.

Step 2. **Small group review.** For each type of data—in small groups, have staff members share what they saw for strengths, challenges, implications for the continuous school improvement plan, and other data they wished they had, recording commonalities on chart paper.

Step 3. **Large group consensus.** Combine the small group results to get a comprehensive set of strengths, challenges, implications for the continuous school improvement plan, and other data they wished they had. This becomes a set of information to which everyone agrees.

Step 4. **Comprehensive analysis for each type of data.** Repeat steps 1-3 for each of the four types of data.

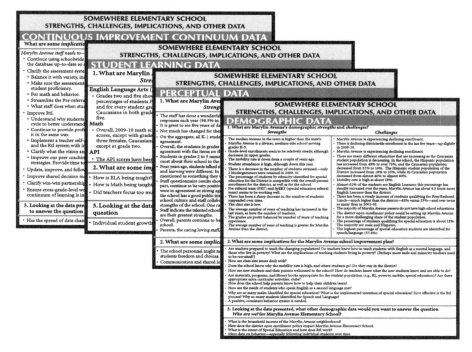

**Step 5. Aggregation of commonalities.** Line up the consolidated implications for demographics, perceptions, student learning, and school processes. Look across the implications and highlight the commonalities. Staff members will be amazed to see there are many things that need to change in demographics, perceptions, and school processes if they want student learning increases.

### SOMEWHERE ELEMENTARY SCHOOL

| DEMOGRAPHICS | STUDENT, STAFF, PARENT QUESTIONNAIRES | STUDENT LEARNING | PROCESS DATA |
|---|---|---|---|
| • Are teachers prepared to teach the changing population? Do teachers know how to teach students with English as a second language, and those who live in poverty? What are the implications of teaching students living in poverty? (Perhaps more male and minority teachers need to be recruited?)<br>• How are class-size issues dealt with, with mobility?<br>• Does the school know why the mobility rate is high, and where students go? Do students stay in the district?<br>• How are new students and their parents welcomed to the school? Do teachers know what the new students know and are able to do?<br>• Are materials, programs, and library books appropriate for the student population (e.g., EL, poverty, mobile, special education), and for getting students college and career ready? Are there appropriate extra-curricular activities, clubs?<br>• How does the school help parents know how to help their children learn?<br>• How are the needs of students who speak English as a second language met? Is there a need for an English Language Development program?<br>• Why are so many males identified for special education? What is the implemented intention of special education? How effective is the RtI process? Why are so many students identified for Speech and Language?<br>• A positive, consistent behavior system is needed. Parents need to be a part of the behavior system.<br>• Instructional assistants, recess and lunch supervisors need professional development in the behavior system. | • Someone should follow-up on the lowest scoring items (K–1)—*The work I do in class makes me think, Students at my school are friendly, I have lots of friends- even though they are still high.*<br>• The school personnel might need professional development in behavior/respect and diversity issues, and how they give students freedom and choices.<br>• Communication and shared leadership need to improve.<br>• Enrichment in learning. | • How is ELA being taught? How is ELA being measured on an ongoing basis?<br>• How is Math being taught? How is Math being measured on an ongoing basis?<br>• Did teachers focus too much on the students not proficient? Do all teachers know what to do when students are proficient?<br>• We need stronger core instruction for all students. | *Somewhere School staff needs to—*<br>• Continue using schoolwide data as they have in the past to help them know how the system is doing. Get and keep the database up-to-date so staff can gauge progress.<br>• Clarify the assessment system to measure the attainment of the Common Core State Standards.<br>  * Balance it with variety, including performance assessments and student self-assessments.<br>  * Make sure the assessments that are used are telling them what they need to hear to know how to ensure student proficiency.<br>  * For math and behavior.<br>  * Streamline the pre-referral process, especially the form completion process.<br>  * What staff do when students are proficient on benchmarks.<br>• Improve RtI:<br>  * Understand why students who have been through interventions are not proficient. Problem-solving cycle can guide this.<br>  * Continue to provide professional development on RtI for all staff so everyone can understand it and implement it in the same way.<br>  * Implement a teacher self-assessment and grade-level self-assessment system to help implement the vision and the RtI system with integrity and fidelity throughout the school. Identify internal quality measures.<br>  * Clarify what the vision and RtI would look like when implemented.<br>  * Improve the peer coaching system: support and provide guidance for new instruction and assessment strategies. Provide time to develop new skills and improve Level 1.<br>• Update, improve, and follow the continuous school improvement plan.<br>• Improve shared decision making and leadership: Define, implement, and communicate.<br>• Clarify win-win partnerships with parents. Make sure parents know the vision and mission of the school, and learning expectations for their children.<br>• Ensure cross-grade-level work improves to implement the standards, vision, and RtI consistently, and to also ensure that a continuum of learning makes sense for all students. |

**Step 6. Aggregate implications.** Aggregate, or consider as a whole, those highlighted commonalities. Make a list of the items that must be addressed in the continuous school improvement plan, based on data. Those aggregated commonalities most often include professional learning for all staff, need for a vision, need for consistency in how students are treated (behavior), support and modeling for implementing learning standards and using data, strategies to welcome students to school, and so on.

### SOMEWHERE ELEMENTARY SCHOOL
### AGGREGATED IMPLICATIONS FOR THE CONTINUOUS SCHOOL IMPROVEMENT PLAN

| INSTRUCTION | ASSESSMENT | CURRICULUM | BEHAVIOR | VISION / PLAN | PROFESSIONAL LEARNING |
|---|---|---|---|---|---|
| • Teachers need to strengthen their instructional strategies in ELA, Math, Science, and Social Studies.<br>• There needs to be deeper implementation of RtI.<br>• Continue to ensure that all teachers are teaching to standards and all students are meeting Common Core State Standards (CCSS) in all subject areas.<br>• Clarify what staff do when students are proficient. | • Clarify a balanced assessment system.<br>• We need to make sure teachers know what the new students know and are able to do when they arrive, so we do not lose instructional time.<br>• We need to collect more systematic formative data in all subject areas. | • Are materials, programs, and library books appropriate for the student population? (EL, poverty, mobile, special education)<br>• Will all materials, etc., help us implement the Common Core State Standards (CCSS)?<br>• We need to document and continue to improve RtI implementation. | • We need a positive, consistent behavior system schoolwide.<br>• We need to set-up dynamic data collection for behavior, monitor it, and change as needed. | • The vision needs to be fully implemented.<br>• Staff need to stay focused on the plan; always have next steps in front of them; create and post a graphic organizer to help us stay focused.<br>• We need to systematically include our parents in quality planning. | • Continue our professional learning in meeting the needs of our students, especially students with English as a second language, those who live in poverty, and males, specifically in ELA and Math learning, for RtI, and for implementing the Common Core State Standards (CCSS).<br>• School personnel need consistent training and implementation of behavior and motivation strategies. |

| COLLABORATION | LEADERSHIP | PARTNERSHIPS | DATA | CLIMATE | RtI / SPECIAL EDUCATION |
|---|---|---|---|---|---|
| • Staff need to strengthen peer coaching and make it and the feedback structure more systematic and defined.<br>• We need to schedule schoolwide articulation more often and make cross-grade-level articulation meetings more systematic.<br>• Staff need to continue cross-grade-level articulation, including agreements about student behavior in terms of motivation, attitude, and effort-also as related to *Students Committed to Excellence.* | • Communication needs to improve among staff and with parents.<br>• Everyone needs to be a part of professional learning and leadership.<br>• We need to improve shared leadership. | • We need to connect student achievement data to partnerships, and look into relationships that might affect student achievement, based on our mission/vision/ plan.<br>• We need to document different ways the community is contributing to the school, and how parent involvement affects student achievement.<br>• We need to make sure parents know how to help meet the learning needs of their children. | • Where do our mobile students go? Do they stay in the district?<br>• We need to gather and monitor behavior data regularly.<br>• We need to continue using schoolwide data teams.<br>• Staff need to become astute in knowing what works so they can predict and ensure successes.<br>• Staff accessibility to data tools needs to be improved. | • We need a system to welcome new students and their parents to the school.<br>• Staff need to continue cross-grade-level articulation, including agreements about student behavior in terms of motivation, attitude, and effort-also as related to *Students Committed to Excellence.*<br>• Staff need to continue to communicate and collaborate. | We need to:<br>• Look into speech and language referrals.<br>• Streamline PRT process.<br>• Get all staff understanding RtI in the same way.<br>• Strengthen core curriculum.<br>• Evaluate and improve RtI implementation.<br>**COMMON CORE STATE STANDARDS**<br>• Continue to learn more about teaching and assessing the Common Core State Standards (CCSS). |

Appendix G shows what we saw in the case study data, and how we got to aggregated implications for the continuous school improvement plan. The implication commonalities provide powerful information for a school's continuous school improvement efforts.

The benefits to using this approach are many, including but not limited, to the following:

◆ Everyone on staff sees all the data about the school and the impact of school processes on student learning results.

◆ When the data are broken into types, the amount of data each person reviews at a time is doable. Even with an inexperienced data analyzer, the comprehensive demographic data profile shown in the case study should take 20 minutes to review. In most schools, it will take no more than 15 minutes.

◆ Staff members get feedback on their analysis of the data as they synthesize what they saw in the data. Each person gets to see what others saw in the data and, collectively, they can create a comprehensive analysis that tells the story of the school.

◆ Everyone on staff contributes to the whole staff analysis through the individual and small-group work. By the time the small groups merge their thinking, the entire group is coming to consensus on what needs to be included in the continuous school improvement plan, some of which gets implemented immediately.

◆ In addition to setting up the continuous school improvement plan, this comprehensive data analysis provides information that must be included in the school vision.

◆ Without a data profile, these data almost never get reviewed, especially together.

Through the staff engagement that takes place with the identification of strengths, challenges, and implications for the continuous school improvement plan, the data profile facilitates staff's understanding of the following:

◆ How the student and teaching populations have changed over time.

◆ Who the students are and what teachers need to learn about the students to help them learn.

◆ Current health of the organization and new ideas to make it healthier.

◆ Impact of philosophies and policies.

◆ How the school is getting the results it is getting now.

**BENEFITS TO ANALYZING YOUR SCHOOL'S DATA PROFILE**

• *Everyone on staff sees all the data about the school and the impact of school processes on student learning results.*

• *When the data are broken into types, the amount of data each person reviews at a time is doable.*

• *Staff members get feedback on their analysis of the data as they synthesize what they saw in the data.*

• *Everyone on staff contributes to the whole staff analysis through the individual and small-group work.*

• *In addition to setting up the CSI plan, this comprehensive data analysis provides information that must be included in the school vision.*

• *Without a data profile, these data almost never get reviewed, especially together.*

**The data profile facilitates staff's understanding of the following:**

• *How the student and teaching populations have changed over time.*

• *Who the students are and what teachers need to learn about the students to help them learn.*

• *Current health of the organization and new ideas to make it healthier.*

• *Impact of philosophies and policies.*

• *How the school is getting the results it is getting now.*

• *What staff members need to study, so new approaches to getting better results will be informed by data.*

• *If students are learning what teachers are teaching.*

• *The importance of having instructional coherence.*

• *How to paint with a broad brush to know how to improve multiple grade levels and subject areas at the same time.*

◆ What staff members need to study, so new approaches to getting better results will be informed by data.

◆ If students are learning what teachers are teaching.

◆ The importance of having instructional coherence.

◆ How to paint with a broad brush to know how to improve multiple grade levels and subject areas at the same time.

## HOW MUCH TIME DOES IT TAKE?

**With a complete data profile available to staff, the analysis of the four types of data might take two hours, with a facilitator who keeps the work moving.**

## REFLECTION QUESTIONS

1. Why is it important to look across all types of data for continuous school improvement?

2. Who needs to do the work of analyzing the data across the four types?

3. What are the benefits of using this approach with your staff?

## APPLICATION OPPORTUNITIES

1. Using Appendix H, *Analyzing Data for Continuous School Improvement Planning,* analyze each type of data with your staff. Come to consensus on strengths, challenges, implications, and other data you wish you had for the continuous school improvement plan.

2. Look across all the planning implications and determine the commonalities.

3. Aggregate the commonalities. What needs to be included in the vision and continuous school improvement plan for your learning organization?

# WHAT IS WORKING AND WHAT IS NOT WORKING:
## DELVING DEEPER INTO THE DATA

**8**

**CHAPTER**

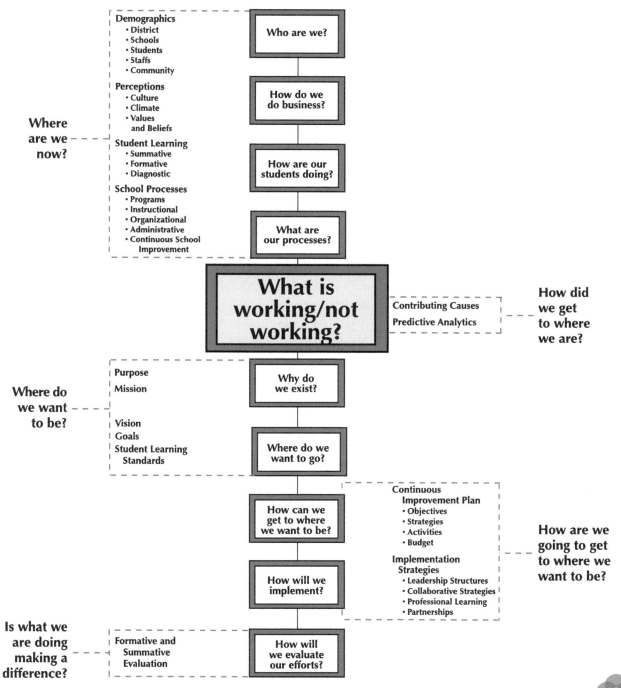

*How can anyone be sure that a particular set of new inputs will
produce better outputs if we do not at least study what happens inside?*

Paul Black and Dylan Wiliam
*Beyond the Black Box*

*To understand how the organization is getting the results it is getting now, what is working/ what is not working, and to learn more about what to do differently to get different results, we need to go deeper into the data to get answers to these and other significant questions.*

The data analyses described in the preceding chapters are crucial for knowing where a learning organization is right now, and for cleaning up the system so the organization can operate with greatest efficiency. To understand how the organization is getting the results it is getting now, what is working/what is not working, and to learn more about what to do differently to get different results, we need to go deeper into the data to get answers to these and other significant questions. We need to look across multiple measures of data to gain insights that are actionable.

Let's start by talking about the intersections, or crossing over, of the four categories of data, which will be at the center of all deeper analyses.

## INTERSECTIONS OF MULTIPLE MEASURES OF DATA

The multiple measures of data graphic, shown in Chapter 2, Figure 2.2, is a Venn diagram that shows the many ways one can look across school data. On the next page is a table (Figure 8.1) of possible two-way and three-way intersections across the four different types of data, and the all-important four-way intersection that gives us the ability to predict what we need to do to meet the learning needs of *all* students in the school. Each intersection shown is illustrated with a statement of what the intersection of the measures can tell us, and a real-school example. There are, of course, endless possibilities for what intersecting these measures can tell a school. As you read the table, keep in mind that complex intersections can mean different things depending upon the perspective from which one looks at them—and what it is one wants to know. When clear on what you want to know, intersections can provide powerful insights into continuous school improvement.

Intersections allow us to look closely at and better understand the results we are getting in a school.

### Multiple Measures of Data

The individual multiple measures, shown in Chapters 3 through 6, are easy to understand. As Figure 8.1 shows, we can understand each of the multiple measures more deeply when we combine two, three, and four measures together.

Figure 8.1
SUMMARY OF DATA INTERSECTIONS

| Intersections | Can Tell Us— | For Example |
|---|---|---|
| **Two-Way Intersections** | | |
| **Demographics by Student Learning** | If subgroups of students perform differently on student learning measures. | *Do students who attend school every day get better grades than students with absences?* |
| **Demographics by Perceptions** | If subgroups of students are experiencing school differently. | *What are the differences in students' perceptions of the learning environment, by number of student absences?* |
| **Demographics by School Processes** | If all subgroups of students are represented in the different programs offered by the school. | *What are the differences in attendance by program enrollment? In other words, what are the attendance rates of students in AP, Gifted, Basic Math, etc.* |
| **Student Learning by School Processes** | If different programs are achieving similar student learning results. | *Did students who were enrolled in interactive math programs this year perform better on standardized achievement tests than those who took traditional math courses?* |
| **Student Learning by Perceptions** | If student perceptions of the learning environment have an impact on their learning results. | *Do students with positive attitudes about school do better academically, as measured by teacher-assigned grades?* |
| **Perceptions by School Processes** | If students perceive programs and processes differently. | *Is there a difference in how students enrolled in different programs perceive the learning environment, by teacher, by student reading level, and by type of differentiation?* |
| **Three-Way Intersections** | | |
| **Demographics by Student Learning by Perceptions** | The impact demographic factors and attitudes about the learning environment have on student learning. | *Do students of different ethnicities perceive the learning environment differently, and do they score differently on standardized achievement tests in patterns consistent with these perceptions?* |
| **Demographics by Student Learning by School Processes** | The impact of specific programs on different subgroups of students, as measured by subgroup learning results. | *Which program is making the biggest difference this year with respect to student achievement for at-risk students, and is there one group of students that is responding "better" to the processes?* |
| **Demographics by Perceptions by School Processes** | What programs different students like best, or the impact different programs have on student attitudes. | *What instructional process did high absentee students respond to best with respect to perceptions?* |
| **Student Learning by School Processes by Perceptions** | The relationship between the processes students prefer and learning results. | *Is there a difference in students' reports of what they like most about the school that is connected to whether they participate in extracurricular activities? Do these students have higher grade point averages than students who do not participate in extracurricular activities?* |
| **Four-Way Intersections** | | |
| **Demographics by Student Learning by Perceptions by School Processes** | What processes or programs have the greatest impact on different subgroups of students' learning, according to student perceptions, and as measured by student learning results. | *Of the students with higher than desired absentee rates, which instructional processes did they prefer, and which ultimately helped them perform well?* |

How do educators use intersections to go deeper into their data? A school would not set out to do all intersections for the sake of doing intersections. Let purpose drive the analyses. It is easy to keep gathering and analyzing and forget the question one is striving to answer. If you keep sight of the purpose, you'll know when to stop. A two-way intersection, or two two-way intersections, might answer the question better than a three-way intersection. Intersections set us up for deeper analyses.

Step 1. **Start with purpose.** What is it you want to know? The purpose can be presented as a statement or question. For example: *Grade 8 students are not scoring well on the state math assessment,* or *Why are students not scoring better on the state 8th grade math assessment?*

Step 2. **Questions and data.** Think logically about the questions you need to answer to know more about the issue, and consider the data you need to analyze to answer each question. This will lead you into two way, three-way, and four-way intersections very quickly.

| Deeper questions for: *Why are students not scoring better on the state 8th grade math assessment?* | Intersections Needed |
|---|---|
| How did 8th grade students score on the state math assessment? How did previous 8th graders score, and how did these 8th graders score as 3rd, 4th, 5th, 6th, and 7th graders? | Student learning math results analyzed by proficiency levels and grade, over time. |
| Which students are proficient and which ones are not, by demographics? | Student learning results by demographics, e.g., gender, ethnicity/race, language proficiency, learning disabilities, indicators of poverty, mobility. |
| Of the students not proficient, what do they know, what do they not know? Is it different for different student groups? | Student learning results by item analysis, and by demographics, e.g., gender, ethnicity/race, language proficiency, learning disabilities, indicators of poverty, mobility. |
| Are there differences by teacher and student group? | Student learning results by item analysis, by teacher (school process), and by student group (demographics). |
| How are math concepts being taught? | School processes data by teacher. |
| What are students' perceptions of why they did not score well? What are teachers' perceptions of why students did not score well? | Student and teacher perceptions. |

Step 3.   **Gather and analyze the data.** This analysis should lead to understanding the processes that create the results for the different student groups.

Variation.   A variation would be to start with one type of data and consider a question you can answer with that data; add another type of data and grow the questions, then add another type of data until you use all four types of data. Example follows.

### *Why are students not scoring better on the state 8th grade math assessment?*

| Types of Data | Question You Answer With This Type of Data | Data to Gather |
|---|---|---|
| **Student Learning** | What do our 8th graders know and not know on the Grade 8 math assessment? | Student learning results by item analysis, for the past three years |
| **Student Learning by Demographics** | Who are the students who are not scoring well on the Grade 8 math assessment? | Student learning results by item analysis, and by demographics, e.g., gender, ethnicity/race, language proficiency, learning disabilities, indicators of poverty, mobility. |
| **Student Learning by Demographics by School Processes** | Are there differences in results on the Grade 8 math assessment for the different subgroups of students, by the way math is taught? | Student learning results by demographics, and by classroom. |
| **Student Learning by Demographics by School Processes by Perceptions** | Do student perceptions of how they are learning math have any relationship to the scores they are getting? | Student learning results by demographics, by classroom, and student perceptions. |

## USING INTERSECTIONS IN CONTRIBUTING CAUSE ANALYSES

*Problems cannot be solved by the same level of thinking that created them.*

Albert Einstein

Intersections of multiple measures of data are powerful. They show us how much more we can see when we open our eyes wide and use all of our lenses. A way to tap into the power of intersections is through a problem-solving cycle. The problem-solving cycle facilitates powerful exploration of the intersections while helping us uncover contributing causes of our undesirable results (AKA, problems or challenges). There is seldom a single root cause for an undesirable result—there are usually several contributing causes. When combining multiple causes or predictors of risk, a compounding effect takes place. That is why it is necessary to look at all potential causes by looking at all data available.

*The problem-solving cycle facilitates powerful exploration of the intersections while helping us uncover contributing causes of our undesirable results (AKA, problems or challenges).*

**Steps in Solving a Problem**

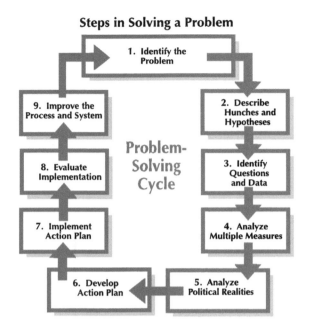

**THE FIRST FOUR STEPS IN THE PROBLEM-SOLVING CYCLE**

**Step 1.** *Identify the problem.*
**Step 2.** *Staff members brainstorm at least 20 reasons they believe the problem exists.*
**Step 3.** *Identify questions and data needed to answer each question.*
**Step 4.** *Analyze the data.*

The problem-solving cycle uses effective problem-solving strategies to engage staff in:

◆ their preconceptions,

◆ new levels of thinking about a problem/challenge,

◆ making deeper data analysis their idea,

◆ making improving processes their idea,

◆ showing what the data are saying, and

◆ data-informed solutions.

The first four steps in the problem-solving cycle are the most important for thinking broader about a "problem" before solving it.

Step 1. **Identify the problem.** The process begins with the identification of the problem, or undesirable results. For example: *Not enough students are proficient in Mathematics.*

Step 2. **Staff members brainstorm at least 20 reasons they believe the problem exists.** Getting to 20 is very important for effective brainstorming. The deep thinking that gets us to numbers 17-20 begin to uncover contributing causes of the problem. Resist the urge to "prioritize" the twenty hunches. This brainstorming gets us to where we want to be for the next step.

## THE PROBLEM-SOLVING CYCLE: Example Hunches and Hypotheses

| *List hunches and hypotheses about why the problem exists.* | |
|---|---|
| 1. Too many students live in poverty. | 11. We don't know what data are important. |
| 2. There is a lack of parent support. | 12. We don't know how to use the data. |
| 3. There is too much student mobility in our school. | 13. We don't get the data soon enough to make a difference. |
| 4. The students aren't prepared for school. | 14. Not all our curriculum is aligned to the standards. |
| 5. Many of our students are not fluent in English. | 15. Teachers don't know how to setup lessons to teach to the standards. |
| 6. Even if the students don't speak English, they have to take the test in English. | 16. We need to know sooner what students know and don't know. |
| 7. Students don't do their homework. | 17. We are not teaching to the standards. |
| 8. Students do not like to read. | 18. Our expectations are too low. |
| 9. There is no district support. | 19. We need to collaborate to improve instruction. |
| 10. There are budget problems at the school and district levels. | 20. Teachers need professional learning to work with students with backgrounds different from our own. |

**Step 3.** Identify questions and data needed to answer each question. Next, staff members go back to the problem: *Not enough students are proficient in Mathematics,* and identify the questions that they must answer with data, and the data they must gather to answer each question.

### THE PROBLEM-SOLVING CYCLE
### Example Questions and Data Needed

| Questions | Data Needed |
|---|---|
| 1. Who are the students who are not performing? | Student achievement results by student groups. |
| 2. What do the students know and what do they not know? | Student achievement results by standards. |
| 3. Are all teachers teaching to the standards? | Standards questionnaire. |
| 4. How are we teaching Mathematics, ELA—actually, everything? | Teacher reports about teaching strategies to grade-level teams. |
| 5. What is the impact of our instruction? | We need to follow student achievement by teachers and by course. |
| 6. What do teachers, students, and parents think we need to do to improve? | Teacher, student, and parent questionnaires and follow-up focus groups. |
| 7. What does our data analysis tell us about what we need to do to improve? | Study data analysis results. |

**Step 4.** Analyze the data. Staff follow up with the data and analyze what needs to change to get different results.

When schools discover gaps or undesirable results, they naturally want to identify solutions immediately to close the gaps. To permanently eliminate the gaps, schools must uncover root causes, or contributing causes (we believe there is more than one cause for undesirable results), and eliminate them—not the surface issues.

The problem-solving cycle is a great activity for getting all staff involved in thinking through undesirable results, or problems, before jumping to solutions. By starting with brainstorming hunches and hypotheses, all staff can be heard. When all voices are expressed, and heard, there is a better chance of all staff using the information later. During the brainstorming, all staff members hear what they believe are the reasons for the undesirable results. There is also an important opportunity to acknowledge challenges facing teachers, which usually show up as the first five to ten hunches. Once those hunches are written down, staff can go past them. As they go past those hunches that they feel have been holding them back, staff begin to think how their current programs and processes might be contributing to the causes of

*To permanently eliminate the gaps, schools must uncover root causes, or contributing causes (we believe there is more than one cause for undesirable results), and eliminate them— not the surface issues.*

*By starting with brainstorming hunches and hypotheses, all staff can be heard.*

*Deeper data analyses show what processes need to improve to get different results.*

undesirable results. Next, staff will need to determine what questions must be answered with data (and what data) before the "problem" can be solved. It is their idea to go deeper into the data—sometimes into areas they might not go to under typical situations. Staff members naturally use the multiple measures of data with this process, and they might not without the process. Deeper data analyses show what processes need to improve to get different results.

**Effective data analyses and problem-solving methodologies embrace the following key principles of organizational improvement:**

- *Encourage staff identification and ownership of the process(es) at the root.*
- *Empower those that need to carry out change.*
- *Focus on comprehensive data analysis.*
- *Streamline the improvement process.*

Effective data analyses and problem-solving methodologies embrace the following key principles of organizational improvement:

- *Encourage staff identification and ownership of the process(es) at the root.* People come to learning with preconceptions based on existing understanding and practices. If these initial understandings are not explicitly engaged, the result will be outright resistance or superficial compliance (at best) and a perpetuation of the status quo. Therefore, existing understandings and practices have to get on the table. (Katz, 2012)

- *Empower those that need to carry out change.* Using data should be inclusive of and engaging to those who must embrace and carry out change. This represents an important shift towards systemic and systematic improvement, away from personality focused, top-down driven methods.

- *Focus on comprehensive data analysis.* Staff members need to think through a problem in an informed way, considering all data, before simply jumping to a solution.

- *Streamline the improvement process.* Empowerment requires that all staff see the immediate impact of their work—the data analysis. A structured process that makes big problems manageable and facilitates a quick move to resolution is required. Because all staff are involved in the process and are following along, improvement can be made quickly.

## PREDICTIVE ANALYTICS

The concepts and activities presented thus far in this book can be performed by teachers and administrators to know how the learning organization got to where it is now, and to provide valuable information about how to get different results. Staff can put together a descriptive data profile, look for trends and commonalities across multiple measures of data, and perform an intersection analysis or contributing cause analysis, at any time, to go deeper into their data.

*At the highest levels of data use is prediction and optimization. We want to use data to predict and ensure success, and to predict and prevent failure.*

At the highest levels of data use is prediction and optimization. We want to use data to predict and ensure success, and to predict and prevent failure. With this information, we can optimize our processes to enhance our results. We can do a great deal of this descriptively and relationally; however, to understand the probable relationships of different data in predicting results requires someone knowledgeable of advanced multivariate statistics (regression analysis), and a lot of data. If the data profile and the database behind it is comprehensive, your school will be set to do powerful, predictive analyses.

Predictive analytics uses a variety of statistical techniques and research models to analyze current and historical data to make predictions about the likelihood of future outcomes. Historical data help us see the probabilities within the predictions. We use the past and current data to create the predictive models. We might want to predict the following:

◆ How students will do on the state standards assessments.

◆ If there are students at-risk of not advancing to the next grade level, or to graduation.

◆ How attendance and course grades predict high school graduation.

◆ If students are being adequately prepared for college and careers.

These statistical models analyze massive amounts of data to understand what data predict the outcome. These models can identify a set of predictors (i.e., marks on report cards, attendance, gender, etc.) and inform practitioners of the importance of some data. With that information, staff can intervene in a preventive manner to ensure positive outcomes by acting either on predictors when possible (like attendance), or by implementing remedial programs in order to mitigate the risk.

Predictive analytics also constitutes a powerful scientific technique (Popper, 2002) for the purpose of program evaluation. By anticipating the outcome of a group of individuals, one can scientifically measure the impact of a particular program by verifying if the outcomes of the students, after engaging in the program, are significantly superior to what was predicted.

## Early Warning Systems

Many school districts are creating *Early Warning Systems* to predict potential "failures," and then to change their processes to turn the situation around to ensure success. While it is ideal to have a statistician to support the complex analyses, schools can do some things on their own:

Step 1. **Determine what you want to predict.** Example: High school dropouts.

Step 2. **Read the research about what predicts the results.** for example: *Research shows* **course performance** *and* **attendance** *during the first year of high school are powerful predictors of whether or not a student will graduate from high school.* (Allensworth and Easton, 2005; 2007) (Also see *http://www.betterhighschools.org.*)

*Predictive analytics uses a variety of statistical techniques and research models to analyze current and historical data to make predictions about the likelihood of future outcomes.*

*By anticipating the outcome of a group of individuals, one can scientifically measure the impact of a particular program by verifying if the outcomes of the students, after engaging in the program, are significantly superior to what was predicted.*

**THE STEPS IN CREATING AN EARLY WARNING SYSTEM**

**Step 1.** *Determine what you want to predict.*

**Step 2.** *Read the research about what predicts the results.*

**Step 3.** *Review your historical data to look for patterns to see if those indicators were and are true in your school.*

**Step 4.** *Locate students in pipeline.*

*The power of the Early Warning Systems and predictive analytics does not come from the numbers, but from what staff do to prevent the undesirable results.*

Step 3.  Review your historical data to look for patterns to see if those indicators were and are true in your school. It is important to take an objective look at the data, and make no assumptions. District staff often assume that students not attending school are the lowest performing. There are many places where that is not true. Sometimes the students not attending are those doing well, but are bored with school.

Step 4.  Locate students in pipeline. After identifying the predictors, determine which students in the pipeline have these same characteristics, and do something about it—change the processes. Interview the students to find out the issues, and work to ensure each student's success. Figure 8.2 shows a school's *Early Warning System,* spelled out in the *Measuring Programs and Processes Table.* Figure 8.3 shows the school's Early Warning System to prevent dropouts in a flowchart.

The power of the Early Warning Systems and predictive analytics does not come from the numbers, but from what staff do to prevent the undesirable results. (See *http://www.betterhighschools.org/pubs/ews_guide.asp* for more information and support.)

Figure 8.2

SOMEWHERE HIGH SCHOOL'S EARLY WARNING SYSTEM TO ENSURE THAT *ALL* STUDENTS GRADUATE

| PURPOSE | | PARTICIPANTS | | IMPLEMENTATION | | RESULTS |
|---|---|---|---|---|---|---|
| *What is the purpose of the program or process?* | *How will you know the purpose is being met? (What are the outcomes?)* | *Who is the program/process intended to serve?* | *Who is being served? Who is not being served?* | *What will it look like when the program/process is fully implemented?* | *How is implementation being measured?* / *To what degree is the program being implemented?* | *What are the results?* |
| The purpose of this Early Warning System is to: • Identify factors that contribute to our students not completing high school. • Identify students at-risk of dropping out of high school. • Understand why students are dropping out. • Offer processes to get students back on track. • Provide programming to meet the needs of all students, get them on-track for graduation, and prepare them to be successful in postsecondary education/training, and/or become successful in a chosen career. | When the purpose of the Early Warning System is met— • All students will graduate. • Students at-risk will be identified early. • Students will attend and want to attend school. • High quality programming will be provided so all students can succeed. • Students will be satisfied with the programs and processes of the school. • All students will be prepared to be successful in college and/or careers. • Staff will feel satisfied that they have done everything they can to provide a quality education for every student. • Students will successfully apply for postsecondary education/training. • Will become successful in gaining employment and in their chosen careers. | All students at-risk to graduate from high school. | The students currently not being served are those who are dropping out of high school, failing courses, and missing more than 10% of classes. | When the program is fully implemented: • Staff will review the data of all students to identify those at-risk of dropping out of Somewhere High School. • After interviewing each student, staff will determine processes and procedures for getting individuals or groups of students on-track to graduate. • High-quality strategies that engage students in learning will be employed. • Programs will be monitored and students will be interviewed regularly to ensure that students are on track. • A support system for families will be established and implemented. (See Flowchart.) | The Early Warning monitoring system will ensure that all students at-risk of dropping out of high school are identified and that processes and procedures are put into place to prevent these students from dropping out. <br><br> The degree of implementation will be measured by reviewing the integrity and fidelity of implementation, by reviewing the data and asking the students. | When the program is fully implemented, students will: • attend school regularly. • behave appropriately at school. • be motivated to learn and complete high school. • graduate from high school. • be satisfied with the programs offered. • be prepared for college and/or careers. • be admitted to postsecondary education institutions. • succeed in college without remediation. <br><br> Staff will be happy because they are doing something for students who would otherwise fail. <br><br> Parents will be happy because— • they know how to support their child's education and future. • their child is graduating from high school and on track for a productive life. |

**NEXT STEPS:** Develop programs and processes in cooperation with colleges, universities, career preparatory programs, and businesses in the areas to understand their expectations for student success.

## Figure 8.3
## SOMEWHERE HIGH SCHOOL'S EARLY WARNING SYSTEM TO PREVENT DROPOUTS

Review schoolwide data to know how many students are not completing high school.

How many students have dropped out of this high school, by grade level, subject area, credits, GPA, attendance, behavior, over time.  Ⓐ

Assign a committee to learn more about predictors of dropping out, to determine our school's predictors by reviewing data, study the data to find our students at-risk of dropping out, and recommendations on next steps.

The Committee should include staff who like to work with data and have time to work on the project, and community members with influential roles in student success.

Identify factors that contribute to students dropping out of high school.

The Committee will need to review the research to understand what others have found over time, and their own data to understand more about Somewhere's dropouts.

Review what the research says about the factors that contribute to students dropping out of high school.

The research says that Grade 9 is a predictor of dropping out, specifically: course performance, failing one or more course, over age for grade, retentions, attendance (especially in the first 30 days), and getting behind in credits, especially second semester.

Identify factors that contribute to students dropping out of this high school.

Using the research as a starting point, review the data of former dropouts to see if the data from the research fit this school. Also, look at all the data about our dropouts to find other factors that may have contributed to their dropping out of high school. Check both first and second semesters.

*Administer student and staff questionnaires that assess:*
- Feelings of belonging to the school;
- Perceptions of teacher caring;
- Positive relationships with adults or peers at the school;
- Participation in extra-curricular activities;
- Ability/desire to get along with peers;
- Commitment to postsecondary education;
- Commitment to finish high school;
- Motivation to do well in high school;
- Perception of the value and relevance of high school;
- Interest in content of courses;
- Interest in how courses are taught;
- Preparation to meet the academic demands of college coursework;
- College and career aspirations;
- Perceptions of the value or relevance of college;
- Parents college and career aspirations for the student;
- Knowledge of postsecondary options;
- Preparation to meet the academic demands of postsecondary education/training; and
- Perceptions of college costs outweighing the benefits.

The questionnaires can help identify students that do not have the motivation or aspirations to do high school or college work. The questionnaires will also help staff check their perceptions against student perceptions.

**Figure 8.3** *(Continued)*

## SOMEWHERE HIGH SCHOOL'S EARLY WARNING SYSTEM TO PREVENT DROPOUTS

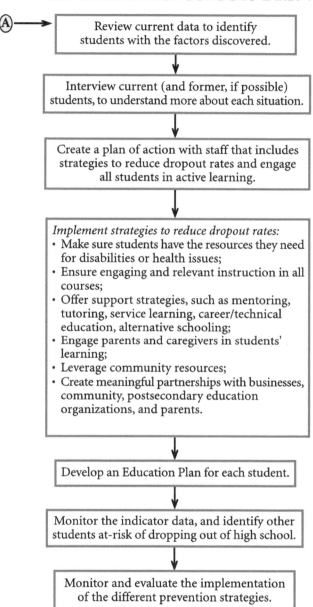

Review the data to identify students at-risk of dropping out of high school, by grade level, and demographic categories.

Ask students what the school and teachers can do to prevent them from dropping out? Or why they dropped out.

Involve classroom teachers, guidance counselors, administrators, and support staff, along with parents and student, in discussion about a sustainable plan of action.

Adjust the implementation strategies to meet the needs of the students identified for being at-risk of dropping out of high school.

Involve identified students in developing an education plan to ensure their success.

Make sure the indicators are identifying the right students and that other students who need to be identified are included.

Evaluate the entire Early Warning System to make sure everything is on-track as planned. Make adjustments and start over.

## HOW MUCH TIME DOES IT TAKE?

*Staff can perform an intersection analysis or use the problem-solving cycle any time to go deeper into the data. Each analysis will probably take twenty to thirty minutes. The predictive analytics will require a team or a statistician to devote the time to do the deeper analytic work.*

## REFLECTION QUESTIONS

1. What does it take to understand how we got to where we are now?

2. Why is it important for continuous school improvement to understand how we got our current results?

3. What do intersection and contributing cause analyses do for the learning organization?

4. Why are predictive analytics important for continuous school improvement?

## APPLICATION OPPORTUNITIES

1. Identify one of your school's undesirable results. Consider one of the multiple measures of data, such as student learning. What questions can you answer about that undesirable result? Add another measure. How do the questions change? Keep adding different types of data and grow the questions until you use all four types of data.

2. Identify an undesirable result. Use the problem-solving cycle, Appendix I, with staff to think broader about your school's most undesirable result(s), and to determine the questions that must be answered with data before you can solve that problem.

3. Think about predictive analytics—What results would you like to predict? And what do you think explains and predicts these results?

# *WHERE DO WE WANT TO BE:*
## CREATING A SHARED VISION AND MONITORING ITS IMPLEMENTATION

**CHAPTER 9**

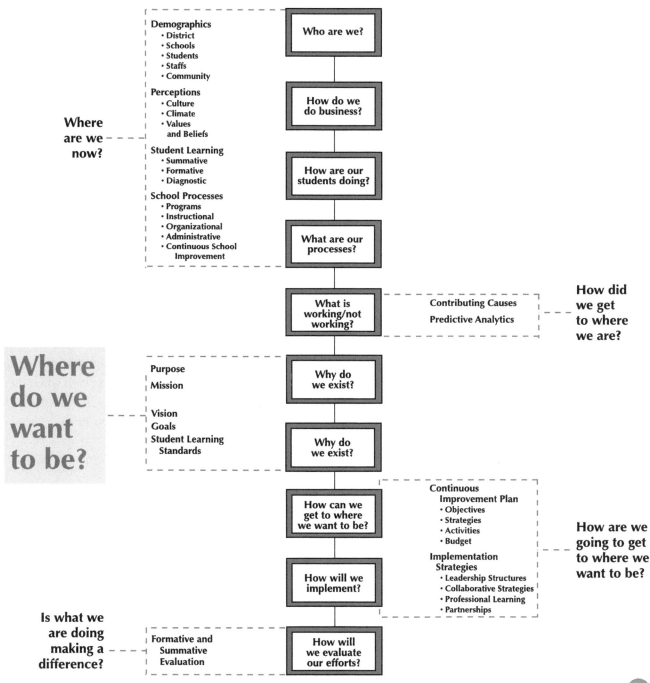

**Where are we now?**

**Demographics**
- District
- Schools
- Students
- Staffs
- Community

**Perceptions**
- Culture
- Climate
- Values and Beliefs

**Student Learning**
- Summative
- Formative
- Diagnostic

**School Processes**
- Programs
- Instructional
- Organizational
- Administrative
- Continuous School Improvement

Who are we?

How do we do business?

How are our students doing?

What are our processes?

What is working/not working?

**How did we get to where we are?**

Contributing Causes

Predictive Analytics

**Where do we want to be?**

Purpose
Mission

Vision
Goals
Student Learning Standards

Why do we exist?

Why do we exist?

How can we get to where we want to be?

How will we implement?

**How are we going to get to where we want to be?**

**Continuous Improvement Plan**
- Objectives
- Strategies
- Activities
- Budget

**Implementation Strategies**
- Leadership Structures
- Collaborative Strategies
- Professional Learning
- Partnerships

**Is what we are doing making a difference?**

Formative and Summative Evaluation

How will we evaluate our efforts?

*Shared visions emerge from personal visions.*
*This is how they derive their energy and how they foster*
*commitment. . . . If people don't have their own vision,*
*all they can do is 'sign up' for someone else's.*
*The result is compliance, never commitment.*

Peter Senge
Author, *The Fifth Discipline*

*Staff need to study and discuss the implications of teaching the current and future student populations, and the changes needed in the school's curriculum, instruction, assessment, and environmental approaches to implement best practices, and then create a vision for where they want to go.*

After analyzing the school data profile, clarifying where the learning organization is right now, and learning what is and is not working and why, it is important to study different approaches to improving results. Staff need to study and discuss the implications of teaching the current and future student populations, and the changes needed in the school's curriculum, instruction, assessment, and environmental approaches to implement best practices, and then create a vision for where they want to go. With new knowledge, a staff can implement new thinking and new strategies—as opposed to signing up for the same thing and getting the same results, or adding interventions and programs to "solve" each problem.

## WHY THE SHARED VISION IS IMPORTANT FOR CONTINUOUS SCHOOL IMPROVEMENT

*If a school does not have a clear, shared vision, it has as many visions as it has people.*

If a school does not have a clear, shared vision, it has as many visions as it has people. Consequently, the most the school could ever hope for are random acts of improvement. Figure 9.1 shows that *Random Acts of Improvement* result when there is no specific target. A vision which is based on guiding principles, is shared, and to which all staff are committed is the key to getting *Focused Acts of Improvement* (Figure 9.2).

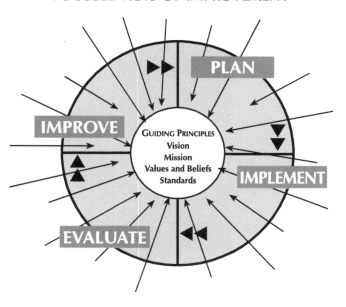

A school defines its future through its mission, vision, goals, and student expectations. The school's vision, goals, and student expectations must reflect the core values and beliefs of the staff, merged from personal values and beliefs. This level of reflection is paramount. If educators are not cognizant of what they value and believe about being educators, and do not come together on these beliefs, it is impossible to create a shared vision/mission. Creating a vision from core values and beliefs ensures a vision to which all staff members can commit. Without a vision to which all staff members commit, a school's collective efforts have no target.

*The school's vision, goals, and student expectations must reflect the core values and beliefs of the staff, merged from personal values and beliefs.*

To create a school vision that is truly shared, we must begin with the personal and move to the collective. To create a school vision that is committed to unanimously and understood in the same way—we must build on the values and beliefs of the school staff to create core values and beliefs, a core purpose, and a mission for the school. With core values and beliefs, purpose and mission established, a vision for the school can be created.

*With core values and beliefs, purpose and mission established, a vision for the school can be created.*

## INSPIRING A SHARED VISION

Effective visions have the following characteristics. Effective visions are:

- ◆ based on comprehensive data analysis that show how the school is getting its current results for its students;
- ◆ grounded in research on best practices that show staff how they might get different results with different processes;

> **Effective visions are:**
>
> • *based on comprehensive data analysis;*
> • *grounded in research on best practices;*
> • *created from shared personal values and beliefs;*
> • *reflective of core values and beliefs;*
> • *organized on what teachers do;*
> • *specific, detailed, and clear; and*
> • *supported by structures to implement the vision.*

◆ created from shared personal values and beliefs about the factors that impact learning for the school's students;

◆ reflective of core values and beliefs that can be transported into action;

◆ organized on what teachers do, such as implement curriculum, instructional and assessment strategies, and create learning environments that encourage learning by all students;

◆ specific, detailed, and clear so everyone can understand them and implement them in the same way; and they are

◆ supported by structures that ensure that everyone understands that her/his job is to implement the vision.

*A vision, which is clear and detailed, based on core values and beliefs and best practice research, with support structures gets implemented.*

A vision, which is clear and detailed, based on core values and beliefs and best practice research, with support structures gets implemented. Many schools think of vision as a paper exercise that results in a statement. In over two decades of working with schools on continuous school improvement, I have never seen a vision *statement* get implemented. While schools and districts may develop a vision *statement* to post in public areas, to use on stationery and other publications, a vision statement is simply too narrow to drive continuous school improvement. It is impossible for everyone on staff to understand and implement a statement in the same way unless the details have been agreed to and spelled out.

An example follows that leads us through the creation of a shared vision that will get implemented. (The process for *Creating a Shared Vision* is in Appendix J.)

## HOW TO CREATE A SHARED VISION

The steps in creating a shared mission and vision are illustrated using Somewhere School, a school committed to having all staff implement the Common Core State Standards (CCSS).

Step 1.  **Review comprehensive data and read Best Practices.** Prior to the visioning work, staff members reviewed their comprehensive school data analysis, problem-solving cycle work, and read Best Practices related to areas of need and implementing the CCSS. Because they want to get better end results, they had book studies, attended workshops, worked with consultants, and shared their learnings with each other.

Step 2.  **Seat staff members.** On the day of their visioning session, the facilitator placed staff members, mixed by subject area and grade level, at tables of six. The ground rules and the agenda for the day were reviewed.

Step 3.   Review the big picture of creating a shared vision. Staff learned that a shared vision is based on a system of fundamental motivating assumptions, and principles.

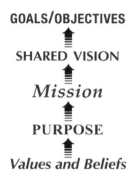

**GOALS/OBJECTIVES**

**SHARED VISION**

*Mission*

**PURPOSE**

*Values and Beliefs*

Step 4.   Create individual values and beliefs. The first order of business was to create a solid foundation with core values and beliefs—the shaping forces behind the shared vision.

Each staff member jotted down the first ideas that came to her/him, with respect to—

*What are the curriculum, instruction, assessment, and environmental factors that support effective learning for our students?*

Step 5.   Merge individual thinking into small groups. Staff members at each table merged their thinking about these factors, and wrote their ideas on chart papers that were posted on the wall.

Step 6.   Merge small group thinking to whole group. The small group values and beliefs were merged into core values and beliefs for the staff, shown in Figure 9.3. In less than one hour, staff members created an outstanding foundation for their shared vision.

Step 7.   Agree on purpose of school. To get to mission, an exercise that many staff members were worried about because of the terrible time they had word smithing the last mission statement, they started with purpose.

*What is the purpose of our Somewhere School?*
*Why does our Somewhere School exist?*

It was quickly agreed that the purpose of Somewhere High School is:

*To educate all students so that they may achieve their dreams and better the world.*

---

**HOW TO CREATE A SHARED VISION**

Step 1.   *Review comprehensive data and read Best Practices.*

Step 2.   *Seat staff members.*

Step 3.   *Review the big picture of creating a shared vision.*

Step 4.   *Create individual values and beliefs.*

Step 5.   *Merge individual thinking into small groups.*

Step 6.   *Merge small group thinking to whole group.*

Step 7.   *Agree on purpose of school.*

Step 8.   *Develop mission statement.*

Step 9.   *Record independent thoughts about vision.*

Step 10.  *Merge individual thoughts to small group.*

Step 11.  *Merge small group thinking into large group.*

Step 12.  *Determine school goals.*

Step 13.  *Staff reflections.*

Figure 9.3
SOMEWHERE SCHOOL CORE VALUES AND BELIEFS

| CURRICULUM<br>*What we teach.* | INSTRUCTION<br>*How we teach the curriculum.* | ASSESSMENT<br>*How we assess learning.* | ENVIRONMENT<br>*How each person treats every other person.* |
|---|---|---|---|
| **Curriculum should be:**<br>• *Accessible* and aligned to evidence-based instructional strategies and assessments.<br>• Dynamic, rigorous, and coherent, aligned to the knowledge and skills required to be productive citizens and workers in the 21st Century.<br>• Designed to develop literacy across content areas.<br>• Technology supportive (e.g., computer adaptive and accessible).<br>• Evidence-based, vertically and horizontally aligned, and based on learning progressions.<br>• *Collaboratively* agreed upon in Communities of Professional Practice and supported by *all* teachers in the school.<br>• At the core of a Continuous School Improvement Model and served by an effective RtI system designed to promote student success and prevent school failure, ensuring that *all* students attain or exceed the pre-set performance standards.<br>• Designed to motivate critical thinking, creativity, and innovation. | **Instruction should be:**<br>• Aligned to curriculum and assessment as part of a coherent *learning system* that is responsive to all learners and makes sense to students.<br>• Grade level *accessible* and available to *all* students.<br>• Engaging to students, providing them with *authentic* work that prepares them for citizenship, college, and careers in the 21st Century.<br>• Helpful to students to make cross-curricular connections, providing students with opportunities to demonstrate their *literacy* across content areas.<br>• Technology supportive (e.g., computer adaptive, accessible by variety of technologies, employing Universal Design principles, etc.).<br>• Differentiated to address the needs of *all* students so that grade-level instruction is accessible to everyone.<br>• *Enacted*, matching the content and intent of the written curriculum.<br>• At the core of the Continuous School Improvement Model and at the center of the RtI system, designed to promote success and prevent school failure, ensuring that *all* students attain, or exceed, the pre-set performance standards.<br>• *Collaboratively* developed, implemented, evaluated, and continually revised for improvement.<br>• Motivating, encouraging students to think, create, and innovate. | **Assessment should be:**<br>• Multi-faceted, employing diagnostic, formative, and summative assessments.<br>• Used for the purposes of the assessment design, and *multiple criteria* always used to make critical decisions regarding student's lives (e.g., graduation, promotion to next grade, etc.).<br>• Aligned to the school's curriculum, instruction, and student learning resources.<br>• Designed to assess cross-curricular standards–*literacy* across content areas.<br>• Accessible via technology and developed using the principals of *Universal Design*[1], particularly for summative assessments.<br>• Designed to provide qualitative, as well as quantitative information to students and the school's instructional staff, as well as to parents and community.<br>• Primarily formative and *lesson-embedded*, providing teachers with data to inform instructional modifications and re-teaching, and to provide students with useful information to improve their work.<br>• Designed to provide the kind of data that will help school staff answer the questions: *How well are the Continuous School Improvement and RtI systems serving our students? What is working? What isn't working?* | **The school environment should:**<br>• Provide a safe and nurturing environment for learning and encourage creativity and innovation.<br>• Focus on *learning*, rather than delivering instruction.<br>• Provide appropriate technology to support 21st Century learning.<br>• Develop students who respect diversity (e.g., ideas, people, cultures).<br>• Provide a highly-effective Response to Intervention (RtI) Model that provides *timely* assistance to *all* students so that *all* students succeed.<br>• Develop the *whole* child.<br>• Listen to and provide assistance to parents, bringing them into the life of the school and their children's learning.<br>• Be truthful and clear about where a student is academically and socially and what the student needs in order to be ready for citizenship, college, and career in the 21st Century.<br>• Be a place where students want to come each day–a place where they gain respect for themselves and others because they are successful learners in all respects: academically, as citizens, and as members of a community. |

[1] "Universally designed assessments are designed and developed to allow participation of the widest possible range of students, in a way that results in valid inferences about performance on grade-level standards for all students who participate in the assessment." -Thurlow and Malouf, *Creating Better Tests for Everyone Through Universally Designed Assessments.* Retrieved from: http://www.testpublishers.org/assets/documents/volume%206%20issue%201%20Creating%20%20better%20tests.pdf

*Example provided by Cheryl Z. Tibbals, Consultant, cztibbalsconsulting@gmail.com*

**Step 8.** **Develop mission statement.** After a healthy debate, a teacher synthesized what colleagues were saying they liked, and recommended wording for the mission statement, which was accepted wholeheartedly:

> *To provide all students with the knowledge*
> *and tools they will need to be successful*
> *citizens and workers in the 21st Century.*

If staff members had not quickly agreed to the mission, they would have delegated its writing to the English teachers to develop a draft, so the visioning work could continue. They already agreed on core values and beliefs and purpose.

**Step 9.** **Record independent thoughts about vision.** While staff members were agreeing on purpose and mission statements, the facilitator had the core values and beliefs typed and copied for each staff member to use to inform thinking about a school vision. The task of staff was to jot down what each thought the school would look like, sound like, and feel like when the mission is implemented, with our core values and beliefs, in terms of—

> *Curriculum, what we teach;*
> *Instruction, how we teach the curriculum;*
> *Assessment, how we assess learning;*
> *and Learning Environment, how each*
> *person treats every other person.*

**Step 10.** **Merge individual thoughts to small group.** One more time, staff members merged their individual thinking with their small group teammates.

**Step 11.** **Merge small group thinking into large group.** The consensus was that the core values and beliefs were excellent and should be elaborated for their shared vision. (The Leadership Team refined the language after the visioning day, shown in Figure 9.4.)

**Step 12.** **Determine school goals.** Goals are the outcomes of the vision. Given the staff's core values and beliefs, mission, and vision, the following goals represent what staff believe will result from vision.

> *Ensure that ALL students graduate from high school,*
> *college and career ready for citizenship*
> *and success in the 21st Century workplace.*

Figure 9.4
SOMEWHERE SCHOOL VISION

| CURRICULUM *What we teach.* | INSTRUCTION *How we teach the curriculum.* | ASSESSMENT *How we assess learning.* | ENVIRONMENT *How each person treats every other person.* |
|---|---|---|---|
| The curriculum is a living document that represents what will be important to know and be able to do in the future. It provides a *learning roadmap* that guides teachers in *what* they will teach and students in what they will learn. It paves a way through the fields of content knowledge that is direct, efficient, rich, and deep while, at the same time, connecting one disciplinary path to another so the learner arrives at high school graduation a *literate citizen* across content areas, ready to take on the 21st Century. | Instruction is truly *student-centered.* Students are *engaged* in *authentic, meaningful, rigorous, deep work* where they must consistently analyze, synthesize, evaluate, develop, build, and create. They work on learning tasks individually and in teams, with the continual assistance of teachers who are effective at guiding student learning as coach and facilitator, as well as instructor. *All* students in the district are met *where they are* and are taken to *where they need to be.* Students have at their disposal the instructional resources, including technology, that they need to develop the knowledge and skills required to graduate from high school-prepared for success in college and career. Teachers collaboratively develop and deliver lessons that transform the curriculum into a learning landscape that encourages students to *think outside the box,* to take the knowledge and skills they have learned to the next dimension, to invent the next dynamic technology, to develop the needed vaccines, to put, as Steve Jobs wanted to do, that "ding in the universe." | Assessment is used as a tool, not a bludgeon. Assessment is a vital part of Continuous School Improvement, providing the information needed to identify where the school is performing well, where its performance needs improvement, and where there are major problems that must be addressed immediately. Assessment is conducted in a variety of ways and via a variety of approaches (e.g., technology) that meet the needs of each student. Diagnostic, formative, and summative assessments provide a constant flow of data that informs instruction. *Formative* assessment is embedded in every lesson. The results are used by teachers to provide *just-in-time* corrections and re-teaching, to identify students in need of secondary or tertiary RtI, and to inform revisions in instructional materials, as well the CSI and RtI systems. Students use the results of formative assessment (e.g., teacher, peer, or self-evaluation) to improve their work, and to develop metacognitive skills and the habits of mind that enable them to master standards in elementary and secondary school, preparing them for citizenship and success in college and career in the 21st Century. Using multiple assessment types enables the school staff to develop a clearer picture of how effective the CSI and RtI systems are. The *focus on formative* assessment is to provide the staff and students with the powerful tool that revolutionizes classroom instruction and *learning,* resulting in consistent, statistically significant, across-the-board yearly improvement in mastery of the CCSS. | *All* students enjoy school every day because they are learning skills and knowledge for which they see a connection to their present and future lives. Engaged in their own learning, working closely with teachers who guide and nurture their intellectual and emotional development, students have learned the importance and personal satisfaction that grows out of mutual respect for others–teachers, parents, and peers. They value collaboration, teamwork, innovation, and persistence because they have experienced it in an environment where not succeeding at first, does not mean failure but, instead, an opportunity to learn and a step closer to ultimate success. These real-life scenarios prepare these students for citizenship and work in the 21st Century. Schools become the "hubs" of their communities, as parents and community members participate in a partnership with their school staffs, galvanizing what might once have been disparate groups into a unified effort to see that truly no child leaves school unprepared for a successful and productive life. |

*Example provided by Cheryl Z. Tibbals, Consultant, cztibbalsconsulting@gmail.com*

Staff will:

- provide a learning environment that develops life-long learners.

- build a collaborative professional community that values and strives for continuous organizational improvement.

- provide resources that support work typical of the 21st Century workplace (e.g., technology).

- help all parents support their students for success.

- develop an insatiable hunger for self-improvement among staff, students, and community.

- bring the community into the life of the school and the school into the life of the community.

- provide a physically, emotionally, and intellectually safe environment that encourages students to become creators and innovators that improve the world.

Step 13. **Staff reflections.** Our final job of the day was to reflect on two questions, shown below with our merged responses. We can see how this work, along with the data analysis work, leads us directly into our continuous school improvement plan.

*What will it look like, sound like, and feel like when the vision is implemented?*

Staff reflections:

- Every student will be on track for high school graduation and will be prepared for citizenship, college, and career in the 21st Century workplace.

- Students will be inquisitive and accustomed to using critical thinking skills and technology in their daily work.

- Classroom observations will reveal students engaged in deep and authentic tasks (constructivism) with teachers serving as facilitators who are continually collecting formative assessment data that enable them to provide the just-in-time instructional adjustments and re-teaching (direct instruction) required to ensure success and prevent school failure.

- Students are found in after-school programs that build on what they learned in class, offer assistance with homework, and provide extended resources (e.g., computers).

- Student attendance is very high, tardies very low, and drop-outs nonexistent.

◆ In faculty meetings and in the school's Communities of Professional Practice sessions, teachers and leaders, like their students, are engaged in deep work, analyzing standards, developing an aligned curriculum/instruction/assessment system that is focused, coherent, and explainable to parents and community.

◆ Teachers and leaders work collaboratively to build a school environment that is inviting and dynamic—a fun place to work and learn for students and staff.

◆ Parents and community members participate monthly in classroom sessions where teachers explain what their students will be learning in the next month and why.

◆ In the teachers' workroom, teachers talk excitedly about successes in their classrooms that morning, ask others for advice, share information and strategies, and offer help to each other.

◆ Student assessment results reflect an effective instructional program implemented with fidelity. No teacher or leader wants to leave this school.

*What do your learning organization
and/or classroom need in order to
fully implement the shared vision?*

Some of the things the organization would need to implement the shared vision include the following:

◆ Time to establish a Community of Professional Practice for collaborative work in the following areas:

  ∗ to dig deeper into school data to determine what is working and not working and for whom, as well as to determine what data are still needed as the school moves into CCSS implementation;

  ∗ to conduct Standards Studies across the school;

  ∗ to institute grade-level Lesson Study;

  ∗ to research and establish an evidence-based research data base for professional learning; and

  ∗ to re-examine the school's Continuous School Improvement and RtI System in light of implementing the CCSS.

◆ Funds for the following:

  * bring in outside experts/assistance to challenge
    our thinking;

  * purchase the needed CCSS-aligned
    instructional resources;

  * infuse classrooms with appropriate learning
    technology; and

  * work with coaches.

Once the vision work was cleaned up, shared, and approved in the next staff
meeting, a group of staff members volunteered to create a flowchart of how the
parts of the vision work together so all staff can understand it in the same way. The
flowchart is shown in Figure 6.3. (Also see Appendix E, *Flowcharting School
Processes.*)

This same group of staff members was also tasked with determining how the vision
would be monitored when the details of the vision are fleshed out. (See Appendix K
for the *Monitoring Vision Implementation.*)

## HOW MUCH TIME DOES IT TAKE?

**With the comprehensive data analysis and the study of
Best Practices complete, the actual visioning process
should take under three hours, depending upon the size of staff
and how much they have worked together in the past.**

## REFLECTION QUESTIONS

1. What is a shared vision?

2. Why is a shared vision important to continuous school improvement?

3. How can your staff create a shared vision?

## APPLICATION OPPORTUNITIES

1. Schedule time for your staff to create a shared vision.

2. Follow Appendix J, *Creating a Shared Vision*, to facilitate the creation of a shared vision for your school.

3. Follow Appendix E, *Flowcharting School Processes*, to facilitate the creation of a flowchart to show what the vision will look like when implemented.

4. Use Appendix K, *Monitoring Vision Implementation*, to create a tool to monitor the implementation of your vision.

# HOW ARE WE GOING TO GET TO WHERE WE WANT TO BE:
## IMPLEMENTING THE SHARED VISION BY CREATING A PLAN FOR CONTINUOUS SCHOOL IMPROVEMENT

**Where are we now?**

Demographics
- District
- Schools
- Students
- Staffs
- Community

Perceptions
- Culture
- Climate
- Values and Beliefs

Student Learning
- Summative
- Formative
- Diagnostic

School Processes
- Programs
- Instructional
- Organizational
- Administrative
- Continuous School Improvement

Who are we?

How do we do business?

How are our students doing?

What are our processes?

What is working/not working?

**How did we get to where we are?**

Contributing Causes

Predictive Analytics

**Where do we want to be?**

Purpose

Mission

Vision

Goals

Student Learning Standards

Why do we exist?

Where do we want to go?

How can we get to where we want to be?

Continuous Improvement Plan
- Objectives
- Strategies
- Activities
- Budget

Implementation Strategies
- Leadership Structures
- Collaborative Strategies
- Professional Learning
- Partnerships

How will we implement?

**Is what we are doing making a difference?**

Formative and Summative Evaluation

How will we evaluate our efforts?

How are we going to get to where we want to be?

128

CHAPTER **10**
HOW ARE WE GOING TO GET TO WHERE WE WANT TO BE: IMPLEMENTING THE
SHARED VISION BY CREATING A PLAN FOR CONTINUOUS SCHOOL IMPROVEMENT

*Vision without action is merely a dream.*
*Action without vision just passes the time.*
*Vision with action can change the world.*

Joel A. Barker
Author and Futurist

*If the vision clarifies what we are going to teach, how we are going to teach, how we are going to assess, and how everyone is going to treat each other, then the continuous school improvement plan must spell out how all of these actions are going to occur.*

If the vision clarifies what we are going to teach, how we are going to teach, how we are going to assess, and how everyone is going to treat each other, then the continuous school improvement plan must spell out how all of these actions are going to occur. To get the shared vision implemented, a strong plan based on collaborative structures and data use is necessary to improve learning for *all* students.

The continuous school improvement plan to implement a vision is very different from a plan to close a gap or to meet a target. A continuous school improvement plan moves the whole system forward to a vision, as opposed to just closing a gap. Effective continuous school improvement plans—

*A continuous school improvement plan moves the whole system forward to a vision, as opposed to just closing a gap.*

◆ Implement the shared vision.

◆ Include all staff from where they are. In other words, what teachers know and are able to do are taken into consideration. The plan includes strategies to move all staff forward.

◆ Support staff in implementing the vision.

◆ Are grounded in standards implementation.

◆ Focus on teacher/administrator actions, not student actions.

◆ Include ways to monitor vision implementation.

## HOW WILL WE IMPLEMENT

**The most powerful approaches to implementing a school vision and plan focus on three supportive implementation strategies:**

• *Leadership*
• *Professional Learning*
• *Partnerships*

The most powerful approaches to implementing a school vision and plan focus on three supportive implementation strategies:

◆ Leadership

◆ Professional Learning

◆ Partnerships

These elements must be woven throughout the continuous school improvement plan.

*Leadership* assists schools in creating shared decision making structures to implement the vision. A leadership structure defines how teachers and administrators are going to implement the vision, when they are going to meet to collaborate, align resources, review data and support each others' instruction, and review their progress toward the implementation of the vision.

Ongoing, job-embedded *Professional Learning* helps teachers, administrators, and staff members learn in order to change/improve the manner in which they work, i.e., how they make decisions; gather, analyze, and utilize data; plan, teach, and monitor achievement; meet the needs of students; collaborate with each other; evaluate personnel; and assess the impact of instruction and assessment on student learning.

*Partnership Development* lays out the purposes of, approaches to, and planning for educational partnerships with business and community groups, parents, and other educational professionals to increase student learning and prepare all students for college and careers. When schools are clear about their outcomes, others can more effectively contribute to that end.

## Creating the Continuous School Improvement Plan

A continuous school improvement plan lays out how to implement a vision, including strategies and activities, person(s) responsible, measurement, expenditures, estimated costs, funding sources, and timelines.

An example *Somewhere Continuous School Improvement Plan* is shown in Figure 10.1. Steps in creating a continuous school improvement plan follows: (See Appendix L, *Continuous School Improvement Plan.*)

Step 1.　**Enroll a Planning Team.** It is not necessary to have every staff member involved in creating a continuous school improvement plan. While it is important that all staff agree with the strategies, which they did while using data to create the shared vision, it can become cumbersome and inefficient if too many people are working on the plan at the same time. We recommend that a representative group, such as the Leadership Team or a Planning Team draft the plan, take it to staff for review, improvement, acceptance, and commitment to its implementation. Never should one person draft the plan in isolation.

Step 2.　**Review the Data.** The planning team reviews the analyses of data that the entire staff examined together.

Step 3.　**Reflect on the School Vision.** When the vision is done well, it will be very clear what needs to be put in the plan and implemented, with respect to curriculum (what we teach), instruction (how we teach the curriculum), assessment (how we measure learning), and environment (how each person treats every other person)—generally, what we hope to accomplish together.

130

CHAPTER 10
HOW ARE WE GOING TO GET TO WHERE WE WANT TO BE: IMPLEMENTING THE
SHARED VISION BY CREATING A PLAN FOR CONTINUOUS SCHOOL IMPROVEMENT

## Figure 10.1
### EXAMPLE: SOMEWHERE SCHOOL CONTINUOUS SCHOOL IMPROVEMENT PLAN ~ 2013-14

**Goal 1:** Ensure the *all* students graduate from high school, college, and career ready for citizenship and success in the 21st Century workplace.
- Provide a learning environment that develops *life-long learners.*
- Build a collaborative professional community that values and strives for continuous organizational improvement.
- Provide resources that support work typical of the 21st Century workplace (e.g., technology).
- Help *all* parents help their students to succeed.
- Develop an insatiable hunger for self-improvement among staff, students, and community.

**Goal 2:** Bring the community into the life of the school and the school into the life of the community.

**Goal 3:** Provide a physically, emotionally, and intellectually safe environment that encourages students to become creators and innovators that will improve the world.

**Goal #1: Ensure that all students graduate from high school, college and career ready for citizenship and success in the 21st Century workplace.**

| Strategy/Action | Person(s) Responsible | Measurement | Resources Needed | Due Date | Timeline (Aug Sept Oct Nov Dec Jan Feb Mar Apr May Jun Jul) |
|---|---|---|---|---|---|
| *Align instruction and materials with Common Core State Standards (CCSS):* All grade levels have studied the essential standards they will teach for each curricular area. Each essential standard has been scaffolded (to feature needed skills, concepts, and materials), vertically aligned, mapped, and paced for all curricular areas. | Whole Staff/ Ongoing | Essential standards are documented for all curricular areas for all grade levels. Grade-level teams agree on the standards. Cross-grade-level teams agree on the standards. Documentation of all essential standards show them to be scaffolded, mapped, vertically aligned, and paced. | Instructional materials. Technology spelled out in the technology budget plan. | Start of the school year. | X (Aug) |
| *Improve instructional strategies and student learning:* All teachers will use the CCSS to target instruction. A. Learning objectives will be clearly stated. B. Students will understand the importance of the learning objective. C. Teachers will frequently check for understanding and adjust instruction as needed. D. Instruction is student-centered, technology infused, with students engaged in authentic, meaningful, higher level thinking. E. Attainment of learning objectives will be based on student performance data. F. Partnerships with the community will be incorporated in the learning, as spelled out in the Partnership Plan, and Goal #2. | Teachers / Ongoing Principal | Classroom observations that describe what instruction and the classroom would look like when the CCSS are implemented will also determine if, and how, teachers are: • using the essential standards to target instruction; • creating clear learning objectives to teach the essential standards and to make sure students understand their importance; • checking for understanding and adjusting instruction as needed. | Substitute time for classroom observations, feedback, and support. | Ongoing | X X X X X X X X X (Sept–May) |

## Figure 10.1 (Continued)

### EXAMPLE: SOMEWHERE SCHOOL CONTINUOUS SCHOOL IMPROVEMENT PLAN ~ 2013-14

**Goal 1:** Ensure the *all* students graduate from high school, college, and career ready for citizenship and success in the 21st Century workplace.
- Provide a learning environment that develops *life-long learners.*
- Build a collaborative professional community that values and strives for continuous organizational improvement.
- Provide resources that support work typical of the 21st Century workplace (e.g., technology).
- Help *all* parents help their students to succeed.
- Develop an insatiable hunger for self-improvement among staff, students, and community.

**Goal 2:** Bring the community into the life of the school and the school into the life of the community.

**Goal 3:** Provide a physically, emotionally, and intellectually safe environment that encourages students to become creators and innovators that improve the world.

**Goal #1: Ensure that all students graduate from high school, college and career ready for citizenship and success in the 21st Century workplace.**

| Strategy/Action | Person(s) Responsible | Measurement | Resources Needed | Due Date | Aug | Sept | Oct | Nov | Dec | Jan | Feb | Mar | Apr | May | Jun | Jul |
|---|---|---|---|---|---|---|---|---|---|---|---|---|---|---|---|---|
| *Each grade level uses assessments that are embedded in every lesson, as well as common, formative assessments that are administered frequently.*<br><br>A. Grade levels assess each essential standard, every 2–3 weeks, and conduct data team meetings to discuss performance for most of them.<br><br>B. Grade level teams and the Data Leadership Team look at the data from our assessments to determine alignment, within and across grade levels, and the effectiveness of instructional strategies and programs.<br><br>C. Grade level teams and the Data Leadership Team look at the data from our assessments to determine which students are not meeting proficiency, those that are, and what to do about it.<br><br>D. Agreements are made on the skill levels and benchmarks for at-risk students in all subject areas for all grades.<br><br>E. Results from assessments will be shared with students and parents, and merged with student self-assessments.<br><br>F. Feedback to students will be timely and specific.<br><br>G. Proficiency and growth will be acknowledged and celebrated on a regular basis.<br><br>H. Student goals will be based on assessments, and will be shared with students and parents at goal-setting conferences. | Subject-Area Grade-Level Teams/ Ongoing | Classroom observations that describe what instruction and the classroom would look like when the CCSS and the school vision are implemented will also determine if, and how, teachers are:<br>• using grade level assessments of each standard;<br>• administering common formative assessments every 2–3 weeks;<br>• attending data team meetings about the assessment of each essential standard;<br><br>Documentation exists that grade-level teams and then schoolwide-data-team meetings review the results of the assessments, and check for alignment.<br><br>Evidence exists that the meeting minutes are shared with all teachers, and that needed adjustments are made in classrooms. | Some substitute time for classroom observations, feedback, and support. |  | X |  | X | X | X | X | X | X | X | X |  |  |

132

CHAPTER 10
HOW ARE WE GOING TO GET TO WHERE WE WANT TO BE: IMPLEMENTING THE
SHARED VISION BY CREATING A PLAN FOR CONTINUOUS SCHOOL IMPROVEMENT

Figure 10.1 (*Continued*)

## EXAMPLE: SOMEWHERE SCHOOL CONTINUOUS SCHOOL IMPROVEMENT PLAN ~ 2013-14

**Goal 1:** Ensure the *all* students graduate from high school, college, and career ready for citizenship and success in the 21st Century workplace.
- Provide a learning environment that develops *life-long learners*.
- Build a collaborative professional community that values and strives for continuous organizational improvement.
- Provide resources that support work typical of the 21st Century workplace (e.g., technology).
- Help *all* parents help their students to succeed.
- Develop an insatiable hunger for self-improvement among staff, students, and community.

**Goal 2:** Bring the community into the life of the school and the school into the life of the community.
**Goal 3:** Provide a physically, emotionally, and intellectually safe environment that encourages students to become creators and innovators that improve the world.

**Goal #1: Ensure that all students graduate from high school, college and career ready for citizenship and success in the 21st Century workplace.**

| Strategy/Action | Person(s) Responsible | Measurement | Resources Needed | Due Date | Aug | Sept | Oct | Nov | Dec | Jan | Feb | Mar | Apr | May | Jun | Jul |
|---|---|---|---|---|---|---|---|---|---|---|---|---|---|---|---|---|
| *Professional development and collaboration:* Professional development and collaboration is frequent and ongoing. | | | | | | | | | | | | | | | | |
| A. Grade levels meet every Wednesday from 1:45 to 3:00. Collaboration is focused on results of formative assessments and on effective instructional strategies. | All staff | Leadership structure and process flowcharts detail how collaboration will work for all teachers. | Early release Wednesday support. | | X | | X | X | X | X | X | X | X | X | | |
| B. Cross-grade-level teams meet alternate Wednesdays from 3:05 to 4:15. | | | | | | | | | | | | | | | | |
| C. Leadership Team meets Thursdays from 3:05 to 4:30. | | | | | | | | | | | | | | | | |
| D. Data Leadership Team will meet as needed to prepare assessment results for grade level teams. | | | | | | | | | | | | | | | | |
| E. Whole staff meets once a month for ongoing professional development aligned to our vision and plan. | | | | | | | | | | | | | | | | |
| F. Schoolwide, we will use peer coaching to support deep implementation of vision strategies and the CCSS. | | | | | | | | | | | | | | | | |

**Step 4.** **Set Goals.** Schoolwide goals need to be set with the whole staff before the actual writing of the plan commences. It is ideal to set schoolwide goals while creating the shared vision. Goals are intended outcomes of the vision. They are stated in broad, general, abstract, and largely measurable terms. Schools should have only two or three school goals. Goals should:

◆ Give the school a long term vision.

◆ Be realistic, but ambitious at the same time.

◆ Drive action to the purpose and vision of the school.

◆ Have at least one objective that describes how the goal will be measured.

◆ Help the school reach district and state goals.

Goals should not specify how the schools will achieve the goal.

**EXAMPLE: Somewhere School Goal**

*Ensure that all students graduate from high school, college and career ready for citizenship and success in the 21st Century workplace.*

**Step 5.** **Identify Objectives.** Draft objectives that will close the gap between where the school is right now and where it wants to be, for each of the goals. Objectives are goals that are redrafted in clearly tangible terms, to close gaps. They must be grounded in the data. Objective statements are narrow, specific, concrete, and measurable. When writing objectives, it is important to describe the intended results, rather than the process or means to accomplish them. Objectives are SMART[1] goals: *Specific, Measurable, Attainable, Realistic,* and *Trackable.*

**EXAMPLE: Somewhere School Objective**

*Decrease the number of students at risk of dropping out of school to zero by the end of the school year.*

**STEPS IN CREATING A CONTINUOUS SCHOOL IMPROVEMENT PLAN**

Step 1. *Enroll a planning team.*
Step 2. *Review the data.*
Step 3. *Reflect on the school vision.*
Step 4. *Set goals.*
Step 5. *Identify objectives.*
Step 6. *Identify and group strategies to achieve the objectives.*
Step 7. *Actions required to implement the strategies.*
Step 8. *Arrange strategies and activities.*
Step 9. *Determine how achievement of the actions will be measured.*
Step 10. *Use a planning template.*
Step 11. *Establish due dates.*
Step 12. *Determine resources.*
Step 13. *Refine the plan.*
Step 14. *Communicate the plan.*
Step 15. *Monitor the implementation of the plan.*
Step 16. *Evaluate the plan.*

---

[1]Conzemius, A., & O'Neill, J. (2005). *The power of SMART goals: Using goals to improve student learning.* Bloomington, IN: Solution Tree.

134

CHAPTER 10

HOW ARE WE GOING TO GET TO WHERE WE WANT TO BE: IMPLEMENTING THE
SHARED VISION BY CREATING A PLAN FOR CONTINUOUS SCHOOL IMPROVEMENT

Step 6. **Identify and Group Strategies to Achieve the Objectives.** Brainstorm and discuss different strategies to reach the objectives, making sure the vision is reviewed, contributing causes of undesirable results have been analyzed, and aggregated commonalities from your comprehensive data analysis are considered as well. Group the strategies under the objectives.

Step 7. **Actions Required to Implement the Strategies.** Below each strategy, list the actions that need to be accomplished to implement the strategy (i.e., *identify students at risk of dropping out of school, review the student-level data*). Think in terms of what the strategy looks like right now, and what you want the strategy to look like when the vision is implemented. What will it take to get there?

Step 8. **Arrange Strategies and Activities.** Arrange the strategies and activities in chronological order. (Keep the first version for later reference and fine-tune the plan in chronological summary form, starting with the action to be taken first.)

Step 9. **Determine How Achievement of the Actions Will Be Measured.** For each activity, determine how you will know if the action is being implemented and the impact of its implementation.

Step 10. **Use a Planning Template.** Using a planning template with labeled columns—strategy/ action, person(s) responsible, measurement, resources, due date, and timeline—place the reorganized strategies and actions in the action column in a manner that is easiest for staff to utilize later. In the column next to each action, identify the person ultimately responsible for the action. Try not to use team names like *Language Arts Action Team* in the person responsible column. Accountability is most effective if the responsibility is delegated to an individual. Responsible persons determine how accountability reviews are conducted, and how to talk with one another about fostering and demonstrating accountability.

Step 11. **Establish Due Dates.** In the column next to "person(s) responsible," write in the due dates. For each strategy or activity (depends on the topic and structure for implementation), determine when the activity must be completed. If your plan has columns that represent months, weeks, and sometimes days, make notations that will indicate when each activity will begin and when it will be completed, by showing an "X" in the cell. Indicate the duration by marking a line between the "Xs" across the months.

Step 12. **Determine Resources.** Determine the financial resources required of each strategy and activity. These budgets, developed in conjunction with the continuous school improvement plan, determine the financial feasibility of the actions for each year. Alterations are made simultaneously and balanced back and forth, while looking for items that can leverage other items. Dollars sometimes limit activities. School staff are often surprised, however, to discover that many times what they have to spend is equivalent to what they can do in a year's time, once they spell out the components and costs. If the latter does not hold true, staff has important and specific information (i.e., the vision, plan, and budget) to utilize in seeking additional support for their efforts. Note that the budget is a part of the continuous school improvement plan and that all school funds are used with the one resulting plan. Everything in the school should be working toward that one continuous school improvement plan and the one school vision. The planning team must have a clear understanding of all budget resources.

Step 13. **Refine the Plan.** With the first draft of the continuous school improvement plan complete, review the elements and the big picture of the plan. Below are some guiding questions:

- Are the objectives about improved student learning for all students?

- Will this plan lead to student learning for all students?

- Will this plan support staff in implementing the vision?

- Will the strategies lead to attainment of the objectives?

- What evidence do we need to know if the objectives are being met?

- Do the strategies address contributing causes?

- Are there strategies/actions that can be further collapsed?

- Will all staff members know what is expected of them?

- Does the plan include new learning required of staff? If so, has training and support been incorporated for each area?

- Are the time frames realistic?

- How will the ultimate goal of improved student learning for all students be kept at the forefront of everything we do?

- How often will the plan and strategies be monitored?

136

CHAPTER 10
HOW ARE WE GOING TO GET TO WHERE WE WANT TO BE: IMPLEMENTING THE
SHARED VISION BY CREATING A PLAN FOR CONTINUOUS SCHOOL IMPROVEMENT

- ◆ Whose job is it to monitor the implementation of the plan?
- ◆ How will new staff members learn about the plan?

Step 14. **Communicate the Plan.** Determine how the continuous school improvement plan will be documented, communicated, reported, and updated. Communicate progress towards the attainment of the school improvement goals and objectives in newsletters, staff bulletins, websites, and bulletin boards.

Step 15. **Monitor the Implementation of the Plan.** A part of refining the continuous school improvement plan is ensuring that everything in the plan is aligned to the implementation of the vision, including the leadership structure, curriculum, instruction, assessment, professional learning, etc. When staff members begin to implement the plan, all parts of the plan need to be monitored regularly. The measurement column for the strategies and activities provides a means for monitoring. We recommend that the Leadership Team check the plan for implementation each month, remembering that implementation of a continuous improvement plan requires collaboration and flexibility on the part of the monitors. (See Appendix M, *Monitoring Plan.*)

Step 16. **Evaluate the Plan.** The entire continuous school improvement plan must be evaluated, with the vision and school goals as targets. This comprehensive evaluation will evaluate the parts and the whole of the plan to indicate if the goals, objectives, and strategies are leading to the attainment of the vision. (See Chapter 12, and *Evaluation of Plan*, Appendix U.)

## A Leadership Structure With Clear Roles And Responsibilities For All Staff

*Leadership is the capacity to translate vision into reality.*

Warren G. Bennis

*Every school should have a structure in place that will help every staff member implement the vision, as well as collaborate with colleagues to help each other review data and implement the vision.*

We believe the job of leaders is to help everyone in the organization implement the vision. We also believe that each teacher is a leader. Every school should have a structure in place that will help every staff member implement the vision, as well as collaborate with colleagues to help each other review data and implement the vision. These structures are often called "leadership structures" because they also support shared decision making. The important elements of effective leadership structures include:

◆ *Partitioning of the school staff in a manner that makes sense for supporting the implementation of the vision.* For example, in elementary schools, establishing grade-level teams and cross-grade-level teams to implement the vision makes sense. This is especially effective since the focus is to make sure each teacher is implementing grade level standards, and to ensure that the standards are calibrated across grade levels. Most traditional high schools and middle schools have departments which could represent an effective leadership structure—if that structure supports the implementation of the vision. However, if the middle school or high school is trying to integrate subjects, individual subject-specific departments might keep the school from implementing its vision. The leadership structure must reflect the vision, and include all staff.

◆ *Clarifying purposes and roles and responsibilities of all teacher teams.* Getting the teachers to create and agree on the purpose and roles and responsibilities of each team helps them know the intricacies of that team, as well as contribute to the successful implementation of each team. A part of identifying roles and responsibilities is to set structures for norms, timed agendas, and rotating roles (facilitator, timekeeper, and recorder) to keep the team focus on student learning.

◆ *Identifying times to meet and keeping them sacred.* The teams meet, no matter what. There can be no cancellations because of other meetings. It is important to not put the principal as lead of any team. We find that the principal is often pulled out at the last minute, and then the team thinks the meeting has to be cancelled. However, the principal should participate in as many meetings as possible. To implement the vision with a strong leadership structure, the team meeting times and agendas must be adhered to. At least one hour per week needs to be dedicated to grade-level or subject-area teams to review data and update instruction. Additional time needs to be protected for leadership team meetings and other leadership teams. Time must be created. Many schools bank time by extending the school day four days a week, providing an early dismissal or late start for students, so teachers can meet for part of one day a week. An example of a Leadership structure follows (Figure 10.2). (See Appendix N, *Leadership Structure.*)

> **THE IMPORTANT ELEMENTS OF EFFECTIVE LEADERSHIP STRUCTURES**
>
> • *Partitioning of the school staff in a manner that makes sense for supporting the implementation of the vision.*
>
> • *Clarifying purposes and roles and responsibilities of all teacher teams.*
>
> • *Identifying times to meet and keeping them sacred.*

CHAPTER 10
HOW ARE WE GOING TO GET TO WHERE WE WANT TO BE: IMPLEMENTING THE
SHARED VISION BY CREATING A PLAN FOR CONTINUOUS SCHOOL IMPROVEMENT

## Figure 10.2
### EXAMPLE: SOMEWHERE ELEMENTARY SCHOOL LEADERSHIP STRUCTURE

**Somewhere Elementary School's** leadership structure is four-pronged:
- Grade-Level Teams
- Data Leadership Team
- Cross-Grade-Level-Teams
- Leadership Team

The mission and vision of the school guide all leadership components. The work of each team is guided by data and the continuous school improvement plan, with a focus on implementing the Common Core State Standards.

All meetings are scheduled on the school calendar. All meetings are open to all staff members; therefore, agendas will be sent in advance or with the current meeting minutes. In the event of additions and/or deletions to agendas, staff will be informed by e-mail.

### Meeting Times

| Team | Time | Day |
|------|------|-----|
| Grade-Level Teams | 1:45 to 3:00 PM | Wednesdays |
| Cross-Grade-Level Teams | 3:05 to 4:15 PM | Alternate Wednesdays |
| Data Leadership Team | (Calendared by the team) | (Calendared by the team) |
| Leadership Team | 3:05 to 4:30 PM | Thursdays |
| Whole Staff Meetings | 3:05 to 4:15 PM | Every other Friday, and as needed |

### Roles and Responsibilities

It is the collective responsibility of all teachers, in grade-level teams and cross-grade-level teams, to work together to implement all aspects of the shared vision. All classroom teachers participate in grade-level team meetings on a weekly basis.

One teacher at each grade level serves as the Grade-Level Lead; this teacher sits on the Leadership Team. One teacher at each grade level serves on the Cross-Grade-Level Team. One teacher at each grade level serves on the Data Leadership Team.

### Grade-Level Teams

The purpose of Grade-Level Teams is to maintain the cohesion of curriculum, instruction, assessment, and environment spelled out in the shared vision. Grade-Level Teams will:
- create, adopt, review, and revise norms as needed, in support of working effectively together;
- study together, coach each other, and support one another in the implementation of the Common Core State Standards and the school's vision;
- use data to update and improve each teacher's teaching;
- seek support from one another;
- study and support each other's implementation of best practices; and
- seek support from specialists on staff, as needed.

Grade-Level Team meetings will be conducted in each other's classrooms on a rotating basis and will follow the norms and support strategies.

### Cross-Grade-Level Teams

The purpose of the Cross-Grade-Level Team is to focus on all teachers effectively implementing the Common Core State Standards. This structure is made up of representative grade-level team members and, as such, must practice clear and objective communication to the grade level they represent. Its members facilitate this team's work. The responsibilities of the Cross-Grade-Level Team include:
- focusing on instructional coherence for all core instruction;
- reviewing and clarifying the implementation of Common Core State Standards as they apply to stregthening effective classroom instruction schoolwide;
- working to strengthen the cross-grade-level alignment of curriculum instruction, assessment, and environment;
- sharing best practices and effective lessons toward the goal of bringing these to respective grade-level teams;
- making decisions about schoolwide instructional and assessment practices, related to consistency;
- planning and implementing professional learning.
- making budgetary recommendations to the Leadership Team in support of Common Core State Standards resource alignment; and
- planning and implementation of schoolwide programs.

## Figure 10.2 *(Continued)*
### EXAMPLE: SOMEWHERE ELEMENTARY SCHOOL LEADERSHIP STRUCTURE

**Data Leadership Team**

The Data Leadership Team leads the classroom data analysis process. The team makes sure the work of the grade level and cross-grade level teams is conducted smoothly. The Data Leadership Team is comprised of educators from across grade levels and subject areas who enjoy working with data.

The purposes of the Data Leadership Team include:
- ensuring that data are available to teachers in an appropriate fashion for review, on schedule;
- supporting and facilitating dialogue with colleagues in analyzing data and student work to improve teaching and learning;
- enabling teacher ownership of the data review process that motivates teachers to implement and monitor new strategies;
- ensuring exploration of current processes, based on data, before identifying solutions; and
- ensuring the implementation, monitoring, and follow-through of next steps.

**Leadership Team**

The Leadership Team is a decision-making body and, as such, members must practice clear and objective communication with the staff members whom they represent, and to fellow Leadership Team members as representatives for other staff members.

The Leadership Team is made up of the Principal, the Principal's Secretary, the Resource Specialist, and the lead from each grade-level team. Input from teachers will be communicated to the Grade-Level Lead, input from Instructional Assistants will be communicated via the Resource Specialist, and input from non-teaching staff will be communicated via the Principal's Secretary. The Issues Bin and the Anonymous Comments envelope are additional avenues for all staff to give input to the Leadership Team.

The purposes of the Leadership Team are to:
- support the implementation of Common Core State Standards within and across grade levels;
- guide, support, and reinforce the continuous school improvement plan using multiple sources of data;
- plan for the Data Leadership Teams to monitor use of data for the improvement of teaching and learning, schoolwide;
- provide ongoing input into budgetary decisions, all of which are based on data and available resources;
- oversee and approve the design of agendas for professional learning;
- disseminate information;
- troubleshoot the concerns of grade levels and individuals;
- improve and support school climate by modeling effective communication and leadership skills; and
- calendar schoolwide assessments and events.

**Whole Staff Meetings**

The entire staff will meet every other week to discuss the schoolwide implementation of the vision.

**Principal**

The role of the principal is to ensure:
- the implementation of the vision, plan, and leadership structure;
- staff receive the professional learning they need;
- all staff use data to impact learning for all students;
- quality instruction in every classroom;
- staff members collaborate to improve instruction; and
- communication is often and of high quality.

140

CHAPTER 10

HOW ARE WE GOING TO GET TO WHERE WE WANT TO BE: IMPLEMENTING THE
SHARED VISION BY CREATING A PLAN FOR CONTINUOUS SCHOOL IMPROVEMENT

## Professional Learning Calendar Created from the Continuous School Improvement Plan and Leadership Structure

*Through learning we re-create ourselves. Through learning we
become able to do something we never were able to do.
Through learning we re-perceive the world and our relationship
to it. Through learning we extend our capacity to create,
to be part of the generative process of life.*

Peter M. Senge

*Many principals have found the Professional Learning Calendar to be extremely valuable in keeping the whole school on target with implementing the vision, plan, and leadership structure.*

Once the plan, based on the data analysis, vision, and leadership structure, is completed, school staff can benefit from a Professional Learning Calendar. A Professional Learning Calendar starts with those agreed upon times for the teams to meet, and then pulls from the plan what the teams should be working on at any point in the school year calendar; thereby setting the topic for each meeting. Many principals have found the Professional Learning Calendar to be extremely valuable in keeping the whole school on target with implementing the vision, plan, and leadership structure. Some principals say the use of the calendar makes things happen that have never happened before, even though the activities had been "planned." All the purposes or topics in the calendar are derived from the continuous school improvement plan. An example of a Professional Learning Calendar follows (Figure 10.3). (See Appendix O, *Professional Learning Calendar.*)

## Figure 10.3
## EXAMPLE: SOMEWHERE SCHOOL PROFESSIONAL LEARNING CALENDAR

*The first month of the Somewhere School 2013-14 Professional Learning Calendar is shown in the example below. During 2013-14, the focus is on implementing the Core Curriculum State Standards. Every Wednesday, students will be dismissed at 1:30 pm for collaborative team meetings.*

| Date | Who Should Attend | Purpose |
|---|---|---|
| July 22-26 All day | Data Leadership Team | Attend the *Education for the Future Data Institute.* Create the School Data Profile, and plan for data analysis and use during the year. Reroster student data for current teachers and students. |
| August 19-23 8:00 AM to 4:00 PM | Professional Learning for all staff | Expectations for the year. Review of continuous school improvement. Analyze schoolwide, grade level, and classroom level data with staff. Clarify curriculum and instructional strategies that must change, based on the data analysis. Establish team members and team leaders. Review roles and responsibilities. Professional learning on analyzing and implementing the CCSS. Review where staff is on aligning curriculum and instructional resources to CCSS, and continue with standards analysis. Learn the elements of effective CCSS lessons, how to assess the lessons, and how to conduct lesson studies. Grade-level teams work to lay out the curriculum, lesson designs, and assessments for the year. Cross-grade-level teams meet to ensure alignment across grade levels. Leadership Team meets to establish how they will work during the year to monitor CCSS and vision implementation and student attainment. |
| August 26 | Data Leadership Team | Determine how to support staff during the administration of the screening assessments and the retrieval of results. |
| August 27 | First Day of School | School starts. |
| August 28 | Initial Screener Administration | All teachers administer short online screening assessments to students to understand what they know and do not know. |
| August 28 1:45 to 3:00 PM | Grade-Level Teams | Meet to discuss the results of the screening assessments and to adjust planned lessons. |
| August 28 3:05 to 4:15 PM | Cross-Grade-Level Teams | Review grade level assessments for alignment. Establish a system to monitor assessment data and ensure the alignment of standards across grade levels, throughout the year. |
| August 29 3:05 to 4:30 PM | Leadership Team | Review grade level and cross-grade level team assessment results. Prepare agenda for all staff meetings. |
| August 30 3:05 to 4:15 PM | All staff meeting. Leadership Team facilitates. | Review Meet to discuss the first week. Plan for diagnostic assessments and additional support for students in need. Approve monitoring system for assessments and standards alignment. |
| September 2 | School Closed | Labor Day. |

142

CHAPTER 10
HOW ARE WE GOING TO GET TO WHERE WE WANT TO BE: IMPLEMENTING THE
SHARED VISION BY CREATING A PLAN FOR CONTINUOUS SCHOOL IMPROVEMENT

**Figure 10.3** *(Continued)*
### EXAMPLE: SOMEWHERE SCHOOL PROFESSIONAL LEARNING CALENDAR

| Date | Who Should Attend | Purpose |
|---|---|---|
| September 4<br>1:45 to 3:00 PM | Grade-Level Team | Review diagnostic assessment data. Agree on lesson plans and learning structures for students in need. Review instructional resource requirements. |
| September 5<br>3:05 to 4:30 PM | Leadership Team | Review grade-level team status. Continue planning for the provision of instructional and technology resources so each grade level can implement the CCSS with integrity and fidelity. |
| September 11<br>1:45 to 3:00 PM | Grade-Level Teams | Conduct lesson studies in implementing the CCSS. Determine what support each teacher needs and how it will be provided. |
| September 11<br>3:05 to 4:15 PM | Cross-Grade-Level Team | Verify CCSS implementation across grade levels. Share grade level needs and discuss commonalities to present to the Leadership Team. |
| September 12<br>3:05 to 4:30 PM | Leadership Team | Review grade level and cross-grade level team progress, concerns, and support requirements. Continue planning for the year. |
| September 13<br>3:05 to 4:15 PM | All Staff Meeting<br>Leadership Team facilitates | Review the schoolwide implementation of the CCSS and school vision. Staff members report on CCSS implementation. Discuss staff needs and adjustments required. Introduce a communication protocol for lesson study. |
| September 18<br>1:45 to 3:00 PM | Grade-Level Team | Conduct lesson study. |
| September 19<br>3:05 to 4:30 PM | Leadership Team | Determine how to prepare teachers for the first sets of common formative assessments. |
| September 19<br>3:05 to 4:30 PM | Data Leadership Team | Prepare to support teachers in implementing the first sets of common formative assessments. Determine assessment reports that will assist staff in implementing and assessing standards attainment.<br>Begin the search for the questionnaires to administer in October. |
| September 25<br>1:45 to 3:00 PM | Grade-Level Team | Review progress. Teachers begin to take turns presenting their student work, data, and questions for team member support. |
| September 25<br>3:05 to 4:15 PM | Cross-Grade-Level Team | Monitor assessment data and ensure the alignment of standards across grade levels |

## Plan for Partners

*Never doubt that a small group of thoughtful,*
*concerned citizens can change the world.*
*Indeed it is the only thing that ever has.*

Margaret Mead

Continuous school improvement calls for real partnerships among the schools' parents, businesses, and the community—partnerships that are consistent, organized, and centered on meaningful communication. This communication allows partners to play important roles in childrens' education across academic, behavioral, and social domains and help them be College and Career Ready. (See Appendix P for *Creating Partnerships*.) A *Somewhere Elementary School Example Partnership Plan* follows in Figure 10.4.

Leadership structures, professional learning, and partnership work together to help everyone on staff implement the vision. All of these components are a part of the continuous school improvement plan.

*Leadership structures, professional learning, and partnership work together to help everyone on staff implement the vision.*

### Figure 10.4
### EXAMPLE: SOMEWHERE ELEMENTARY SCHOOL PARTNERSHIP PLAN

Somewhere Elementary School staff created a Partnership Team to develop strategic partnerships to support 21st Century Learning in our classrooms. The Partnership Team is striving for win-win partnerships with our colleagues, parents, the community, and businesses to support and build student creativity, collaboration, critical thinking, and communication skills.

Our plan is to have an open meeting each semester with parents, community, and business to:

1. Provide awareness of the Common Core State Standards.
2. Define 21st Century Skills and why they are important.
3. Describe what it might look like if we were implementing the standards together.
4. Brainstorm ideas about how we can work together to help all students meet the Common Core Standards and gain 21st Century Skills.

Teachers need to plan partnership lessons in terms of student understandings of how systems work, how communities operate, where materials come from, and what students can do to become contributing members of society. Consider how to incorporate the following in lessons:

- Museums and libraries
- Health Clubs
- City Works
- Technology
- Internships with Businesses
- Tours of local businesses
- Colleges and Universities
- Music and dance performances
- Parks

- Speakers Bureau for Students
- Blogs to discuss skills required for different careers
- Book in common discussions
- Meetings with Politicians
- Hospitals
- TV and radio
- Service learning projects
- Grocery stores
- Farms and Farmers' Markets

144

CHAPTER 10
HOW ARE WE GOING TO GET TO WHERE WE WANT TO BE: IMPLEMENTING THE
SHARED VISION BY CREATING A PLAN FOR CONTINUOUS SCHOOL IMPROVEMENT

## HOW MUCH TIME DOES IT TAKE?

*It will take a couple of hours to create a Leadership Structure, complete with roles and responsibilities, if your school does not have something like this in place. The actual writing of the comprehensive continuous school improvement plan could take a week of going back and forth with staff.*

## REFLECTION QUESTIONS

1. What are the differences between a continuous school improvement plan and a school improvement plan focused on closing gaps?

2. Why is a continuous school improvement plan important to continuous school improvement?

3. Why are leadership, professional learning, and partnership development important to continuous school improvement and the continuous school improvement plan?

## APPLICATION OPPORTUNITIES

1. Create a continuous school improvement plan to implement your shared vision. (Use *Continuous School Improvement Plan*, Appendix L.)

2. Construct a leadership structure, complete with roles and responsibilities, that will help everyone in the learning organization implement the vision. (Use *Leadership Structure*, Appendix N.)

3. Generate a professional learning calendar by laying out the dates of team meetings and professional learning and who should attend. From the continuous school improvement plan, determine the purpose of the meetings. If the calendar looks undoable, you will need to revise your school plan. (Use *Professional Learning Calendar*, Appendix O.)

4. Produce a plan for partnerships. Start with your standards. What do you want students to know and be able to do? With potential partners, brainstorm what each can do to support students in achieving the standards. (Use *Creating Partnerships*, Appendix P.)

# STRATEGIES FOR TEACHERS:
## USING DATA TO IMPLEMENT THE VISION THROUGH THE CONTINUOUS SCHOOL IMPROVEMENT PLAN TO IMPROVE TEACHING AND LEARNING

**CHAPTER 11**

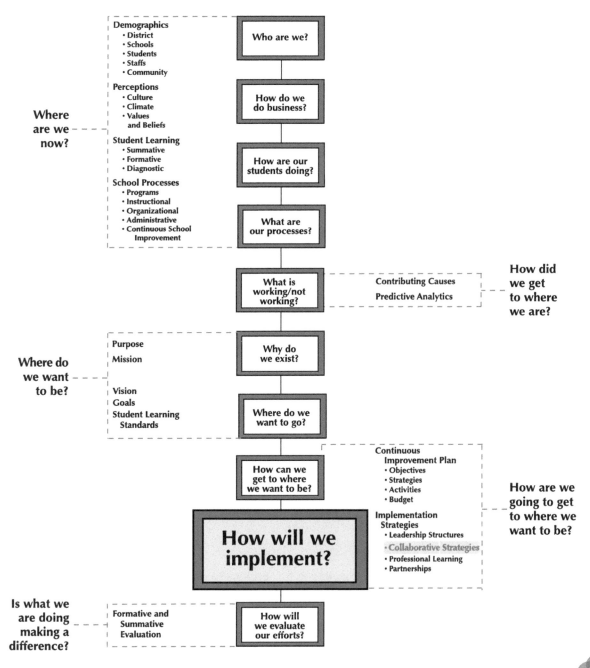

146

CHAPTER **11**

STRATEGIES FOR TEACHERS: USING DATA TO IMPLEMENT THE VISION THROUGH THE
CONTINUOUS SCHOOL IMPROVEMENT PLAN TO IMPROVE TEACHING AND LEARNING

*What would it take to get learning growth for every student,
every year, in your school? Teachers and administrators often tell me
the answer to that question pivots on two difficult elements:*

*1. Teachers and administrators must honestly review and use
their data—ALL their data, not just study a gap here or there.*

*2. Teachers and administrators must truly believe that all
children can learn, or learning cannot and will not happen.*

Victoria L. Bernhardt
Executive Director, *Education for the Future*

These two comments reflect the top elements that teachers and administrators say
need to be in place to get learning increases for every student, every year.

Are the two comments related? Very closely. Do they work hand-in-glove? Most
definitely. Why would any educator not believe that all students can learn; after all,
isn't it her/his job to ensure that all students learn? If we follow the arguments in the
perceptions section (Chapter 4), one of the reasons some teachers might not believe
that all students can learn is because they have never experienced reaching all
students and helping them all learn; and when teachers do have this experience, they
change their belief systems. Enter the effective use of data that can tell teachers what
students know and do not know so teachers can adjust their teaching to help *all*
students learn.

*Why would any
educator not believe
that all students
can learn; after all,
isn't it her/his job?*

Some researchers believe that to get teachers using data, professional
learning facilitators need to provide more instruction to teachers on how
to understand and use the numbers. I disagree. I think teachers do fine
reading data and understanding what students need to know when the
learning data are organized in a manner that they can quickly
comprehend and use. Effective professional learning, instead, has teachers
analyzing and determining how to use the data they gather, as opposed to
talking about how to look at data they do not have in front of them.

**To get teacher to effectively
use data, our challenges are to:**

- *Get appropriate data to the
teachers;*
- *Set-up the structures for
collaboration; and*
- *Establish leadership for
accountability.*

To get teachers to effectively use data, our challenges are to:

- get *appropriate data* to the teachers in a manner that they can use;

- set-up the *structures* for teachers to *collaborate* with professional
colleagues to share challenges and understandings, try strategies, and
reflect; and

- establish *leadership* to hold the process and people accountable.

One thing is clear: *using data to improve teaching and learning will not happen on its own.* We must *lead* the way to build the *collaborative structures,* inspire the *vision* of effective teaching and data use, and encourage *strategies* to make it all happen.

## STRATEGIES THAT LEAD TO EFFECTIVE DATA USE

When a school implements the continuous school improvement framework, it has begun an excellent journey of using data effectively to improve teaching and learning. Staff members know where they are as a school, as well as what processes and programs are working and which ones are not working. They have a shared vision to be carried out through a strong plan, collaborative leadership structures, professional learning, and quality partnerships. The missing piece is what the teachers do in their collaborative teams to gather, analyze, and use student learning data to improve teaching and learning in classrooms, and how the data use is supported.

Five preconditions for the effective use of student learning data by teachers include:

1. the use of appropriate data;

2. a shared vision;

3. leadership encouragement and support;

4. structures for collaboration; and

5. strategies to support each other in the attainment of new teaching skills.

Each of these is discussed on the pages that follow.

### The Use of Appropriate Data

It *does* matter what assessments teachers use.

Quality formative assessments, which can take many different forms, should help teachers know—

- what students know and do not know with respect to what teachers want them to know and be able to do;

- how students are learning;

- how teachers are teaching;

- what teachers need to do differently to get different results; and

- who is getting different (better) results, and why.

If formative assessments are not aligned to learning standards, there will be a problem. One elementary school decided to use an assessment in all grades that

---

**Five preconditions for the effective use of student learning data by teachers include:**

1. *The use of appropriate data;*

2. *A shared vision;*

3. *Leadership encouragement and support;*

4. *Structures for collaboration; and*

5. *Strategies to support each other in the attainment of new teaching skills.*

---

**Quality formative assessments, which can take many different forms, should help teachers know—**

- *what students know and do not know with respect to what teachers want them to know and be able to do;*

- *how students are learning;*

- *how teachers are teaching;*

- *what teachers need to do differently to get different results; and*

- *who is getting different (better) results, and why.*

---

*If formative assessments are not aligned to learning standards, there will be a problem.*

148

CHAPTER **11**
STRATEGIES FOR TEACHERS: USING DATA TO IMPLEMENT THE VISION THROUGH THE
CONTINUOUS SCHOOL IMPROVEMENT PLAN TO IMPROVE TEACHING AND LEARNING

worked well for the lower grades. It banked its year on that assessment. The teachers could see student progress and felt very good about the assessment until the summative test results showed the school had many fewer students proficient than the previous year, in every grade level, except the lowest grades. That assessment was assessing something important, but it was not developmentally keeping up with the grade levels and standards, and was not a good predictor of the summative test, which did assess standards acquisition. The assessment was valid but was not used in a valid fashion.

*Districts and schools must support teachers in adopting formative assessments for every subject area that assess standards attainment.*

Teachers need support in getting real-time formative data to review in a timely fashion. Districts and schools must support teachers in adopting formative assessments for every subject area that assess standards attainment. In addition, we recommend creating a Data Leadership Team to take on the task of assessing the reliability of the data and in getting appropriate data in the hands of teachers in a timely fashion so teachers can spend their time analyzing and discussing the results in their teams, and implementing new strategies. An example of the purposes and responsibilities of a Data Leadership Team is shown in Figure 11.1.

### Figure 11.1
### EXAMPLE: DATA LEADERSHIP TEAM

A Data Team is a meaningfully assigned group of educators (e.g., grade level teams, department teams) who examines student data and student work in collaborative, structured, scheduled meetings that focus on improving teaching and learning—their common mission. The Data Leadership Team leads the data team process, and makes sure the work of the data teams is conducted smoothly. The Data Leadership Team should be comprised of educators from across grade levels and subject areas, who enjoy working with data.

**Purposes**

Purposes of the Data Leadership Team include:

1. Supporting and facilitating dialogue with colleagues in analyzing data and student work to improve teaching and learning.
2. Ensuring that data are available to teachers in an appropriate fashion for review, on schedule.
3. Enabling teacher ownership of the data review process that motivates teachers to implement and monitor new strategies.
4. Ensuring exploration of current processes, based on data, before identifying solutions.
5. Ensuring the implementation, monitoring, and follow-through of next steps.

**Responsibilities**

Responsibilities of the Data Leadership Team include the following:

*Technical*

- Learn the school's data tools and databases, and support others in their uses.
- Make sure appropriate reports and graphs are available in a timely fashion for teacher review.
- Help re-roster or reorganize student achievement results before each meeting.
- Look at all data in perspective to other data, i.e., across grade levels, schoolwide, longitudinal, triangulated with other student learning data, assessed with other types of data. Follow-up with whole school inquiry processes when needed.
- Establish longitudinal reports of individual students, for each teacher, for grade levels, and for the school on multiple measures of data.
- Assist in planning a work calendar that is focused on the best and most immediate use of available data.

**Figure 11.1** *(Continued)*
**EXAMPLE: DATA LEADERSHIP TEAM**

*Ensure the Integrity of the Team*
* Make sure all teachers understand the purpose of the team (e.g., collective responsibility for all teachers to improve learning for all students) and the team meetings.
* Set meeting norms. (See below.)
* Build the conditions for trust.
* Ensure safety to ask challenging questions.
* Make sure all teachers have a chance to participate in the meetings.
* Use time well in meetings.

*Instructional*
* Encourage all staff members to make instructional decisions based on data and standards implementation.
* Help teachers analyze the data, and determine which instructional strategies need to be improved.
* Help teachers target their instruction to meet the needs of the students who are not showing progress.
* Ensure the implementation of instructional strategies across all grade levels.
* Monitor and measure to ensure the desired results are occurring.

## Responsibilities *(Continued)*

*Collaboration and Communication*
* Learn and facilitate the use of protocols for data dialogues.
* Prepare questions for data review protocols.
* Lead the creation of flowcharts or other mechanisms to describe what it would look like if all teachers were implementing the vision or programs as expected and desired.
* Keep administrators informed, if they are not in attendance at data team meetings.

*Follow-through*
* Assist school in creating a vision for continuous school improvement based, in part, on the use of data.
* Help the school staff create the time to learn new instructional strategies.
* Plan for next steps, reflections, and follow-through.
* Monitor and measure the implementation of the State or Provincial Standards and the school vision.
* Set up visits to all classrooms, with feedback.

## Norms for Collaborative Data Analysis
* Arrive at all meetings on time and with all needed materials.
* Start and end each meeting on time.

At least one week prior to the data analysis meeting, distribute, preferably by e-mail, an agenda identifying the data to be analyzed and what participants should bring with them to the data analysis meeting.
* Score all assessments, compile and graph the results prior to the meeting so that the data are ready to be analyzed.
* Support colleagues by asking clarifying questions. Criticism of any kind is inappropriate.
* Cast no blame. Use data solely to help each other determine how to teach more effectively.
* Approach data analysis as a learner. There are no "right" or "wrong" analyses.

## Protocols for Collaborative Data Analysis Review

Protocols are guidelines for dialogue that everyone understands and commits to using in team meetings. Protocols permit conversations to take place that build skills, trust, and the culture for collaborative work, without blame. (See *Communication Protocol,* Appendix Q.)

## Time

One hour every week, minimum.

150

CHAPTER 11
STRATEGIES FOR TEACHERS: USING DATA TO IMPLEMENT THE VISION THROUGH THE
CONTINUOUS SCHOOL IMPROVEMENT PLAN TO IMPROVE TEACHING AND LEARNING

## A Shared Vision

*When school staff agree and commit to a shared vision, they are collaborating on what they know and believe will make a difference for student learning.*

When school staff agree and commit to a shared vision, they are collaborating on what they know and believe will make a difference for student learning. They create common understandings about what to teach, how to teach, how to assess, and how each person will treat each other. They also have common understandings of what they are going to do when students know the information and what they are going to do when students do not know the information. These agreements make data use so much more effective.

A school can use *Measuring a Program or Process* (Appendix D) to ensure a shared vision for data use, such as Somewhere School did in Figure 11.2. They could also use this process to come to agreement on collaboration, differentiating instruction, reteaching, and teaching to learning standards.

## Leadership Encouragement and Support

*A vision will not make a difference unless it is modeled and reinforced by leadership. Leadership structures are based on the premise that it is everyone's job in the organization to implement the vision.*

A vision will not make a difference unless it is modeled and reinforced by leadership. Leadership structures, described in Chapter 10, are based on the premise that it is everyone's job in the organization to implement the vision. While we would never put the Principal of a school in the leadership role for any team (because the team might not meet when the leader is absent and because we want teachers to own the process), the Principal has to lead the cause of implementing the vision and using data. The Principal must:

◆ monitor implementation of the vision and data use;

◆ facilitate shared leadership and implementation of the vision;

◆ ensure that the appropriate use of data is taking place in each classroom;

◆ ensure that strategies within the leadership structures are effective;

◆ reinforce collaboration and teacher ownership of the results;

◆ hold structured collaboration time sacred;

◆ monitor schoolwide data throughout the year to ensure instructional coherence; and

◆ hold individuals and collaborative teams accountable for the results.

Figure 11.2

EXAMPLE: SOMEWHERE SCHOOL TEACHERS USING DATA TO IMPROVE TEACHING AND LEARNING

| PURPOSE | | PARTICIPANTS | IMPLEMENTATION | | RESULTS |
|---|---|---|---|---|---|
| *What is the purpose of the program or process?* | *How will you know the purpose is being met? (What are the outcomes?)* | *Who is the program/process intended to serve?* | *What would it look like when the program/process is fully implemented?* | *How is implementation being measured?* | *What are the results?* |
| The purpose of teachers *using data* is to use multiple measures of student assessment data to continuously improve teaching and learning.<br><br>Teachers, in collaborative teams, review student learning data and support each other's teaching to ensure that all students are learning.<br><br>Teachers follow the cycle of trying new strategies and reflecting on results. | When the purpose for using data is met:<br>• *all* students will show learning growth on meeting standards;<br>• teachers will adjust their instruction to meet the needs of students who are not meeting standards and challenging those who do;<br>• attendance and behavior will improve because students' needs are being met, and they want to be at school;<br>• teachers will work collaboratively to help all students, not just the students in their own classroom;<br>• teachers and students feel that they belong to the school, that students are challenged, and that the school is helping to prepare students for the 21st Century;<br>• teachers feel that they know how to teach to standards, regardless of where students are on the proficiency scale.<br><br>When using data is implemented as intended, there will be a continuum of learning that makes sense for all students. There will be instructional coherence in every subject area. | Using data is for all teachers so they may make a positive impact on the learning of all students.<br><br>*Who is being served? Who is not being served?*<br><br>According to our results, not all students are being served.<br><br>The students not being served are those who are not meeting grade level standards. | When teachers are working collaboratively to use data to improve teaching and learning, they will, together, determine—<br>• what concepts and skills students need to know and be able to do, and when.<br>• how they will know that students know these concepts and skills.<br>• a timeline for giving assessments during the year.<br>• which instructional strategies will make a difference.<br>• a plan/flowchart for what teachers will do when students do not know the concepts and do not have the skills, and what teachers will do when students know the concepts and have the skills.<br>• times, strategies, and roles and responsibilities for grade-level/subject-area work during the year.<br><br>At the beginning of the year, semester, unit, teachers administer post-assessments as pre-assessments.<br>In addition, they—<br>• monitor student progress throughout the course of the unit.<br>• review results with team members.<br>• determine how to support students who are not proficient, and students who are proficient in specific skills.<br>• review/update curriculum maps.<br>At predetermined times, teachers will review student learning progress across grade levels to ensure instructional coherence. | Teachers will create a monitoring tool to support the implementation of these strategies.<br><br>Teachers are held accountable to implementing standards and reaching every student, through classroom observations.<br><br>Administrators monitor and encourage the implementation of the using data structure and strategies throughout the school.<br><br>*To what degree is the program being implemented?*<br><br>All teachers are a part of a using data team and participate fully in all strategies. | Results show that teachers are assessing student growth in all subject areas, sharing the challenges of teaching with each other, implementing new strategies to meet the needs of all students, and supporting each other in meeting the needs of all students.<br><br>End of year achievement results show that all students are making at least a year's growth.<br><br>Teacher morale is high because teachers feel excited about being able to predict and prevent failure with their actions. |

**NEXT STEPS:**

This school needs to ensure that:
• appropriate formative assessments are being used in every subject area and every grade level.
• leadership is following through with monitoring and observations of the intent of the using data structure.
• instructional coherence is being monitored throughout the year.

152

CHAPTER 11
STRATEGIES FOR TEACHERS: USING DATA TO IMPLEMENT THE VISION THROUGH THE
CONTINUOUS SCHOOL IMPROVEMENT PLAN TO IMPROVE TEACHING AND LEARNING

## Structures for Collaboration

*Peter Senge says, "Collaboration is vital to sustain what we call profound or really deep change, because without it, organizations are just overwhelmed by the forces of the status quo."*

Peter Senge says:

> *Collaboration is vital to sustain what we call profound or really deep change, because without it, organizations are just overwhelmed by the forces of the status quo.*

Most schools say they encourage and have many opportunities for collaboration among their teachers. However, what they do in these collaborative communities is as varied as the schools. What we want teachers to do in these communities include:

◆ Agree and commit to working with each other to help all students learn.

◆ Agree on what they want students to know and be able to do, and how they will know that each student has learned it.

◆ Agree on how and when they will assess student knowledge.

◆ Establish a plan/flowchart for what teachers will do when students do not know the concepts and do not have the skills, and what teachers will do when students know the concepts and have the skills.

◆ Review data, discuss results, and support each other in trying new strategies to ensure students are learning.

◆ Share professional knowledge, understanding, experience, vision, and goals.

◆ Support each other in the challenges of practice.

◆ Hold themselves and the collaborative teams accountable for results.

◆ Improve teaching and learning.

**WHAT WE WANT TEACHERS TO DO IN COLLABORATIVE COMMUNITIES, INCLUDE—**

- *Agree and commit to working with each other to help all students learn.*
- *Agree on what they want students to know and be able to do, and how they will know that each student has learned it.*
- *Agree on how and when they will assess student knowledge.*
- *Establish a plan/flowchart for what teachers will do when students do not know the concepts and do not have the skills, and what teachers will do when students know the concepts and have the skills.*
- *Review data, discuss results, and support each other in trying new strategies to ensure students are learning.*
- *Share professional knowledge, understanding, experience, vision, and goals.*
- *Support each other in the challenges of practice.*
- *Hold themselves and the collaborative teams accountable for results.*
- *Improve teaching and learning.*

Collaboratively, teachers and administrators must determine, commit to, and hold sacred when they will meet, preferably once a week, to review student learning results for their grade levels, subject areas, and individual students, and work on next steps.

At the beginning of the year, semester, unit, it would be great to have all teachers administer common post-assessments as pre-assessments, review the results, discuss and alter their teaching plans to better meet the needs of the students. Then on a regular basis—

◆ Assess student progress.

◆ Review results.

◆ Determine how to support students who are not proficient, and students who are proficient in specific skills and knowledge.

◆ In teacher teams, review grade-level/subject-area results.

◆ Determine how teachers will support each other.

◆ Re-establish goals for the year, quarter, month, unit.

◆ Review/update curriculum maps.

## Strategies to Support Each Other in the Attainment of New Teaching Skills

To make a difference with teaching and learning, and to use what little time teachers have to collaborate, the work in collaborative teams must be structured. Many strategies exist for encouraging collaboration among team members so they can help each other improve their teaching and their students' learning. Below are three favorites.

### The Communication Protocol

One strategy that was started by the Coalition of Essential Schools has helped many schools engage in hard conversations about improving teaching and learning is a communication protocol. With a communication protocol, team members take turns bringing lesson plans, student learning results, examples of student work, case studies, and any other samples of materials to the team to critique, as well as two questions they would like the team members to consider. In the timed protocol, team members reflect, discuss, and offer suggestions. The presenting team member makes a plan for improvement and reports back to the team about progress. A version of the formal *Communication Protocol* is shown as Appendix Q.

### Examining Student's Work for Instructional Coherence

One of the goals of continuous school improvement is instructional coherence; in other words, making sure that grade levels and subject areas have horizontal and vertical alignment. There are many ways to ensure this alignment. *Examining Students' Work* (Appendix R) is a very powerful way to assess and ensure alignment, and to engage staff in conversations about standards, student work, and working together for the benefit of the students.

The protocol for this activity starts by explaining the purpose for looking at student work is to determine how to improve instructional practices to ensure all students meet the student learning standards. Have grade level teams purposefully choose examples of student work related to a specific content area or

**PROTOCOL TIMING**

15 min: *Presenter sets context for the work; uses examples of student work, student data, case studies, lesson plans, etc. Presenter poses two key questions she/he wants colleagues to address.*

5 min: *Participants ask clarifying questions.*

5 min: *Participants and presenter spend time in reflective writing, organizing notes and thoughts.*

15 min: *Participants discuss their observations and thoughts, and begin to explore options, consider gaps, and seek solutions or recommendations among themselves with no input from the presenter.*

15 min: *Presenter reflects verbally on participants' discussion while team members silently take notes. Presenter describes next steps.*

10 min: *Facilitator debriefs the session.*

154

CHAPTER **11**
STRATEGIES FOR TEACHERS: USING DATA TO IMPLEMENT THE VISION THROUGH THE
CONTINUOUS SCHOOL IMPROVEMENT PLAN TO IMPROVE TEACHING AND LEARNING

standard. A rubric, or some other criteria, can be used to get a selection of performance levels. On the wall, place vertically, the number 4, under it the number 3, followed by the number 2, and ending with the number 1 (the same as the scoring criteria you are using). Horizontally, across the top, place numbers or descriptions that spell out grade levels. Line up the student work by grade level and achievement level (see photo in Appendix R). After the student work has been posted, have teachers review the work and write on chart paper, answering questions, such as:

Question 1. What did the student know and understand at this level? What did the student not know or not understand?

Question 2. What questions would you ask this student to learn more about what she/he understands and knows?

Question 3. What strategies would you use to help this student understand the concepts and move to at least the next level?

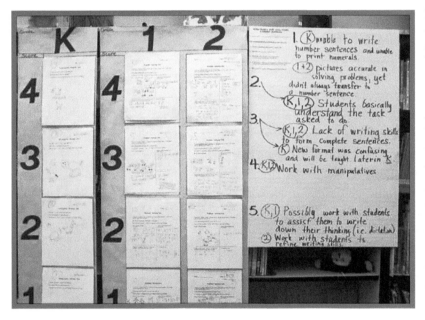

Have staff members look at the student work (also called exemplars) at a "4 level" to understand what the standards require across the grade levels. Make sure they look at all the grade levels, not just their grade level. Ask participants to reflect on which concepts need to be taught in more depth and determine at which grade level. The more practice in structured settings that teachers have together examining student work, the more likely it will be that they will spend time informally looking at student work in pairs or in teams. This activity will lead to improved teaching at all levels and in all subject areas.

> *Teachers upon occasion state that some students do not have the ability to achieve, and that the teachers have to work extremely hard to move those students' learning forward.*

## Ability to Achievement

The purpose of this activity is to engage teachers in discussions with colleagues about how to improve learning for all students in the classroom. (See Appendix S.)

Teachers, on occasion, state that some students do not have the ability to achieve, and that the teachers have to work extremely hard to move those students' learning forward. This activity helps teachers come to grips with their perceptions of students' abilities, then collaboratively consider additional ways to improve students' achievement. A summary of steps follow.

DEFINITIONS ~ **Ability:** *Perceived aptitude*

**Achievement:** *Evidence of attainment of knowledge*

*Mathematics*
*Ability +*

| List the names of the students you feel **have the ability to achieve and do *not* achieve.** | List the names of the students you feel **have the ability to achieve and *do* achieve.** |
|---|---|
| *Achievement -* | *Achievement +* |
| List the names of the students you feel **do not have the ability to achieve and do *not* achieve.** | List the names of the students you feel **do not have the ability to achieve, but *do* achieve.** |

*Ability –*

Step 1. **Have teachers complete matrix.** Before the meeting day, by grade levels or subject areas, have teachers choose a subject area, write the names of their students on self-stick dots, and then place each dot in one of the ability achievement quadrants, with respect to teachers' opinions of each student's ability to do the work and to achieve. Teachers might line up the dots for their class, color code the dots by gender or proficiency levels on an achievement measure, or any other meaningful way.

Step 2. **List common characteristics.** During the meeting, have teachers discuss and list the common characteristics of the students who fall into each of these quadrants. If possible, add past proficiency levels next to the names of students.

Step 3. **Brainstorm what processes need to be put into place in order to help all students achieve.** A question such as *What can we do in every quadrant to move these students forward?* might start the discussion. If possible, have the longitudinal individual student growth profile available for each child during this discussion.

Step 4. **Determine what needs to be done schoolwide to move all students to the highest quadrant.** For example: one school determined that they needed to clarify their RtI process and improve their diagnostic assessments so they cold have the structures in place to close basic skills gaps for all students. If done well, this activity will help teachers see what processes need to change in order to get different results. It will also, hopefully, change some belief systems about student abilities. Perceived abilities might be clouding the teachers' interactions with students and, therefore, students' achievement levels.

156

CHAPTER 11
STRATEGIES FOR TEACHERS: USING DATA TO IMPLEMENT THE VISION THROUGH THE
CONTINUOUS SCHOOL IMPROVEMENT PLAN TO IMPROVE TEACHING AND LEARNING

## HOW MUCH TIME DOES IT TAKE?

*The collaborative work of teachers is ongoing.
Teachers should be working together in their
teams for no less than an hour a week.*

### REFLECTION QUESTIONS

1. What does it take to get teachers to use data to improve teaching and learning?

2. Why is data use important to continuous school improvement?

3. Why are collaborative structures important to data use?

4. Why is vision important to data use?

5. What types of collaborative learning structures to use data exist in your school? How might you improve them?

### APPLICATION OPPORTUNITIES

1. How do your teachers use data now? How can you improve the use of data to improve teaching and learning? Use the *Measuring a Program or Process* table, Appendix D, to spell out the purposes for using data and how implementation will be monitored.

2. How do your teachers collaborate now and how might you improve the collaboration? (Consider and commit to trying at least one of the activities described in Appendices Q, R, S.)

3. Create a flowchart of collaborating for data use. (Use *Flowcharting a School Process*, Appendix E.)

# IS WHAT WE ARE DOING MAKING A DIFFERENCE: EVALUATING OUR EFFORTS

**12**

**CHAPTER**

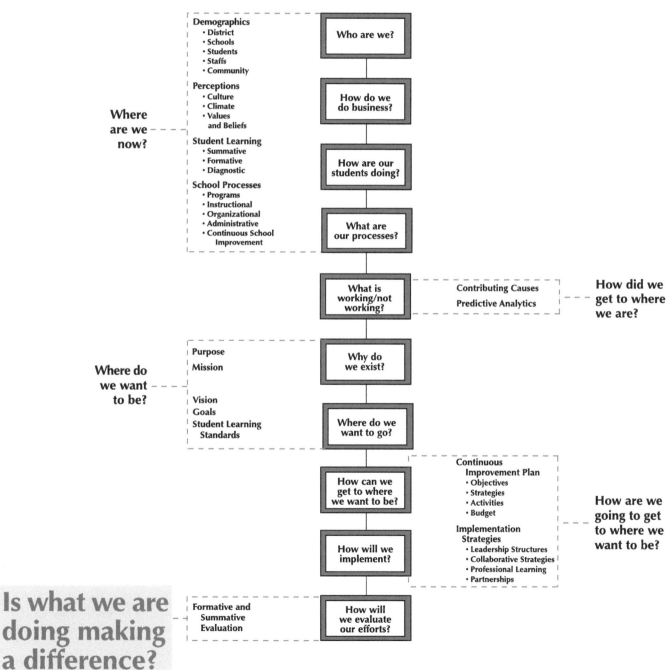

**Where are we now?**

**Demographics**
- District
- Schools
- Students
- Staffs
- Community

**Perceptions**
- Culture
- Climate
- Values and Beliefs

**Student Learning**
- Summative
- Formative
- Diagnostic

**School Processes**
- Programs
- Instructional
- Organizational
- Administrative
- Continuous School Improvement

Who are we?

How do we do business?

How are our students doing?

What are our processes?

What is working/not working?

**How did we get to where we are?**

Contributing Causes

Predictive Analytics

**Where do we want to be?**

Purpose

Mission

Vision

Goals

Student Learning Standards

Why do we exist?

Where do we want to go?

How can we get to where we want to be?

How will we implement?

**How are we going to get to where we want to be?**

**Continuous Improvement Plan**
- Objectives
- Strategies
- Activities
- Budget

**Implementation Strategies**
- Leadership Structures
- Collaborative Strategies
- Professional Learning
- Partnerships

**Is what we are doing making a difference?**

Formative and Summative Evaluation

How will we evaluate our efforts?

157

*If you are not monitoring and measuring program*
*implementation, the program probably doesn't exist.*
*You cannot evaluate a program you cannot describe.*

*Education for the Future*

*"Evaluation means asking good, critical questions about programs to improve programs and help them be accountable for the wise use of resources."*

At the bottom of the continuous school improvement framework is the all-important question: *Is what we are doing making a difference?* which requires us to evaluate the parts of continuous school improvement as well as the whole.

"Evaluation means asking good, critical questions about programs to improve programs and help them be accountable for the wise use of resources." (University of Wisconsin-Extension) Evaluation also means assessing the impact of the vision.

### WHY KNOWING IF WHAT WE ARE DOING IS MAKING A DIFFERENCE IS IMPORTANT TO CONTINUOUS SCHOOL IMPROVEMENT

Evaluation is a fundamental component of continuous school improvement. Continuous school improvement uses evaluation to review where the school is on multiple sources of data, where it wants to go as it creates its vision, and where it is going as it implements its plans. Continuous school improvement uses evaluation to know how the school got to where it is now, as well as which programs and processes are working and not working, and how to ensure the attainment of the school goals using the most effective processes and programs. Evaluation in continuous school improvement provides real-time feedback for development and implementation.

*Continuous school improvement uses evaluation to know how the school got to where it is now, as well as which programs and processes are working and not working, and how to ensure the attainment of the school goals using the most effective processes and programs.*

### HOW TO KNOW IF WHAT WE ARE DOING IS MAKING A DIFFERENCE?

To continuously improve a school, we need to evaluate the parts and the whole; make sure the parts equal what we are trying to do overall; and ensure that what we are doing overall is what we intend to be doing. It sounds like a daunting task; however, when schools create a data profile such as the one shown in Appendix F, they make a great start with their comprehensive evaluation. They simply need to use the analyses in the data profile to go deeper into the data and to answer specific questions.

*To continuously improve a school, we need to evaluate the parts and the whole; make sure the parts equal what we are trying to do overall; and ensure that what we are doing overall is what we intend to be doing.*

In this chapter, we start the process of evaluation by thinking about how we would evaluate the following:

- ◆ the impact of programs and processes;
- ◆ the effectiveness of the continuous school improvement plan; and
- ◆ the attainment of school goals.

## EVALUATING PROGRAMS AND PROCESSES

You and your staff might be thinking that conducting a full-blown program evaluation is too difficult to do in-house. A very easy and powerful start to evaluating all programs is to make a list of the programs and processes that are being implemented, or intended to be implemented, in your school (described in Chapter 6, and shown in the School Process Data Inventory, Appendix B4). Then use the *Measuring Programs and Processes* Table (Appendix D). This same process can be used very powerfully to evaluate the school mission and vision. In Chapter 9, you saw Somewhere School's vision in creation. Figure 12.1 shows how Somewhere School used the *Measuring Programs and Processes* Table to set up the evaluation of their vision. This table is a very powerful way to lay out the evaluation of the vision. The creation of the table before implementation helps ensure a more robust implementation.

*A very easy and powerful start to evaluating all programs is to make a list of the programs and processes that are being implemented, or intended to be implemented, in your school.*

Figure 12.1
SOMEWHERE ELEMENTARY SCHOOL VISION

| PURPOSE | | PARTICIPANTS | | IMPLEMENTATION | RESULTS |
|---|---|---|---|---|---|
| *What is the purpose of our school?* | *What are the outcomes of the purpose?* | *Who is the program/process intended to serve?* | | *What will it look like when the purpose is fully implemented?* | *What are the results?* |
| The purpose of Somewhere School is— **To educate *all* students so that they may achieve their dreams and better the world.** **The mission of Somewhere Elementary School is to provide all students with the knowledge and tools they will need to be successful citizens and workers in the 21ˢᵗ Century.** | When the purpose of Somewhere School is met, all students will— • be on track to graduate from high school, college and career ready for citizenship and success in the 21st Century; • become *life-long learners;* • learn with resources that support work typical of the 21st Century workplace (e.g., technology). Teachers will— • become a part of a collaborative professional community that values and strives for continuous school improvement. • help *all* parents support their children's success. • bring the community into the life of the school and the school into the life of the community. • provide a physically, emotionally, and intellectually safe environment that encourages students to become creators and innovators who improve the world. | *All* students will be served by all teachers who are committed to implementing the vision. *Who is being served? Who is not being served?* Currently, not all students are being served in the fashion Somewhere Elementary School wants them to be served. We still have students not proficient in all subjects, students who do not feel challenged with the work provided, and students who do not feel respected by other students. | | Every student would be on track for high school graduation and would be prepared for citizenship, college and career in the 21st Century workplace. Students would be inquisitive and accustomed to using critical thinking skills and technology in their daily work. Classroom observations would reveal students engaged in deep and authentic tasks (constructivism) with teachers serving as facilitators who are continually collecting formative assessment data that enable them to provide the just-in-time instructional adjustments and re-teaching (direct instruction) required to ensure success and prevent school failure. Students are found in after-school programs that build on what they learned in class, offer assistance with homework, and provide extended resources (e.g., computers). Student attendance is very high, tardies very low, and drop-outs nonexistent. Students feel respected. In faculty meetings and in the school's Communities of Professional Practice sessions, teachers and leaders, like their students, are engaged in deep work, analyzing standards, developing an aligned curriculum/instruction/assessment system that is focused, coherent, and explainable to parents and community. Teachers and leaders work collaboratively to build a school environment that is inviting and dynamic - a fun place to work and learn for students and staff. Parents and community members participate monthly in classroom sessions where teachers explain what their students will be learning in the next month and why. In the teachers' workroom, teachers talk excitedly about successes in their classrooms that morning, ask others for advice, share information and strategies, and offer help to each other. Student assessment results reflect an effective instructional program implemented with fidelity. No teacher or leader wants to leave this school. | Our current results are our baseline. As our school data profile shows, we have many areas to work on. Student proficiency in all subject areas. Instructional coherence. Behavior. Collaboration. Integrating technology meaningfully in classwork. |

*How is implementation being measured? (Should it be measured differently?)*

The implementation of the Somewhere School vision and mission will be measured through a vision monitoring tool created by staff.

*To what degree is the program being implemented?*

We are just starting, however, the vision, plan, leadership structures, data teams, and partnerships are in place. We just need to keep implementing as intended.

**NEXT STEPS:** Our next steps are spelled out nicely in our continuous school improvement plan, vision, and data profile.

## EVALUATING THE CONTINUOUS SCHOOL IMPROVEMENT PLAN

High quality continuous school improvement plans tell staff how to implement the school vision. Most school improvement plans have a measurement column that indicates whether or not an activity has been completed. Many staff think the measurement column represents an evaluation of the effectiveness of the plan. It does not. The measurement column is very important for determining if the parts of the plan are being implemented and are on schedule. It does not, however, tell staff if what they are planning or doing is effective.

*High quality continuous school improvement plans tell staff how to implement the school vision.*

---

**EXAMPLE: Continuous School Improvement (CSI) Plan**

**Goal 1:** All students will exhibit their best effort for themselves, their families, and the community, including a demonstration of respect for their peers and for property.
**Goal 2:** Create an environment where every student, family, staff member, and community member will be excited to be at Marylin Avenue School; and be flexible in order to accommodate the educational needs of all.
**Goal 3:** All students will be *Proficient* or *Advanced* in Language Arts and Math by the end of fifth grade.

> **Objective 1:** The percentage of students achieving proficiency in ELA, as measured by CSTs, will increase from 51% to 61% by Spring of 2010, measured through student learning results.
> **Objective 2:** The percentage of students achieving proficiency in Math, as measured by CSTs, will increase from 63% to 70% by Spring of 2010, measured through student learning results.
> **Objective 3:** The precentage of English learner students achieving proficiency in ELA, as measured by CSTs, will increase from 36% to 46% by Spring of 2010, measured through student learning results.

**Planned Improvements in Student Performance**

| Strategies and Activities | Person(s) Responsible | Measurement | Expenditures | Estimated Cost |
|---|---|---|---|---|
| **Alignment of instruction with content standards:**<br>All grade levels have identified essential standards for all curricular areas. Each essential standard has been unwrapped (in order to feature needed prerequisite skills and concepts), vertically aligned, mapped, and paced for all curricular areas. | Whole Staff / Ongoing | Essential standards are documented for all curricular areas for all grade levels. Grade-level teams agree on the standards. Cross-grade-level teams agree on the standards. Documentation of all essential standards show them to be unwrapped, mapped, vertically aligned, and paced. | | |
| **I. Improvement of instructional strategies and materials:**<br>A. All teachers will use the unwrapped essential standards to target instruction.<br>  1. Learning objectives will be based on assessment data.<br>  2. Learning objectives will be clearly stated.<br>  3. Students will understand the importance of each learning objective.<br>  4. Teachers will frequently check for understanding and adjust instruction as needed.<br>B. Each grade level uses balanced assessments that are common, formative, and administered frequently. Assessment will be varied—performance, multi-choice, short answers.<br>  1. Grade levels assess each essential standard and conduct data team meetings for most of them.<br>  2. Grade levels and our schoolwide-data team look at the data from our assessments to determine the effectiveness of instructional strategies and programs.<br>  3. Grade levels administer CFAs every 2-3 weeks. | Teachers / Ongoing<br><br><br><br>Grade-Level Teams Ongoing | Classroom observations that describe what instruction and the classroom would look like if RtI implemented will also determine if teachers are:<br>using the unwrapped essential standards to target instruction<br>creating clear learning objectives to teach the unwrapped essential standards and to make sure students understand their importance<br>checking for understanding and adjusting instruction as needed<br>using grade level assessments of each essential standard<br>administering CFAs every 2-3 weeks<br>attending data team meetings about the assessment of each essential standard<br>using CAFÉ/Literacy Studio system with fidelity focusing on nonfiction reading and writing | Grade Level Articulation—two articulation days per grade level<br><br>Leadership Team Stipends | $7,000<br><br><br><br>$9,000 |

---

To evaluate the implementation of the plan, one needs to think about how staff will know that the planned strategies were implemented. To evaluate the effectiveness of the plan, one needs to consider how staff will know if the plan was effective and if the goals were achieved.

To evaluate a continuous school improvement plan, design a three column template. In the first column, place activities and strategies from the school improvement plan. In the second column, place the measurements for these activities and strategies, also from the plan, which answer the question *How will we know if this got done?* Then create a third column that asks a deeper question than the measurement column addresses: *How will we know if what we are doing is effective?* Have staff members brainstorm and come to consensus on how they will know if what they are doing is effective.

Figure 12.2 shows the first iteration of the evaluation design of the Somewhere Elementary School plan for the first part of the school's first goal. To complete the effectiveness evaluation, staff members will need to analyze the data spelled out in the effectiveness column.

*To evaluate the implementation of the plan, one needs to think about how staff will know that the planned strategies were implemented.*

## Figure 12.2

### EXAMPLE: EVALUATION OF THE SOMEWHERE ELEMENTARY SCHOOL CONTINUOUS SCHOOL IMPROVEMENT PLAN

**Goal 1:** Ensure that all students graduate from high school, college and career ready for citizenship and success in the 21st Century workplace.

- Provide a learning environment that develops *life-long learners*.
- Build a collaborative professional community that values and strives for continuous organizational improvement.
- Provide resources that support work typical of the 21st Century workplace (e.g., technology).
- Help *all* parents help their students to succeed.
- Develop an insatiable hunger for self-improvement among staff, students, and community.

**Goal 2:** Bring the community into the life of the school and the school into the life of the community

**Goal 3:** Provide a physically, emotionally, and intellectually safe environment that encourages students to become creators and innovators that improve the world.

**Goal 1—***Ensure that all students graduate from high school, college and career ready for citizenship and success in the 21st Century workplace.*

| Description of Specific Actions to Improve Educational Practice | Measurement of Strategies ~ Is It Done? | Evaluation ~ How Effective? |
|---|---|---|
| **Align instruction and materials with Common Core State Standards (CCSS):**<br><br>All grade levels have studied the essential standards they will teach for each curricular area. Each essential standard has been scaffolded (to feature needed skills, concepts, and materials), vertically aligned, mapped, and paced for all curricular areas. | Essential standards are documented for all curricular areas for all grade levels. Grade-level teams agree on the standards. Cross-grade-level teams agree on the standards. Documentation of all essential standards show them to be scaffolded, mapped, vertically aligned, and paced. | Have the *most essential* standards been identified? Is there horizontal as well as vertical alignment? Is there vertical and horizontal alignment with the implementation of the standards? Are students proficient? Do student scores continue to increase over time? |
| ***Improve instructional strategies and student learning:***<br>1. All teachers will use the CCSS to target instruction.<br>  A. Learning objectives will be clearly stated.<br>  B. Students will understand the importance of the learning objective.<br>  C. Teachers will frequently check for understanding and adjust instruction as needed.<br>  D. Instruction is student-centered, technology infused, with students engaged in authentic, meaningful, higher level thinking.<br>  E. Attainment of learning objectives will be based on student performance data.<br>  F. Partnerships with the community will be incorporated in the learning, as spelled out in the Partnership Plan, and Goal #2. | Classroom observations that describe what instruction and the classroom would look like when the CCSS are implemented will also determine if, and how, teachers are:<br>• using the essential standards to target instruction;<br>• creating clear learning objectives to teach the essential standards and to make sure students understand their importance;<br>• checking for understanding and adjusting instruction as needed. | Classroom observations will ensure standards work and the degree of implementation. Alignment can be determined through classroom observations and assessment results. How do students feel about the learning? Do they understand the learning objectives? Do Common Formative Assessments parallel the curriculum and state assessments to predict student performance and inform instruction? What do grade-level teams do when they meet? How effective are the grade-level teams? What makes grade level teams most effective? |

Figure 12.2 (*Continued*)

EXAMPLE: EVALUATION OF THE SOMEWHERE ELEMENTARY SCHOOL CONTINUOUS SCHOOL IMPROVEMENT PLAN

**Goal 1—*Ensure that all students graduate from high school, college and career ready for citizenship and success in the 21st Century workplace.***

| Description of Specific Actions to Improve Educational Practice | Measurement of Strategies ~ Is It Done? | Evaluation ~ How Effective? |
|---|---|---|
| 2. Each grade level uses assessments that are embedded in every lesson, as well as common, formative assessments that are administered frequently.<br><br>A. Grade levels assess each essential standard, every 2-3 weeks, and conduct data team meetings to discuss performance for most of them.<br><br>B. Grade level teams and the Data Leadership Team look at the data from our assessments to determine alignment, within and across grade levels, and the effectiveness of instructional strategies and programs.<br><br>C. Grade level teams and the Data Leadership Team look at the data from our assessments to determine which students are not meeting proficiency, those that are, and what to do about it.<br><br>D. Agreements are made on the skill levels and benchmarks for at-risk students in all subject areas for all grades.<br><br>E. Results from assessments will be shared with students and parents, and merged with student self-assessments.<br><br>F. Feedback to students will be timely and specific.<br><br>G. Proficiency and growth will be acknowledged and celebrated on a regular basis.<br><br>H. Student goals will be based on assessments, and will be shared with students and parents at goal-setting conferences. | Classroom observations that describe what instruction and the classroom would look like when the CCSS and the school vision are implemented will also determine if, and how, teachers are:<br>• using grade level assessments of each standard;<br>• administering common formative assessments every 2-3 weeks; and<br>• attending data team meetings about the assessment of each essential standard.<br><br>Documentations exist that grade-level teams and then schoolwide-data-team meetings review the results of the assessments, and check for alignment.<br><br>Evidence exists that the meeting minutes are shared with all teachers, and that needed adjustments are made in classrooms. | Do the assessments reveal what students know and are able to do?<br><br>Is there assessment alignment across grade levels? Is a continuum of learning being created?<br><br>How effective is student feedback? |
| *Professional development and collaboration:*<br>Professional development and collaboration is frequent and ongoing.<br><br>A. Grade levels meet every Wednesday from 1:45 to 3:00. Collaboration is focused on results of formative assessments and on effective instructional strategies.<br><br>B. Cross grade level teams meet alternate Wednesdays from 3:05 to 4:15.<br><br>C. Leadership Team meets Thursdays from 3:05 to 4:30.<br><br>D. Data Leadership Team will meet as needed to prepare assessment results for grade level teams.<br><br>E. Whole staff meets once a month for ongoing professional development aligned to our vision and plan.<br><br>F. Schoolwide, we will use peer coaching to support deep implementation of vision strategies and the CCSS. | Leadership structure and process flowcharts detail how collaboration will work for all teachers. | What do the grade level teams do during their times together? Is the time used effectively? What do they need to make their times more effective? How do staff members feel about these meetings?<br><br>Is whole staff professional learning effective? Is it tied to the vision and plan? Does the information get implemented? Does the professional development lead to more effective teaching?<br><br>How effective is peer coaching? Are CCSS strategies included in the peer coaching? To what degree are teachers implementing CCSS deeply? How effective is the deep implementation? Is CCSS implementation leading to student achievement increases? |

## EVALUATING THE CONTINUOUS SCHOOL IMPROVEMENT PLAN

*School improvement plans typically document how goals and objectives will be carried out through actions, strategies, person(s) responsible, and due dates, with a measurement column for strategies and activities.*

School improvement plans typically document how goals and objectives will be carried out through actions, strategies, person(s) responsible, and due dates, with a measurement column for strategies and activities. Again, it would be nice if the measurement column added up to a comprehensive evaluation of the goals and objectives; however, it does not. While these measurements are appropriate and required to know that activities are accomplished, it is also important to stand back and think about the big picture of what we are trying to do with the entire plan.

This evaluation requires you to go back to the school goals, the outcomes of the vision, and objectives, which are redrafted goals to close the gaps between where the school is right now and where it wants to be. Determine how you will know the goals and objectives will be met, and how these outcomes will be measured.

### Evaluating Your School Goals and Objectives

To know if your goals and objectives are being met—

- ◆ Lay out the school goals and objectives.
- ◆ Logically think of how you will know the objectives will be met, and how they can be measured.
- ◆ When the data become available, analyze and determine if your objectives have been met.
- ◆ Adjust your school improvement plan to ensure that all goals and objectives are met.

## AN EXAMPLE EVALUATION OF SCHOOL GOALS

Following is Somewhere Elementary School's evaluation plan for its school goals (Figure 12.3). Somewhere School now needs to gather its data to see if it achieved its goals and objectives.

**Figure 12.3**
EXAMPLE: SOMEWHERE ELEMENTARY SCHOOL EVALUATION PLAN FOR SCHOOL GOALS

**THE MISSION OF SOMEWHERE ELEMENTARY SCHOOL**
*To provide ALL students with the knowledge and tools they will need*
*to be successful citizens and workers in the 21st Century.*

SCHOOL GOALS

- Ensure that all students graduate from high school, college and career ready for citizenship and success in the 21st Century workplace.
  * Provide a learning environment that develops *life-long learners.*
  * Build a collaborative professional community that values and strives for continuous organizational improvement.
  * Provide resources that support work typical of the 21st Century workplace (e.g., technology).
  * Help *all* parents help their students to succeed.
  * Develop an insatiable hunger for self-improvement among staff, students, and community.
- Bring the community into the life of the school and the school into the life of the community.
- Provide a physically, emotionally, and intellectually safe environment that encourages students to become creators and innovators that improve the world.

Somewhere Elementary School staff believe that the three school goals are very closely related, and that the achievement of the first two goals is critical for the staff and students to be successful with the third goal.

| SCHOOL GOAL | WHEN THIS GOAL IS IMPLEMENTED— | MEASURED BY— |
|---|---|---|
| *Students will exhibit their best efforts for themselves, their families, and the community, including a demonstration of respect for their peers and for property.* | *All* students will be— <br>• on track to graduate from high school; <br>• proficient at each grade level in reading, writing, math, science, social studies, and technical subjects; <br>• able to demonstrate study and organizational skills; <br>• able to self-assess; <br>• knowledgeable of careers; <br>• able to apply creativity, collaboration, critical thinking, and communication skills; <br>• challenged, and therefore engaged, in school activities, so they will want to attend school and behave according to school expectations. | • Graduation rates <br>• State assessments, disaggregated by all student groups <br>• Teacher observations and assessments <br>• Teachers assessments, student self-assessments, student questionnaires <br>• Behavior and attendance indicators |
| | *All* teachers will: <br>• provide instruction aligned to the CCSS, and create a continuum of learning that makes sense to students; <br>• assess student progress on an ongoing basis, and adjust instruction to allow all students to learn the material; <br>• collaborate with each other to study data and improve instruction; <br>• work with parents to help them help their child learn. | • Teachers observations, student questionnaires, student formative assessments <br>• Student formative assessments, grade level team meeting minutes <br>• Grade level team discussions, staff questionnaire <br>• Parent questionnaire, staff questionnaire |
| *Bring the community into the life of the school and the school into the life of the community.* | Students will be learning with community partners: <br>• at business and community locations; <br>• at museums, city parks; <br>• at home; and <br>• using technology. | • Parent questionnaire, staff questionnaire, student questionnaire, partner questionnaire. |
| *Provide a physically, emotionally, and intellectually safe environment that encourages students to become creators and innovators that improve the world.* | Students will have the opportunities to: <br>• create and innovate; <br>• fail, and learn from their failures; <br>• be challenged by the work that is asked of them. | • Parent, staff, student, partner questionnaires. |

### HOW MUCH TIME DOES IT TAKE?

*Setting up the evaluation of the plan, vision, or program/process using the Measuring Programs and Processes Table will take thirty minutes. Following through with the data analysis will take a couple of hours, depending upon the availability of the data.*

## REFLECTION QUESTIONS

1. What is evaluation in the context of continuous school improvement?

2. Why is evaluation important to continuous school improvement?

3. How do you evaluate your programs, processes, and vision, and how should you?

4. How do you evaluate your continuous school improvement plan, goals and objectives, and how should you?

5. How can predictive analytics help determine the impact of the program (see Chapter 8).

## APPLICATION OPPORTUNITIES

1. Use the Measuring a Program or Process table, Appendix D, to evaluate your vision, programs and processes.

2. Review your continuous school improvement plan. Is effectiveness being measured? Are the goals and objectives being measured?

3. Create an evaluation of your school improvement plan and goals.

4. Analyze your data to determine if goals and objectives have been met.

# CONTINUOUS SCHOOL IMPROVEMENT TIMELINE:
## MAKING TIME TO DO THE WORK

**13**

CHAPTER

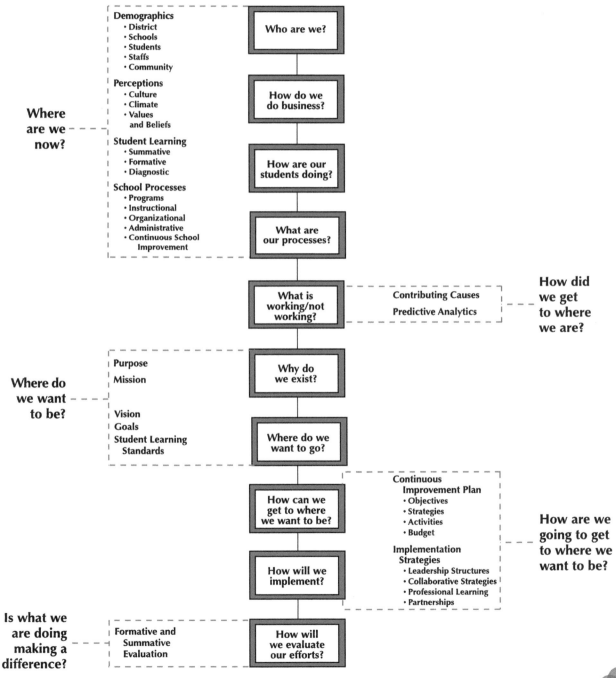

**Where are we now?**

**Demographics**
- District
- Schools
- Students
- Staffs
- Community

**Perceptions**
- Culture
- Climate
- Values and Beliefs

**Student Learning**
- Summative
- Formative
- Diagnostic

**School Processes**
- Programs
- Instructional
- Organizational
- Administrative
- Continuous School Improvement

Who are we?

How do we do business?

How are our students doing?

What are our processes?

What is working/not working?

**How did we get to where we are?**
- Contributing Causes
- Predictive Analytics

**Where do we want to be?**

Purpose
Mission

Vision
Goals
Student Learning Standards

Why do we exist?

Where do we want to go?

How can we get to where we want to be?

How will we implement?

**How are we going to get to where we want to be?**

**Continuous Improvement Plan**
- Objectives
- Strategies
- Activities
- Budget

**Implementation Strategies**
- Leadership Structures
- Collaborative Strategies
- Professional Learning
- Partnerships

**Is what we are doing making a difference?**

Formative and Summative Evaluation

How will we evaluate our efforts?

*In the beginning you think. In the end you act.*
*In-between you negotiate the possibilities.*
*Some people move from complexity to simplicity and on into*
*catastrophe. Others move from simplicity to complexity and onward*
*into full-scale confusion. Simplification makes action possible*
*in the face of overwhelming complexity. It also increases the odds*
*of being wrong. The trick is to let a sense of simplicity inform our*
*thinking, a sense of complexity inform our actions,*
*and a sense of humility inform our judgments.*

Michael Quinn Patten
Author and Evaluation Thought Leader

*To systemically improve, a school must do all the hard work of gathering and analyzing data, getting all staff on board to create a shared vision, develop empowering structures to implement the vision and effectively use data, and to continually monitor and improve.*

To systemically improve, a school must do all the hard work of gathering and analyzing data, getting all staff on board to create a shared vision, develop empowering structures to implement the vision and effectively use data, and to continually monitor and improve—all those components spelled out in the continuous school improvement framework.

*Cutting out parts of the continuous school improvement framework is really not an option if you want systemic results*

Cutting out parts of the continuous school improvement framework is really not an option if you want systemic results. However, the process can be simplified by understanding who needs to be involved with components of the process, and when. This chapter is devoted to pulling together all the pieces of continuous school improvement in a timeline that spells out what needs to be done, when, and by whom, as well as the tools that are available for you to use to do the work. (See Appendix T for the *Timeline for Continuous School Improvement Work.*)

## THE TIMELINE

Developing a timeline for continuous school improvement implementation isn't just about the time, it's about determining how to:

◆ Convey knowledge and information so staff members know why they are doing the work.

◆ Utilize a formal framework to align efforts.

◆ Effectively use data, schoolwide, and in classrooms.

◆ Get organizational structures in place to support the work.

◆ Allocate time to accomplish the work.

Schools need to understand where they are right now to know how they are getting the results they are getting, so processes can be improved to get even better results. All staff members need to review schoolwide data. However, not all staff members need to be involved in gathering and organizing the data. Perhaps a data team can be assigned to organize the data to be reviewed by all staff. If a shared vision does not exist, staff must gather together and create one.

The following is a discussion about how the work of continuous school improvement and comprehensive data analysis can be completed the first time. Start wherever you are, with what you have, and move forward.

## Before the School Year Begins

We recommend starting the process by organizing the school's data into graphs and a data profile before the school year begins so staff members can review the data to set the context for the school year, and so they can create plans for continuous school improvement during the year.

Long before the first staff meeting, where the data will be reviewed and analyzed, assign a Data Leadership Team (see Chapter 11) to pull together a data profile that summarizes the schoolwide data currently available. The Data Leadership Team needs to use rules for getting the data consistent with the needs of the data systems they will be using. Data most available are demographic and student learning data. Five years of these data are preferred, but not necessary to begin. Summer usually is a good time to do this work, perhaps in Institute format, so the Data Leadership Team can learn the overall framework and work together to organize the rest of the year. In addition to the schoolwide data profile, have the data teams "re-roster" individual student learning data over time by current teachers' classrooms. In other words, create a report of previous scores for this year's class lists. (Use the *Data Inventories*, Appendix B, and *Case Study*, Appendix F, to guide the data collection and graphing work.) Figure 13.1 summarizes the when, who, what, tools, data sources, and artifacts for *Before School Begins*.

*Schools need to understand where they are right now to know how they are getting the results they are getting, so processes can be improved to get even better results.*

*Long before the first staff meeting, where the data will be reviewed and analyzed, assign a Data Leadership Team to pull together a data profile that summarizes the schoolwide data currently available.*

## Figure 13.1
### CONTINUOUS SCHOOL IMPROVEMENT AND DATA ANALYSIS TIMELINE
### BEFORE SCHOOL BEGINS

| WHEN | WHO | WHAT | TOOLS | DATA SOURCES | ARTIFACTS |
|---|---|---|---|---|---|
| **Before School Begins.** | *Data Leadership Team. (AKA Data Team.)* | *Create Data Leadership Team:* At minimum, data leadership team will be responsible for making sure appropriate data reports are available for teachers in a timely fashion. Team members will ensure that teachers in grade-level/subject-matter teams understand how to analyze data and can target instruction based on the data. | *Data Leadership Team.* | School assessment databases. | Identification of members, clarification of roles and responsibilities. |
| | | *Provide data team training:* Data analysis and continuous school improvement (CSI) overview.<br>*Case study:* Practice analyzing schoolwide data and see what it looks like when a school is doing the work and using it for continuous school improvement planning. Model how to do the work with staff.<br>*Analyze data:* Pull together longitudinal demographic and student learning data for your school. Should be able to get these from your State Longitudinal Data System (SLDS). Add, and plan to add, additional data.<br>*Analyze school data and detail observations about next steps:* Analyze the school's demographic and student learning data, along with any process and questionnaire data the school might have.<br>*Inventory* the school's data, assessments, and programs.<br>*Re-roster individual student learning data* overtime by current teachers' classrooms, or plan to have grade-level/subject-area teams do this before school starts.<br>*Create a plan* to review data and assess on the *Continuous Improvement Continuums* with staff.<br>*Create a plan* to complete this work during the school year. | Overview of continuous school improvement and data analysis in book.<br>*Case Study.*<br>*Analyzing Data for Continuous School Improvement Planning.*<br>Introduction to the data tools and how to use them.<br>Inventories.<br>*Timeline for Continuous School Improvement Work.* | Student information system.<br>State Longitudinal Data System.<br>School databases. | The beginning of a data profile for the school.<br>A plan to analyze schoolwide data with staff.<br>Inventories of the school's data, assessments, and programs.<br>A plan to help staff analyze student learning data during the school year.<br>A plan to schedule continuous school improvement work during the year. |

### As School Begins

The Data Leadership Team can organize and then facilitate a whole-staff meeting to provide an overview of the *Continuous School Improvement Framework* and comprehensive data analysis, and to have staff analyze the schoolwide data in the data profile. Figure 13.2 summarizes the when, who, what, tools, data sources, and artifacts for *As School Begins.* Use *Data Analysis for Continuous School Improvement,* Third Edition, Chapter 2, to prepare the overview and *Analyzing Data for Continuous School Improvement,* Appendix H, to complete a comprehensive analysis of strengths, challenges, and implications for the school improvement plan. If there is a chance staff members will be jumping to solutions as they are analyzing the data instead of just recording strengths and challenges, or if it is determined that staff need to practice analyzing an objective set of data, use the case study to practice on a data set that is not theirs. (*Case Study,* Appendices F and G.)

After reviewing the data, use the *Problem-Solving Cycle* (Appendix I) to understand the contributing causes of undesirable results. You might wish to divide staff into groups to tackle multiple challenges. It is important that the groups share with the whole staff.

*After reviewing the data, use the Problem-Solving Cycle to understand the contributing causes of undesirable results.*

From the comprehensive data analysis and problem-solve cycle, determine—

◆ new strategies to get different results and to meet the needs of *all* students.

◆ implications for the continuous school improvement plan and professional learning for the year.

◆ what new instructional and assessment strategies staff must learn.

◆ time to learn new concepts.

## Figure 13.2
### CONTINUOUS SCHOOL IMPROVEMENT AND DATA ANALYSIS TIMELINE AS SCHOOL BEGINS

| WHEN | WHO | WHAT | TOOLS | DATA SOURCES | ARTIFACTS |
|---|---|---|---|---|---|
| As School Begins. | *Entire staff.* | *Data team facilitates,* with staff, the analysis of the school's data.<br>• Provide overview of continuous school improvement and comprehensive data analysis:<br> * Five essential questions.<br> * Four types of data.<br>• Analyze schoolwide results, over time (3 to 5 years):<br> * What are our strengths, challenges, implications for the continuous school improvement plan, and what other data should we be gathering and analyzing?<br> * How is our student population changing?<br> * What/where did we do well?<br> * What/where did we not do well?<br> * Use contributing cause, prediction, and optimization analyses, to understand how school is getting undesirable results, and to consider how to get different results.<br>• Determine—<br> * new strategies to get different results and to meet the needs of all students.<br> * implications for the continuous school improvement plan and professional learning for the year.<br> * what new instructional and assessment strategies staff must learn.<br> * time to learn new concepts. | *Continuous School Improvement Framework.*<br><br>*Multiple Measures* chapter.<br><br>*Analyzing Data for Continuous School Improvement Planning.*<br><br>*Problem-Solving Cycle.* | Data profile (created in the summer).<br><br>State Longitudinal Data System.<br><br>Assessment database application. | Data profile completed.<br><br>The consensus analysis of the school's data.<br><br>*Problem-Solving Cycle.*<br><br>Prediction and optimization analyses (if available). |

## Figure 13.2 *(Continued)*
### CONTINUOUS SCHOOL IMPROVEMENT AND DATA ANALYSIS TIMELINE
### AS SCHOOL BEGINS

| WHEN | WHO | WHAT | TOOLS | DATA SOURCES | ARTIFACTS |
|---|---|---|---|---|---|
| As School Begins. | *Entire staff.* | • Set up Professional Learning Communities/Data Team/Leadership Teams/Grade-Level/Subject Area Teams.<br>• Grade-level/subject-area breakouts:<br> * What concepts and skills do students need to know. Agree on essential standards to teach, when.<br> * What do we want students to know and be able to do this year, quarter, month, week? (Review core curriculum standards and update curriculum maps.)<br> * How will we know that students know these concepts and skills?<br> * Create common post-assessments.<br> * Adopt timelines for giving assessments throughout the year.<br> * Determine which instructional strategies will make a difference.<br> * Establish plan/flowchart for what teachers will do when students do not know the concepts and do not have the skills, and what teachers will do when students know the concepts and have the skills.<br> * Determine times, strategies, and roles and responsibilities for grade-level/subject-area work during the year.<br>• Discuss grade-level/subject-area breakout work with full staff for cross-grade-level congruence.<br>• Reinforce intentions of programs and interventions, how they are to be implemented, and the results expected.<br>• Create flowcharts of processes expected to be used.<br>• Assess on *Continuous Improvement Continuums.*<br>• Look across the implications for the continuous school improvement plan that come from the data analysis work and *Continuous Improvement Continuum* assessment. | *Leadership Structure.*<br>Inventory.<br>*Measuring a Program or Process.*<br>*Flowcharting School Processes.*<br>*Continuous Improvement Continuums Self-Assessment.*<br>*Analyzing Data for Continuous Improvement Planning.* | State Longitudinal Data System.<br>Assessment database application. | Professional Learning Community/Data/Leadership Team Structure, including roles and responsibilities.<br>Inventories of school programs and assessments.<br>Flowcharts that show how standards will be implemented, and what teachers will do when students do not know the concepts and do not have the skills, and what teachers will do when students know the concepts and have the skills.<br>Plan for teams to review their students' data throughout the year.<br>*Continuous Improvement Continuums* assessment.<br>Data analysis results with aggregated implications for the continuous school improvement plan. |

*Determine how teachers will work, in teams, with classroom and student level data, during the school year.*

Determine how teachers will work, in teams, with classroom and student level data, during the school year. Have them meet to review student learning results for their grade levels and subject areas, and individual students, over time, and begin working on next steps, such as:

◆ Determine what concepts and skills students need to know.

◆ Agree on essential learning standards to teach, and when.

◆ What do we want students to know and be able to do this year, quarter, month, week? (Review core curriculum standards and update curriculum maps.)

◆ How will we know that students know these concepts and skills?

◆ Create common post-assessments, including timeline for giving assessments during the year.

◆ Determine which instructional strategies will make a difference.

◆ Establish plan/flowchart for what teachers will do when students do not know the concepts and do not have the skills, and what teachers will do when students know the concepts and have the skills. (*Flowcharting School Processes*, Appendix E.)

◆ Determine times, strategies, and roles and responsibilities for grade-level/subject-area work during the year.

While in the whole staff meeting:

◆ Discuss grade-level/subject-area breakout work for cross grade-level congruence.

◆ Reinforce intentions of programs and processes, how they are to be implemented, and the results expected. (*Measuring a Program or Process*, Appendix D.)

◆ Create flowcharts of processes expected to be used. (*Flowcharting School Processes*, Appendix E.)

◆ Assess on the *Education for the Future Continuous Improvement Continuums* to understand what staff members are thinking about where the school is on continuous school improvement, and to make plans for improvement. (See Appendix A, *Continuous Improvement Continuums Self-Assessment*.)

◆ Look across the implications that come from all the data analysis work for the school improvement plan. Determine new strategies to get different results to meet the needs of all students, and determine what has to go into the continuous school improvement plan for the year. (*Analyzing Data for Continuous School Improvement*, Appendix H.)

◆ Present the finished product, with recommended revisions for the continuous school improvement plan, to the full staff for approval and implementation.

◆ Determine when and how staff can continue to list programs and processes, their intended/desired results, and what each would look like, separate and together, if they were implemented with 100% integrity and fidelity. (See *Measuring a Program or Process*, Appendix D.)

## After School Begins

### *Determine Questionnaires to Administer*

Sometime after the beginning of the school year, staff members need to agree on what questionnaires they would like to use to learn about student, staff, and parent perceptions. A small team, perhaps the Data Leadership Team, can do the research to determine what questionnaires are available to administer, or to design a questionnaire as a last resort, and how they will be administered. With staff approval, the questionnaire team can set up the details of administering the questionnaires. (*Designing Questionnaires*, Appendix C1.) Figure 13.3 summarizes the when, who, what, tools, data sources, and artifacts for questionnaire design to analysis and use.

### Figure 13.3
#### CONTINUOUS SCHOOL IMPROVEMENT AND DATA ANALYSIS TIMELINE
#### AFTER SCHOOL BEGINS

| WHEN | WHO | WHAT | TOOLS | DATA SOURCES | ARTIFACTS |
|---|---|---|---|---|---|
| **After School Begins.** *Administer no earlier than a month into the school year.* | *Data Team.* | Determine questionnaires to administer to students, staff, and parents. Research existing, adapt, or create questionnaires. <br><br> Review with staff and approve to administer. | *Designing Questionnaires.* | Research. | Questionnaires to administer. |
| | *Staff.* | Administer staff school improvement questionnaires. (Staff meeting, 20 minutes.) | Questionnaires. *Administering Questionnaires.* | Questionnaire administration, analysis, presentation tool (online). | Questionnaire. |
| | *Students: Strategic administration.* | Administer student school improvement questionnaires. (Organized class time, 20 minutes.) | Questionnaires. *Administering Questionnaires.* | | Questionnaire. |
| | *Parent-Teacher Conference. In person.* <br><br> *Data teams.* | Administer parent school improvement questionnaires. (20 minutes.) <br><br> Merge open-ended results. | Questionnaires. *Administering Questionnaires.* *Analyzing Open-Ended Responses.* | Questionnaire administration, analysis, presentation tool (online). | Questionnaire. |
| | *Entire staff.* | Review/share questionnaire results, along with the data profile and analysis, and current assessment results. <br><br> Adjust continuous school improvement plan and vision to improve school climate. | *Analyzing Data for Continuous School Improvement Planning.* *Analyzing Questionnaire Results.* | | Questionnaire analysis, with other data. <br><br> Adjustments to the school improvement plan. |

## Administering Questionnaires

We recommend administering the staff questionnaire first so staff members can see what the questionnaires are like to take and so they can determine how to administer the questionnaires to students quickly and easily. If the staff questionnaire is administered in a staff meeting, you can get one hundred percent responses in less than thirty minutes. Administer the student questionnaires during organized school time for as close to a one hundred percent response rate as you can get. It is also recommended that the parent questionnaire be administered when most of the parents are in the school. In elementary schools and most middle schools, it is Parent-Teacher Conference time. That way, students can meet the parents at the door, take them to the questionnaire completion area, and then on to their conference when they have completed the questionnaire. The response rate will be high. (*Administering Questionnaires,* Appendix C2.)

*We recommend administering the staff questionnaire first so staff members can see what the questionnaires are like to take and so they can determine how to administer the questionnaires to students quickly and easily.*

## Analyzing Questionnaires

Hopefully the questionnaires are administered online with a program that automatically analyzes the results. The questionnaire team will need to analyze the open-ended results, however. (*Analyzing Questionnaires,* Appendix C3 and C4.)

The questionnaire team can set-up and facilitate the review of the questionnaire results with the entire staff. Adjust the continuous school improvement plan and vision, as needed, to improve school climate. (*Presenting and Using Questionnaire Results,* Appendix C5.)

*Hopefully the questionnaires are administered online with a program that automatically analyzes the results.*

## On-Going

At the beginning of the year, semester, unit teachers, in their collaborative teams, will want to establish goals, administer post-assessments as pre-assessments, and review what they want students to know and be able to do. Figure 13.4 summarizes the when, who, what, tools, data sources, and artifacts for this on-going team work.

Throughout the semester, teachers will—

◆ Monitor student progress.

◆ Review results in collaborative teams.

◆ Determine how to support students who are not proficient, and students who are proficient in specific skills.

◆ In teacher teams, review grade-level/subject-area results.

◆ Determine how teachers will support each other.

◆ Establish goals for the year, quarter, month, unit.

◆ Review/update curriculum maps.

◆ Ensure the implementation of the vision.

*At the beginning of the year, semester, unit, teachers, in their collaborative teams, will want to establish goals, administer post-assessments as pre-assessments, and review what they want students to know and be able to do.*

Figure 13.4
CONTINUOUS SCHOOL IMPROVEMENT AND DATA ANALYSIS TIMELINE
ON-GOING

| WHEN | WHO | WHAT | TOOLS | DATA SOURCES | ARTIFACTS |
|---|---|---|---|---|---|
| On-going. | Teachers. | • At the beginning of the year, semester, unit, teachers, in their collaborative teams will want to establish goals, administer post-assessments as pre assessments, review what they want students to know and be able to do.<br>• Throughout the semester, teachers will—<br>  * Monitor student progress.<br>  * Review results in collaborative teams.<br>  * Determine how to support students who are not proficient, and students who are proficient in specific skills. | *Flowcharting School Processes.*<br>*Analyzing Student Learning Data.* | Data profile.<br>State Longitudinal Data System.<br>Assessment databases. | Pre-assessments of standards knowledge and skills.<br>Flowcharts that show what teachers will do when students do not know the concepts and do not have the skills, and what teachers will do when students know the concepts and have the skills. |
| | Data team. | • Assist teachers in analyzing student and classroom level data.<br>• Make sure appropriate reports are available to teachers. | *Analyzing Student Learning Data.* | Assessment database application. | Assessment reports. |
| | Grade-level/subject-area teams. | • Review/share grade-level/subject-area results.<br>• Determine how teachers will support each other.<br>• Establish goals for the year, quarter, month, unit.<br>• Review/update curriculum maps.<br>• Ensure the implementation of programs/vision. | *Analyzing Student Learning Data.*<br>*Strategies for teachers to support each other.*<br>*Communication Protocol.* | Data profile.<br>Data warehouse/State Longitudinal Data System.<br>Assessment databases. | Student achievement results graphed by teachers, students, grade-level/subject-area/leadership teams/school.<br>Analysis of student learning results by grade levels and across grade levels. |
| | School Leadership Team. | • Review/share grade-level/subject-area results and teachers' plans to ensure instructional congruence.<br>• Discuss adjustments required with grade-level/subject-area teams.<br>• Reinforce with staff the intentions of programs and interventions, how they are to be implemented, and the results expected. | *Analyzing Student Learning Data.*<br>*Strategies for teachers to support each other.*<br>*Measuring a Program or Process.* | Data profile.<br>Data warehouse/State Longitudinal Data System.<br>Assessment databases. | Plan to ensure instructional coherence.<br>Evidence of instructional coherence. |

During this time, the Data Leadership Team will make sure appropriate reports are available to the teachers, and assist teachers in analyzing student and classroom level data.

School Leadership Teams will—

◆ Review grade-level/subject-area results and teachers' plans to ensure instructional congruence. Discuss needed adjustments with grade-level/subject-area teams.

◆ Reinforce with staff intentions of programs and processes, how they are to be implemented, and the results expected.

## Professional Learning Days and Meetings

During a professional learning day, with the entire staff, create or revisit the school mission and vision. (Use Appendix J, *Creating a Shared Vision* and *Creating a Shared Vision Guide* to support the work.) Figure 13.5 summarizes the when, who, what, tools, data sources, and artifacts for on-going professional learning days and meetings. During a visioning professional learning day, staff need to come to agreement on—

* Core values and beliefs.
* Purpose and mission.
* Shared vision for curriculum, instruction, assessment, and environment.
* School goals.
* A flowchart to show how to implement the vision.
* How the vision will be monitored and evaluated.
* Create/adopt monitoring/evaluation tools.

*During a professional learning day, with the entire staff, create or revisit the school mission and vision.*

### Spell out Program and Process Intentions

As a whole staff, or departments, or grade levels, depending on the programs:

* Spell out the intentions of each program/process, expected outcomes, and how the program/ process will be implemented and evaluated. (*Measuring a Program or Process*, Appendix D.)
* Create flowcharts for programs and processes to support implementation. (*Flowcharting School Processes*, Appendix E.)

### Create Leadership Teams

Create leadership teams to ensure the implementation of the vision. (*Leadership Structure*, Appendix N.)

* Determine roles and responsibilities, and dedicated meeting times.
* Establish a partnership plan to include parents, community, and business in achieving the vision. (*Creating Partnerships*, Appendix P.)

## Figure 13.5
### CONTINUOUS SCHOOL IMPROVEMENT AND DATA ANALYSIS TIMELINE
### PROFESSIONAL LEARNING DAYS AND MEETINGS

| WHEN | WHO | WHAT | TOOLS | DATA SOURCES | ARTIFACTS |
|---|---|---|---|---|---|
| Professional Learning Day. | *Entire staff.* | • Revisit/create the school vision.<br>  *Values and beliefs.<br>  *Purpose and mission.<br>  *Shared vision for curriculum, instruction, assessment, and environment.<br>• Create flowchart for vision.<br>• Determine how the vision will be monitored and evaluated.<br>• Create monitoring/evaluation tools. | *Creating a Shared Vision.*<br>*Flowcharting School Processes.*<br>*Monitoring Vision Implementation.*<br>Assessment and Program Inventories. | Data profile.<br>State Longitudinal Data System.<br>Assessment tools. | Core values and beliefs, mission, vision for the school.<br>Flowchart of the vision.<br>Monitoring and evaluation plan for vision.<br>Updated inventory of assessments and programs. |
| Delegated or staff meeting. | *Staff members.* | • Spell out the intention of each program/process, expected outcomes, and how the program/process will be implemented and evaluated.<br>• Create flowcharts for programs and processes to support implementation, within the context of the vision. | *Measuring a Program or Process.*<br>*Flowcharting School Processes.* | Data profile.<br>State Longitudinal Data System.<br>Assessment tools. | Program intention and assessment plan established for programs.<br>Program flowcharts. |
| Professional Learning Day, unless it can be done during the vision process. | *Entire staff.* | Create structures to implement the vision.<br>• Review all the implications from the data.<br>• Review purpose, mission, vision, and values and beliefs.<br>• Revisit leadership structure.<br>• Determine roles and responsibilities.<br>• Establish a relationship plan to include parents, community, and business in achieving the vision.<br>• Begin the school improvement plan for the year. | *Leadership Structure.*<br>*Creating Partnerships.* | Data profile.<br>State Longitudinal Data System. | Leadership structure.<br>Plan for building relationships, with parents, community, and business. |

## Figure 13.5 (*Continued*)
### CONTINUOUS SCHOOL IMPROVEMENT AND DATA ANALYSIS TIMELINE
### PROFESSIONAL LEARNING DAYS AND MEETINGS

| WHEN | WHO | WHAT | TOOLS | DATA SOURCES | ARTIFACTS |
|---|---|---|---|---|---|
| Create and Use a Continuous School Improvement Plan. | *Work with Leadership Team to create and bring back to staff.* | • Create/update the continuous school improvement plan to implement the vision.<br>• Determine goals, objectives, strategies, activities, measurement, persons responsible, timelines, and evaluation of the plan.<br>• Get all staff committed to implementing the plan.<br>• Develop professional learning calendar. | *Continuous School Improvement Plan.*<br>*Professional Learning Calendar.* | Data profile.<br>State Longitudinal Data System. | School improvement plan.<br>Professional learning calendar. |
| On-going. | *Leadership Team.* | • Assess the implementation of the vision and plan, and make adjustments to implement better. | *Evaluating a Continuous School Improvement Vision and Plan.* | Vision monitoring tool. | On-going monitoring of the vision and plan reports and analysis. |
| End of Year. | *Data team or data analysis personnel, with staff.* | • Review/share data results:<br>• Clarify new learning required for all teachers over the summer.<br>• Determine changes required in the vision and plan. | *Analyzing Data for Continuous School Improvement Planning.* | Data profile.<br>State Longitudinal Data System.<br>Assessment database application. | Analysis of data and analysis of changes required. |

### Create Continuous School Improvement Plan

Create/update the continuous school improvement plan (*Continuous School Improvement Plan,* Appendix L) to implement the vision. The Leadership Team, or an assigned Planning Team, should do this work and bring it back to the entire staff:

*Create/update the continuous school improvement plan to implement the vision.*

◆ Determine objectives, strategies, activities, measurement, persons responsible, timelines, and evaluation of the plan.

◆ Get all staff committed to implementing the plan.

◆ Get all staff to reflect on the impact of implementing the plan in their classrooms.

◆ Develop professional learning calendar. (*Professional Learning Calendar,* Appendix O.)

### On-Going During the School Year

Throughout the school year, the Leadership Team will work with Teacher Teams to monitor the implementation of the vision and plan. (*Monitoring Vision Implementation,* Appendix K; and *Monitoring the Implementation of the Plan,* Appendix M.)

### End of the School Year

Having the evaluation of the achievement of goals and the implementation of the vision already set up, a team, probably the Data Leadership Team, will analyze the data and present results to staff. (Chapter 13.)

During a staff meeting, staff will—

◆ Review data results.

◆ Clarify new learning required for all teachers over the summer.

◆ Determine changes required in the vision and plan.

### Abbreviated Timeline

*While the complete timeline for continuous school improvement work can seem overwhelming, when staff get into the work, they will see it is logical and includes many things they are already doing.*

While the complete timeline for continuous school improvement work can seem overwhelming, when staff get into the work, they will see it is logical and includes many things they are already doing. They will also see that much of the work can be delegated and presented to the whole staff, as opposed to the whole staff doing everything all the time. Figure 13.6 shows the tasks of the timeline, by who will do the work.

## Figure 13.6
## TIMELINE FOR CONTINUOUS SCHOOL IMPROVEMENT WORK

**Columns:** DATA LEADERSHIP TEAM | WHOLE STAFF | TEACHER TEAMS | LEADERSHIP TEAM

**Rows:** BEFORE THE SCHOOL YEAR BEGINS | ON-GOING | QUESTIONNAIRE WORK | END OF SCHOOL YEAR

---

### BEFORE THE SCHOOL YEAR BEGINS

**DATA LEADERSHIP TEAM**

*Before First Staff Meeting*
Assign a data leadership team to—
- understand the concepts of continuous school improvement and comprehensive data analysis.
- pull together a data profile that summarizes the schoolwide data currently available.
- re-roster individual student learning data, over time, by current teachers' classrooms.
- inventory assessments, data, and programs.
- create a plan to do this work with staff.

**WHOLE STAFF**

*Whole-Staff Meeting*
- Provide overview of continuous school improvement framework and comprehensive data analysis.
- Analyze the schoolwide data in the data profile.
- Use the Problem-Solving Cycle Activity to understand the contributing causes of undesirable results.
- Determine how teachers will work, in teams, with classroom and student-level data during the school year.
- Allow time for grade-level/subject-area teams to work.
- Discuss grade-level/subject-area breakout work with full staff for cross-grade-level congruence.
- Assess on the CICs to understand what staff members are thinking about where the school is on continuous school improvement.
- Look across the implications that come from the data analysis work for the school improvement plan.
- Determine new strategies to get different results to meet the needs of *all* students, and determine what has to go into the school improvement plan for the year.
- Determine when and how staff can list programs and processes, their intended/desired results, and what each would look like, separate and together, if they were implemented with 100% integrity and fidelity.

**TEACHER TEAMS**

*Grade-Level/Subject-Area Team/PLC Breakout Session*
Determine—
- what concepts and skills students need to know.
- agree on essential standards to teach, when.
- what do we want students to know and be able to do this year, quarter, month, week?
- core curriculum standards and update curriculum maps.
- how we will know that students know these concepts and skills.
- common assessments, including timeline for giving assessments during the year.
- which instructional strategies will make the difference.
- an established plan/flowchart for what teachers will do when students do not know the concepts and do not have the skills, and what teachers will do when students know the concepts and have the skills.
- times, strategies, and roles and responsibilities for grade-level and subject-area work during the year.

---

### ON-GOING

**DATA LEADERSHIP TEAM**

*On-Going*
Help teachers review student learning data by—
- creating reports.
- coaching their interpretation of results.
- listening to, and creating, others ways teachers may want the data displayed.

**WHOLE STAFF**

*Create/Revisit a Mission and Vision*
- Review implications from all the data.
- Values and beliefs.
- Purpose and mission.
- Shared vision for curriculum, instruction, assessment, and environment.
- Determine school goals and objectives.
- Create flowchart for vision.
- Get staff to reflect on the impact of implementing the vision in her/his classroom.
- Determine how the vision will be monitored and evaluated.
- Create/adopt monitoring/evaluation tools. (Leadership Team may have to finish and bring it back to staff.)
- Create Leadership Teams to implement the vision.
- Determine roles and responsibilities for Leadership Teams.
- Establish a partnership plan to include parents, community, and business in achieving the vision.
- Begin the school improvement plan for the year. (Leadership Team can finish and bring back to staff.)

**TEACHER TEAMS**

*At the Beginning of the Year*, semester, unit, administer post-assessments as pre-assessments.

*On-Going*
- Monitor student progress.
- Review results.
- Determine how to support students who are not proficient, and students who are proficient in specific skills.
- Determine how teachers will support each other.
- Establish goals for the year, quarter, month, unit.
- Review/update curriculum map.
- Monitor the implementation of the vision and plan.

**LEADERSHIP TEAM**

*Regularly Scheduled Meetings*
- Review grade-level/subject-area results and teachers' plans to ensure instructional congruence.
- Discuss needed adjustments with grade- level/subject-area teams.
- Reinforce with staff the intentions of programs and interventions, how they are to be implemented, and the results expected.
- Monitor the implementation of the vision and plan.

*Create a School Improvement Plan to Implement the Vision*
- Get all staff committed to implementing the vision and plan.
- Develop professional learning calendar from the plan.
- Get staff approval of plan and professional learning calendar.
- Ensure all staff have appropriate professional learning.

---

### QUESTIONNAIRE WORK

**DATA LEADERSHIP TEAM**

*Questionnaires*
- Research existing questionnaires.
- Adopt or develop questionnaires to administer.
- Gain staff approval to administer questionnaires.

- Organize and administer questionnaires.

**WHOLE STAFF**

*Program Analysis*
- List the programs operating in the school.
- Spell-out the intentions of each program/process, expected outcomes, and how the program/process will be implemented and evaluated.
- Create flowcharts for programs and processes to support implementation.

- *Analyze Questionnaire* results with the other data.

*Professional Learning*
- Engage all staff in appropriate professional learning.

**TEACHER TEAMS**

*Administer Questionnaires*
- Support the administration of questionnaires.
- Review results with respect to grade level/subject areas.

**LEADERSHIP TEAM**

*Use Results*
- Adjust school improvement plan and vision to improve school climate.
- Clarify new learning required for all teachers over the summer.

---

### END OF SCHOOL YEAR

**DATA LEADERSHIP TEAM**

*Evaluate Achievement of Continuous School Improvement* goals and the implementation of the vision.
- Review data results.
- Clarify new learning required for all teachers over the summer.
- Determine changes required in the vision and plan.

**LEADERSHIP TEAM**

*Evaluate Achievement of Continuous School Improvement* goals and the implementation of the vision.
- Review data results.
- Clarify new learning required for all teachers over the summer.
- Determine changes required in the vision and plan.

## HOW MUCH TIME DOES IT TAKE?

*Creating a timeline for doing the continuous school improvement work might take two hours of adjusting and organizing the school year schedule.*

### REFLECTION QUESTIONS

1. Why is a timeline for continuous school improvement important to a school?

2. What type of work can be done by a team, and what type of work must be done by the entire staff?

### APPLICATION OPPORTUNITIES

1. Create a timeline for your school to do this work of continuous school improvement. Who is going to lead the work? (Use the *Timeline for Continuous School Improvement Work,* Appendix T.)

# THE TRANSFORMATION FROM A COMPLYING SCHOOL TO A LEARNING ORGANIZATION

**14**

**CHAPTER**

*Learning organizations are…*
*"organizations where people continually expand*
*their capacity to create the results they truly desire,*
*where new and expansive patterns of thinking are nurtured,*
*where collective aspiration is set free, and where people*
*are continually learning how to learn together."*

Peter Senge
Author, *The Fifth Discipline*

The ultimate goal of continuous school improvement is to create learning organizations that have the ability to develop their capacity to create the results they truly desire. This book is about helping schools become true learning organizations by moving them from focusing solely on gaps, compliance, and being "Adequate," to becoming learning organizations that create the vision, commitment, and results they want for all their students.

After reading the previous thirteen chapters, you might become overwhelmed with the many things that need to be done to become a continuously improving learning organization. Some schools do not enter into the work of comprehensive data analysis and continuous school improvement because they believe it is "over their heads" and too technical. The work of comprehensive data analysis and continuous school improvement is not just a technical task. In reality, it is more about getting all people on the same page committing to move the system forward, and then doing it. While the tasks may seem difficult, they are doable, and the outcome is surely worth the effort. Let's review what it takes to become a continuously improving learning organization.

*The ultimate goal of continuous school improvement is to create learning organizations that have the ability to develop their capacity to create the results they truly desire.*

*The work of comprehensive data analysis and continuous school improvement is not just a technical task. In reality, it is more about getting all people on the same page committing to move the system forward, and then doing it.*

## BECOMING LEARNING ORGANIZATIONS

As stated in Chapter 1, this book is a call to action. It is about inspiring schools and districts to commit to continuous school improvement by providing a framework that will result in improving teaching for every teacher, and learning for every student, in one year, through the comprehensive use of data. It provides a new definition of improvement, away from compliance, toward a commitment to excellence. Inherent in this work are the following non-negotiables:

◆ *Commit and engage staff throughout the entire process.* Continuous school improvement does not happen from the top-down. Leadership must work to get *commitment,* which is NOT enlisting, recruiting, or getting staff to buy-in. It is leading and encouraging staff to commit to do the best they can for every student. Engaging the staff throughout the process keeps the commitment fresh.

◆ *Empower all staff with schoolwide data.* When staff see all the data, they understand why and how they are getting the results they are getting now. They understand linkages, what is working, and what is not working. Collectively, they can see what they need to learn and change to get better results for their students. It is easier to understand why some things have to change when all staff see the data pointing them in a certain direction. It is also easier to move the entire staff in that direction when the data analysis process supports their understanding of the data.

◆ *Provide data tools.* It is critical to have the technological capacity and data tools that support the analyses described in this book, so staff can spend their time analyzing the data rather than organizing the data. Empowering staff requires that data are easily accessible, clean and reliable, and the systems are focused on supporting the framework for continuous school improvement.

◆ *Create a shared vision.* A shared vision is the power that drives learning organizations. The vision clarifies the strategies and actions that learning organizations propose to do to get their desired results. Shared means that everybody understands the vision in the same way, so it can be implemented in the same way. When staff are a part of the creation of the vision, they will implement it. Leadership must focus on facilitating the vision.

◆ *Develop a continuous school improvement plan to implement the vision.* A continuous school improvement plan shows everyone on staff how to implement the vision, as opposed to just closing a gap for compliance.

*Leadership must work to get commitment, which is NOT enlisting, recruiting, or getting staff to buy-in.*

*It is easier to understand why some things have to change when all staff see the data pointing them in a certain direction.*

*A shared vision is the power that drives learning organizations.*

*A continuous school improvement plan shows everyone on staff how to implement the vision, as opposed to just closing a gap for compliance.*

- *Create a true shared decision-making structure.* A true shared decision-making structure clarifies and supports everyone's job in implementing and helping everyone else to implement the vision. Clarifying and monitoring roles and responsibilities in the implementation of the vision cements commitment.

- *Identify change agents to lead and carry out specific improvement tasks.* Some staff members have more interest and talents in data analysis, others in collaborative structures. Find the staff leaders for the work that needs to be done, and let them lead.

- *Create a collaborative work culture.* Collaborative work is vital to overcoming the status quo. To get improved results for all students, teachers must be able to prescribe and implement immediate improvement. Together, staff can review student, grade, and school level performance data, utilize problem-solving strategies, study program and process implementation, create process flowcharts, and coach each other to ensure implementation to get the results they want for all students.

- *Support for the improvement process through professional learning and partnerships.* Staff need support to improve teaching and learning for all students. Structures need to be in place so staff can learn new concepts, and tap into parent, community, and business support.

- *Engage staff in evaluating processes, programs, and the vision to make sure they are making a difference.* By being involved in the evaluation process, on-going reflection becomes the way work is done, and ensures that staff are making the intended difference.

The continuous school improvement framework provided in this book helps staff do all these things to create a desirable learning organization and stay on course. To continuously improve a school, staff must agree on what they want students to know and be able to do, want the same outcomes, share the same vision, determine how they are going to get to where they want to be, and know that they got there, together. Then, as spelled out in the *Plan–Implement–Evaluate–Improve Cycle,* they must adjust, and start again to do things even better the next time. The framework, along with the tools in the chapters and appendices, are intended to guide and support staff in bringing together the technical elements with the facilitation necessary for effective staff engagement.

The framework also helps staff look at the whole organization and get away from focusing on gaps only. The completion of the elements of the continuous school improvement framework is *the* way to get student learning for every student, in every grade level, and in every subject area. When this work is thorough, a school will transform into a true learning organization and can step away from a narrow focus on compliance only. When staff can see the whole system, they are able to understand what they can do to get better results across the board and not just focus

*A true shared decision-making structure clarifies and supports everyone's job in implementing and helping everyone else to implement the vision.*

*Collaborative work is vital to overcoming the status quo.*

*By being involved in the evaluation process, on-going reflection becomes the way work is done, and ensures that staff are making the intended difference.*

*The completion of the elements of the continuous school improvement framework is the way to get student learning for every student, in every grade level, and in every subject area.*

on one subject or subgroup at a time. Schools and school districts/boards are bound by government politics regarding the reduction of gaps between specific subgroups. If the staff look at the whole organization and get all students to learn, the rest will follow and the gaps will disappear.

## LOGIC IN THE LEARNING ORGANIZATION

What I am asking you to do in this book is very logical. I am asking you to pay attention to the results your school is getting now, understand how and why you are getting these results, and adjust your processes to get better results for your students. I want you to reflect on the big picture and how the parts lead to the whole, and then to be intentional about creating a learning organization that will make a difference for *all* of your students.

*A logic model is a tool to clarify and graphically display what your learning organization plans to do and what it hopes to accomplish, given its context.*

A logic model is a tool to clarify and graphically display what your learning organization plans to do and what it hopes to accomplish, given its context. This tool is useful for planning, implementation, and for evaluation.

Logic models provide us with the opportunity to see the whole learning organization and the components that make up that big picture. They enable us to improve all aspects of the learning organization, and ultimately, produce the results we want. They are a way to pull everything together—to get a systems view. A logic model shows how we "do" school and why.

Putting together a logic model for a learning organization requires:

◆ clarification of the results we want to get for all students *(short and long-term outcomes);*

◆ listing the *inputs* that must be taken into consideration for staff to create the processes to achieve the desired outcomes; and

◆ the adaptation and implementation of programs, processes, and procedures *(processes)* to achieve those *outcomes,* given whom we have as students, staff, parents, and community *(inputs).*

*One of the greatest benefits in using a logic model is to enable a review of the big picture to determine how you can improve the results your school is getting for all students.*

The logic model is an ideal structure for reflecting on linkages. If you do not know the impact of your current processes, take the time to study those results. One of the greatest benefits in using a logic model is to enable a review of the big picture to determine how you can improve the results your school is getting for *all* students. If you are not getting the results you expect or anticipated, you must understand how to change the processes to create the results you want for *all* students.

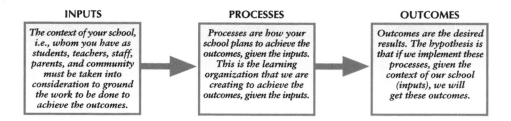

| INPUTS | PROCESSES | OUTCOMES |
|---|---|---|
| *The context of your school, i.e., whom you have as students, teachers, staff, parents, and community must be taken into consideration to ground the work to be done to achieve the outcomes.* | *Processes are how your school plans to achieve the outcomes, given the inputs. This is the learning organization that we are creating to achieve the outcomes, given the inputs.* | *Outcomes are the desired results. The hypothesis is that if we implement these processes, given the context of our school (inputs), we will get these outcomes.* |

Figure 14.1 shows a logic model for a typical school. On the left side are the *inputs* that spell out the context of the school. In the middle are the *processes* that create the results. On the right side are the short-term and long-term *outcomes*. This is how to read the reasoning within the logic model.

The following steps indicate how to create a logic model for your learning organization. It might be fitting for you to start with the example logic model in Figure 14.1 and adapt it to fit your data.

## Creating the Logic Model of Your Learning Organization

Step 1. *Assemble a Team to Create a Logic Model.* You will want the team to consist of individuals familiar with all aspects of the learning organization and the school data, and who are committed to achieving the outcomes.

Step 2. *Determine Short-Term and Long-Term Outcomes.* Schools are pretty clear about their outcomes for K-12. Often, however, they have never listed them all before. The short-term and long-term outcomes listed in the example are a starting place. Review these and add to the outcomes.

> **CREATING THE LOGIC MODEL OF YOUR LEARNING ORGANIZATION**
>
> 1. *Assemble a team to create a logic model.*
> 2. *Determine short-term and long-term outcomes.*
> 3. *Layout the inputs.*
> 4. *List high-quality processes and programs to create the results you want.*
> 5. *Review the big picture.*
> 6. *Revise the parts.*

It is important to know where your school is with respect to your desired outcomes, so processes can be adjusted, given the inputs. Your work with the multiple measures of data (Chapters 3, 4, 5, 6, 7, and 8) should help you uncover the answer to the question, "how are we doing with respect to these outcomes?"

As professional educators, your challenge is to determine how you are going to get better results. With collective and shared knowledge, you determine how to put together your school—curriculum, instruction, assessment, environment, processes, procedures, and programs—given your inputs. This is where the school processes come in, but not until the inputs are taken into consideration.

## Figure 14.1 ~ EXAMPLE SCHOOL LOGIC MODEL

**INPUTS — PROCESSES — OUTCOMES**

### INPUTS

**School**
- Enrollment—total and disaggregated
- Enrollment by programs
- Attendance
- Mobility rates
- Graduation rates
- Dropout rates
- Special education
- Accountability ratings
- Grade-level expectations
- Resources
- Culture/environment/safety
- Predictive analytics identifying at-risk students

**Students**
- Who the students are: gender, ethnicity/race, socio-economic status, first language, second language, migrant, students with disabilities, gifted
- Attitudes
- Learning styles
- Retentions
- Pre-K attendance
- Early readiness (social, emotional, cognitive)
- Health
- Mobility
- Behavior
- Attendance
- Tardies
- Extracurricular activity participation

**Teachers**
- Gender, ethnicity
- Qualifications, training, experience
- Assignments
- Numbers of years of teaching
- Teaching styles
- Attitudes
- Core values and beliefs
- Attendance
- Retention rate

**Principals**
- Gender, ethnicity
- Qualifications, training, experience
- Number of years as principal
- Leadership style
- Attitudes
- Core values and beliefs

**Parents**
- Social economic status
- Participation in school events
- Educational attainment
- Attitudes
- Number of children in the home
- Number of parents in the home
- Language spoken at home

**Community**
- Businesses
- School Board
- Involvement in student learning

### PROCESSES

**Instructional**
- Curriculum
- Instruction
- Assessment (common, formative, grades, standards)
- Alignment of standards, curriculum, instruction, assessment
- Academic conversations with students
- Career planning/readiness
- Career/technology education
- Classroom assignments (types of tasks, choices, projects, collaboration)
- Classroom discussions (teacher talk, student-to-student talk, student-to-teacher talk)
- Culture/environment/safety
- Differentiated instruction
- Direct instruction
- Flipped classrooms
- Grading
- Homework
- Immersion
- Inquiry process
- Internships
- Standards implementation
- Student reflection and self-assessment
- Student teamwork
- Technology integration
- Tutoring

**Organizational Processes**
- Teacher collaboration
- Data Teams
- Data use
- Healthy breakfasts and lunches
- Healthy activities
- Inquiry process
- Instructional coaching
- Leadership structure (Leadership Teams)
- Professional Learning Communities
- Mentoring
- Mission
- Parent involvement
- Pathways for graduation
- Policies and procedures
- Problem solving
- Professional discussions and support
- Professional reflection
- Referral process
- Response to Intervention (RtI)
- Teaching assignments
- Teacher evaluation
- Teacher hiring and recruitment
- Teacher observations
- Teacher renewal (professional learning)
- Vision
- Work training

**Administrative**
- Attendance program
- Class sizes
- Data collection
- Discipline strategies
- Dropout rates
- Enrollment in different courses/ programs, program offerings
- Graduation rates
- Leadership turnover rates
- Number of support personnel
- Student groupings
- Policies and procedures
- Retentions
- Scheduling of classes
- Teacher hiring
- Teacher assignments
- Teacher certification
- Teacher turnover

**Programs**
- AVID
- A+
- Accelerated Reader/Math
- Advanced Placement
- After School
- At-Risk
- Bilingual
- College Credit
- Dropout Prevention
- Extracurricular activities
- Gifted and Talented
- International Baccalaureate
- Interventions
- Ninth Grade Academy
- Science Fairs
- Service Learning
- Special Education
- Other remedial programs
- Programs that address identified risk factors

**Continuous School Improvement**
- Data analysis and use
- Contributing cause analysis
- Vision
- Mission
- Continuous school improvement planning
- Leadership
- Professional learning
- Partnership
- Evaluation
- Self-assessment

### OUTCOMES

**Short-Term**

**Students**
- Graduation—on time
- Student growth at all grade levels
- Improved early learning outcomes
- Employment
- No remedial courses in college
- Positive attitudes about learning
- Enrollment in college—2 year, 4 year
- Successful SAT/ACT/State assessment results
- Ability to plan for the future
- Leadership abilities
- Feeling that they belong
- Feelings that teachers care about them
- Positive behavior
- Good attendance
- Positive self-esteem
- Motivated to learn
- Love to learn
- Engaged in learning/school
- Dropout (credit) recovery
- Positive grades
- Community involvement
- Involvement in extracurricular activities
- Involvement in school activities
- Involvement in service learning
- Winning scholarships
- Able to write effectively
- Able to think scientifically
- Able to think critically
- Able to read
- Able to compute
- Speaking
- Listening
- Problem solving
- Logical reasoning
- Ability to use technology effectively
- Appreciation for the arts and music
- Ability to integrate subjects
- Ability to make healthy choices and stay fit

**Principals and Teachers**
- Satisfied with services they are providing
- Good morale
- Program alignment to college and the work force
- Caring relations with students
- Able to understand the impact of their actions/policies on students
- Collaborative with each other
- Engaged in partnerships with parents and community
- Able to predict and ensure student success
- Able to analyze the impact on results of a particular program implementation

**Parents / Families**
- Satisfied with services provided by the school
- Involved with their child's learning
- Knowledgeable of strategies to enhance children's learning
- Engaged in partnerships with teachers, principals, and students

**Long-Term**

**Students**
- Successful completion of post-secondary education/training
- Successful in work
- Successful in life
- Healthy and fit
- Life-long learners

**Parents**
- Able to support their childrens' lifelong ambitions

**Community**
- Benefiting from having great schools and employees
- High levels of confidence in public education

Step 3. *Layout the Inputs.* Using the data inventories located in Appendix B that follow the information provided in Chapters 3, 4, 5, and 6, list the data that must be considered as your school adapts it programs, processes, and procedures to meet the needs of all students. The example school logic model inputs are a good start.

The Logic Model can look overwhelming, even before we think about looking at all the data implied within it. However, if a school is working on continuous school improvement, it has much of the data work done already. Inputs describe where we are now and are documented in the learning organization's data profile. The update of the results of the data profile becomes the outcomes. For example, student attendance is an input that we would also want to see improved, as an outcome.

Step 4. *List High-Quality Processes and Programs to Create the Results You Want.* Following the work outlined in Chapter 6, you will have a list of school processes; i.e., programs, processes, and procedures that your school is using right now. Hopefully, you will also have an assessment of the impact of each of these programs, processes, and procedures so only those that are impacting students positively will be used. List those processes, procedures, and programs that your staff believe everyone should be implementing, and then make sure the implementation is occurring. The school processes data inventory, the school vision, leadership structures, and partnerships will help you spell out the processes.

Step 5. *Review the Big Picture.* To improve thinking about how to get better results, it is important to review the whole system that the logic model helps us see. Engage staff in this review. Ask and answer questions like, W*ill the processes get the results we want, given the inputs?, Are we doing the right things for all of our students?,* and *Is this our best theory of change?* If not, we must change the processes that create the results.

Step 6. *Revise the Parts*

Given the review in step 5, the analyses of processes, procedures, and programs completed in previous chapters and current and past results, adjust your logic model in the best way you can to get better outcomes.

## BENEFITS OF CONTINUOUS SCHOOL IMPROVEMENT AND BECOMING A LEARNING ORGANIZATION

*The most important benefit of continuous school improvement is that through this hard work, a school can become a true learning organization committed to continuous improvement.*

The benefits of continuous school improvement are many. The most important benefit is that through this hard work, a school can become a true learning organization committed to continuous improvement. More specifically:

1.  We are able to clarify who our students are.

2.  We understand how we are getting our results, and how to get better results for our students.

3.  We have cleaned up the system to work as effectively and efficiently as possible.

4.  We do business in a manner that will allow all students to achieve success.

5.  We have created a vision that is truly shared and to which all staff are committed.

6.  We are able to clarify roles and responsibilities and the work we do.

7.  We implement common strategies with integrity and fidelity.

8.  We implement structures that get all staff working together and that make a difference.

9.  We collaboratively improve teaching and learning through the ongoing use of data.

10. We truly understand if what we are doing is making a difference.

11. We are focused on the creation of a true learning organization.

*Imagine not continuously improving…. If you are not creating a learning organization that is continuously improving, you are not doing enough for your students.*

With this, learning organizations are able to ensure increased learning for every student, in every grade level, in every subject area, and with every student group.

Imagine not continuously improving…. If you are not creating a learning organization that is continuously improving, you are not doing enough for your students.

## HOW MUCH TIME DOES IT TAKE?

*The work of continuous school improvement is ongoing
and should be a continuous part of every school year.*

## REFLECTION QUESTIONS

1. What is a learning organization?

2. How does the Logic Model help with the understanding of continuous school improvement?

3. How does the continuous school improvement framework help a school become a true learning organization?

4. What are the benefits of doing the hard work of continuous school improvement?

## APPLICATION OPPORTUNITIES

1. Reflect with your staff members on their progress in becoming a true learning organization.

2. Review the Logic Model presented in this chapter. Adjust it to reflect the data from your school. How will this Logic Model help your school become a learning organization?

3. How has the continuous school improvement framework helped your school become a learning organization?

4. What have been the benefits of your school engaging in continuous school improvement?

5. What specific strategies can you put in place to help all staff members move from compliance to commitment of the school vision?

# CONTINUOUS IMPROVEMENT CONTINUUMS SELF-ASSESSMENT

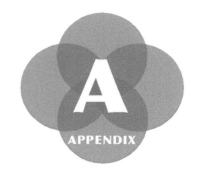

## OVERVIEW OF THE CONTINUUMS

Measuring a school's progress against identified criteria—such as the *Education for the Future Continuous Improvement Continuums*—provides a benchmark that schools can use to see if their actions have created the results they intended. These measures are supported by analyzing data gathered through questionnaires, performance measures, and observations of the learning environment. When these measures are used on a regular basis, the data clearly document trends and provide information that assist schools in determining next steps for improvement.

The seven *Education for the Future Continuous Improvement Continuums* represent the theoretical flow of systemic continuous school improvement. The Continuous Improvement Continuums (CICs) take the theory and spirit of continuous school improvement, interweave educational research, and offer practical meaning to the components that must change, simultaneously and systematically, throughout the learning organization.

These *Education for the Future Continuous Improvement Continuums,* adapted from the *Malcolm Baldrige Award Program for Quality Business Management,* provide an authentic means for measuring schoolwide improvement and growth. Schools use these Continuums as a vehicle for ongoing self-assessment. They use the results of the assessment to acknowledge their accomplishments, to set goals for improvement, and to keep school districts and partners apprised of the progress they have made in their continuous school improvement efforts.

### Understanding the Continuums

These Continuums, extending from one to five horizontally, represent a range of expectations related to continuous school improvement with respect to an *Approach* to the Continuum, *Implementation* of the approach, and the *Outcome* that results from the implementation. A one rating, located at the left of each Continuum, represents a school that has not yet begun to improve. Five, located at the right of each Continuum, represents a school that is one step removed from "world class quality." The elements between one and five describe how that Continuum is hypothesized to evolve in a continuously improving school. Each Continuum moves from a reactive mode to a proactive mode—from fire fighting to prevention. The five in *Approach, Implementation,* and *Outcome* in each Continuum is the target.

Vertically, the *Approach, Implementation,* and *Outcome* statements, for any number one through five, are hypotheses. In other words, the implementation statement describes how the approach might look when implemented, and the outcome is the "pay-off" for implementing the approach. If the hypotheses are accurate, the outcome will not be realized until the approach is actually implemented.

**194**

Purpose
: Assessing on the *Continuous Improvement Continuums* will help staff members see where their systems are right now with respect to continuous improvement, and ultimately show that they are making progress over time. The discussion that leads to consensus is the most valuable piece of this activity. In addition to helping the entire staff see where the *school or district* is, the process lays out next steps for continuous school improvement.

Target Audience
: School or district staff.

Time
: Three hours for the first assessment; 90 minutes for subsequent assessments.

Materials
: One set of the school or district *Continuous Improvement Continuums* (CICs), enlarged to poster size, a copy of the CICs for staff members, chart pad paper, markers, masking tape or push pins to hang the large *Continuums*, colored dots, 2x2 self-stick notes, and computer for notetaking. Reserve a room with big blank walls for this activity. (Do not bother laminating the posters or making them really big unless you can do so inexpensively. The posters serve as a chart. They will be used once.)

## Overview

Use the *Continuous Improvement Continuums* (CICs) to understand where your school is with respect to continuous school improvement, and to determine next steps. The results will provide that sense of urgency needed to spark enthusiasm for your school improvement efforts.

Be sure each table has a supply of markers, colored dots, and self-stick notes. Do not try to assign any one group the same color dots. The color of the dots has no particular meaning, and we want to ensure a feeling of one cohesive organization.

Remember that where your school is at any time is just where it is. Do not worry about being lower than you thought. The important thing is what you do with this information. Continuous school improvement is a never-ending process which, when used effectively, will ultimately lead your school, or district, toward providing a quality program for all students.

## Process Protocol

Hang the enlarged posters of the *Continuous Improvement Continuums* around the room. Read about where the *Continuous Improvement Continuums* came from, that they represent the theoretical flow of continuous improvement, going from reactive (1) to proactive (5). Have a person available to record the highlights of the conversation.

Step 1.  Establish ground rules for the assessment. We want to make sure everyone understands that the conversation is safe and confidential. Also clarify why it is important to do this activity.

Step 2.  Introduce the first section of the *Continuums—Information and Analysis*. Ask staff members to independently read the *Information and Analysis Continuous Improvement Continuum* and see if they can recognize where the *school or district* is right now, with respect to *Approach, Implementation*, and *Outcome*. Ask them to read left to right with a one and move to a five. Keep the group moving and try to avoid rewording the descriptions of the continuums. Also ask them to select a whole number, as opposed to a "between" number like 2.5.

Step 3.  Direct staff members to walk over to the *Information and Analysis Continuum* on the wall and place a colorful dot where they believe the school/district is with respect to *Approach, Implementation*, and *Outcome*. We call this "dot mocracy."

Step 4.  After everyone has placed her or his dot, review what you see. Focusing on *Approach*, ask for discussion of why staff thought the school/district was a 1, 2, 3, 4, or *5*.

Step 5.  After the discussion, if one number is becoming clearly favored, ask if there is anyone who could not live with this number as a baseline assessment of this school's or district's *Approach* to *Information and Analysis*. If no one opposes, write that number on a post- it and place it on the large continuum to represent the consensus decision of the group. If there is not a number that is clearly favored after the first discussion, continue the discussion. You can assist if there is a stalemate by systematically asking what the organization has for *Information and Analysis,* and walking through each number in *Approach,* clarifying what the organization would have to have to be a specific number. Ask again for a show of hands.

Step 6.  Continue with *Implementation* and *Outcome*.

Step 7.  When consensus on the three sections is complete, ask for the "Next Steps." *What do we need to do to move up? Or to become the next solid number?* (See *Coming to Consensus,* after *Comments to the Facilitator.)*

Step 8.  Continue with the next six *Continuums.* After *Information and Analysis,* you can usually introduce two *Continuums* at a time. (If you are familiar with the *Continuums,* you could read and dot two at the same time. You will need to discuss each one separately to list "Next Steps.") It is effective to have one-half of the group read one *Continuum,* place their dots, and then come back and read the next *Continuum,* while the other half of the group is reading the second *Continuum* first, putting up their dots, and then reading the first *Continuum.*

## Process Protocol *(Continued)*

Step 9.    As staff members are reading the next *Continuum*, use the time to type highlights of the discussion of the just completed *Continuum*. You will be able to leave the session with a complete report that summarizes the assessment results that day.

Step 10.   Add digital pictures of the assessment charts to the report to watch the staff thinking come together over time.

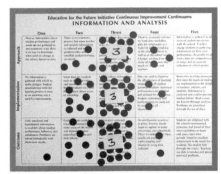

**Fall Assessment**

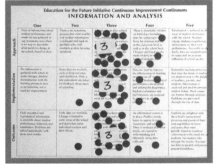

**Spring Assessment**

## Comments to the Facilitator

Make sure everyone knows the emphasis is on *consensus* and not just a vote. We want everyone to win! We want the *Continuous Improvement Continuums* to add a sense of urgency for improvement. To that end, do not let staff members average their scores or rate themselves too high. Averaging the scores does not inspire change—especially on the first assessment. If the discussion hangs between two numbers, go to the lower number, and write solid next steps to become the next number.

Periodic (regular) assessment sessions will help staff see that they are making progress. We recommend assessing on the *Continuous Improvement Continuums* at least once a year.

## Figure A-1

## COMING TO CONSENSUS

*Consensus is reached when everyone in the group can buy into, or live with, the decision without feeling compromised in any way.*

Michael Doyle and David Straug
*How to Make Meetings Work: The New Interaction Method (1993)*

Any group's goal should be to reach decisions that best reflect the thinking of all group members. We call this *reaching consensus.* It is easy to be confused about what consensus is and isn't, so here are some guidelines:

*Consensus is...*
♦ Finding a proposal acceptable enough that all members can support it; no member opposes it.

*Consensus is not...*
♦ A unanimous vote—a consensus may not represent everyone's first priorities.
♦ A majority vote—in a majority vote, only the majority gets something with which they are happy, while those in the minority may get something they don't want at all.
♦ Everyone is totally satisfied.

*Consensus requires...*
♦ Time to discuss ideas.
♦ The active participation of all group members.
♦ Good communication skills (listening, clarification, conflict resolution, and facilitation for both discussion and dialogue).
♦ Creative thinking and open-mindedness.

How do you know when you have reached consensus? Probably no one will be completely satisfied with the decision, but everyone can live with it.

Not every decision needs consensus. Your group should decide ahead of time when you will push for consensus. Decisions that may have a major impact on the direction of the project or conduct of the team—such as which problem to study, or what ground rules to establish—should belong to the whole team and be supported by consensus.

*Benefits of Consensus*
• Decisions are more accurate and usually of higher quality.
• People are more willing to support decisions.
• Disagreement can be explored rather than avoided.

*Why Not Vote?*
• Voting causes an individual to establish a position. It is difficult for anyone to publicly change her or his position.
• Voting ignores the opinions of the minority.
• Voting avoids conflict and discussion. Voting denies the group the benefit of understanding others and the natural synergism created by group interaction.

## Continuous Improvement Continuums for Schools
## INFORMATION AND ANALYSIS

| | One | Two | Three | Four | Five |
|---|---|---|---|---|---|
| **Approach** | Data or information about student performance and needs are not gathered in any systematic way; there is no way to determine what needs to change at the school, based on data. | There is no systematic process, but some teacher and student information is collected and used to problem solve and meet accountability expectations. | School collects all types of data, including demographics, student learning, perceptions, and school processes. The information is used to drive the strategic quality plan for school change. | There is systematic reliance on data (including data for subgroups) as a basis for decision making at the classroom level as well as at the school level. Changes are based on the study of data to meet the needs of students and teachers. | Information is gathered in all areas of student interaction with the school. Teachers engage students in gathering information on their own performance. Accessible to all levels, data are comprehensive in scope and an accurate reflection of school quality. |
| **Implementation** | No information is gathered with which to make changes. Student dissatisfaction with the learning process is seen as an irritation, not a need for improvement. | Some data are tracked, such as student learning results, attendance, and behavior. Only a few individuals are asked for feedback about areas of schooling. | School collects information on current and former students (e.g., student achievement, demographics, perceptions), analyzes and uses it in conjunction with future trends for planning. Identified areas for improvement are tracked over time. | Data are used to improve the effectiveness of teaching strategies on all student learning. Students' historical performances are graphed and utilized for diagnostics. Student evaluations and performances are analyzed by teachers in all classrooms, along with process data. | Innovative teaching processes that meet the needs of students are implemented to the delight of teachers, parents, and students. Information is analyzed and used to prevent student failure. Contributing causes are known through analyses. Problems are prevented through the use of data. |
| **Outcome** | Only anecdotal and hypothetical information are available about student performance, behavior, and satisfaction. Problems are solved individually with short-term results. | Little data are available. Change is limited to some areas of the school and dependent upon individual teachers and their efforts. | Information collected about student and parent needs, assessments, and instructional practices is shared with the school staff and used to plan for change. Information helps staff understand pressing issues, analyze information for "contributing causes," and track results for improvement. | A comprehensive information system is in place. Positive trends begin to appear in many classrooms and schoolwide. There is evidence that these results are caused by understanding and effectively using data, systemwide. | Students are delighted with the school's instructional processes and proud of their own capabilities to learn and assess their own growth. Good to excellent achievement is the result for all students. No student falls through the cracks. Teachers use data to predict and prevent potential problems, and optimize their results. |

*Updated 2013*

*Education for the Future Initiative, Chico, CA (http://eff.csuchico.edu).*

## Continuous Improvement Continuums for Schools
## STUDENT ACHIEVEMENT

| | One | Two | Three | Four | Five |
|---|---|---|---|---|---|
| **Approach** | Instructional and organizational processes critical to student success are not identified. Little distinction of student learning differences is made. Some teachers believe that not all students can achieve. | Some data are collected on student background and performance trends. Learning gaps are noted to direct improvement of instruction. It is known that student learning standards must be used to guide instruction and learning. | A shared vision is created. Each staff agree and commit to what they are going to teach, how they are going to teach, how they will assess, and how they and students will treat each other and students (teachers). Student learning standards are identified for implementation, and a continuum of learning is created throughout the school. Student performance data are collected and compared to the standards in order to analyze how to improve learning for all students. | Data on student achievement and the achievement of student learning standards are used throughout the school to pursue the improvement of student learning. Teachers collaborate to implement appropriate instruction and assessment strategies for meeting student learning standards articulated across grade levels. All teachers believe that all students can learn. | School makes an effort to exceed student achievement expectations. Innovative instructional changes are made to anticipate learning needs and improve student achievement. Teachers are able to predict characteristics impacting student achievement and to know how to perform from a small set of internal quality measures. |
| **Implementation** | All students are taught the same way. There is no communication with students about their academic needs or learning styles. There are no analyses of how to improve instruction. | Some effort is made to track and analyze student achievement trends on a schoolwide basis. Teachers begin to understand the needs and learning gaps of students. | Teachers commit to effective instruction and assessment strategies to implement standards and to increase their students' learning. Student feedback and analysis of achievement data are used in conjunction with implementation support strategies, such as lesson study and demonstration lessons. | There is a systematic focus on implementing student learning standards and on the improvement of student learning schoolwide. Effective instruction and assessment strategies are implemented in each classroom. Teachers support one another with peer coaching, lesson study, and/or action research focused on implementing strategies that lead to increased achievement and the attainment of the shared vision. | All teachers correlate critical instructional and assessment strategies with objective indicators of quality student achievement. A comparative analysis of actual individual student performance to student learning standards is utilized to adjust teaching strategies to ensure a progression of learning for all students. |
| **Outcome** | There is wide variation in student attitudes and achievement with undesirable results. There is high dissatisfaction among students with learning. Student background is used as an excuse for low student achievement. | There is some evidence that student achievement trends are available to teachers and are being used. There is much effort, but minimal observable results in improving student achievement. | There is an increase in communication between students and teachers, and teachers and teachers, regarding student learning. Teachers learn about effective instructional strategies that will implement the shared vision, student learning standards, and meet the needs of their students. They make some gains. | Increased student achievement is evident schoolwide. Student morale, attendance, and behavior are good. Teacher morale is high. Teachers converse often with each other about preventing student failure. Areas for further attention are clear. | Students and teachers conduct self-assessments to continuously improve performance. Improvements in student achievement are evident and clearly caused by teachers' and students' understandings of individual student learning standards, linked to appropriate and effective instructional and assessment strategies. A continuum of learning results. No students fall through the cracks. |

*Updated 2013*

# Continuous Improvement Continuums for Schools
## QUALITY PLANNING

*Updated 2013*

| | One | Two | Three | Four | Five |
|---|---|---|---|---|---|
| **Approach** | No quality plan or process exists. Data are neither used nor considered important in planning. | The staff realize the importance of a mission, vision, and one comprehensive school plan; however, the current school improvement plan focuses on solving problems and closing gaps. | A comprehensive continuous school improvement plan to achieve the shared vision is developed. Plan includes evaluation and continuous improvement. | One focused and integrated continuous school improvement plan for implementing the shared vision is put into action. All school efforts are focused on the implementation of this plan that represents the achievement of the vision. | A plan for the continuous improvement of the school, with a focus on students, is put into place. There is excellent articulation and integration of all elements in the school due to quality planning. Leadership team ensures all elements are implemented by all appropriate parties. |
| **Implementation** | There is no knowledge of or direction for quality planning. Budget is allocated on an as-needed basis. Many plans exist. | School community begins continuous school improvement planning efforts by laying out major steps to create a shared vision, and implementing student learning standards. | Implementation goals, responsibilities, due dates, and timelines are spelled out in the comprehensive continuous school improvement plan to implement the shared vision. Support structures to implement the vision, such as teams, for implementing the plan are set in place. | The continuous school improvement plan is implemented through effective procedures in all areas of the school. Everyone commits to implementing the plan aligned to the vision, mission, and values and beliefs. All share responsibility for accomplishing school goals. | Schoolwide goals, mission, vision, and student learning standards are shared and articulated throughout the school and with feeder schools. The attainment of identified student learning standards is linked to planning and implementation of effective instruction and assessments that meet students' needs. Leaders at all levels are developing expertise because planning is the norm. |
| **Outcome** | There is no evidence of comprehensive planning. Staff work is carried out in isolation. A continuum of learning for students is absent. | The school community understands the benefits of working together to implement a comprehensive continuous school improvement plan. Current improvements are neither systematic nor integrated schoolwide. | There is evidence that the continuous school improvement plan is being implemented in some areas of the school. Schoolwide improvements are starting to show. | A continuous school improvement plan to implement the vision is known to all. Results from working toward the quality improvement goals are evident throughout the school. Planning is ongoing and inclusive of all stakeholders. | Evidence of effective teaching and learning results in significant improvement of student achievement attributed to continuous school improvement planning at all levels of the school organization. Teachers and administrators understand and share the school mission and vision. Quality planning is seamless and all demonstrate evidence of accountability. |

## Continuous Improvement Continuums for Schools
## LEADERSHIP

| | One | Two | Three | Four | Five |
|---|---|---|---|---|---|
| **Approach** | Principal as decision maker. Decisions are reactive to state, district, and federal mandates. There is no knowledge of continuous school improvement. | A shared decision-making structure is put into place and discussions begin on how to achieve a school vision. Most decisions are focused on solving problems and are reactive. | Leadership teams are created and committed to continuous school improvement. Leadership seeks inclusion of all school sectors and supports teams by making time provisions for their collaboration. | Leadership teams represent a true shared decision-making structure. All teams understand their roles and carry them out in the implementation of a comprehensive continuous school improvement plan. | A strong continuous school improvement structure is set into place that allows for input from all sectors of the school, district, and community, ensuring strong communication, flexibility, and refinement of approaches and beliefs. The school vision is student-learning focused, based on data, and appropriate for school/ community values, and meeting *all* student needs. |
| **Implementation** | Principal makes all decisions, with little or no input from teachers, the community, or students. Leadership inspects for mistakes. | The shared decision-making structure is implemented in some places and not others. Structure is mostly used to solve problems or close gaps. | School values and beliefs are identified; the purpose of school is defined; a school mission, vision, and student learning standards are agreed upon. A leadership structure for implementing approaches to achieving student learning standards and the shared vision is established. | Decisions about budget and implementation of the vision are made within teams, by the principal, by the leadership team, and by the full staff as appropriate. All decisions are communicated to the full staff. | The vision is implemented and articulated across all grade levels and into feeder schools. Quality standards are reinforced throughout the school. All members of the school community understand and apply the quality standards. Leadership team has systematic interactions and involvement with district administrators, teachers, parents, community, and students about the school's direction. Necessary resources are available to implement and measure staff learning related to student learning standards. |
| **Outcome** | Decision-making process is clear and known; however, decisions lack focus and consistency. There is no evidence of staff commitment to a shared vision. Students and parents do not feel they are being heard. | Quality leadership techniques are used sporadically. Critical areas for improvement are identified. | The mission provides a focus for all school improvement, and guides the action to the vision. The school community is committed to continuous school improvement. Faculty feel included in shared decision making. | There is evidence that the leadership team listens to all levels of the organization. Implementation of the continuous school improvement plan is linked to student learning standards and the shared vision. Leadership capacities for implementing the vision among teachers are evident. | Site-based management and shared decision making truly exists. Teachers understand and display an intimate knowledge of how the school operates. Teachers support and communicate with each other in the implementation of quality strategies. Teachers implement the vision in their classrooms and can determine how their new approach meets student needs and leads to the attainment of student learning standards. Leaders are standards-driven at all levels. Instructional coherence results. |

*Updated 2013*

# Continuous Improvement Continuums for Schools
## PROFESSIONAL LEARNING

| | One | Two | Three | Four | Five |
|---|---|---|---|---|---|
| **Approach** | There is no professional learning. Teachers, principals, and staff are seen as interchangeable parts that can be replaced. Professional learning is external and usually equated to attending a conference alone. Hierarchy determines "haves" and "have-nots." | The "cafeteria" approach to professional learning is used, whereby individual teachers choose what they want to take, without regard to an overall school plan, or vision. | The shared vision, school plan, and student needs are used to target focused professional learning for all employees. Staff is inserviced on relevant instructional, assessment, and leadership strategies. | Professional learning and data are used by all teachers and are directed toward the goals of the shared vision and the continuous improvement of the school. Teachers have ongoing conversations about student achievement data. Other staff members receive training in their content areas. Systems thinking is considered in all decisions. | Leadership and staff continuously improve all aspects of the learning organization through an innovative, data-informed, and comprehensive continuous school improvement process that prevents student failures. Effective job-embedded professional learning is ongoing for implementing the vision for student success. Teachers engage in collegial coaching and action research focused on student learning standards. Policies set professional learning as a priority budget line-item. Professional learning is planned, aligned, and leads to the achievement of student learning standards and the shared vision. |
| **Implementation** | Teacher, principal, and staff performance is controlled and inspected. Performance evaluations are used to detect mistakes. | Teacher professional learning is sporadic and unfocused, lacking an approach for implementing new procedures and processes. Some collaborative training begins to take place. | Teachers are involved in year-round quality professional learning. The school community is trained in shared decision making, team building concepts, effective communication protocols, and data analysis at the classroom level. | Teachers, in teams, continuously set and implement student achievement goals. Leadership considers these goals and provides necessary support structures for collaboration. Teachers utilize effective support approaches as they implement new instruction and assessment strategies. Coaching and feedback structures are in place. Use of new knowledge and skills is evident. | Teams passionately support each other in the pursuit of quality improvement at all levels. Teachers make bold changes in instruction and assessment strategies focused on student learning standards and student learning styles. Staffwide conversations focus on systemic reflection and improvement. Teachers are strong leaders. |
| **Outcome** | No professional growth and no staff or student performance improvement. There exists a high turnover rate of employees, especially administrators. Attitudes and approaches filter down to students. | The effectiveness of professional learning is not known or analyzed. Teachers feel helpless about making schoolwide changes. | Teachers, working in teams, feel supported and begin to feel they can make changes. Evidence shows that collaboration to improve student learning works. | A collegial school is evident. Effective classroom strategies are practiced, articulated schoolwide, are reflective of professional learning aimed at ensuring student achievement, and the implementation of the shared vision, that includes student learning standards. | True systemic change and improved student achievement result because teachers are knowledgeable of and implement effective, differentiated teaching strategies for individual student learning gains. Teachers' repertoire of skills are enhanced, and students are achieving. Professional learning is driving learning at all levels. |

*Education for the Future Initiative, Chico, CA (http://eff.csuchico.edu).*

*Updated 2013*

## Continuous Improvement Continuums for Schools
## PARTNERSHIP DEVELOPMENT

| | One | Two | Three | Four | Five |
|---|---|---|---|---|---|
| **Approach** | There is no system for input from parents, business, or community. Status quo is desired for managing the school. | Partnerships are sought, but mostly for money and things. | School has knowledge of why partnerships are important and seeks to include businesses and parents in a strategic fashion related to student learning standards for increased student learning. | School seeks effective win-win business and community partnerships and parent involvement to implement the vision. Desired outcomes are clearly identified. A solid plan for partnership development exists. | Community, parent, and business partnerships become integrated across all student groupings. The benefits of outside involvement are known by all. Parent and business involvement in student learning is refined. Student learning *regularly* takes place beyond the school walls. |
| **Implementation** | Barriers are erected to close out involvement of outsiders. Outsiders are managed for least impact on status quo. | A team is assigned to get partners and to receive input from parents, the community, and business in the school. | Involvement of business, community, and parents begins to take place in some classrooms and after school hours related to the vision. Partners begin to realize how they can support each other in achieving school goals. School staff understand what partners need from the partnership. | There is a systematic utilization of parents, community, and businesses schoolwide. Areas in which the active use of these partnerships benefit student learning are clear. | Partnership development is articulated across all student groupings. Parents, community, business, and educators work together in an innovative fashion to increase student learning and to prepare students for college and careers in the 21st Century. Partnerships are evaluated for continuous improvement. |
| **Outcome** | There is little or no involvement of parents, business, or community at-large. School is a closed, isolated system. | Much effort is given to establishing partnerships. Some spotty trends emerge, such as receiving donated equipment. | Some substantial gains are achieved in implementing partnerships. Some student achievement increases can be attributed to this involvement. | Gains in student satisfaction with learning and school are clearly related to partnerships. All partners benefit. | Previously non-achieving students enjoy learning with excellent achievement. Community, business, and home become common places for student learning, while school becomes a place where parents come for further education. Partnerships enhance what the school does for students. |

*Updated 2013*

## Continuous Improvement Continuums for Schools
# CONTINUOUS IMPROVEMENT AND EVALUATION

| | One | Two | Three | Four | Five |
|---|---|---|---|---|---|
| **Approach** | Neither goals nor strategies exist for the evaluation and continuous improvement of the school organization or for elements of the school organization. | The approach to continuous improvement and evaluation is problem solving. If there are no problems, or if solutions can be made quickly, there is no need for improvement or analyses. Changes in parts of the system are not coordinated with all other parts. | Some elements of the school organization are evaluated for effectiveness. Some elements are improved on the basis of the evaluation findings. | All elements of the school's operations are evaluated for improvement and to ensure congruence of the elements with respect to the continuum of learning students experience. | All aspects of the school organization are rigorously evaluated and improved on a continuous basis. Students, and the maintenance of a comprehensive learning continuum for students, become the focus of all aspects of the school improvement process. |
| **Implementation** | With no overall plan for evaluation and continuous improvement, strategies are changed by individual teachers and administrators only when something sparks the need to improve. Reactive decisions and activities are a daily mode of operation. | Isolated changes are made in some areas of the school organization in response to problem incidents. Changes are not preceded by comprehensive analyses, such as an understanding of the contributing causes of problems. The effectiveness of the elements of the school organization, or changes made to the elements, is not known. | Elements of the school organization are improved on the basis of comprehensive analyses of contributing causes of problems, client perceptions, and operational effectiveness of processes. | Continuous improvement analyses of student achievement and instructional strategies are rigorously reinforced within each classroom and across learning levels to develop a comprehensive learning continuum for students and to prevent student failure. | Comprehensive continuous improvement becomes the way of doing business at the school. Teachers continuously improve the appropriateness and effectiveness of instructional strategies based on student feedback and performance. All aspects of the school organization are improved to support teachers' efforts. |
| **Outcome** | Individuals struggle with system failure. Finger pointing and blaming others for failure occurs. The effectiveness of strategies is not known. Mistakes are repeated. | Problems are solved only temporarily and few positive changes result. Additionally, unintended and undesirable consequences often appear in other parts of the system. Many aspects of the school are incongruent, keeping the school from reaching its vision. | Evidence of effective improvement strategies is observable. Positive changes are made and maintained due to comprehensive data and process analyses and evaluation. | Teachers become astute at assessing and in predicting the impact of their instructional strategies on individual student achievement. Sustainable improvements in student achievement are evident at all grade levels, due to continuous improvement. | The school becomes a congruent and effective learning organization. Only instruction and assessment strategies that produce quality student achievement are used. A true continuum of learning results for all students and staff. The impact of improvements is increasingly measurable. |

*Updated 2013*

# DEMOGRAPHIC DATA INVENTORY

**Purpose** The purpose of the *Demographic Data Inventory* is to guide schools in gathering demographic data, and/or making their collection of demographic data robust, relevant, clean, consistent, and known.

**Target Audience** Data Leadership Team, person/people responsible for entering data in the student information system, administrators.

**Time** Completing the inventory can be done in less than an hour by someone who knows what data are available. Determining what data you want to gather that are not being gathered may take longer. Pulling the data together into a data profile may take quite some time depending on the student information system the school/district is using.

**Materials** Copy of demographic inventory.

## Overview

The *Demographic Data Inventory* helps staff think about what data are available, and what data they want to have available. These data should describe the school completely, as well as provide complete information about programs. For example, a behavior program would need to contain the who, what, when, and where of behavior incidents. Beginning on the next page are the most common demographics used in schools. This is not a list to say you should have everything. It is a list to jog your thinking about potential demographic data that could support your continuous school improvement efforts.

## Process Protocol

Steps in establishing a *Demographic Data Inventory* include:

Step 1. Determine who in your school will complete the inventory.

Step 2. Have the inventory completers indicate all the demographic data that are currently available.

Work with staff to determine what other demographic data would be helpful, and how the school will get consistency in gathering, analyzing, and using its demographic data.

## Comments to the Facilitator

After the *Demographic Data Inventory* is completed, begin graphing and organizing the data into a data profile for staff use. Make sure the final list of demographic data will help teachers and administrators know how students are doing with respect to the things that influence how the students experience school.

Figure B1–1

| DEMOGRAPHIC DATA INVENTORY (Possible Demographic Data to Gather) | | | |
|---|---|---|---|
| **Demographic Data** | Where Does This Info Reside? | Number of Years of Data Available | Number of Years of Data Desired |
| **Community (Descriptive)**<br>• Location and history<br>• Economic base, population trends, and community resources (www.census.gov is a great resource for getting information about the community, as is your local chamber of commerce)<br>• Community involvement<br>• Business partnership | | | |
| **School District (Descriptive)**<br>• Description and history<br>• Number of schools, administrators, students and teachers over time, and by grade level | | | |
| **School (Descriptive)**<br>• Description and history, attendance area, location<br>• Type of school, e.g., magnet, alternative, charter, private, private management<br>• Number of administrators, students and teachers over time, and by grade level<br>• Number of students electing to come to the school from out of the attendance area<br>• Grants and awards received<br>• Title 1/Schoolwide<br>• Safety/crime data<br>• State designation as a dangerous school<br>• Class sizes<br>• Extracurricular activities<br>• After-school programs/summer school<br>• Tutoring/peer mentoring<br>• Community support-services coordinated<br>• Counseling opportunities<br>• Facilities: equipped for networked computers and handicapped<br>• Facilities: age, capacity, maintenance<br>• Availability of supplies and necessities<br>• Uniqueness and strengths | | | |
| **Students, Over Time, and by Grade Level**<br>• Living situation/family structure/family size/homeless<br>• Preschool/Head Start/Even Start<br>• Preschool attendance<br>• Gender of students<br>• Race/ethnicity, numbers and percentages<br>• Free/reduced lunch, numbers and percentages<br>• Language fluency by language<br>• Migrant/immigrants, by country, home languages | | | |

Figure B1–1 *(Continued)*

| DEMOGRAPHIC DATA INVENTORY (Possible Demographic Data to Gather) | | | |
|---|---|---|---|
| **Demographic Data** | Where Does This Info Reside? | Number of Years of Data Available | Number of Years of Data Desired |
| **Students, Over Time, and by Grade Level (Continued)**<br>• Special Education by disability, gender, ethnicity, language fluency, free/reduced lunch<br>• Attendance/tardies<br>• Mobility (where students go/come from)<br>• Retention rates by gender, ethnicity, language fluency, free/reduced lunch<br>• Dropout rates by gender, ethnicity, free/reduced lunch, migrant, and special education (where students go/what they do)<br>• Number of students leaving middle school overall for grade, by gender, ethnicity, language fluency, free/reduced lunch<br>• Extracurricular activity participation/clubs/service learning by gender, ethnicity, language fluency, free/reduced lunch<br>• Number and types of participants in programs, such as AP, IB, Honors, Upward Bound, Gear-up, college-prep, vocational<br>• Number and types of participants in any programs<br>• Number of home schoolers associated with school<br>• Number of students electing to come to the school from out-of-attendance area<br>• Number of bus riders<br>• Student employment<br>• Discipline indicators (e.g., suspensions, referrals, types of incidences, number of students carrying weapons on school property, who, what, when, where)<br>• Number of drugs on school property (offered, sold, or given drugs)<br>• Graduation rates by gender, ethnicity, language proficiency, free/reduced lunch, migrant, and special education (where students go/what they do)<br>• Dropout rates, by gender, ethnicity, language proficiency, free/reduced lunch, migrant, and special education (where students go/what they do/how many come back to finish)<br>• Number of students concurrently enrolled in college courses<br>• Number of students meeting college course entrance requirements, by gender, ethnicity, language fluency, free/reduced lunch<br>• Number of scholarships, by gender, ethnicity, language fluency, free/reduced lunch<br>• Number of students completing GEDs<br>• Adult education program<br>• Number and percentage of students going on to college; postgraduate training; and/or employment<br>• Grade-point average in college<br>• Number of graduates enrolled in college remedial classes | | | |

**Figure B1–1** *(Continued)*

| DEMOGRAPHIC DATA INVENTORY (Possible Demographic Data to Gather) | | | |
|---|---|---|---|
| **Demographic Data** | **Where Does This Info Reside?** | **Number of Years of Data Available** | **Number of Years of Data Desired** |
| **Staff Over Time**<br>• Number of teachers, administrators, instructional specialists, support staff by assignments<br>• Grade/subjects teachers are teaching<br>• Years of experience, by grade level and/or role, in this school/in teaching<br>• Ethnicity, gender, languages spoken<br>• Retirement projections<br>• Types of certifications/licenses/teacher qualifications/ percentage of time teaching in certified area(s)<br>• National Board for Professional Teaching Standards (NBPTS) teachers<br>• Degrees<br>• Educational training of paraprofessionals<br>• Teacher-student ratios by grade level<br>• Teacher turnover rates<br>• Attendance rates<br>• Teacher involvement in extracurricular activities, program participation<br>• Number of teachers receiving high-quality professional development that impact classroom performance | | | |
| **Parents**<br>• Educational levels, home language, employment, socioeconomic status<br>• Involvement with their child's learning<br>• Involvement in school activities<br>• Incarceration | | | |
| **Other Demographic Data** | | | |

# PERCEPTIONS DATA INVENTORY

B2

APPENDIX

**Purpose** The purpose of the *Perceptions Data Inventory* is for a school to take stock of the perceptions data being gathered across grade levels and subject areas, and to get agreement and consistency on gathering perceptions throughout the school.

**Target Audience** Teachers, program directors.

**Time** Completing the inventory can probably be done in less than an hour. Determining improvements will take longer.

**Materials** Copies of data inventories.

## Overview

Not every teacher knows what perceptions data are being collected from other teachers, administrators, and program directors, or how the data are being used. The perceptions data inventory helps all teachers know who is asking common students, parents, staff, and partners information as well as the variety of information available. Some efforts can be merged; some subjects might need additional perceptions data.

## Process Protocol

Steps in establishing a *Perceptions Data Inventory* include:

Step 1. Determine how your school will complete the inventory. Perhaps, by grade-level teams.

Step 2. Have the inventory completers list the names of all the perceptions data they are currently using, the purpose of the survey, grade levels targeted, the number of people expected to be reached, dates of collection, and then comments about each perception result uses.

Step 3. In grade-level teams, and then ultimately cross-grade level teams, determine where there are overlaps in asking for perceptions, where the efforts can be streamlined, what other perceptions data would be helpful, and how the school will get consistency with its perceptions data.

## Comments to the Facilitator

After the *Perceptions Data Inventory* is completed, make sure staff determine the appropriate administration and use perception data in each subject area and grade level. Some requests for perceptions responses might need to be discontinued because they are not fulfilling a need, or another request is fulfilling that need. Make sure the final list of perceptions data will help teachers know what it is they want and need to know. Integrate the findings into the data profile.

Figure B2-1
PERCEPTIONS DATA INVENTORY

| QUESTIONNAIRE OR OTHER FORMAT | PURPOSE/INTENT | GRADE LEVEL(S) | NUMBER BEING REACHED | | | | DATE(S) GIVEN | COMMENTS |
|---|---|---|---|---|---|---|---|---|
| | | | Students | Staff | Parents | Other | | |
| | | | | | | | | |
| | | | | | | | | |
| | | | | | | | | |
| | | | | | | | | |
| | | | | | | | | |
| | | | | | | | | |
| | | | | | | | | |
| | | | | | | | | |
| | | | | | | | | |
| | | | | | | | | |
| | | | | | | | | |
| | | | | | | | | |

# STUDENT LEARNING
# DATA INVENTORY

**B3**

APPENDIX

| | |
|---|---|
| **Purpose** | The purpose of the *Student Learning Data Inventory* is for a school/district to take stock of the assessments being used across grade levels and subject areas, and to make the inventory of assessments robust and consistent across grade levels. |
| **Target Audience** | Teachers, Testing Coordinators. |
| **Time** | Completing the inventory can probably be done in an hour. Determining improvements may be done in grade-level or subject-area meetings and then shared. |
| **Materials** | Copies of assessment inventories. |

## Overview

Even though formative assessments, and assessments imbedded in learning are used throughout schools, not every teacher knows what assessments other teachers are using, or even how the assessments they are using should be used. The assessment inventory helps all teachers know the variety of information available. Some subjects might need additional assessments. All assessments need to be used as intended. The most common types of assessments are described below.

*Types of Assessments*

- *Screening* involves brief assessments that are valid, reliable, and evidence-based. They are conducted with all students or targeted groups of students to identify students who are at risk of academic failure and, therefore, likely to need additional or alternative forms of instruction to supplement the conventional general education approach.

- *Assessments for Learning* are in-class measures, usually given frequently, to determine student success with the curriculum and for teachers to determine what additional or modified instruction is needed. These assessments are embedded in the curriculum or created by teachers as common short assessments with specific scoring criteria.

- *Progress Monitoring* assessments provide teachers with the information needed to regroup students for leveled/tiered instruction or remediation after a major segment of instruction. They allow a teacher to track students in a specific skill area or could be more general tests of grade level curricula. Progress monitoring is conducted at least monthly to (a) estimate rates of improvement, (b) identify students who are not demonstrating adequate progress, and/or (c) compare the efficacy of different forms of instruction to design more effective, individualized instruction.

- *Summative* assessments provide a bottom line of learning as related to established grade level standards. Most summative assessments are given yearly or pre-and post during a year. Summative assessments are developed and scored in ways that ensure reliability and validity, and may be norm or criterion referenced. Summative or outcome assessments are used for student screening, accountability, or pre-post measures of a major program.

## Process Protocol

How this inventory gets completed is less important than getting it completed, sharing it with staff, and then implementing a comprehensive assessment system that will help teachers and students know what students need to learn to enable mastery of student learning standards. Steps in establishing an assessment inventory include:

Step 1. Determine how your school will complete the inventory. Perhaps, by grade-level teams.

Step 2. Have the inventory completers list the names of all the assessments they are currently using, their targeted assessment area, dates of collection and length of assessment, grade level, who has access to the results, the uses for the assessment, and then comments about each assessment's uses.

Step 3. In grade-level teams, and then ultimately across grade level teams, determine where there are gaps in assessments, where the efforts can be streamlined, what other assessments would be helpful, and how the school will get consistency with the assessments.

## Comments to the Facilitator

After the *Student Learning Data Inventory* is completed, make sure staff determine the appropriate assessments to use in each subject area and grade level. Some assessments might need to be discontinued because they are not fulfilling a need. Make sure the final list of assessments will help teachers know how students are achieving with respect to standards, and if the curriculum and instructional strategies are meeting the needs of the students.

Create a *Student Learning Data Inventory* for each applicable subject (i.e., Mathematics, English Language Arts, Science, Social Studies, Other Assessments). Analyze the data to integrate into the data profile.

Figure B3-1
ASSESSMENT INVENTORY

SUBJECT:

| ASSESSMENT NAME (e.g., MAP) | TARGETED ASSESSMENT AREA (e.g., Math: Fractions) | DATES OF COLLECTION AND LENGTH OF ASSESSMENT (e.g., date or number of times administered, for how long) | GRADE LEVEL(S) | WHO HAS ACCESS TO RESULTS | USES — Screening | USES — Diagnostics | USES — Instruction-Imbedded | USES — Progress Monitoring | USES — Summative | COMMENTS |
|---|---|---|---|---|---|---|---|---|---|---|
| | | | | | | | | | | |
| | | | | | | | | | | |
| | | | | | | | | | | |
| | | | | | | | | | | |
| | | | | | | | | | | |
| | | | | | | | | | | |
| | | | | | | | | | | |
| | | | | | | | | | | |

# SCHOOL PROCESSES DATA INVENTORY

| Purpose | The purpose of the *School Processes Data Inventory* is for a school to take stock of the programs and processes being used across grade levels and subject areas, to eliminate overlap and ineffective processes, and to solidify programs and processes that need to be implemented throughout the school. |

**Target Audience**  Teachers and administrators.

**Time**  Completing the inventory will probably take a couple of hours. Determining improvements will take longer, depending upon how much consistency is currently in your school.

**Materials**  Copies of *School Processes Data Inventory*.

## Overview

The *School Processes Data Inventory* helps all teachers know the variety of programs and processes being implemented (as well as not implemented) in a school. There are some programs and processes that everyone should be implementing. This inventory will reinforce the implementation of the programs and processes that need to be implemented throughout the school.

There are four types of processes to consider, as well as programs:

 ◆ **Instructional**—the techniques and strategies that teachers use in the learning environment.

 ◆ **Organizational**—those structures the school puts in place to implement the vision.

 ◆ **Administrative**—elements about schooling that we count, such as class sizes.

 ◆ **Continuous School Improvement**—the structures and elements that help schools continuously improve their systems.

Programs are school processes too. Programs are planned series of activities and processes, with specific goals. See the lists of example processes and programs in Figure B4-1.

Figure B4-1
SCHOOL PROCESSES EXAMPLES

| Instructional Processes | Organizational Processes | Administrative Processes | Continuous School Improvement Processes | Programs |
|---|---|---|---|---|
| • Curriculum (what we teach)<br>• Instructional Strategies (how we teach)<br>• Assessments (how we know students are learning what we teach)<br>• Differentiated Instruction<br>• Direct Instruction<br>• Flipped Classrooms<br>• Grading<br>• Homework<br>• Immersion<br>• Academic conversations with students<br>• Classroom discussions (teacher talk, student-to student talk, student-to teacher talk)<br>• Classroom assignments (types of tasks, choices, projects, collaboration)<br>• Inquiry process<br>• Student reflection and self-assessment<br>• Standards Implementation<br>• Technology Integration<br>• Tutoring | • Teacher Collaboration<br>• Data Teams<br>• Data Use<br>• Leadership Structure (Leadership Teams)<br>• Professional Learning Communities<br>• Response to Intervention (RtI)<br>• Mentoring<br>• Instructional Coaching<br>• Referral Process<br>• Policies and Procedures<br>• Parent Involvement<br>• Teacher Hiring<br>• Teaching Assignments<br>• Teacher renewal (professional learning)<br>• Professional reflection<br>• Teacher evaluation<br>• Inquiry process<br>• Problem-solving<br>• Professional discussions and support<br>• Teacher observations<br>• Mission<br>• Vision | • Scheduling of classes<br>• Class sizes<br>• Discipline strategies<br>• Student groupings<br>• Policies and procedures<br>• Enrollment in different courses/programs/program offerings<br>• Retentions<br>• Attendance Program<br>• Dropout rates<br>• Graduation rates<br>• Teacher hiring<br>• Teacher assignments<br>• Teacher certification<br>• Teacher turnover rates<br>• Leadership turnover rates<br>• Number of support personnel<br>• Data collection | • Data analysis and use<br>• Contributing cause analysis<br>• Vision<br>• Mission<br>• Continuous school improvement planning<br>• Leadership<br>• Professional learning<br>• Partnership<br>• Evaluation<br>• Self-assessment | • AVID<br>• A+<br>• Accelerated Reader/Math<br>• Advanced Placement<br>• After School<br>• Advanced Placement<br>• At-Risk<br>• Bilingual<br>• Dropout Prevention<br>• Gifted and Talented<br>• International Baccalaureate<br>• Interventions<br>• 9th Grade Academy<br>• Science Fairs<br>• Service Learning<br>• Special Education |

## Process Protocol

A recommended process for completing the *School Processes Data Inventory* is described below.

**Step 1.** Determine how your school will complete the inventory. Perhaps by assigning a school process category to small meaningful groups.

**Step 2.** Have the groups make lists of all programs and processes in the different categories, using the school processes data inventory.

**Step 3.** Have each team share their list and have staff add more to the lists.

**Step 4.** In grade-level teams, and then ultimately cross grade-level teams, determine where there are gaps in instructional processes and programs, where the efforts can be streamlined, what other programs would be helpful, and how the school can get consistency.

**Step 5.** Determine which school processes will be described in the *Measuring Programs and Processes Table*, and who will do the work.

## Comments to the Facilitator

After the inventory of school processes is completed, make sure staff determine the appropriate programs and processes to use in each subject area and grade level. Some programs and processes might need to be discontinued because they are not fulfilling a need (Figure B4-2). Make sure the final list of school processes will help teachers know how students are achieving with respect to standards, and if the curriculum and instructional strategies are meeting the needs of the students.

Follow through by completing the *Measuring Programs and Processes Table*, for each school process (Appendix D).

Figure B4-2
SCHOOL PROCESSES INVENTORY

| Instructional Processes | Organizational Processes | Administrative Processes | Continuous School Improvement Processes | Programs | |
| --- | --- | --- | --- | --- | --- |
| | | | | Name | Grade Level |
| | | | | | |

# GETTING TO PERCEPTIONS THROUGH QUESTIONNAIRES

One of the four types of data that schools will want to gather, analyze, and use is *Perceptions* data, gathered through the use of questionnaires. Questionnaires are an excellent way to determine student, staff, parent, and alumni perceptions. The overall process for developing, administering, analyzing, and using the results is outlined in the graphic below. The attached activities show the processes for:

- ◆ *Designing Questionnaires*
- ◆ *Administering Questionnaires*
- ◆ *Analyzing Questionnaire Results*
- ◆ *Analyzing Open-Ended Responses*
- ◆ *Presenting and Using Questionnaire Results*

**QUESTIONNAIRE PROCESS
OVERVIEW**

**DETERMINE PURPOSE:**
What do you want to learn? How do
you want to use the results in conjunction with
your continuous school improvement plan?

↓

**DETERMINE CONTENT:**
What content is desired
and from whom?

↓

**DEVELOP INSTRUMENT AND PILOT:**
Create instrument, pilot, and revise
as necessary. Is the questionnaire
working the way you want it to work?

↓

**COLLECT THE DATA:**
How will the questionnaire
be administered and when?

↓

**ANALYZE RESULTS:**
How can the results be analyzed to
show the information gleaned
from the questionnaire?

↓

**REPORT RESULTS:**
How can the data be graphed and
reported to effectively show the results?

↓

**SHARE AND REVIEW RESULTS:**
How and when are you going to
share results with stakeholders?

↓

**USE RESULTS:**
How can you use the results
for continuous school improvement?

| Purpose | The purpose of the *Perceptions Data Inventory* is for a school to take stock of the perceptions data being gathered across grade levels and subject areas, and to get agreement and consistency on gathering perceptions throughout the school. |
|---|---|
| Target Audience | Teachers, program directors. |
| Time | Completing the inventory can probably be done in less than an hour. Determining improvements will take longer. |
| Materials | Copies of data inventories. |

## Overview

Not every teacher knows what perceptions data are being collected from other teachers, administrators, and program directors, or how the data are being used. The perceptions data inventory helps all teachers know who is asking common students, parents, staff, and partners information as well as the variety of information available. Some efforts can be merged; some subjects might need additional perceptions data.

## Process Protocol

Steps in establishing a *Perceptions Data Inventory* include:

Step 1: Determine how your school will complete the inventory. Perhaps, by grade-level teams.

Step 2: Have the inventory completers list the names of all the perceptions data they are currently using, the purpose of the survey, grade levels targeted, the number of people expected to be reached, dates of collection, and then comments about each perception result uses.

Step 3: In grade-level teams, and then ultimately cross-grade level teams, determine where there are overlaps in asking for perceptions, where the efforts can be streamlined, what other perceptions data would be helpful, and how the school will get consistency with its perceptions data.

## Comments to the Facilitator

After the *Perceptions Data Inventory* is completed, make sure staff determine the appropriate administration and use perception data in each subject area and grade level. Some requests for perceptions responses might need to be discontinued because they are not fulfilling a need, or another request is fulfilling that need. Make sure the final list of perceptions data will help teachers know what it is they want and need to know. Integrate the findings into the data profile.

# DESIGNING QUESTIONNAIRES

| | |
|---|---|
| **Purpose** | The purpose of this activity is to lay out the steps in designing a questionnaire. |
| **Target Audience** | Committee, who will take the draft product to staff for review and approval. |
| **Time** | It will take at least a week of solid work for a committee to design questionnaires. The draft questionnaire will then need to be reviewed by staff, rewritten and reviewed again until the questionnaire contains all that staff want it to contain. |
| **Materials** | Paper and pens, or computer and projector, examples of other questionnaires. |

Good questionnaires have the following features:

## Overview

♦ A strong purpose so participants will want to complete the questionnaire.

♦ Short and to the point (both questions and questionnaire).

♦ Questions that everyone can understand in the same way.

♦ Questions that proceed from general statements to more specific statements.

♦ Response options that make sense for the questions.

Whatever type of questionnaire you decide to use for data gathering, the questionnaire must be based upon the underlying assumption that the respondents will give truthful answers. To this end, you must ask questions that are—

♦ valid—ask the right questions.

♦ reliable—will result in the same answers if given more than once.

♦ understandable—respondents know what you are asking.

♦ quick to complete—brain-compatible, designed well, and short.

♦ able to get the first response from the respondent—quality administration and setup.

♦ justifiable—based on a solid foundation.

**Figure C1–1**

**QUESTIONNAIRE PROCESS OVERVIEW**

**DETERMINE PURPOSE:**
What do you want to learn? How do you want to use the results in conjunction with your continuous school improvement plan?

**DETERMINE CONTENT:**
What content is desired and from whom?

**DEVELOP INSTRUMENT AND PILOT:**
Create instrument, pilot, and revise as necessary. Is the questionnaire working the way you want it to work?

**COLLECT THE DATA:**
How will the questionnaire be administered and when?

**ANALYZE RESULTS:**
How can the results be analyzed to show the information gleaned from the questionnaire?

**REPORT RESULTS:**
How can the data be graphed and reported to effectively show the results?

**SHARE AND REVIEW RESULTS:**
How and when are you going to share results with stakeholders?

**USE RESULTS:**
How can you use the results for continuous school improvement?

## Process Protocol

**Step 1. Outline Content.** Begin by thinking about what you want to know and by pulling together concepts or key theories that you want to test through the questionnaire. For example, the *Education for the Future* student questionnaires were suggested by teachers who wanted this questionnaire to be about what they wanted their students to be able to say by the time they had implemented their vision—that they feel safe at school, have freedom, fun, and like school. Once you determine what you want to know, outline the key points and jot down ideas related to the key points. (See *Education for the Future* questionnaire resources:
> *http://eff.csuchico.edu/html/questionnaire_resources.html*)

**Step 2. Draft the Questions.** Look first for existing questionnaires. If there is no existing questionnaire to adapt, formulate questions that address issues based upon what you want to know. There are many different ways to ask questions. Figure C1-2, at the end of this activity, describes different types of questions, advantages and disadvantages for each type, and when it is appropriate to use each type of question. You can create forms that will allow you to use different types of questions; however, it is probably not wise to use more than two or three different types of questions in a form. The key to successful questionnaires is to make them interesting, easy, and quick to complete. Be sure to:

+ Ask purposeful questions—don't just ask questions for the sake of asking questions.
+ Make sure the questions will be interpreted the same way by many different people.

Think about the impact of every question on your respondents. *Will it offend anyone?* Hints in developing the questions are summarized below.

Helpful hints include—

+ Simple is best.
+ Phrase all questions positively. Movement up the scale indicates a more positive result; respondents will not be required to constantly reorient themselves as to how the question relates to the scale, and results can be analyzed and graphed.
+ Ask all questions in the same way (e.g., all positive so double negatives are not possible).
+ Keep items and the questions short (definitely less than 20 words).
+ Eliminate all jargon and bureaucratic wording.
+ Spell out abbreviations and acronyms.
+ Be sure that phrasing does not suggest a response.
+ Use a logical sequence in asking questions (general to specific).
+ Ask questions that everyone understands in the same way.
+ Make sure that, if necessary, your questions will allow you to disaggregate responses in your analyses.
+ List question first and response options second (left-to-right is brain-compatible for most of the world).
+ List response options from left (least positive) to right (most positive).

### Process Protocol *(Continued)*

Avoid—

♦ Trying to assess a little bit of everything.

♦ Conjunctions (and, or) in questions.

♦ Adverbs such as "sometimes," "nearly," and "always" in the questions—let the response options discriminate responses.

♦ Leading questions.

♦ Jumping around, content-wise.

♦ Showing response options first and then the question—you are asking respondents to skip a part of the process and then come back to it—not efficient.

♦ Asking the same question more than once.

Step 3.   **Determine the Scales.** Questionnaires are collections of items or questions intended to reveal levels of information not readily observable. Scales are used with items so responses can describe phenomena more specifically. Most questionnaires that utilize scales have a question or statement and then a series of response options. Those response options are types of scales. If you want to notice subtle differences in your analyses, you will want to use some sort of scale.

Many types of scales can be used with questionnaires. What type is used depends on the purpose of the questionnaire item and how the results will be used. General terms related to scales include *nominal, ordinal, interval,* and *ratio.*

If you want to notice subtle differences in your analyses, your item options will need to discriminate among responses. Consider these questions about the items you put together:

♦ How many response options does it take to discriminate meaningfully?

♦ How many response options will confuse or bore respondents?

♦ Presented with many response options, will respondents use only those responses that are multiples of five, for instance, reducing the number of options anyway?

There are several kinds of response options. The response option chosen depends upon the purpose for using the questionnaire and the types of questions desired. For the majority of questionnaires, five-point options are adequate. Possible labels include—

♦ *Endorsement:* strongly disagree, disagree, neutral, agree, strongly agree.

♦ *Frequency:* never, almost never, sometimes, very often, always.

♦ *Intensity:* really apprehensive, somewhat apprehensive, mixed feelings, somewhat excited, really excited.

♦ *Influence:* big problem, moderate problem, small problem, very small problem, no problem.

♦ *Comparison:* much less than others, less than others, about the same as others, more than others, much more than others; much worse than others, worse than others, no difference, better than others, much better than others.

## Process Protocol *(Continued)*

Each scale implies how it can be analyzed. Equal interval scales can be averaged. The others must be displayed as frequency distributions or summed in bar graphs. Please note that if more than one scale is used in a questionnaire, the results will need to be analyzed separately—in other words, questions with different scales will probably need to be graphed separately. An often-neglected, but very important, factor that must be taken into consideration when establishing a scale and format for a questionnaire is the age and attention span of the respondent. Young children do best with two or three response options—smiling faces versus frowning faces. Adults will not finish a questionnaire that requires over thirty minutes of their time.

The *Education for the Future* questionnaires utilize a five-point endorsement scale. Each item is presented as a declarative sentence, followed by response options that indicate varying degrees of agreement with the statement—from *strongly disagree* to *strongly agree*. The questionnaires go from *strongly disagree* to *strongly agree* because it is our opinion that this direction is left-to-right— the way our western brains work. That is also why our response options are to the right of the questions.

People often ask about the center option. They worry that most individuals will use the middle response option if it is made available. *Education for the Future's* experience with thousands of questionnaires shows that people do not automatically choose the middle response. If participants commit to responding to a questionnaire, they will typically respond with precision. When responses on a questionnaire do appear in the middle, the questionnaire constructor needs to examine the questions to determine if it is causing indecision, if the response option and the statement do not go well together, or if, indeed, the respondent does not have a definite response to the question. One of the first things to check is whether there is a conjunction or an adverb in the statement that would cause people to *say: Well, I agree with this part of the question, and I disagree with that part of the question.* Researchers often add the middle response to give respondents a legitimate response option for opinions that are divided or neutral, and to make the scale an equal interval scale. If you prefer to force your respondents to make a decision, you can always use an even-point scale that has no middle point. You will not be able to be average the responses if you do this because you will no longer have an equal interval scale. We add that middle-response option because we think it is a reasonable response option, and because it creates an interval scale giving us the ability to average. We want to graph all the item averages together to show relationships.

*Education for the Future* has piloted many different scales, including 100, 10, 7, 6, 5, 4, and 3-point scales. We ultimately and easily chose a 5-point scale. Any scale that had more than 5 points upset the respondents—it was too fine a distinction, too hard for participants to respond. Respondents give us less information and do not complete the questionnaire when they do not like the response options. The even-numbered scales did not allow us to average the responses. Averaging provides the easiest understanding of the relationship of the responses to each other. The even-numbered scales did not allow respondents to give a response that indicated half the time "yes" and half the time "no," or "just do not have an opinion at this time." The 3-point scale did not discriminate enough.

What about offering "don't know" or "not applicable" as a response option? Some researchers say that "don't know" does not affect the proportion of responses. Depending upon the question, a "not applicable" response might give you more information than getting no response. We tend to stay away from both these response options.

## Process Protocol *(Continued)*

**Step 4.** **Create the Form.** Appearance and arrangement of the questionnaire frequently determine whether respondents will complete it. In fact, research shows that individuals determine within five seconds whether or not they will respond to a questionnaire. Think about what would get you to psychologically commit to completing a questionnaire, and build in those same considerations for your respondents. The good news is that once respondents take the effort to read a questionnaire, they make a psychological commitment to complete it.

Upon first glance, we definitely want the questionnaire to be appealing to the eye. We want to have white space. We want to keep the questionnaire consistent. Never split questions, instructions, or the responses from the questions between pages. Use an easy-to-read, equally spaced font for the questions themselves. Avoid italics. Make the questionnaire look professional. We typically want to end the questionnaire by giving each respondent a chance to *comment on the topic* as a paper questionnaire. Figure C1-3 offers tips to consider when creating the paper form (as a paper questionnaire). Figure C1-4 offers tips to consider when writing and placing open-ended questions in a questionnaire. Take the time to make the appearance pleasing and the instructions clear to the respondent. Also, take the time to make the questionnaire brain-compatible. Written in a common sense, logical fashion like our western brains work, i.e., left-to-right, top-to-bottom.

**Step 5.** **Review and Revise Your Instrument.** Examine the content in relation to the other steps in the process: type of questions, scaling, respondents, the potential data analysis and presentation of results. Revise to the best of your abilities. Figure C1-5 describes design considerations for online questionnaires.

**Step 6.** **Pilot the Questionnaire.** No matter how many times you review the questionnaire after your construct it, you won't know how the questions will actually be interpreted until you administer them to a small number of respondents in your target group as a pilot test. We highly recommend piloting the questionnaire and analyzing the data to understand if you are asking questions that respondents understand and questions that provide responses that lead to your purpose. We also recommend piloting an already developed questionnaire that you might decide to use to make sure it is doing what you want it to do.

To pilot the questionnaire, you can use one of two approaches. One, organize a small group of respondents who are similar to the larger target group. Administer the questionnaire and analyze the results. Include questions on the pilot questionnaire to help you know if the pilot group understood everything on the questionnaire, if they thought the questions were relevant, if there are other questions they feel you should be asking, if they feel the questionnaire was easy to respond to, and to solicit their general overall comments. Another approach would be to administer the questionnaire individually to two or three people from each major demographic subgroup. Have each person read the items aloud, offer responses, and tell you orally what she/he thinks the question is asking, and what her/his responses mean. This is a very powerful information gatherer and quicker than traditional pilot tests. If you are going to use open-ended responses on your questionnaire, be sure to include them as part of the pilot.

**Step 7.** **Analyze Pilot Results.** After you have piloted the questionnaire, look at each of the questions with responses to see if each item was understandable. Look at the open-ended responses for clues to responses that may not seem logical. If respondents are available, ask them to tell you why particular questions were hard to understand.

## Process Protocol *(Continued)*

Step 8.   **Revise, Review Again, and Finalize.** After you study the responses from the pilot group, revise the questionnaire to reflect what you have learned. If you feel that the questions need to be piloted again, do so. It is much better to try out a questionnaire on a different, small group again than to administer a poor questionnaire to a large group. Have several people review the final version of the questionnaire to ensure there are no typographical errors and to ensure that the content flow is as you intend. When you feel that all of the bases have been covered, print the forms and post them online for the "real" questionnaire administration.

## Comments to the Facilitator

Creating a questionnaire can be an arduous task. Many people who want to design questionnaires often stop when it comes to writing the questions. It is definitely one of those tasks that looks much easier than it actually is. However, questionnaires provide us with valuable information that is well worth the effort.

## Figure C1–2

| Types of Questions | | | |
|---|---|---|---|
| **Types of Questions** | **Advantages** | **Disadvantages** | **Appropriate When—** |
| **Written**<br>*(Open-ended)*<br><br>Example:<br>*What do you like about this school?*<br>(Write your response in the space provided below.) | • Spontaneity of the response.<br>• Can understand what the respondent thinks.<br>• Can get deep into the topic. Can use to build multiple choice items.<br>• Sometimes respondents provide quotable material.<br>• Can ask all types of individuals, regardless of language differences. | • Must pay for someone's time to transcribe and synthesize.<br>• Takes time—on everyone's part.<br>• Coding can be unreliable.<br>• Cannot always read the response.<br>• Some handicapped people might have difficulty responding.<br>• Language translations are expensive.<br>• Difficult to interpret.<br>• Many people might have said the same thing with prompting.<br>• Difficult to categorize when taking frequencies of types of responses. | • Not sure about what respondents are thinking and feeling about a topic.<br>• Want to gain insight into the respondents' thinking.<br>• Are in the process of designing closed-ended questions.<br>• Want to supplement or better understand closed-ended responses. |
| **Multiple Choice**<br>*(Nominal, Closed-ended)*<br><br>Example:<br>Suppose you are a school board member. What is the most important concept you think the school should focus on to ensure well-prepared students?<br><br>(Circle the one response option below that best represents your position.)<br>1. Basic skills<br>2. Technology<br>3. Problem-solving skills<br>4. Lifelong learning<br>5. Collaborating with others | • Fast to complete.<br>• Respondents do not need to write.<br>• Relatively inexpensive.<br>• Easy to administer.<br>• Easy to score.<br>• Can compare groups and disaggregate easily.<br>• Responses can be scanned and interpreted easily. | • Unless one has thought through how the items will be scored and has the capabilities of scoring items mechanically before sending out the questionnaires, it can be expensive to do, time-consuming, and easy to make mistakes.<br>• Lose spontaneity.<br>• Don't always know what you have as results.<br>• Respondents are not always fond of these questions.<br>• Some respondents may resent the questioner's pre-selected choices.<br>• Multiple-choice questions are more difficult to write than open-ended.<br>• Can make the wrong assumption in analyzing the results when response options are not the same as what respondents are thinking. | • Want to make group comparisons.<br>• Know some of the responses that the sample is considering, and want to know which option they are leaning toward.<br>• Have large samples.<br>• Want to give respondents finite response choices. |
| **Ranking**<br>*(Ordinal, Closed-ended)*<br><br>Example:<br>*Why did you choose to enroll your child in this school?*<br>(Mark a 1 by the most important reason, 2 by the second most important reason, etc.)<br>• It is our neighborhood school<br>• Reputation as a quality school<br>• Know someone else who attends<br>• I went there when I was in elementary school<br>• My child needs more challenge<br>• My child needs more personal help | • Allows understanding of all reasons in priority order. | • More than seven response options will confuse respondents.<br>• May leave out important item response options.<br>• Relatively hard to analyze—you will know the number of respondents who rated item one as 1, etc. | • Want to know all responses in an order.<br>• Are clear on common response options.<br>• Do not want people to add to list. |

## Figure C1–2 *(Continued)*

| Types of Questions *(Continued)* | | | |
|---|---|---|---|
| **Types of Questions** | **Advantages** | **Disadvantages** | **Appropriate When—** |
| **Rating** *(Interval, Closed-ended)*<br><br>Example:<br>(Write your response in the space provided below.)<br><br>*I feel like I belong at this school.*<br><br>Strongly Disagree 1  Disagree 2  Neutral 3  Agree 4  Strongly Agree 5 | • Allows you to see the passion behind respondents' feelings, i.e., *Strongly Agree/Strongly Disagree.*<br>• Easy to administer.<br>• Easy to score.<br>• Can compare group responses.<br>• If an ordinal scale is created similar to the 5-point example, one can average the results.<br>• There are many ways one can analyze the results.<br>• Since there are usually only five options, frequencies of each response can be taken, along with the mode to determine most popular responses. | • Do not know if every respondent is reading the question and response options in the same way.<br>• Do not know what you have when *neutral* is circled—might be a bad question or the respondent doesn't care, or it might be a viable option.<br>• Unless one has thought through how the items will be scored and has the capability of scoring items mechanically before sending out the questionnaires, it can be expensive to do, time-consuming, and easy to make mistakes.<br>• Questions are more difficult to write than open-ended.<br>• If charted together, questions must be written so the desired responses fall in the same direction (in other words—all written positively). | • Want respondents to rate or order choices, such as: *strongly disagree* to *strongly agree,* or show passion.<br>• Want to make group comparisons.<br>• Have large samples.<br>• Want to understand where problems are in the organization. |
| **Yes – No** *(Closed-ended)*<br><br>Example:    Yes    No<br>*I like this school*    ☺    ☹ | • Very young children can answer questions with these response options.<br>• Very easy to score, analyze, and chart. | • Not sure how meaningful the data are.<br>• Responses do not give enough information. | • Want all or nothing responses.<br>• Have a sample that would have difficulty responding to more options. |
| **Nominal** *(Categorical)*<br><br>Example:<br>*I am–*<br>    Male    ○<br>    Female    ○ | • Factual: no value judgment.<br>• Useful for disaggregating other question responses.<br>• Lets you know if sample is representative of the total population. | • Some people will not respond to these types of questions.<br>• Some people respond falsely to these questions.<br>• With small groups, one might be able to identify the respondent on an anonymous questionnaire because of the demographic information given. | • Want to disaggregate data by male/female, ethnicity, program.<br>• Want to know the impact of a program on different types of individuals.<br>• Want to know if respondents resemble the population. |

## Figure C1–3

### Design Considerations for Multiple Choice Paper Questionnaires

The appearance and arrangement of the questionnaire frequently determine whether or not the respondents will complete it. Try to fit the questions and answers onto one page, if possible. You want the questionnaire to be quick to complete so that the respondent will answer all of the questions.

The majority of western respondents read from left to right. If the layout of the questions and responses is consistent with this pattern, it will increase the accuracy, and will be easier and faster for respondents to complete.

Placing response options close to the questions decreases the chance of error due to respondents mismatching lines.

If the questions are worded so that the answers fit into one scale, it will be easier for the respondent to complete and for you to analyze and graph later.

Make it obvious where respondents should make their mark.

A clear label shows respondents for whom the questionnaire is intended.

Begin with more general questions and lead up to the more specific.

Write instructions that tell your respondents what you would like them to do.

Leaving white space makes the questionnaire easier to read.

Do not use questions that have conjunctions. Use two separate questions instead.

Ask questions to address the issues that are based on what you want to know, and that cannot be gathered from other sources.

For evidence of school improvement, ask questions that you want to ask over time to see growth.

Think about the impact of every question on your respondent. Make sure the questions will not offend anyone.

Make the questions simple, short, and free of jargon/bureaucratic words.

Avoid:
- trying to assess a little of everything
- leading questions
- jumping around content-wise
- double negatives

*Education for the Future*

# Parents

*Please complete this form using a No. 2 pencil. Be sure to completely fill in the circle that describes best what you think or how you feel. Thank you!*

PLEASE USE NO. 2 PENCIL.
RIGHT · ▪ ▪ ▪   WRONG ⊘ ⊘ ⊙ ⊚

|  | Strongly Disagree | Disagree | Neutral | Agree | Strongly Agree |
|---|---|---|---|---|---|
| I feel welcome at my child's school | ① | ② | ③ | ④ | ⑤ |
| I am informed about my child's progress | ① | ② | ③ | ④ | ⑤ |
| I know what my child's teacher expects of my child | ① | ② | ③ | ④ | ⑤ |
| My child is safe at school | ① | ② | ③ | ④ | ⑤ |
| My child is safe going to and from school | ① | ② | ③ | ④ | ⑤ |
| There is adequate supervision during school | ① | ② | ③ | ④ | ⑤ |
| There is adequate supervision before and after school | ① | ② | ③ | ④ | ⑤ |
| Teachers show respect for the students | ① | ② | ③ | ④ | ⑤ |
| Students show respect for other students | ① | ② | ③ | ④ | ⑤ |
| The school meets the social needs of the students | ① | ② | ③ | ④ | ⑤ |
| The school meets the academic needs of the students | ① | ② | ③ | ④ | ⑤ |
| The school expects quality work of its students | ① | ② | ③ | ④ | ⑤ |
| The school has an excellent learning environment | ① | ② | ③ | ④ | ⑤ |
| I know how well my child is progressing in school | ① | ② | ③ | ④ | ⑤ |
| I like the school's report cards/progress report | ① | ② | ③ | ④ | ⑤ |
| I respect the school's teachers | ① | ② | ③ | ④ | ⑤ |
| I respect the school's principal | ① | ② | ③ | ④ | ⑤ |
| Overall, the school performs well academically | ① | ② | ③ | ④ | ⑤ |
| The school succeeds at preparing children for future work | ① | ② | ③ | ④ | ⑤ |
| The school has a good public image | ① | ② | ③ | ④ | ⑤ |
| The school's assessment practices are fair | ① | ② | ③ | ④ | ⑤ |
| My child's teacher helps me to help my child learn at home | ① | ② | ③ | ④ | ⑤ |
| I support my child's learning at home | ① | ② | ③ | ④ | ⑤ |
| I feel good about myself as a parent | ① | ② | ③ | ④ | ⑤ |

**Children's grades:**
○ Kindergarten
○ First Grade
○ Second Grade
○ Third Grade
○ Fourth Grade
○ Fifth Grade
○ Sixth Grade
○ Seventh Grade
○ Eighth Grade
○ Ninth Grade
○ Tenth Grade
○ Eleventh Grade
○ Twelfth Grade

**Number of children in this school:**
① ② ③ ④ ⑤ ⑥ ⑦ ⑧ ⑨

**My native language is:**
○ Chinese
○ Eastern European
○ English
○ Japanese
○ Korean
○ Spanish
○ Vietnamese
○ Other _____

**Number of children in the household:**
① ② ③ ④ ⑤ ⑥ ⑦ ⑧ ⑨

**Ethnic background:**
(fill in all that apply)
○ Black
○ American Indian
○ Asian
○ White
○ Hispanic/Latino
○ Other _____

**Responding:**
○ Mother
○ Father
○ Guardian
○ Other

Make sure that, however you wish to disaggregate the data later, the information is captured on the form.

In other words, if you want to know the difference between males and females on their responses to particular questions, ask your respondents their gender on the questionnaire.

## Figure C1–4

### Design Considerations for Open-ended Questions

Ask only two to three open-ended questions because of the length of time it takes respondents to reply and because of the difficulty of analyzing the responses. Open-ended questions usually appear at the end of the questionnaire. If all scannable items can be put on one page, place the open-ended on the back.

Place open-ended section at the end of the questionnaire.

Leave enough space for respondents to comment.

Do not use lines. Lines limit feedback. Do provide sufficient space for comments.

What are the strengths of your child's school?

What needs to be strengthened at your child's school?

## Figure C1–5

### Design Considerations for Online Questionnaires

In addition to the same considerations regarding the content of paper questionnaires, you will also want online questionnaires to be quick to complete and easy to navigate so that respondents will answer all of the questions.

Customize for the school and type of respondent.

Write a purpose for the questionnaire.

Write instructions that tell the respondents what you would like them to do.

Always thank respondents for taking the questionnaire.

When there is a stem, group few items together. When scrolling, respondents will forget the stem if more than 5 items are in a group.

Set up the questions so respondents read left-to-right. It is brain-compatible.

Do not use questions that have conjunctions. Use two separate questions instead.

If the questions are worded so that the answers fit into one scale, it will be easier for the respondents to complete and for you to analyze and graph later.

Make it obvious where respondents should make their mark.

---

(Name Here) **Middle School Staff Questionnaire**

This questionnaire is designed to gather general information about what staff members think and feel about the school and their relationship with the school.

In response to the questions asked below, please click on the button next to the answer that is closest to what you think or feel.

## Thank you!

| I feel: | Strongly Disagree | Disagree | Neutral | Agree | Strongly Agree |
|---|---|---|---|---|---|
| like I belong at this school | ○ | ○ | ○ | ○ | ○ |
| that the staff cares about me | ○ | ○ | ○ | ○ | ○ |
| that learning can be fun | ○ | ○ | ○ | ○ | ○ |
| that learning is fun at this school | ○ | ○ | ○ | ○ | ○ |

| I feel: | Strongly Disagree | Disagree | Neutral | Agree | Strongly Agree |
|---|---|---|---|---|---|
| recognized for good work | ○ | ○ | ○ | ○ | ○ |
| intrinsically rewarded for doing my job well | ○ | ○ | ○ | ○ | ○ |
| clear about what my job is at this school | ○ | ○ | ○ | ○ | ○ |
| that others are clear about what my job is at this school | ○ | ○ | ○ | ○ | ○ |

| I work with people who: | Strongly Disagree | Disagree | Neutral | Agree | Strongly Agree |
|---|---|---|---|---|---|
| treat me with respect | ○ | ○ | ○ | ○ | ○ |
| listen if I have ideas about doing things better | ○ | ○ | ○ | ○ | ○ |

## Figure C1–5 *(Continued)*

### Design Considerations for Online Questionnaires

If you want, you may add two to three open-ended questions to the questionnaire after the multiple-choice questions and before the demographic options.

> What are the strengths of this school?
>
> What needs to be improved?
>
> **DEMOGRAPHIC DATA**
> For each item, please select the description that applies to you.
> These demographic data are used for summary analyses;
> some descriptions will not be reported if groups are so small
> that individuals can be identified.

Do not use certain demographics if individuals can be identified (i.e., some demograhic groups might be so small they would identify individuals)

> **I am:**
> (fill in all that apply)
> ☐ African-American
> ☐ American Indian
> ☐ Asian
> ☐ Caucasian
> ☐ Hispanic/Latino
> ☐ Other
>
> **I am a(n):**
> ○ classroom teacher
> ○ instructional assistant
> ○ certificated staff (other than a classroom teacher)
> ○ classified staff (other than an instructional assistant)

Make sure that, however you wish to disaggregrate the data later, the information is captured on the form.

In other words, if you want to know the differences among grade levels on their responses to particular questions, ask your respondents the grade level they teach on the questionnaire.

> **I teach:**
> ○ pre K
> ○ primary grades
> ○ upper elementary grades
> ○ middle school grades
> ○ high school grades 9-10
> ○ high school grades 11-12
>
> **I have been teaching:**
> ○ 1-3 years
> ○ 4-6 years
> ○ 7-10 years
> ○ 11 or more years

*Reference:* Excerpts taken from from V.L. Bernhardt & B.J. Geise (2009). *Questions to Actions: Using Questionnaire Data for Continuous School Improvement.* Larchmont, NY: Eye On Education, Inc.

# C2 APPENDIX

# ADMINISTERING QUESTIONNAIRES

| | |
|---|---|
| **Purpose** | The purpose of this activity is to guide staff members in setting up the administration of questionnaires. |
| **Target Audience** | School staff are the target audience. However, a Leadership Team or Data Team can make the plans and take them back to the full staff for approval and implementation. |
| **Time** | Approximately two hours. |
| **Materials** | Computer and projector. |

## Overview

The most efficient and effective method of administering questionnaires is online through an Internet server. With online questionnaires, respondents visit a website that uses form submission web pages that funnel response data to a database or other container for data housed on a server. With online questionnaires, the data collection process is streamlined for a variety of reasons:

**Figure C2-1**

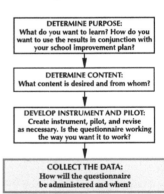

DETERMINE PURPOSE:
What do you want to learn? How do you want to use the results in conjunction with your school improvement plan?

DETERMINE CONTENT:
What content is desired and from whom?

DEVELOP INSTRUMENT AND PILOT:
Create instrument, pilot, and revise as necessary. Is the questionnaire working the way you want it to work?

COLLECT THE DATA:
How will the questionnaire be administered and when?

- ◆ Paper is eliminated, as are the administrative oversight and other costs associated with the use of paper.
- ◆ Most schools and districts already have the hardware and software necessary to administer online questionnaires.
- ◆ A district can administer questionnaires and monitor the entire process for all of its schools from a single location.
- ◆ Administrative oversight is minimal. Communication can take place through e-mail.
- ◆ Duplication of effort is minimized. Files set up for administering questionnaires can be used as templates for data collection and analysis, requiring minimal setup time especially when used with multiple schools.
- ◆ The costs associated with administering questionnaires depend less on the number of responses, as opposed to using scannable forms, hand-entry, or online methods. Receiving 50 or 500 responses online does not significantly impact time spent in analysis.
- ◆ Responses are converted to numeric data at the same time that they are submitted to the server. Results can be turned around as soon as the last respondent completes her/his submission.
- ◆ Questionnaires are administered within a controlled environment, such as a computer lab, to ensure that responses are valid.
- ◆ Checking the reliability of submissions is streamlined as responses are collected within a structured database environment. The responses are visually easy to check.
- ◆ Open-ended responses are collected in the server database and are easily exported to text documents. With paper, you must type each open-ended response to analyze and report the results.
- ◆ The technology and files used for online questionnaire administration can be retasked and used for other data collection projects.

## Process Protocol

### Steps in Setting Up a Data Collection Process

Step 1. **Communicate the purpose, procedures, and content to stakeholders well in advance.** In order for any data work to be successful, the purpose, procedures, and content must be clearly communicated to stakeholders well before data collection begins. Anticipating and answering all of the what, why, when, where, and how questions will go a long way toward helping you obtain a high response rate with honest responses.

When collecting data online, the easiest way to communicate about your questionnaire project is to set up a demonstration site on your server. The demonstration site can consist of a general information page that contains links to demo versions of each of the questionnaires that you will be administering. The general information page can contain information to satisfy the why and when, and the links to demonstration questionnaires can help satisfy the what, where, and how questions. The demonstration sites allow staff members to experience the online method to decrease anxiety about the use of technology, to review the content for each of the questionnaires that will be administered, and to visualize how the respondent groups will submit their responses.

Step 2. **Select the best time to administer questionnaires.** There is really no "best" time of year to administer questionnaires (when administering questionnaires that truly measure environmental perceptions). Significant differences are rarely seen in student and parent perception data that are collected in the Fall versus the Spring. It is more important that questionnaires be administered at generally the same time each year, every year.

If you choose to administer your questionnaires in the Fall, allow enough of the school calendar to pass so that respondents will have adequate experience with the school to inform their responses. If the school year starts in late August, you should not administer your questionnaires before mid October. If you choose to administer your questionnaires in the Spring, be careful not to overwhelm respondents during a time that is heavy with testing.

A key consideration in scheduling your parent questionnaire administration is determining when you are most likely to have parents onsite in large enough numbers that collecting their responses online becomes a viable option. For elementary schools, Fall parent-teacher conferences provide a great opportunity to collect parent responses because these conferences are usually the most highly attended parent-onsite activity of the year. We like to put the students in charge of ushering parents to the computer lab, getting them comfortable with the questionnaire process, and then escorting the parents to their conferences when finished with the questionnaire. For middle or high schools, parent-teacher conferences, curriculum nights, or even athletic/music/drama events might be considered as times to collect parent responses if the opportunity is well publicized.

Step 3. **Select the environment for administration.** A carefully selected environment for completing questionnaires can help facilitate a good return, honest responses, and can also provide facilitators to provide administrative oversight and assistance.

Staff members can submit their responses in a computer lab setting during a staff meeting; in short order, you have a 100% response rate. An e-mail link can be used for convenience, but then you won't know who did not respond and cannot follow-up with individuals to give them the opportunity to respond. Students and parents can submit their responses in a computer lab as well where large numbers can respond simultaneously, and facilitators can provide oversight and assistance as needed.

## Process Protocol *(Continued)*

Schedule staff questionnaire administration first. In submitting their responses, staff members will become familiar with the process of submitting responses and will be better able to organize and lead students through the process. When students submit their responses, they become equally familiar, and they are then available to help parents with the technology and language. If using scannable forms for parents, students are more likely to take parent questionnaires home and return the completed forms to staff in a timely manner after they have completed their own online submissions.

Step 4. **Establish a manageable schedule for administration.** With the impact of administration order in mind, use the school calendar to identify a target date for parents (during conferences); schedule students at least a week before parent conferences and staff at least a week before the student administration.

For school districts facilitating questionnaires for a large number of schools, the timeline for data collection should depend largely upon the amount of oversight and troubleshooting that can be provided by those facilitating data collection. Scheduling questionnaires for every school in a large district for the same week could seriously impact the ability to provide schools with needed oversight and assistance. If facilitators at the district level can effectively communicate with only five schools per week about their student questionnaires, and there are 20 schools in the district, schedule the administration of student questionnaires over a four-week period. Figure C2-2 on the next page is a sample questionnaire administration planning sheet.

Step 5. **Provide a narrow window of administration for each questionnaire.** Selecting a narrow window of administration will help focus your administrative and support efforts and allow you to respond to low response rates or other issues quickly. Opening questionnaire administration to a broad timeline usually decreases the ability to identify exactly who has responded and how to provide additional access or resources.

The window for administration depends largely upon the respondent pool. For students responding online, for instance, it is realistic to allocate a week for the collection of submissions, even at the high school level. Staff and parents may be isolated to a specific event, such as a staff meeting or a parent-teacher conference.

Step 6. **Provide additional language access.** Providing access to questionnaires in multiple languages can be facilitated online by providing respondents with the opportunity to select from a variety of pages that contain the same questionnaire in different languages. Each questionnaire page can be submitted to the same database or another resource on the server where the responses are converted to numeric data. For scannable forms, multiple versions of the same form can be produced for each language and, when scanned, can be combined into a single data file for analysis.

Producing the translated content should not be taken lightly. If care and consideration are not taken to acknowledge the colloquial or regional use of the language, the result may be that the process is more exclusive than inclusive.

A larger issue than translation can be access to the technology for data collection for second language groups. Respondents who require assistance with language may be more likely to require assistance in using the technology to submit their responses. A solution is to ask students or staffs who are able to address both the language and technology issues to facilitate questionnaires for respondents.

## Figure C2-2
## QUESTIONNAIRE INFORMATION PROJECT PLANNING AND TRACKING FORM

| District Name | Kelly River County School District | | |
|---|---|---|---|
| Contact Information | Jane Smith | jsmith@krcsd.org | 555-555-5555 |
| | CONTACT NAME | CONTACT E-MAIL | CONTACT TELEPHONE NUMBER |

### ELEMENTARY

| School | Grades | STUDENTS (3-point Q) | | | | STUDENTS (5-point Q) | | | | STAFF | | | | PARENTS | | | |
|---|---|---|---|---|---|---|---|---|---|---|---|---|---|---|---|---|---|
| | | Desired Ns | Date(s) | Online | Paper | Desired Ns | Date(s) | Online | Paper | Desired Ns | Date(s) | Online | Paper | Desired Ns | Date(s) | Online | Paper |
| Belle Aire | 1st - 5th | 95 | 10/20 – 10/24 | x | | 78 | 10/20 – 10/24 | x | | 30 | 10/20 – 10/24 | x | | 175 | 10/24 – 10/28 | x | |
| Cherry Hill | 1st - 5th | 470 | 11/3 – 11/7 | x | | 325 | 11/3 – 11/7 | x | | 72 | 10/20 – 10/24 | x | | 600 | 10/24 – 10/28 | x | |
| Eastside | 1st - 5th | 70 | 10/27 – 10/31 | x | | 75 | 10/27 – 10/31 | x | | 28 | 10/20 – 10/24 | x | | 120 | 10/24 – 10/28 | x | |
| Rose Avenue | 1st - 5th | 650 | 11/3 – 11/7 | x | | | 11/3 – 11/7 | x | | 20 | 10/20 – 10/24 | x | | 780 | 11/24 – 10/28 | x | |
| Sunnyside | K | 680 | 11/3 – 11/14 | x | | 500 | 11/3 – 11/14 | x | | 60 | 10/20 – 10/24 | x | | 795 | 10/24 – 10/28 | x | |

### MIDDLE

| School | Grades | STUDENTS (3-point Q) | STUDENTS (5-point Q) | | | | STAFF | | | | PARENTS | | | |
|---|---|---|---|---|---|---|---|---|---|---|---|---|---|---|
| | | | Desired Ns | Date(s) | Online | Paper | Desired Ns | Date(s) | Online | Paper | Desired Ns | Date(s) | Online | Paper |
| Eastside Middle | 6th - 8th | N/A | 1,322 | 10/20 – 10/24 | x | | 54 | 10/20 – 10/24 | x | | 1,300 | 10/20 – 10/24 | x | |
| Kelly River Middle | 6th - 8th | | 1,600 | 10/20 – 10/24 | x | | 74 | 10/20 – 10/24 | x | | 1,500 | 10/20 – 10/24 | x | |
| King Middle | 6th - 8th | | 1,749 | 10/20 – 10/24 | x | | 78 | 10/20 – 10/24 | x | | 1,600 | 10/20 – 10/24 | x | |

### HIGH

| School | Grades | STUDENTS (3-point Q) | STUDENTS (5-point Q) | | | | STAFF | | | | PARENTS | | | |
|---|---|---|---|---|---|---|---|---|---|---|---|---|---|---|
| | | | Desired Ns | Date(s) | Online | Paper | Desired Ns | Date(s) | Online | Paper | Desired Ns | Date(s) | Online | Paper |
| Eastside High | 9th - 12th | N/A | 1,822 | 10/20 – 10/24 | x | | 68 | 10/24 – 10/24 | x | 600 | 1,524 | 10/20 – 10/28 | x | |
| Kelly River High | 9th - 12th | | 1,907 | 10/20 – 10/24 if needed 11/5 and 11/6 | x | | 74 | 10/24 – 10/24 | x | 600 | 1,642 | 10/20 – 10/28 if needed 11/5 and 11/6 | x | |

## Process Protocol *(Continued)*

Step 7. **Test the data collection tools prior to administration.** A critical part of effectively collecting questionnaire data involves thoroughly testing the tools to be used before releasing them to respondents. For collecting data online, testing involves submitting responses to each of the questionnaire sites. If using scannable forms, pull forms from various points within the print run, fill them out, and run them through the OMR scanner to make sure data are recorded accurately. Any work associated with the testing that is completed before actually collecting data will pale in comparison to the efforts required if you experience problems with online data submission or form scanning.

Step 8. **Verify the data.** In verifying the data, consider the number of people who were given the questionnaire and the number of responses received. If the number of responses is low, follow-up with those who received the questionnaire originally to get more responses. If your parent questionnaire was given at parent–teacher conferences and only 60% of your parents attended (identified through a guest book or sign-in sheets in each classroom), you could use another format to get additional responses from the parents who did not attend. Only with in person administration procedures can you know exactly who responded to an anonymous questionnaire. You could send scannable questionnaires to those who did not attend. Figure C2-3 shows Figure C2-2 completed to document response numbers to ensure the best possible sample.

For each of the approaches to gathering questionnaire data, you will need to verify the accuracy of the data collection. For online data collection, remove any duplicates, tests, or otherwise errant responses from your sample. For scannable forms, recheck the reliability of your scanning process by checking responses from a few of the scannable forms against the data file produced by the scanner.

Figure C2-3

## QUESTIONNAIRE INFORMATION RESPONSE DETAIL REPORT

| District Name | Kelly River County School District |
| --- | --- |
| Date | Fall 2008 |

### ELEMENTARY

| | STUDENTS (3-point Q) | | | | STAFF | | | | PARENTS | | | |
| --- | --- | --- | --- | --- | --- | --- | --- | --- | --- | --- | --- | --- |
| | Desired Ns | 10/26 | 11/3 | 11/10 | Desired Ns | 10/27 | 11/3 | 11/10 | Desired Ns | 10/27 | 11/3 | 11/10 |
| Belle Aire Elementary | 95 | 0 | 22 | 89 | 30 | 8 | 10 | 28 | 175 | 13 | 136 | 166 |
| Cherry Hill Elementary | 470 | 90 | 186 | 470 | 72 | 24 | 24 | 68 | 600 | 19 | 311 | 541 |
| Eastside Elementary | 70 | 0 | 0 | 70 | 28 | 9 | 9 | 24 | 120 | 0 | 92 | 120 |
| Rose Avenue Elementary | 650 | 209 | 209 | 647 | 20 | 6 | 6 | 18 | 780 | 95 | 480 | 698 |
| Sunnyside Elementary | 680 | 222 | 429 | 678 | 60 | 20 | 28 | 58 | 795 | 140 | 621 | 744 |

### MIDDLE

| | STUDENTS (5-point Q) | | | | STAFF | | | | PARENTS | | | |
| --- | --- | --- | --- | --- | --- | --- | --- | --- | --- | --- | --- | --- |
| | Desired Ns | 10/27 | 11/3 | 11/10 | Desired Ns | 10/27 | 11/3 | 11/10 | Desired Ns | 10/27 | 11/3 | 11/10 |
| Eastside Middle | 1,322 | 704 | 1,122 | 1,309 | 54 | 0 | 36 | 54 | 1,300 | 0 | 894 | 1,196 |
| Kelly River Middle | 1,600 | 509 | 509 | 509 | 74 | 32 | 64 | 74 | 1,500 | 0 | 246 | 1,403 |
| King Middle | 1,749 | 609 | 1,376 | 1,739 | 78 | 0 | 58 | 78 | 1,600 | 0 | 1,146 | 1,688 |

(STUDENTS 3-point Q: N/A)

### HIGH

| | STUDENTS (5-point Q) | | | | STAFF | | | | PARENTS | | | |
| --- | --- | --- | --- | --- | --- | --- | --- | --- | --- | --- | --- | --- |
| | Desired Ns | 10/27 | 11/3 | 11/10 | Desired Ns | 10/27 | 11/3 | 11/10 | Desired Ns | 10/27 | 11/3 | 11/10 |
| Eastside High | 1,822 | 0 | 1,493 | 1,819 | 68 | 0 | 29 | 68 | 1,524 | 0 | 495 | 1,516 |
| Kelly River High | 1,907 | 391 | 1,249 | 1,859 | 74 | 34 | 68 | 74 | 1,642 | 33 | 1,249 | 1,608 |

(STUDENTS 3-point Q: N/A)

*Note:* Numbers above do not account for test or duplicate submissions to be removed prior to analysis.

## Comments to the Facilitator

A secure environment for collecting questionnaire data online can be achieved either through technology or by setting up an effective process.

With technology, we can build elaborate systems to validate users with checks such as unique user names and passwords. This technology requires a greater degree of knowledge and experience with technology, and it often results in the transition from a static (simple) data model to a dynamic (complex) model.

In designing an effective process for collecting responses, however, we can achieve a comparable level of security. A few guiding ideas can help facilitate a secure process:

- Set up data collection websites for each school, each with its own separate staff, student, and parent questionnaire sites. Respondents can only submit responses for their particular questionnaire for their school. Their responses are more readily trackable on the server.

- Provide web addresses for access to each questionnaire for each school, and only just before data collection is to take place. Do not provide links to the questionnaires anywhere on the web. By asking respondents to enter a web address into a browser, you are facilitating a degree of validation without having to oversee the distribution of user names and passwords.

- Add auto-entering date and time fields to your data collection databases so you can track exactly when submissions were received. Any responses received outside of the agreed administration time period may be suspect.

- For students and parents, administer questionnaires within a computer lab or other environment where participation can be supervised and support provided as needed. Set the time frame so it is difficult, or impossible, for someone to submit more than one form.

In the end, simple form submission to a database provides us with the greatest amount of security as databases used for collection (hence the raw data) need not be broadcast directly to the web.

As with other data projects, all data collected must be validated prior to analysis regardless of the safeguards in place prior to collection. The databases used on the server provide a great environment for reviewing and validating our data, which ultimately reduces the need to put technology in place to secure data collection. In the end, a secure process will help us more than focusing on technological solutions that may add complex layers to the work.

*Reference:* Excerpts taken from from V.L. Bernhardt & B.J. Geise (2009). *Questions to Actions: Using Questionnaire Data for Continuous School Improvement.* Larchmont, NY: Eye On Education, Inc.

# ANALYZING QUESTIONNAIRE RESULTS

**Purpose** — The purpose of this activity is to guide staff in analyzing questionnaire data.

**Target Audience** — Leadership Team or Data Team can analyze the questionnaires, aggregate the open-ended responses, and take them to the full staff for analysis.

**Time** — Approximately one hour.

**Materials** — Copies of the questionnaire results and questionnaire study questions. Chart pad paper and markers.

## Overview

When creating a questionnaire, one needs to make sure the content and design facilitate effective data analysis and effective use of the results. The structure of the questions dictates how the responses will be analyzed and how the results will be presented.

If we want to be able to see all items in relation to each other, all items need to use the same scale and be phrased in the same way (e.g., stated positively). A single scale for all items allows us to analyze responses to all questions along a single point of orientation (scale) and to place the results together in the same graph.

If different scales are used, and if positively and negatively phrased questions are combined in the body of the questionnaire, different methods are required to analyze and present the results. Like-scaled and/or phrased items need to be grouped into separate files for analysis of results and into separate graphs for presentation.

Sometimes items are different enough that they warrant using different scales and phrasing, but most often phrasing can be adjusted to the use of a single scale. Figure C3-2, shown on the following page, breaks down the steps for analyzing the results of the questionnaire.

## Process Protocol

Establish analysis points that can consistently provide useful and valuable information for each school or building. Disaggregate or sort results by demographics, by year, and by other specific characteristics of the group being surveyed to lead deeper and deeper into issues.

Typical analysis descriptions follow:

*Analysis of total survey respondents* provides a general overview of questionnaire results. This information plots general differences among items and illustrates some general thematic ties among items.

## Figure C3-1

**QUESTIONNAIRE PROCESS OVERVIEW**

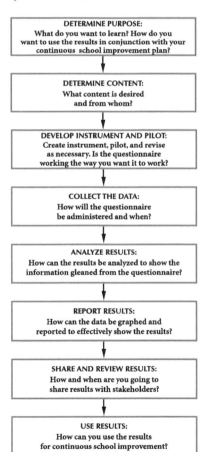

**DETERMINE PURPOSE:**
What do you want to learn? How do you want to use the results in conjunction with your continuous school improvement plan?

**DETERMINE CONTENT:**
What content is desired and from whom?

**DEVELOP INSTRUMENT AND PILOT:**
Create instrument, pilot, and revise as necessary. Is the questionnaire working the way you want it to work?

**COLLECT THE DATA:**
How will the questionnaire be administered and when?

**ANALYZE RESULTS:**
How can the results be analyzed to show the information gleaned from the questionnaire?

**REPORT RESULTS:**
How can the data be graphed and reported to effectively show the results?

**SHARE AND REVIEW RESULTS:**
How and when are you going to share results with stakeholders?

**USE RESULTS:**
How can you use the results for continuous school improvement?

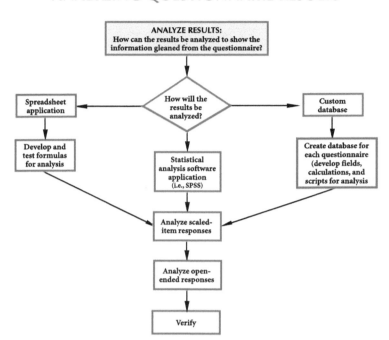

Figure C3-2
ANALYZING QUESTIONNAIRE RESULTS

## Process Protocol *(Continued)*

*Analysis by demographic variables* allows schools to isolate differences in responses by subgroups within the school population. Looking into general demographic subgroups, such as gender, ethnicity, and grade level, provides valuable information about the perceptions of questionnaire respondents. By selecting demographic variables carefully, schools can tie perceptions data to demographic, student learning, and school process data to acquire a clearer picture of how perceptions/climate/ environment influence learning.

*Analysis by year* is perhaps the most powerful level of analysis. Looking at changes over time validates the work a school has done and helps staff members realign their actions. It should be noted that strategies for change should not focus on questionnaire results on their own; perceptions data, along with demographics, student learning, and school process data, can tell the whole story.

When disaggregating or sorting any data for analysis, one needs to take care not to provide analyses where individuals can be identified. Providing any analysis of perceptions data with subgroups fewer than eight can impact the interpretation of the analysis. Potential risks include alienating questionnaire respondent groups by creating a feeling of negative accountability by identifying individuals, or by having readers put undeserved emphasis on results during interpretation.

### Complex Analysis or Simple Statistics?

*Descriptive statistics,* simple summaries used to explain the basic characteristics of the data, are very powerful for analyzing school perceptions. We want to see items in relationship to each other, and to know if different groups are responding to processes in the same or different ways. In addition, producing average statistics for each item, and then eyeballing the relationship of items to each other, can reveal differences and highlight themes. Schools want to know what they are doing well, what they can do better for students, and to know what actions to take. Descriptive statistics can help schools do all of these.

## Process Protocol *(Continued)*

"Significant differences" determined through complex statistical analyses often cement the differences rather than provide information on which to change. For example, if questionnaire results were "significantly different" for classified staff versus certificated classroom teachers on an item related to the school having a shared vision, it would not inspire all staff to work together to revisit and make the vision shared or even to look at other items. It might be perceived that one group should "get on board."

If descriptive statistics showed that items related to working closely together, sharing decisions, and planning were low, in addition to a shared vision, the whole staff would be more likely to work together to revisit the vision and redefine the major parts, such as sharing decisions, planning, collaboration, and analyzing the results of the questionnaire.

## Comments to the Facilitator

At times it seems that unending streams of analyses can be created. The key is to determine what small percentage of these analyses are actionable, and then decide what can be avoided as redundant. Avoid burying users with analyses that do not prompt them to see their results easily, uncover new interpretations of the results, or provide further clarification of the results through disaggregations. We want to focus on analyses that get to the point and relay the results effectively. Perceptions data, unlike other forms of data, may not need to be disaggregated down to multiple subgroups in order to take effective action.

When creating analyses, ask yourself if the analysis is telling you anything beyond what has already been created, or if it is helping you see the data in a new way. Instead of focusing on presenting analyses that are redundant, it would be better to focus energy into other areas of data, tying the perceptions data to other measures. After summarizing the data, integrate into the data profile.

*Reference:* Excerpts taken from from V.L. Bernhardt & B.J. Geise (2009). *Questions to Actions: Using Questionnaire Data for Continuous School Improvement.* Larchmont, NY: Eye On Education, Inc.

# ANALYZING OPEN-ENDED RESPONSES

**APPENDIX**

| | |
|---|---|
| **Purpose** | The purpose of this activity is to share and demonstrate how to analyze open-ended responses from administered questionnaires. |
| **Target Audience** | Committee of teachers. |
| **Time** | One hour. |
| **Materials** | Hard copies of the open-ended questionnaire responses, or computer files; computer on which to record and aggregate responses. |
| **Overview** | Open-ended questions should not be overlooked when assessing perceptions of the learning environment. While open-ended responses to questions are very time-consuming to compile or aggregate, one can get a complete sense of the learning environment by asking students, for instance, two questions: |

+ *What do you like about this school?*

+ *What do you wish was different?*

Or, asking students, staff, and parents, these two questions—

+ *What are the strengths of this school?*

+ *What would make the school better?*

Staff need to be clear on the most common responses; so instead of guessing, they need to aggregate the responses to know how many respondents said the same thing.

## Process Protocol

There is no fast or automated way to analyze open-ended responses. The best way to analyze open-ended responses is to take the list of open-ended responses, review the responses, and tally the number of times students said the same thing. Place the number in parentheses after the statement, eliminate the duplicates, and revise your list. You will need to make judgment calls about how to collapse the items when parts of the responses are different. The table on the next page, *Aggregating Open-ended Responses,* shows the open-ended response list in the left-hand column. The other column shows how the list can be condensed. The right-hand column, labeled "Add Descriptors," shows the number of times teachers were mentioned and in parentheses indicates the descriptions and the number of times the descriptors were mentioned. For example:

+ Teachers (6) (caring, 3; nice, 2; good, 1)

An example of what the aggregated open-ended responses would look like is shown in Figure C4-2.

**Figure C4-1**

**DETERMINE PURPOSE:**
What do you want to learn? How do you want to use the results in conjunction with your continuous school improvement plan?

↓

**DETERMINE CONTENT:**
What content is desired and from whom?

↓

**DEVELOP INSTRUMENT AND PILOT:**
Create instrument, pilot, and revise as necessary. Is the questionnaire working the way you want it to work?

↓

**COLLECT THE DATA:**
How will the questionnaire be administered and when?

↓

**ANALYZE RESULTS:**
How can the results be analyzed to show the information gleaned from the questionnaire?

## Figure C4-2
## AGGREGATED OPEN-ENDED RESPONSES

| All Responses | Aggregated Responses |
|---|---|
| I like the caring teachers and the friendly school | The teachers (8) (e.g., nice, 2; respect/fair, 2; caring, 1; good, 1; way of learning, 1) |
| I like that our school is new and the teachers are nice | The school (3) (e.g., friendly, 1; new, 1; nice, 1) |
| I have a good teacher and friends who treat me nice | My friends (3) (e.g., treat me nice, 1) |
| I like the way teachers make us learn things | Music (2), |
| I feel safe and treated with respect from teachers | My classes (2) |
| I like my teacher and the principal | The principal (2) |
| My teacher treats me with respect | Recess (2) (e.g., playground equipment, 1) |
| I like my friends and my nice teacher | Not too much homework |
| I really like our new principal and my friends | Social Studies, Math, P.E., Reading |
| We have a nice school | |
| I like recess, social studies, P.E., and music | |
| I like recess and the slide and the swings | |
| I like reading and music and math | |
| Not too much homework | |

**Eliminate Duplicates, Add Descriptors, and Rank Order**

## Comments to the Facilitator

Open-ended responses are very helpful in painting the picture of the school. It is important to capture the feelings of the respondents as the responses are aggregated. Make sure responses are aggregated before staff members review the questionnaire results.

*Reference:* Excerpts taken from from V.L. Bernhardt & B.J. Geise (2009). *Questions to Actions: Using Questionnaire Data for Continuous School Improvement.* Larchmont, NY: Eye On Education, Inc.

# PRESENTING AND USING QUESTIONNAIRE RESULTS

| | |
|---|---|
| **Purpose** | The purpose of this activity is to guide staff in presenting questionnaire data so that is will be used by staff. |
| **Target Audience** | Full staff. Leadership Team or Data Team can create the presentation of results and share results with full staff for analysis. |
| **Time** | Approximately 1 hour. |
| **Materials** | Copies of the questionnaire results and questionnaire study questions. |

## Overview

We want to present questionnaire results in a way that facilitates easy interpretation, provides contextual understanding, and creates a "Wow!" moment with data. We know that teachers do not have the time to analyze or use complex questionnaire results. It behooves the preparers of the results to forego complex analyses and to reduce large amounts of information to a single or a small number of graphs that provide powerful information, and to provide a report summarizing the information. The power of graphs comes from their ability to convey data directly to the viewer. Viewers use spatial intelligence to retrieve data from a graph—a source different from the language-based intelligence of prose and verbal presentations.

## Process Protocol

Questionnaires are designed to ask multiple questions to understand the "Big Picture" while defining what needs to improve to get better results. Figure C5-2 shows the steps in reporting questionnaire results.

### Figure C5-1

**DETERMINE PURPOSE:**
What do you want to learn? How do you want to use the results in conjunction with your continuous school improvement plan?

**DETERMINE CONTENT:**
What content is desired and from whom?

**DEVELOP INSTRUMENT AND PILOT:**
Create instrument, pilot, and revise as necessary. Is the questionnaire working the way you want it to work?

**COLLECT THE DATA:**
How will the questionnaire be administered and when?

**ANALYZE RESULTS:**
How can the results be analyzed to show the information gleaned from the questionnaire?

**REPORT RESULTS:**
How can the data be graphed and reported to effectively show the results?

**SHARE AND REVIEW RESULTS:**
How and when are you going to share results with stakeholders?

## Figure C5-2
## REPORTING QUESTIONNAIRE RESULTS PROCESS

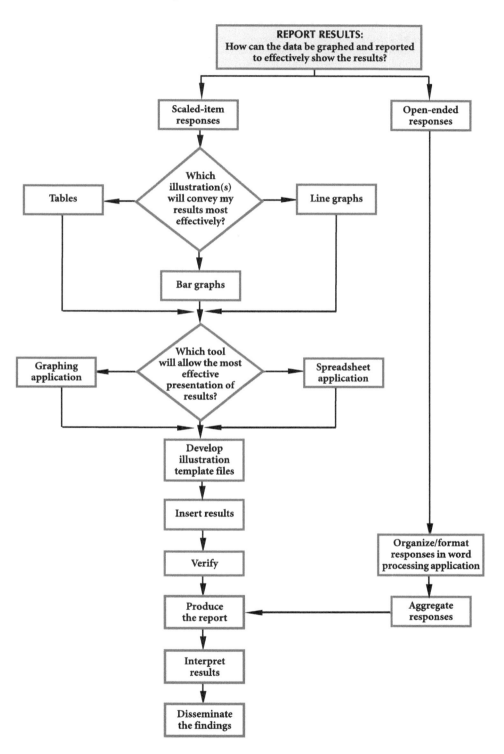

## Figure C5-3
## QUESTIONNAIRE RESULTS TABLE

| ITEM—*When I am at school, I feel:* | Strongly Disagree | Disagree | Neutral | Agree | Strongly Agree |
|---|---|---|---|---|---|
| I belong | 2% | 4% | 22% | 47% | 25% |
| I am safe | 2% | 5% | 10% | 42% | 41% |
| I have fun learning | 4% | 10% | 37% | 32% | 17% |
| I like this school | 2% | 6% | 21% | 27% | 43% |
| This school is good | 1% | 4% | 21% | 38% | 37% |
| I have freedom at school | 7% | 14% | 31% | 30% | 18% |
| I have choices in what I learn | 9% | 20% | 42% | 22% | 8% |
| My teacher treats me with respect | 2% | 3% | 12% | 29% | 55% |
| My teacher cares about me | 3% | 2% | 13% | 29% | 53% |
| My teacher thinks I will be successful | 2% | 3% | 14% | 36% | 44% |
| My teacher listens to my ideas | 2% | 3% | 26% | 44% | 25% |
| My principal cares about me | 2% | 2% | 17% | 31% | 48% |
| My teacher is a good teacher | 2% | 2% | 8% | 26% | 62% |
| My teacher believes I can learn | 1% | 1% | 10% | 29% | 59% |
| I am recognized for good work | 3% | 5% | 29% | 41% | 22% |
| I am challenged by the work my teacher asks me to do | 8% | 8% | 42% | 25% | 17% |
| The work I do in class makes me think | 3% | 4% | 25% | 43% | 24% |
| I know what I am supposed to be learning in my classes | 2% | 1% | 12% | 44% | 40% |
| I am a good student | 1% | 2% | 11% | 39% | 47% |
| I can be a better student | 5% | 5% | 23% | 37% | 30% |
| Quality work is expected at my school | 2% | 4% | 20% | 39% | 35% |
| I behave well at school | 2% | 2% | 17% | 35% | 44% |
| Students are treated fairly by teachers | 7% | 7% | 19% | 28% | 38% |
| Students are treated fairly by the principal | 2% | 2% | 11% | 27% | 58% |
| Students are treated fairly by the people on recess duty | 10% | 13% | 22% | 30% | 24% |
| Students at my school treat me with respect | 8% | 7% | 38% | 30% | 18% |
| Students at my school are friendly | 5% | 7% | 34% | 35% | 18% |
| I have lots of friends | 3% | 4% | 18% | 31% | 44% |
| I have support for learning at home | 2% | 3% | 15% | 35% | 44% |
| My family believes I can do well in school | 2% | 1% | 4% | 19% | 74% |
| My family wants me to do well in school | 1% | 1% | 2% | 12% | 84% |

## Process Protocol *(Continued)*

We are all used to seeing questionnaire results as presented in Figure C5-3. When results are presented in this manner, it is very hard to know which items are most important, highest, or lowest. We don't even think about how the items might work together. It is just too confusing. When using results from this type of presentation, most people pick just one or two items to work on. Even worse, people might ignore them all, especially if they don't understand the "Big Picture."

Results could be provided in individual bar graphs that show the percentage of responses for each response option. Figure C5-4 consists of bar graphs for the first four items listed in Figure C5-3. Again, noting the relationship among items becomes very difficult, each item would have a separate bar graph, which results in many pages; and comparing items to each other would require physically comparing each graph to the others to determine any potential relationship. Therefore, it is difficult to determine what actions to take to eliminate undesirable results or to continuously improve desirable results. Alone, individual bar graphs

## Figure C5-4
### QUESTIONNAIRE RESULTS SHOWN IN BAR GRAPHS

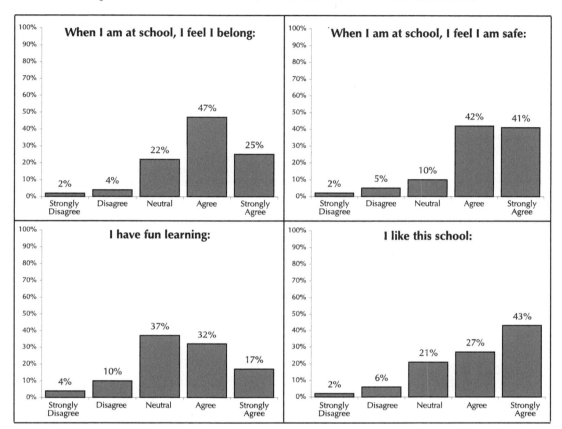

**Process Protocol** *(Continued)*

fail to provide a reference point to take action based on the results because the multi-point scale is not summary enough to quickly see the relationship of items to other items. We want to see what we are doing well in relation to what we could be doing better in order to improve.

The line graph is a very effective tool for presenting all item responses in relation to each other so that those interpreting the graph have a clear idea of the relationship of the low items to each other, and the high items to each other, and how the lows and the highs are related. Figure C5-5 shows a line graph for the same student questionnaire results shown in Figures C5-3 and C5-4.

Seeing the relationship of items to each other allows us to leverage what we are doing well and what it might take for us to do better. Also, the disaggregation can quickly show if there are subgroups with specific issues.

## Figure C5-5
## QUESTIONNAIRE RESULTS SHOWN IN A LINE GRAPH

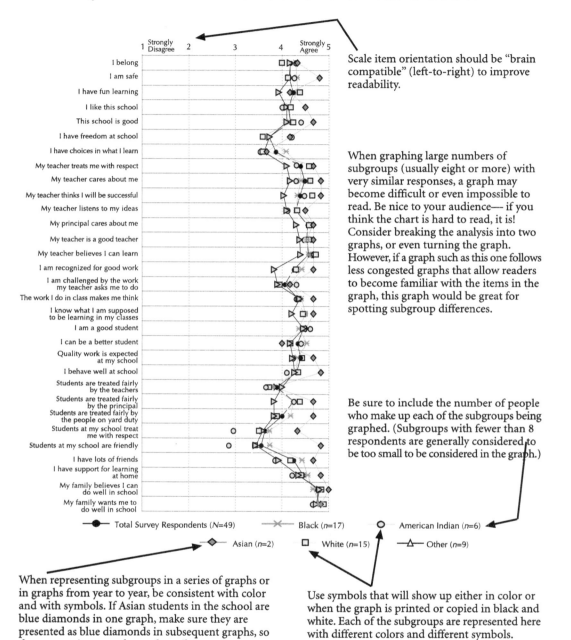

Scale item orientation should be "brain compatible" (left-to-right) to improve readability.

When graphing large numbers of subgroups (usually eight or more) with very similar responses, a graph may become difficult or even impossible to read. Be nice to your audience— if you think the chart is hard to read, it is! Consider breaking the analysis into two graphs, or even turning the graph. However, if a graph such as this one follows less congested graphs that allow readers to become familiar with the items in the graph, this graph would be great for spotting subgroup differences.

Be sure to include the number of people who make up each of the subgroups being graphed. (Subgroups with fewer than 8 respondents are generally considered to be too small to be considered in the graph.)

When representing subgroups in a series of graphs or in graphs from year to year, be consistent with color and with symbols. If Asian students in the school are blue diamonds in one graph, make sure they are presented as blue diamonds in subsequent graphs, so that comparisons can be made easily.

Use symbols that will show up either in color or when the graph is printed or copied in black and white. Each of the subgroups are represented here with different colors and different symbols.

*Note:* When disaggregating by subgroups, numbers do not always add up to the total number of respondents because some respondents do not identify themselves by the demographic, or they may have the option of indicating more than one subgroup in the demographic.

## Process Protocol *(Continued)*

### Sharing Results with Staff

To be used, the results must be shared with staff. Figure C5-6 breaks down the steps in sharing/reviewing results. Nothing can undermine the staff member's acceptance of data results quicker than reading or hearing about them before the results have been shared with all the staff. There are several ways to share and review questionnaire results with staff. These approaches can be done with just the questionnaire results or with all the data in a data profile. All approaches start with each faculty member having her/his own copy of the questionnaire results. Some effective approaches include the following, which are briefly described below. You and your staff will need to determine which approaches will work the best.

- ◆ Committee review meetings
- ◆ Fish bowl
- ◆ Gallery walk
- ◆ Small groups with protocol
- ◆ Data party
- ◆ Review as a part of overall data profile

### Committee Review Meetings

Staff members could serve on committees assigned to review the student, staff, or parent questionnaire results. The committees' charges would be to thoroughly review the results of the questionnaire to look for the strengths, challenges, and implications for the continuous school improvement plan. Each committee would report its findings to the entire staff. Staff members not on a specific committee could add what they saw. Implications across the three questionnaires will be melded into one set of overall implications/recommendations for improvement.

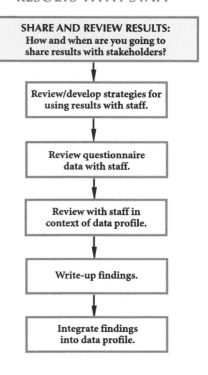

**Figure C5-6**
**SHARE AND REVIEW RESULTS WITH STAFF**

### Fish Bowl

*Fishbowls* are used for dynamic group involvement. The most common configuration is an "inner ring," consisting of four to five chairs arranged in an inner circle, which is the discussion group, surrounded by concentric circle "outer rings," which is the observation group. Just as people observe the fish in the fishbowl, the outer rings observe the inner ring. The people in the inner ring (volunteers) discuss what they see in a graph (five minutes each), while the outer rings listen. The individuals in the outer rings are not allowed to speak until they join the inner circle. When an individual in the inner ring is finished speaking or finished with her/his observations, she/he moves to the empty outer ring chair, and someone from the outer ring wanting to say something moves to the empty chair in the inner ring. A questionnaire could be reviewed and discussed in 30 minutes. The facilitator could make variations to the rules to get input from all observers.

## Process Protocol *(Continued)*

### Gallery Walk

With the questionnaire graphs grouped by respondent and posted on the wall, along with sheets of chart paper with *strengths, challenges,* and *implications* for the continuous school improvement plan written on them, a gallery walk gives staff members an opportunity to look over the data—independently and interdependently—and to write the first things that come to mind when they see the graphs. A facilitator directs staff members to form groups and take turns looking at the student, staff, and parent graphs. The facilitator leads the discussions of findings after everyone has viewed all the graphs.

### Small Faculty Groups with Protocol

Each faculty member could be assigned to a small group of five to seven (with grade level and subject area mixings) to review either the student, staff, or parent questionnaire results. With a protocol for reviewing the results, the conversation can be fun and respectful. A protocol could be something like this: One person speaks for three minutes about what she/he sees in a graph, without questions. Another person takes three minutes to add what she/he observed, and so forth, until the questionnaire has been analyzed. The group is given 15 minutes to discuss what it wants to report to the entire faculty. A recorder documents and reports the highlights to other small groups reviewing the same questionnaire. In 10 minutes they merge their findings and present to the entire staff.

### Data Party

All the disaggregated and total graphs of the student, staff, and parent questionnaires results can be handed out to staff members who would review a graph for highlights and then seek out another disaggregated graph from the other respondents and compare notes. For example, if I got the student graph disaggregated by ethnicity, I would review that data and then seek out the parent questionnaire disaggregated by ethnicity. (There probably will not be a staff questionnaire disaggregated by ethnicity, as the subgroups would be too small.) A facilitator could provide a posted list of different graphs to compare, or use stickers, or draw names to get the faculty talking to each other about the results. This activity could be accompanied with refreshments if staffs would not feel that this trivializes the importance of sharing the data results.

### Review as a Part of the Data Profile

If the timing is right, all data can be a part of the processes described above. The difference is that the implications for demographics, student learning, school processes, and perceptions can then be merged to find the big elements or concepts that must be a part of the continuous improvement plan. (See *Questions to Guide the Study of Questionnaire Results,* Figure C5-7, on the following page.)

Besides looking at the strengths, challenges, and implications for the continuous school improvement plan, staff might choose to use a questionnaire table, such as the one shown in Figure C5-8, on the next page,  to analyze the results across the different respondents.

## Figure C5-7
## QUESTIONS TO GUIDE THE STUDY OF QUESTIONNAIRE RESULTS

| 1. What are your perceptual *strengths* and *challenges?* | |
|---|---|
| *Strengths* | *Challenges* |
| | |

| 2. What are some *implications* for your continuous school improvement plan? |
|---|
| |

| 3. Looking at the data presented, what other perceptual data would you want to answer the question *How do we do business?* for your school? |
|---|
| |

## Comments to the Facilitator

When using questionnaire results to drive continuous school improvement, staff members often want to tackle the most negative item or items first, and sometimes, only. It is important to understand the big picture that the results are showing, and to understand the true meaning behind the responses, so that the results can be dealt with efficiently and effectively.

Consider the relationship of the items to each other. Let's say we have five low items. If we take the items literally and separately, we would be looking at five different things to do, which we probably will not get to. In actuality, the five are most probably related, and a serious consequence to making progress.

In short, to really use the items, staff have to understand the big picture, and determine solutions that can effectively work across the items.

*Reference:* Excerpts taken from from V.L. Bernhardt & B.J. Geise (2009). *Questions to Actions: Using Questionnaire Data for Continuous School Improvement.* Larchmont, NY: Eye On Education, Inc.

Figure C5-8
ANALYSIS OF QUESTIONNAIRE DATA

| | Student Questionnaire | Staff Questionnaire | Parent Questionnaire | Agreements Across Questionnaires | Disagreements Across Questionnaires |
|---|---|---|---|---|---|
| **General Feel of Questionnaire** *(positive, neutral, negative)* | | | | | |
| **Most Positive Items** | | | | | |
| **Neutral Items** | | | | | |
| **Negative Items** | | | | | |
| **On which items are there differences in subgroups?** *(i.e., disaggregated responses)* | | | | | |
| **Comments** | | | | | |

# MEASURING A PROGRAM OR PROCESS

To measure and improve programs and processes, start by making a list of the programs and processes that are being implemented, or intended to be implemented, at your school (Figure B4-1). After listing each program or process, determine if there are some programs that need to be merged, improved, added, or deleted, and note implications for the continuous school improvement plan for each program or process intended to be implemented, complete Figure D-1 to answer these questions.

+ What is the purpose of the program or process?

+ How will you know the intent is being met? (What are the outcomes?)

+ Who is the program/process intended to serve?

+ Who is being served? Who is not being served?

+ What would it look like when the program/process is fully implemented?

+ How is implementation being measured? (Should it be measured differently?)

+ To what degree is the program being implemented?

+ What are the results?

Attached is the Process Protocol for completing Figure D-1. (Figure D-2 is a completed example for RtI implemented in an elementary school, and Figure D-3 is an example for a secondary school.)

To answer the question, *What would the program or process look like if it was fully implemented?,* have your staff create a process flowchart. Process flowcharts show how the program or process is intended to be implemented and/or how it is being implemented now, which is helpful for improving program/process implementation. (See Appendix E, *Flowcharting a School Process.*)

| | |
|---|---|
| **Purpose** | The purpose of this activity is three-fold. To— |

- design programs/processes with purpose, implementation, and evaluation in mind;
- implement programs/processes with integrity and fidelity; and
- establish the evaluation of programs to know if they are working or not working.

| | |
|---|---|
| **Target Audience** | School/School District Staff. |
| **Time** | Two hours or more for each program. |
| **Materials** | Self-stick notes (3x3 and 3x5), chart pad paper, and markers. Reserve a room with big blank walls for this activity. Computers and projectors, and copies of the *Measuring Programs and Processes* Table will work also. |

## Process Protocol

**Step 1.** Before the day staff get together, have a small group make a list of all programs and processes used in the school to improve student learning, using the *School Processes Inventory*, Figure B4-1.

**Step 2.** Make notes of programs to add or delete and implications for the continuous school improvement plan.

**Step 3.** Using the *Measuring Processes and Programs* table, Figure D-1, assign one or more programs to groups of five or so staff members.

**Step 4.** For each program, have the groups lay out the intent/purpose of the program or process, and then brainstorm how you will know the intent is being met. Make sure all aspects of school life are included.

**Step 5.** Document who the program/process is intended to serve.

**Step 6.** Review data and document whom the program is serving and who the program is not serving.

**Step 7.** Use flowcharting tools, or other methods, to describe what each program would look like when fully implemented. (See *Flowcharting a School Process*, Appendix E.)

**Step 8.** Describe how the implementation *is* being measured and if it should be measured differently. (See *Monitoring Vision Implementation*, Appendix K, for suggestions in creating implementation measuring tools.)

**Step 9.** Measure the degree of implementation.

**Step 10.** Document results. This should be the follow-up of the items in the second column.

**Step 11.** Share small group work with staff.

## Comments to the Facilitator

The small group work could be done at times other than full staff meeting times. Then full staff meeting time can be used to share small group work.

Figure D-1
MEASURING PROGRAMS AND PROCESSES

PROGRAM/PROCESS:

| PURPOSE | | PARTICIPANTS | | IMPLEMENTATION | | | RESULTS |
|---|---|---|---|---|---|---|---|
| What is the purpose of the program or process? | How will you know the purpose is being met? (What are the outcomes?) | Who is the program/process intended to serve? | Who is being served? Who is not being served? | What will it look like when the program/process is fully implemented? | How is implementation being measured? (Should it be measured differently?) | To what degree is the program being implemented? | What are the results? |
| | | | | | | | |

NEXT STEPS:

Figure D-2

EXAMPLE: MEASURING RtI EFFECTIVENESS AT MARYLIN AVENUE ELEMENTARY SCHOOL

| PURPOSE | | PARTICIPANTS | | IMPLEMENTATION | | RESULTS |
|---|---|---|---|---|---|---|
| *What is the purpose of the program or process?* | *How will you know the purpose is being met? (What are the outcomes?)* | *Who is the program/process intended to serve?* | *Who is being served? Who is not being served?* | *What would it look like when the program/process is fully implemented?* | *How is implementation being measured? (Should it be measured differently?)* | *What are the results?* |
| The intent of RtI at Marylin Avenue is to:<br>Implement, in every classroom, quality, research-based instruction and assessment strategies that address students' needs and differences, and are based on essential learning standards.<br>Maximize *all students'* learning.<br>Reduce behavior problems.<br>Ensure that *all* students are primarily educated in the general education environment, with access to the general education content, materials, and expectations.<br>Ensure the appropriate identification of students with special needs. | When RtI is implemented as intended, instructional coherence and a continuum of learning that makes sense for all students will be evident. What students learn in one grade level will build on what they learned in the previous grade level:<br>Individual student achievement results will improve each year. All students will be proficient in all areas. No students will need to be retained.<br>Progress monitoring and common formative assessments, conducted within the classroom setting, during the school day, will be utilized to identify struggling students and why they are struggling.<br>Interventions matched to student needs will result in student learning increases for all students.<br>Number of office referrals will be minimal.<br>Students will not be placed in special education for the wrong reasons, such as teachers wanting students out of the classroom because of behavior or lack of learning response, poor test-taking skills, second language learning/ English language proficiency levels not having received high-quality instruction or adequate interventions.<br>Attendance will improve. | RtI is intended to serve all students within the general education environment.<br>When a student has difficulty mastering specific skills, the classroom teacher will adjust instruction in order to assist that child's learning.<br>Classroom teachers, with support from others, will provide additional intensive instruction in small groups for a specified period of time, and then one-on-one. | The California Standards Test (CST) will show which students are proficient and which students are not proficient.<br>Progress monitoring will show which students are and are not making progress, before, during, and after interventions. | When all teachers at Marylin Avenue are implementing RtI as designed by staff, they will:<br>Identify essential student learning standards, in their grade level teams.<br>Create/adopt assessments of the standards, in their grade level teams.<br>Administer agreed-upon assessments in their classrooms to understand what students know and do not know in order to focus their instructional strategies to meet the needs of all students.<br>Provide instruction adjusted to student needs.<br>Assess students every three weeks.<br>Review assessment results with grade level team members.<br>Provide additional instruction and interventions for the students who are not proficient.<br>Provide regular grade level instruction to all students.<br>Only identify students for special education when insufficient progress has been demonstrated.<br>Ensure that students who are proficient continue to grow. | The degree to which teachers are implementing RtI is being measured through the classroom observation tool, and through the results of common formative assessments. These measures are discussed in grade level meetings.<br>Classroom observations show that teachers are implementing the components of RtI.<br>Data are used with the RtI flowcharts to understand if the system is working as intended. | CST results show there is instructional coherence in the school in some subjects.<br>Most students are making the equivalent of one year's growth, or better, on state proficiency tests.<br>There is a reduction of retentions.<br>The percentage of the school population identified for special education services has decreased and does not exceed state or national averages.<br>Students, teachers, and parents feel that students can do the work and that they are learning at adequate rates to prepare them for the future.<br>Student absences were down this year.<br>Teacher morale is good, but lower in 2010.<br>Staff and parents feel the school has a good public image.<br>Teachers are better at meeting needs of the lowest performing students, as measured by progress monitoring assessments. |

Figure D-3

## EXAMPLE: PLANNING FOR RtI AT THE SECONDARY LEVEL, WITH CAREER AND COLLEGE READINESS

| PURPOSE | | PARTICIPANTS | IMPLEMENTATION | | RESULTS |
|---|---|---|---|---|---|
| *What is the purpose of the program or process?* | *How will you know the purpose is being met? (What are the outcomes?)* | *Who is the program/process intended to serve?* | *What will it look like when the program/process is fully implemented?* | *How is implementation being measured? (Should it be measured differently?)* | *What are the results?* |
| The purpose of RtI at the Middle School level is to—<br>• Identify students at risk for failure to be successful in middle school, through an Early Warning System.<br>• Provide differentiated ways of learning so that all students can succeed.<br>• Ensure that all teachers will work with the K-12 curriculum to ensure students are well prepared for high school and beyond.<br>―――――――――<br>The purpose of RtI at the High School level is to—<br>• Identify students at risk for failure to be successful in high school, through an Early Warning System.<br>• Ensure that *all* high school students earn enough credits to graduate, and to get them on track to graduate. This includes low-income and minority students, English Learners, and student with disabilities.<br>• Identify students at risk of failure and get them back on track.<br>• Ensure that every student has the skills and knowledge to complete post-secondary education/training and/or become successful in a chosen career.<br>• Provide a solid core curriculum that will allow all students to succeed.<br>• Provide differentiated ways of learning so that *all* students can succeed.<br>―――――――――<br>An additional intent is that both the Middle School and High School levels will work with feeder schools to ensure students have pre-requisite skills for success in middle school and high school, and therefore are better prepared for high school, careers, and college. | *All* students graduate from high school. No student drops out.<br>*All* students graduate, and are accepted into a college or a career. No student requires remediation in college.<br><br>The school has a successful Early Warning System to identify students at-risk.<br>Students in middle school will be on track to be successful in high school, as measured by course completion, GPA, attendance, no course failures, retentions, credits earned, behavior, and other indicators that keep students from succeeding.<br>Students in each year of high school will be on track to graduate, as measured by course completion, GPA, attendance, no course failures, credits earned, behavior, and other indicators that keep students from succeeding. | RtI at the secondary school level is intended to serve *all* students.<br><br>*Who is being served? Who is not being served?*<br><br>The data will show that all students are being served, as spelled out in the purpose and outcomes, when all students are succeeding. Students who are failing, at-risk of failing, and dropping out are not being served. | 1. All staff *believe* that all students can learn and will be successful when appropriate instruction and supports are provided/available.<br>2. All staff learn and understand the essentials of RtI.<br>3. All staff agree to provide culturally appropriate high quality instruction and a strong core curriculum whereby 80% of all students will do well, without intensive interventions.<br>4. Staff agree on common formative assessments, and an assessment and review cycle.<br>5. All staff review the schoolwide data to see how the school is doing now.<br>6. Given the data analysis results, new learning will be provided to help staff get different results.<br>7. Together staff create a *shared* vision and identify Leadership Teams, and their roles, to guide the overall work of the school.<br>8. All staff will meet together in appropriate teams (e.g., subject area, interdisciplinary, grade level) to agree to—<br>a. academic and behavioral standards to which all teachers are expected to teach, and all students are expected to learn;<br>b. how student knowledge and skills will be assessed;<br>c. what teachers are going to do when students know the information;<br>d. what teachers are going to do when students do not know the information;<br>e. how students will participate in problem-solving;<br>f. what interventions will be used to get students back on track;<br>g. the length of time students will be in different interventions;<br>h. common formative assessments; and<br>i. norms of behavior and meeting etiquette for the collaborative meetings.<br>9. All staff will meet no less than once a week in appropriate teams to—<br>a. review universal screening results,<br>b. place students appropriately,<br>c. review instructional challenges,<br>d. study formative assessment (progress monitoring) results,<br>e. regroup students as needed, and<br>f. support each other in improving the results (given all previous agreements).<br>*(See flowchart.)* | This process will be measured by reviewing the integrity and fidelity of implementation. Data, walk throughs, and observations will show teachers implementing the implementation agreements. Teams will ensure implementation.<br><br>*To what degree is the program being implemented?*<br><br>To be determined through reviewing the data and the formative evaluation results. | Evaluation of core curriculum and intervention implementation and results will include the review of—<br>• The number of students successfully completing the high school curriculum.<br>• Graduation rates:<br>　* 4 and 5 years<br>　* GEDs<br>　* Returning students<br>• Dropout rates.<br>• Number of students accepting and attending college or technical school, by type of college and school.<br>• Number of students requiring remediation in postsecondary classes, by subject and type of school.<br>• Number of students completing college or career preparation.<br>• Number of students at-risk of failure at each grade level.<br>• Course failures by course and grade level.<br>• Attendance rates, by students at risk, and other categories.<br>• Indicators of behavior by at-risk and other breakdowns.<br>• Focus groups and questionnaires of students about how they are learning and what would help them succeed.<br><br>Formative evaluation will monitor the effectiveness of interventions frequently and consistently to determine whether—<br>a. the intervention is working and is no longer needed,<br>b. the intervention is working and should be continued, or<br>c. the intervention is not working and therefore a different (and perhaps more intensive) intervention should be implemented.<br><br>Data are used to guide these decisions. Interventions are commensurate to a student's demonstrated need and are changed or intensified if they are ineffective. |

**NEXT STEPS:** Create an Early Warning System to identify students at-risk of not succeeding in middle and high school. Work with colleges, universities, and career preparatory programs in the area to understand expectations for successful completion.

# FLOWCHARTING
# SCHOOL PROCESSES

**APPENDIX**

**Purpose**

The purpose of this activity is to teach staff how to flowchart processes and programs. Flowcharting will clarify how to implement processes, with integrity and fidelity, and what is being implemented now, so that all staff can understand how they are getting current results. A flowchart allows everyone to see the major steps in a process, in sequence, and then evaluate the difference between the theoretical and actual, or actual and desired.

**Target Audience**

School staff.

**Time**

Usually less than one hour (set aside enough time with staff to do this well and to share).

**Materials**

Display copies of the flowcharting symbols, paper, and pencils for everyone; self-stick notes (large and small), chart pad paper, markers. Computers and projectors if staff are proficient with flowcharting software.

## Overview

School processes data are important for continuous improvement because they are what produce school and classroom results. If different results are desired, processes must be defined, implemented with fidelity, and evaluated for improvement. To implement processes, staff must—

♦ Be clear on the purpose of the process or program.

♦ Become thoroughly familiar with what 100% implementation looks like.

♦ Study the results of these implemented processes over time.

♦ Understand the relationship among processes, results, mission, vision, and actions.

♦ Create plans to achieve different results.

## Process Protocol

**Step 1.** Ask staff to choose a process or program (preferably one that needs to improve).

**Step 2.** Direct them to build "the flow" of how they are teaching students now, using four simple flowcharting symbols. If self stick notes are used, the symbols can be moved around easily for decision and actions.

**Step 3.** Ask staff to:
- Define the beginning of the process being charted.
- Decide on the level of detail to be used.
- Determine the major steps in the process and their sequence.
- Label each step in the process.
- Verify the flowchart. Is it clear?

**Step 4.** Evaluate. Compare the charted version of the process to the "desired" flow.

**Step 5.** Create the desired flow.

## Comments to the Facilitator

There are variations of this activity that give staff a visual pathway for understanding current processes. The first is to show the flow for staff. The second is to show the work process flow for students. Let staff determine which will work best for them.

Remember, if you want different results, you must change the processes that create the results. Three "real" examples follow. These will be helpful in creating your flowcharts.

Figure E-1 is a flowchart of an elementary school vision that is implementing with standards, professional learning communities, and RtI systems.

The Figure E-2 example flowchart shows how a particular high school places its new ninth-grade students in Math courses. The flowchart also shows what the school does when the students are not learning the Math concepts.

Figure E-3 is the first attempt of a school district's curriculum department to define the major concepts related to using data in professional learning communities that they want all schools in their district to implement. Next steps would be to elaborate on each action box.

There are other flowchart examples in the chapters. Figure 6.3 and 6.4 show two different types of flowcharts for implementing the *Common Core State Standards*. One with big steps, and the second one very specific. Figure 8.3 is a flowchart of Somewhere High School's *Early Warning System*.

## Figure E-1
### EXAMPLE ELEMENTARY SCHOOL SHARED VISION FLOWCHART

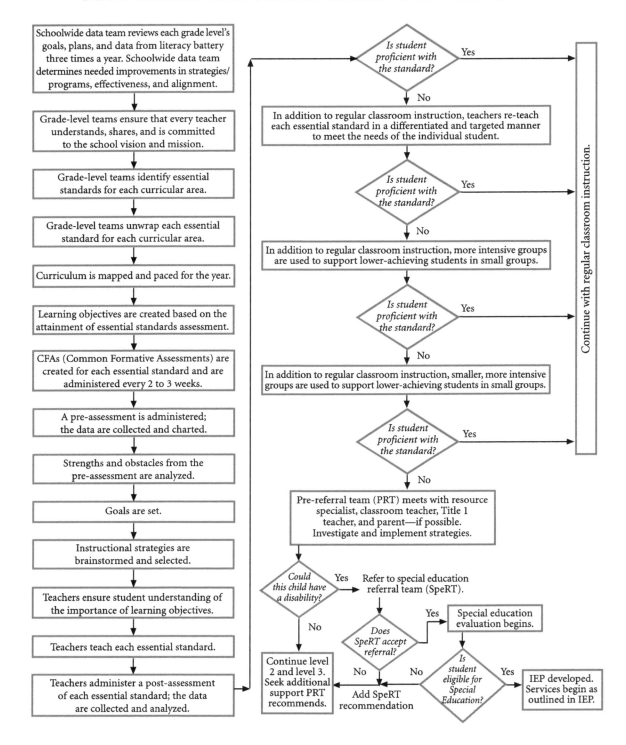

## Figure E-2
## EXAMPLE HIGH SCHOOL PROCESS FLOWCHART

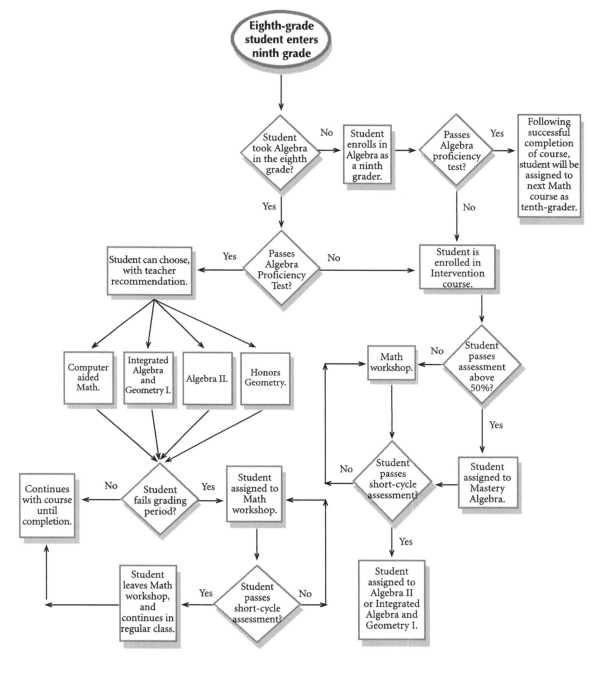

Figure E-3
THE PROCESS OF USING DATA IN
PROFESSIONAL LEARNING COMMUNITIES

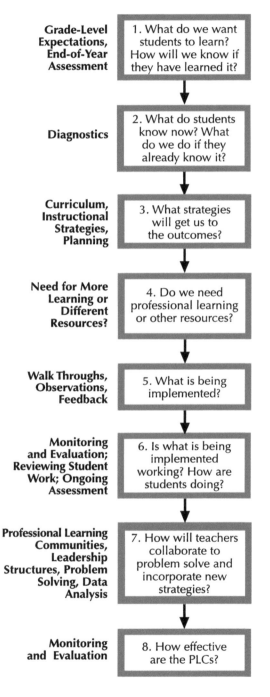

*In this PLC structure, the learning community teams—*

1. Review what they want students to know and be able to do, and how they will know when the students have learned it.

2. Assess what students know now.

3. Determine the best strategies to help students reach those end-of-unit/end-of-course/end of-year expectations.

4. Given #2 and #3 above, identify professional learning and other resources that will help teachers ensure all students' learning.

5. Observe each other and provide feedback, knowing that they can only improve with practice and feedback.

6. Review teaching observation feedback with the student assessment results.

7. Collaborate to determine what needs to change to get different results through problem-solving strategies and deeper analysis.

8. Finally, evaluate the PLC structure to ensure that its intention of improving teaching and learning is achieved.

# CASE STUDY ~ PART 1
# THE CASE STUDY AND
# STUDY QUESTIONS

APPENDIX

**Purpose**　The purpose of this activity is to give staff an opportunity to practice analyzing data with an objective data set, before analyzing their own data. Another purpose is to show what it would look like, from start to finish, when a school engages in continuous school improvement.

**Target Audience**　School staff.

**Time**　Up to three hours, with variations. (See *Comments to the Facilitator,* below.)

**Materials**　Chart pad paper, markers, a copy of the case study and study questions for all staff members.

## Overview

While looking at another school's data, staff can practice, independently and then collectively, assessing strengths, challenges, and implications for the continuous school improvement plan. They can also determine other data that would be helpful to collect and analyze. After analyzing a case study, the staff members will know what data they want to put in their data profile, how to analyze the data, and how to move the implications into a continuous school improvement plan.

## Process Protocol

**Step 1.** Provide an overview of the continuous school improvement and data analysis process.

**Step 2.** Communicate the purpose of looking at the case study.

**Step 3.** Use the process protocol in the *Analyzing Data for School Improvement Planning,* Appendix H, to analyze each type of data, to look for common implications, and then determine the major components that need to go into the continuous school improvement plan. The study questions have been inserted in the case study after each type of data.

## Comments to the Facilitator

There are many benefits to using the process protocol in the *Analyzing Data for School Improvement Planning,* Appendix H, that add to the benefits of using a case study, including:

◆ Requires individuals to review the data independently and determine what they see as strengths, challenges, implications for the continuous school improvement plan, and other data that would be good to collect and analyze, to tell the story of the school.

◆ Allows small groups and then the large group to share and compare what they saw as strengths, challenges, implications for the continuous school improvement plan, and other data that would be good to collect and analyze.

◆ Results in a type of consensus on implications for the school improvement plan, that was achieved quite easily.

## Comments to the Facilitator *(Continued)*

- Next steps are created as a part of the process.
- Individuals will see that, independently, they saw a great deal of information in the data in the case study. They will also see that, collectively, they saw different things and many more things, together, than one person could see alone.

*For time variations:*

We highly recommend using the complete analysis process for reviewing demographic data, at least. In other words, start with individual; move to small groups, and then to the entire group since demographic data set the context for the school. Many schools do not organize their demographic data for review so staff cannot see the power in what the demographic data tell them unless they analyze the data.

After using the process with the demographic data, the process for analyzing the other data types can be altered. For example, one could delegate the student, staff, and parent questionnaire reviews to individuals in the small groups who will then share what they saw with their groups.

The example case study follows.

Part 2 ~ Appendix G: *What We Saw in the Case Study Data,* follows the example case study in Appendix F.

# APPENDIX F
## SOMEWHERE ELEMENTARY SCHOOL PROFILE

## DEMOGRAPHICS

Somewhere Elementary is a kindergarten through grade five school located in Somewhere Valley. Somewhere Elementary School is part of the Somewhere Valley School District, which in 2012-13, served 13,225 students in 19 schools: 9 elementary (K-5), 2 K-8 schools, 3 middle (6-8), 2 comprehensive high (9-12), and 3 alternative schools. In 2003-04, the district served 13,935 students. This decrease (after a few years of increases) in overall district enrollment is shown in Figure F-1.

*Look Fors:* **Increasing, steady, or decreasing enrollment.**

*Planning Implications:* **Is there a need to expand or decrease district/school facilities, services, and/or staff? Are enrollment changes congruent with community population changes?**

## Figure F-1

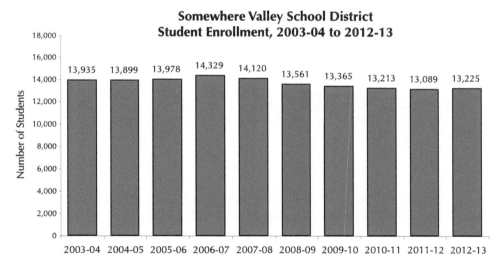

**Somewhere Valley School District Student Enrollment, 2003-04 to 2012-13**

Somewhere Elementary School served 458 students in 2012-13, down 18 students from the previous year (Figure F-2). The lowest enrollment was 445 students in 2004-05; the highest was 529 in 2007-08.

*Look Fors:* **Increasing, steady, or decreasing enrollment.**

*Planning Implications:* **Is there a need to expand or decrease facilities, services, and/or staff? Why is enrollment increasing or decreasing?**

## Figure F-2

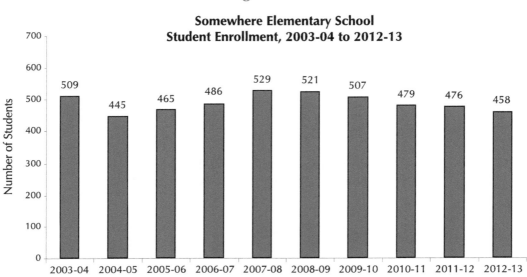

**Somewhere Elementary School Student Enrollment, 2003-04 to 2012-13**

The district student enrollment is shown in Figure F-3 by percent ethnicity. Figure F-4 shows the enrollment by percent ethnicity for the elementary schools in Somewhere Valley School District (excluding Somewhere School). Figure F-5 shows enrollment by percent ethnicity for Somewhere Elementary. In 2012-13, 59% of the district population was Caucasian ($n=7,803$), and 26% was Hispanic ($n=3,439$). The remaining student population was made up of 6% Asian ($n=794$), 3.0% African-American ($n=397$), 3% Filipino ($n=397$), 0.5% Pacific Islander ($n=66$), 0.5% American Indian ($n=66$), and 2% Multiple/Other ($n=265$) ethnicities. In 2012-13, elementary schools (Figure F-4), excluding Somewhere School, had 53.3% of the student population Caucasian ($n=2,977$), 29.4% Hispanic/Latino ($n=1,1,641$), 6.4% Asian ($n=356$), 2.8% African-American ($n=154$), 3.1% Filipino ($n=174$), 0.6% Pacific Islander ($n=33$), 0.5% American Indian ($n=28,$) and 4.0% Multiple/Other ($n=223$) ethnicities.

In 2012-13, 75.3% of Somewhere School students were Hispanic ($n=345$) and 15.9% of students were Caucasian ($n=72$). The remaining student population was made up of 0.9% Asian ($n=4$), 1.5% (African-American ($n=7$), 3.1% Filipino ($n=14$), 0.2% American Indian ($n=1$), and 3.3% Multiple/Other ($n=15$).

*Look Fors:* **Degree of diversity in the school/district population.**

*Planning Implications:* **Are teachers prepared to meet the needs of students from all backgrounds? Are instructional materials geared for all students? Is there a need for diversity programs?**

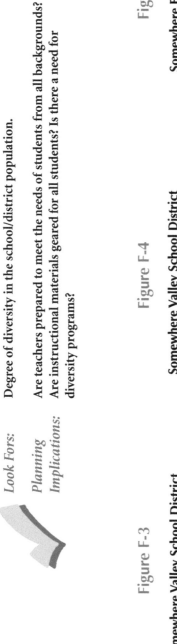

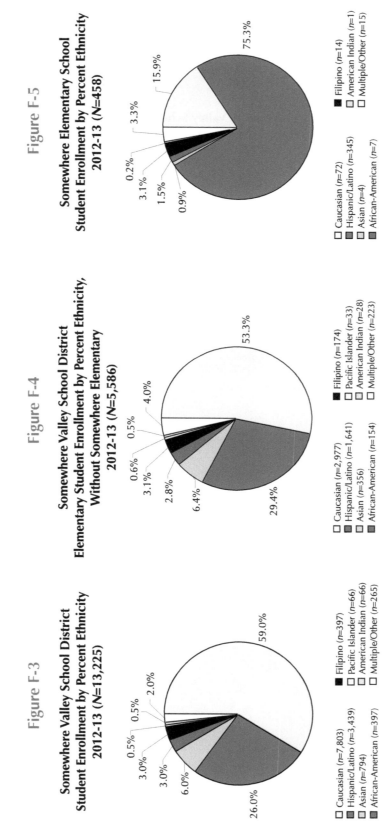

Figure F-3

**Somewhere Valley School District Student Enrollment by Percent Ethnicity 2012-13 (N=13,225)**

Figure F-4

**Somewhere Valley School District Elementary Student Enrollment by Percent Ethnicity, Without Somewhere Elementary 2012-13 (N=5,586)**

Figure F-5

**Somewhere Elementary School Student Enrollment by Percent Ethnicity 2012-13 (N=458)**

The Somewhere Valley School District student enrollment by percent ethnicity since 2007-08 is shown in Figure F-6. The graph shows the diversity of students has changed very little over time, except the percentage of Hispanic/Latino students is increasing while the percentage of Caucasian students is decreasing.

## Figure F-6

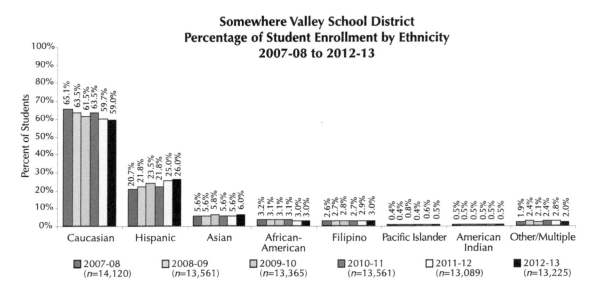

Over the past six years, as shown in Figure F-7, the percentage of Somewhere Elementary Hispanic/Latino students increased from 58.0% to 75.3%, increasing each year. The percentage of Caucasian students decreased from 27.6% to 15.9%, while the percentage of Asian students decreased from 3.4% to 0.9%, African-Americans from 3.4% to 1.5%, and Filipino students from 6.4% to 3.1%. The changes in the other groups were relatively minor.

Figure F-8 shows the Somewhere Elementary School enrollment by ethnicity numbers.

**Look Fors:** Changes in diversity over time.

**Planning Implications:** Is staff equipped to meet the needs of a changing population? What do staff need to know about diversity? Do instructional materials meet the needs of all the students?

## Figure F-7

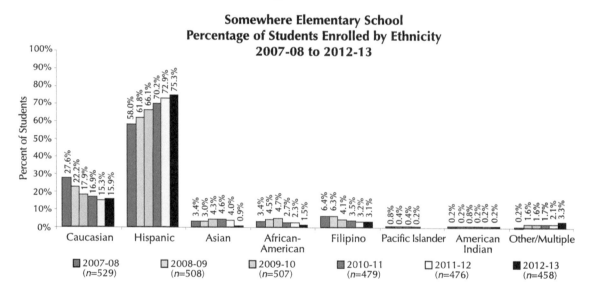

## Figure F-8

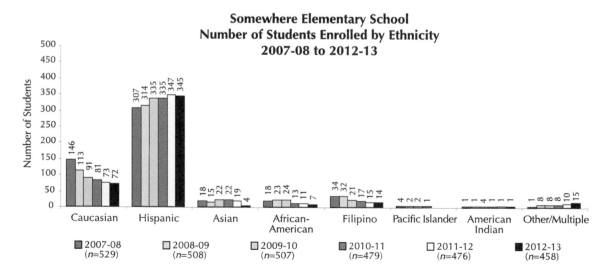

One can see the fluctuations in the numbers within grade levels over time (Figure F-9). Looking at the same grade level over time is called *grade level analysis*. The total number of students in the school is shown in parentheses next to each year in the legend.

*Look Fors:* **Consistency of numbers within and across grade levels.**

*Planning Implications:* **Is there mobility within the school? Are enrollment fluctuations indicators of satisfaction with the services provided? What is the impact of grade-level enrollment on class size?**

## Figure F-9

**Somewhere Elementary School
Student Enrollment by Grade Level
2007-08 to 2012-13**

| | Kindergarten | Grade 1 | Grade 2 | Grade 3 | Grade 4 | Grade 5 |
|---|---|---|---|---|---|---|
| 2007-08 (n=529) | 88 | 99 | 91 | 91 | 78 | 62 |
| 2008-09 (n=508) | 95 | 79 | 87 | 91 | 79 | 77 |
| 2009-10 (n=507) | 79 | 98 | 74 | 88 | 93 | 75 |
| 2010-11 (n=479) | 96 | 77 | 73 | 74 | 73 | 86 |
| 2011-12 (n=476) | 99 | 92 | 75 | 69 | 71 | 70 |
| 2012-13 (n=458) | 97 | 89 | 77 | 68 | 64 | 63 |

Reorganizing the data (Figure F-10) to look at the groups of students progressing through the grades together over time is called a *cohort analysis*. If we were looking at the exact same students (as opposed to the groups of students), the analysis would be called *matched cohorts*. Cohort A starts in kindergarten in 2006-07 and follows the group of students through grade five.

*Cohort A*    Kindergarten 2006-07, grade one 2007-08, grade two 2008-09, grade three 2009-10, grade four 2010-11, grade five 2011-12.

*Cohort B*    Grade one 2006-07, grade two 2007-08, grade three 2008-09, grade four 2009-10, grade five 2010-11.

*Cohort C*    Grade two 2006-07, grade three 2007-08, grade four 2008-09, grade five 2009-10.

*Cohort D*    Grade three 2006-07, grade four 2007-08, grade five 2008-09.

*Cohort E*    Grade four 2006-07, grade five 2007-08.

*Look Fors:*    **Consistency of numbers within cohorts. The degree of mobility and stability.**

*Planning Implications:*    **Do cohort sizes differ greatly from year-to-year? Are additional programs needed, including services to welcome new students to, or to keep them in, the school system? Does the school understand the mobility, particularly why students leave?**

## Figure F-10

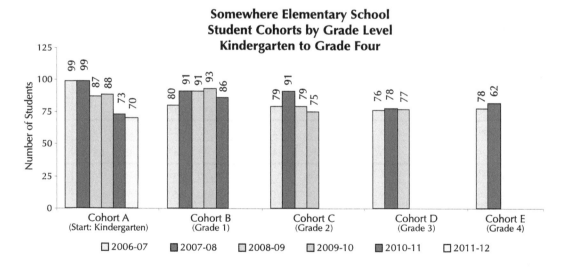

Somewhere Elementary School
Student Cohorts by Grade Level
Kindergarten to Grade Four

By analyzing grade level and gender, one can also see the fluctuations and the differences in the numbers and percentages of males and females over time, within any grade level (Figure F-11).

*Look Fors:* **Fluctuations in enrollment across grade levels and gender over time.**

*Planning Implications:* **What are the enrollment fluctuations over time? Do instructional services and programs meet the needs by gender?**

Figure F-11

### Somewhere Elementary School Enrollment
### Number and Percentage of Students by Grade Level and Gender, 2007-08 to 2012-13

| Grade Level | Gender | 2007-08 (N=529) | | 2008-09 (N=508) | | 2009-10 (N=507) | | 2010-11 (N=479) | | 2011-12 (N=476) | | 2012-13 (N=458) | |
|---|---|---|---|---|---|---|---|---|---|---|---|---|---|
| Kindergarten | Male | 43 | 49% | 43 | 45% | 43 | 54% | 47 | 49% | 48 | 49% | 52 | 54% |
| | Female | 45 | 51% | 52 | 55% | 36 | 46% | 49 | 51% | 51 | 52% | 45 | 46% |
| Grade One | Male | 46 | 47% | 39 | 49% | 49 | 50% | 37 | 48% | 42 | 46% | 41 | 46% |
| | Female | 53 | 54% | 40 | 51% | 49 | 50% | 40 | 52% | 50 | 54% | 48 | 54% |
| Grade Two | Male | 40 | 44% | 35 | 40% | 39 | 53% | 35 | 48% | 33 | 44% | 33 | 43% |
| | Female | 51 | 56% | 52 | 60% | 35 | 47% | 38 | 52% | 42 | 56% | 44 | 57% |
| Grade Three | Male | 46 | 51% | 33 | 36% | 35 | 40% | 35 | 47% | 33 | 48% | 31 | 46% |
| | Female | 45 | 50% | 58 | 64% | 53 | 60% | 39 | 53% | 36 | 52% | 37 | 54% |
| Grade Four | Male | 40 | 51% | 36 | 46% | 40 | 43% | 34 | 47% | 33 | 47% | 30 | 47% |
| | Female | 38 | 49% | 43 | 54% | 53 | 57% | 39 | 53% | 38 | 54% | 34 | 53% |
| Grade Five | Male | 45 | 55% | 44 | 57% | 31 | 41% | 37 | 43% | 27 | 39% | 27 | 43% |
| | Female | 37 | 45% | 33 | 43% | 44 | 59% | 49 | 57% | 43 | 61% | 36 | 57% |
| Totals | Male | 260 | 49% | 230 | 45% | 237 | 47% | 225 | 47% | 216 | 45% | 214 | 47% |
| | Female | 269 | 51% | 278 | 55% | 270 | 53% | 254 | 53% | 260 | 55% | 244 | 53% |

## Mobility

Figure F-12 shows the number of students who moved to or from the school zero, one, two, and more than three times between 2007-08 and 2012-13. Somewhere has a mobility rate of 28% for 2012-13—down from previous years (Figure F-13). School mergers are reflected in the high mobility in 2008-09.

*Note: Student mobility* is defined as students changing schools other than when they are promoted from one school level to the other, such as when students are promoted from elementary school to middle school, or middle school to high school. Somewhere School is looking to gather more specifics about mobility data, such as why students move.

*Look Fors:*  Fluctuations in mobility over time. Differences in mobility percentages over time.

*Planning Implications:*  Does the school need additional support or special services for students moving in and out? Does the school understand its mobility? Where do the students go? Does the school need a common curriculum? Are there effective transfer policies in place?

## Figure F-12

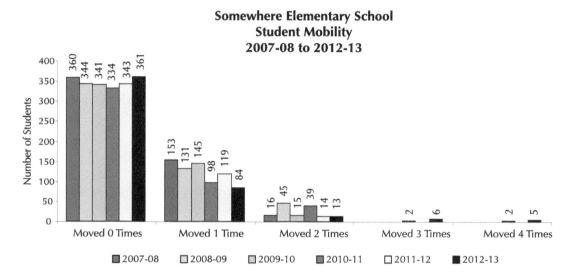

**Somewhere Elementary School**
**Student Mobility**
**2007-08 to 2012-13**

## Figure F-13

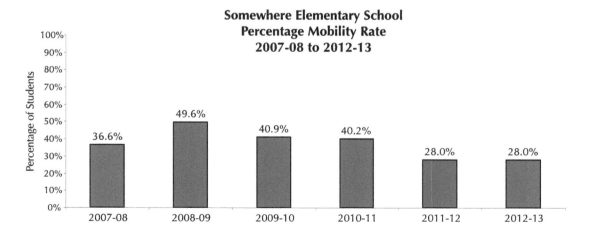

**Somewhere Elementary School**
**Percentage Mobility Rate**
**2007-08 to 2012-13**

*Open Enrollment Policy Change*

It is easy to see the changes in the Somewhere student population over time. There are dramatic increases in the numbers and percentages of English Learners, Hispanic students, and students who qualify for free/reduced lunches (indicating an increased level of poverty at this school). Some of the changes in population may be due to a district open-enrollment policy that permits families to transfer to any school in the district. Some of the changes took place in 2007-08 when one elementary school was closed and two schools were merged.

## Attendance

Somewhere students have maintained an average yearly attendance rate of about 95% over the last six years. The data in Figure F-14 show the 2012-13 school attendance rate to have decreased, compared to the previous years. (*Note:* The school noted a large number of students were absent in the winter of 2012-13, because of a flu virus.) In 2012-13, Somewhere had a total of 3,062 absences and 2,759 tardies. In the same year, the total number of absences for the District was 110,796, with 96,814 tardies. Somewhere is working on an approach to display this information more meaningfully. They are also studying attendance dynamically on their dashboard (i.e., weekly, monthly, quarterly).

*Look Fors:* **High or low average student attendance. Decreasing or increasing attendance rates over time.**

*Planning Implications:* **Why is student attendance *low* or *high*? Why are students missing school? When are students missing school? What can be done to improve attendance?**

## Figure F-14

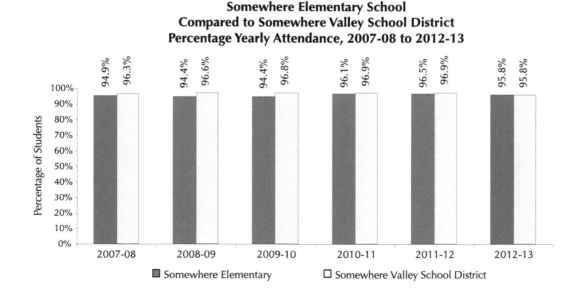

**Somewhere Elementary School
Compared to Somewhere Valley School District
Percentage Yearly Attendance, 2007-08 to 2012-13**

## English Learners

The number of English Learners (EL) by grade level has increased over time, as shown in Figure F-15. Somewhere's student population of English Learners is nearly 4.5 times as many as the District. Ninety percent of English Learners speak Spanish. Other languages in small percentages include Filipino, Vietnamese, Farsi, Gujarati, Punjabi, Mandarin, Indonesian, and Hindi. There is no English Language Development Program at Somewhere Elementary School.

*Look Fors:* **The increases/decreases in the number of English Learner populations.**

*Planning Implications:* **Are additional materials/programs needed to provide services to these students? Do staff need professional learning to meet these students' needs? What are the implications for home school communications? What instructional strategies and approaches should staff use for this population?**

## Figure F-15

**Somewhere Elementary School**
**Percentage of English Learners Compared to Somewhere Valley School District**
**2007-08 to 2012-13**

| | 2007-08 | 2008-09 | 2009-10 | 2010-11 | 2011-12 | 2012-13 |
|---|---|---|---|---|---|---|
| Somewhere Elementary | 49.3% | 59.2% | 55.2% | 62.8% | 60.9% | 60.8% |
| Somewhere Valley School District | 11.7% | 12.6% | 13.6% | 14.1% | 13.4% | 13.9% |

■ Somewhere Elementary    ☐ Somewhere Valley School District

## Free/Reduced Lunch Status

Figure F-16 compares the percentage of Somewhere students qualifying for free/reduced lunch to the overall district and to the other elementary schools in the district. (*Note:* there are 8 other elementary schools in Somewhere Valley School District, including two K-8 schools.) The Somewhere School data show that over a six-year period, the total percentage of students qualifying for Free/Reduced Lunch has increased nearly 30%, from 54% of the school population in 2007-08, to 82% in 2012-13, an indicator of the increased number of families of low socioeconomic levels. Somewhere's free/reduced lunch student percentage is more than 3.5 times that of the district and the other elementary schools, on average. The majority of Somewhere School parents do not have high school educations.

*Look Fors:* **Increases/decreases in the percentage of free/reduced lunch students.**

*Planning Implications:* **Free/reduced lunch count is an indicator of poverty—or an indicator of the degree to which the school is tracking paperwork to get all qualified students signed up to take advantage of free/reduced lunch. Have all students who qualify for free/reduced lunch returned their forms? Do staff need professional learning to meet these students' needs? How do staff best prepare instruction and environment for this population?**

### Figure F-16

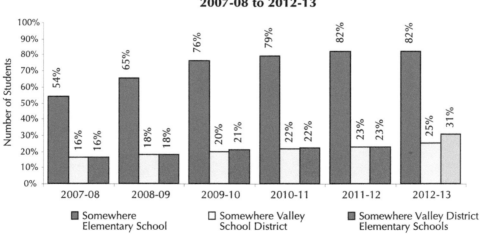

**Somewhere Elementary School
Percentage of Students Receiving Free/Reduced Lunch
Compared to Somewhere Valley School District
2007-08 to 2012-13**

## Retentions

The number of Somewhere Elementary School students retained in a grade level has fluctuated over the past eight years, but has remained low (Figure F-17). No students at any grade level were retained in 2007-08. In 2008-09, 10 students were retained; 13 students in 2009-10; 6 students retained in 2010-11; and four students were retained in 2011-12. Two students (Kindergarten) were retained in 2012-13.

*Look Fors:* Changes in numbers of retentions by grade level over time.

*Planning Implications:* Who are the students that are retained and why? Is retaining helpful/effective? When do we retain?

Figure F-17

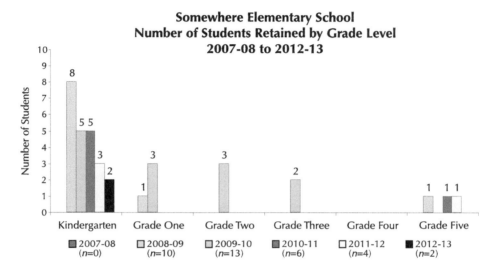

**Somewhere Elementary School**
**Number of Students Retained by Grade Level**
**2007-08 to 2012-13**

## Special Education

Up to 2012-13, Somewhere Elementary School had been serving an increasing number of students classified as needing special education (SE) services. Not all identified students from Somewhere receive services at the school. Some receive services at other schools in the district. The majority of students receiving special education assistance were speech and language impaired, followed by specific learning disabilities. Sixty-four students (12% of the school enrollment) were classified as requiring special education services in 2012-13. Figure F-18 shows the numbers and percentages of students receiving special education services by primary disability for Somewhere, the District, and state. In 2012-13, Somewhere staff began implementing a comprehensive RtI system in English Language Arts (ELA).

278

*Look Fors:* Changes in the number and percentage of students qualifying for special education services over time in the school, district, and state..

*Planning Implications:* Are the numbers increasing or decreasing? Are the services provided meeting the needs of students with learning disabilities? Do teachers have the professional learning required to work with these students?

Figure F-18

## Somewhere Elementary School Compared to the District and State Special Education Numbers by Primary Disability, 2010-11 to 2012-13

| Primary Disability | 2010-11 Somewhere School (N=59) Percent | Number | District (N=1,603) Percent | Number | State (N=677,875) Percent | Number | 2011-12 Somewhere School (N=57) Percent | Number | District (N=1,610) Percent | Number | State (N=677,875) Percent | Number | 2012-13 Somewhere School (N=54) Percent | Number | District (N=1,984) Percent | Number |
|---|---|---|---|---|---|---|---|---|---|---|---|---|---|---|---|---|
| Intellectual disability | | | 3.0% | 48 | 6.4% | 43,113 | | | 3.0% | 48 | 6.3% | 42,646 | 1.9% | 1 | 2.9% | 58 |
| Hard of hearing | 1.7% | 1 | 1.1% | 18 | 1.3% | 8,481 | 3.5% | 2 | 1.2% | 19 | 1.3% | 9,016 | 1.9% | 1 | 1.0% | 19 |
| Deaf | | | 0.1% | 1 | 0.6% | 4,185 | | | 0.1% | 1 | 0.6% | 4,162 | | 0 | 0.2% | 4 |
| Speech/language impairment | 55.9% | 33 | 39.6% | 635 | 26.0% | 176,256 | 50.9% | 29 | 39.9% | 643 | 25.5% | 172,669 | 57.4% | 31 | 40.1% | 795 |
| Visual impairment | 1.7% | 1 | 0.7% | 12 | 0.7% | 4,530 | 1.8% | 1 | 0.8% | 13 | 0.7% | 4,588 | | | 0.7% | 13 |
| Emotional disturbance | | | 3.8% | 61 | 4.0 | 27,199 | | | 4.3% | 70 | 4.0% | 27,124 | | | 4.4% | 88 |
| Orthopedic impairment | 1.7% | 1 | 1.3% | 21 | 2.3% | 15,294 | 1.8% | 1 | 1.4% | 22 | 2.3% | 15,404 | 1.9% | 1 | 1.2% | 23 |
| Other health impairment | 3.4% | 2 | 12.5% | 200 | 7.0% | 47,232 | 8.8% | 5 | 12.7% | 204 | 7.5% | 50,614 | 13.0% | 7 | 13.1% | 259 |
| Specific learning disability | 35.6% | 21 | 31.4% | 504 | 44.0% | 297,933 | 33.3% | 19 | 29.9% | 482 | 43.0% | 291,456 | 25.9% | 14 | 29.8% | 592 |
| Deaf–blindness | | | | | 0.03% | 204 | | | | | 0.03% | 182 | | | | |
| Multiple disability | | | 1.1% | 18 | 0.8% | 5,476 | | | 1.1% | 18 | 0.8% | 5,210 | | | 0.9% | 17 |
| Autism | | | 5.1% | 18 | 6.8% | 49,196 | | | 5.3% | 85 | 7.8% | 53,183 | | | 5.6% | 112 |
| Traumatic brain injury | | | 0.2% | 4 | 0.3% | 1,776 | | | 0.3% | 5 | 0.3% | 1,851 | | | 0.2% | 4 |

Figure F-19 compares the percentage of total student enrollment by ethnicity and special education, by ethnicity, for the district and school.

*Look Fors:* **The percentage of students qualifying for special education services by ethnicity, compared to the overall enrollment by ethnicity.**

*Planning Implications:* **Are the percentages in special education disability numbers across ethnicities congruent with the ethnicity percentages for the district/school?**

## Figure F-19

### Somewhere Valley School District Enrollment and Special Education Enrollment by Ethnicity

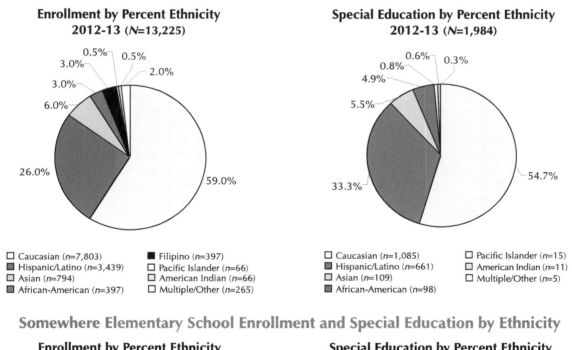

**Enrollment by Percent Ethnicity**
**2012-13 (N=13,225)**

0.5% 0.5%
3.0%
3.0% 2.0%
6.0%
26.0%
59.0%

☐ Caucasian (n=7,803)  ■ Filipino (n=397)
■ Hispanic/Latino (n=3,439)  ☐ Pacific Islander (n=66)
☐ Asian (n=794)  ☐ American Indian (n=66)
■ African-American (n=397)  ☐ Multiple/Other (n=265)

**Special Education by Percent Ethnicity**
**2012-13 (N=1,984)**

0.6% 0.3%
0.8%
4.9%
5.5%
33.3%
54.7%

☐ Caucasian (n=1,085)  ☐ Pacific Islander (n=15)
■ Hispanic/Latino (n=661)  ☐ American Indian (n=11)
☐ Asian (n=109)  ☐ Multiple/Other (n=5)
■ African-American (n=98)

### Somewhere Elementary School Enrollment and Special Education by Ethnicity

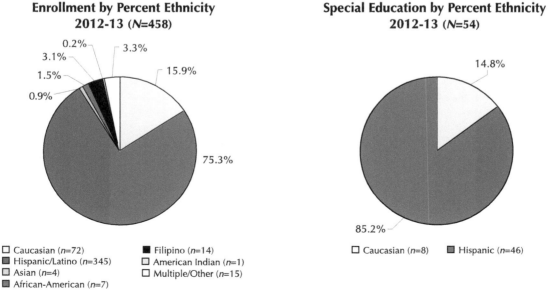

**Enrollment by Percent Ethnicity**
**2012-13 (N=458)**

0.2% 3.3%
3.1%
1.5% 15.9%
0.9%
75.3%

☐ Caucasian (n=72)  ■ Filipino (n=14)
■ Hispanic/Latino (n=345)  ☐ American Indian (n=1)
☐ Asian (n=4)  ☐ Multiple/Other (n=15)
■ African-American (n=7)

**Special Education by Percent Ethnicity**
**2012-13 (N=54)**

14.8%
85.2%

☐ Caucasian (n=8)  ■ Hispanic (n=46)

Figure F-20 shows the number of district special education students by primary disability and ethnicity, over time, while Figure F-21 shows the same data for Somewhere Elementary School.

*Look Fors:*     **Changes in the number of students qualifying for special education services, by type, by ethnicity, over time.**

*Planning Implications:*     **Is the number and percentage identified per ethnicity consistent with overall student population and, if so, how and why are students being identified for special education services? Are assessments used for eligibility determinations appropriate for the populations being assessed? Could there be some testing bias?**

Figure F-20

### Somewhere Valley School District
### Special Education Numbers by Primary Disability and Ethnicity, 2007-08 to 2011-12

| Primary Disability | Ethnicity | | 2007-08 (N=1,622) | 2008-09 (N=1,581) | 2009-10 (N=1,637) | 2010-11 (N=1,603) | 2011-12 (N=1,610) |
|---|---|---|---|---|---|---|---|
| **Intellectual Disability** | Asian | | 3 | 2 | 5 | 1 | 1 |
| | Filipino | | 1 | 0 | 0 | 0 | 0 |
| | Hispanic | | 18 | 17 | 15 | 12 | 18 |
| | African-American | | 4 | 2 | 1 | 1 | 2 |
| | Caucasian | | 35 | 41 | 37 | 34 | 27 |
| | | **Total** | **61** | **62** | **58** | **48** | **48** |
| **Hard of Hearing** | Asian | | 1 | 1 | 2 | 1 | 1 |
| | Filipino | | 1 | 0 | 0 | 1 | 1 |
| | Hispanic | | 0 | 0 | 1 | 5 | 7 |
| | African-American | | 2 | 1 | 1 | 1 | 1 |
| | Caucasian | | 6 | 8 | 7 | 10 | 9 |
| | | **Total** | **10** | **10** | **11** | **18** | **19** |
| **Deaf** | Hispanic | | 0 | 1 | 0 | 0 | 0 |
| | Caucasian | | 1 | 2 | 1 | 1 | 1 |
| | | **Total** | **1** | **3** | **1** | **1** | **1** |
| **Speech or Language Impairment** | American Indian | | 0 | 0 | 1 | 2 | 4 |
| | Asian | | 25 | 24 | 29 | 30 | 30 |
| | Pacific Islander | | 0 | 1 | 5 | 4 | 3 |
| | Filipino | | 17 | 18 | 21 | 21 | 19 |
| | Hispanic | | 148 | 162 | 200 | 209 | 223 |
| | African-American | | 29 | 24 | 20 | 26 | 18 |
| | Caucasian | | 404 | 380 | 400 | 343 | 346 |
| | | **Total** | **623** | **609** | **676** | **635** | **643** |
| **Visual Impairment** | Hispanic | | 4 | 6 | 6 | 6 | 5 |
| | African-American | | 1 | 1 | 1 | 1 | 1 |
| | Caucasian | | 5 | 6 | 4 | 5 | 7 |
| | | **Total** | **10** | **13** | **11** | **12** | **13** |
| **Emotional Disturbance** | American Indian | | 0 | 0 | 0 | 1 | 2 |
| | Hispanic | | 10 | 11 | 10 | 10 | 9 |
| | African-American | | 8 | 4 | 4 | 4 | 3 |
| | Caucasian | | 50 | 49 | 53 | 46 | 56 |
| | | **Total** | **68** | **64** | **67** | **61** | **70** |
| **Orthopedic Impairment** | Asian | | 2 | 3 | 2 | 2 | 2 |
| | Filipino | | 1 | 0 | 0 | 0 | 0 |
| | Hispanic | | 0 | 1 | 2 | 2 | 2 |
| | African-American | | 1 | 1 | 1 | 0 | 0 |
| | Caucasian | | 18 | 19 | 18 | 17 | 18 |
| | | **Total** | **22** | **24** | **23** | **21** | **22** |

Figure F-20 *(Continued)*

## Somewhere Valley School District
## Special Education Numbers by Primary Disability and Ethnicity, 2007-08 to 2011-12

| Primary Disability | Ethnicity | 2007-08 (N=1,622) | 2008-09 (N=1,581) | 2009-10 (N=1,637) | 2010-11 (N=1,603) | 2011-12 (N=1,610) |
|---|---|---|---|---|---|---|
| **Other Health Impairment** | American Indian | 1 | 1 | 0 | 1 | 2 |
| | Asian | 3 | 3 | 5 | 7 | 5 |
| | Pacific Islander | 0 | 0 | 0 | 0 | 1 |
| | Filipino | 2 | 1 | 3 | 2 | 1 |
| | Hispanic | 18 | 23 | 28 | 23 | 40 |
| | African-American | 1 | 1 | 1 | 0 | 0 |
| | Caucasian | 18 | 19 | 18 | 17 | 18 |
| | **Total** | **22** | **24** | **23** | **21** | **22** |
| **Specific Learning Disability** | American Indian | 1 | 2 | 2 | 4 | 5 |
| | Asian | 9 | 8 | 7 | 7 | 9 |
| | Pacific Islander | 1 | 1 | 2 | 2 | 1 |
| | Filipino | 5 | 7 | 3 | 6 | 3 |
| | Hispanic | 123 | 133 | 134 | 138 | 168 |
| | African-American | 38 | 32 | 40 | 34 | 34 |
| | Caucasian | 385 | 337 | 310 | 313 | 262 |
| | **Total** | **562** | **520** | **498** | **504** | **482** |
| **Multiple Disability** | Asian | 0 | 0 | 0 | 1 | 2 |
| | Pacific Islander | 0 | 0 | 1 | 1 | 0 |
| | Filipino | 0 | 0 | 0 | 0 | 1 |
| | Hispanic | 4 | 3 | 4 | 4 | 6 |
| | African-American | 1 | 1 | 1 | 2 | 0 |
| | Caucasian | 18 | 13 | 14 | 10 | 9 |
| | **Total** | **23** | **17** | **20** | **18** | **18** |
| **Autism** | Asian | 7 | 2 | 5 | 9 | 11 |
| | Filipino | 3 | 2 | 2 | 1 | 1 |
| | Hispanic | 4 | 2 | 5 | 7 | 13 |
| | African-American | 1 | 1 | 1 | 2 | 2 |
| | Caucasian | 45 | 55 | 54 | 62 | 58 |
| | **Total** | **60** | **62** | **67** | **81** | **85** |
| **Traumatic Brain Injury** | Asian | 0 | 1 | 1 | 0 | 0 |
| | Hispanic | 0 | 0 | 1 | 2 | 3 |
| | Caucasian | 6 | 7 | 4 | 2 | 2 |
| | **Total** | **6** | **8** | **6** | **4** | **5** |

Figure F-21

### Somewhere Elementary School Special Education
### By Primary Disability and Ethnicity, 2012-13

| Primary Disability | Ethnicity | | 2012-13 (N=54) |
|---|---|---|---|
| Hard of Hearing | Hispanic | | 1 |
| | | Total | 1 |
| Speech or Language Impairment | Hispanic | | 28 |
| | Caucasian | | 3 |
| | | Total | 31 |
| Orthopedic Impairment | Caucasian | | 1 |
| | | Total | 1 |
| Other Health Impairment | Hispanic | | 4 |
| | Caucasian | | 3 |
| | | Total | 7 |
| Specific Learning Disability | Hispanic | | 13 |
| | Caucasian | | 1 |
| | | Total | 14 |

Figure F-22 shows the number of Somewhere students qualifying for special education by primary disability and grade level, over time. The majority of students qualifying for Special Education services are speech and language impaired. Most disabilities are fairly evenly distributed across grade levels.

| | |
|---|---|
| *Look Fors:* | **Changes in the number of students qualifying for special education services, by primary disability and grade level, over time.** |
| *Planning Implications:* | **Is there one grade level that has more students identified than the others? Is there an increase or decrease in special education disability numbers across grade levels, over time? Is there a large group of students with IEPs in any grade level that may influence teacher ability to address needs or allocation of resources?** |

Figure F-22

## Somewhere Elementary School
## Special Education Numbers by Primary Disability and Grade Level, 2007-08 to 2012-13

| Primary Disability | Grade Level | 2007-08 (N=55) | 2008-09 (N=60) | 2009-10 (N=54) | 2010-11 (N=59) | 2011-12 (N=57) | 2012-13 (N=54) |
|---|---|---|---|---|---|---|---|
| Speech or Language Impaired | Kindergarten | 4 | 5 | 1 | 7 | 7 | 3 |
| | Grade One | 3 | 3 | 5 | 4 | 7 | 7 |
| | Grade Two | 4 | 2 | 3 | 5 | 2 | 8 |
| | Grade Three | 11 | 9 | 3 | 5 | 5 | 6 |
| | Grade Four | 8 | 10 | 11 | 2 | 6 | 5 |
| | Grade Five | 5 | 5 | 6 | 10 | 2 | 2 |
| | **Total** | **35** | **34** | **29** | **33** | **29** | **31** |
| Specific Learning Disabilities | Kindergarten | 0 | 0 | 0 | 1 | 1 | |
| | Grade One | 2 | 1 | 0 | 0 | 0 | 1 |
| | Grade Two | 2 | 3 | 2 | 3 | 2 | 0 |
| | Grade Three | 2 | 7 | 4 | 6 | 4 | 1 |
| | Grade Four | 2 | 4 | 7 | 5 | 4 | 5 |
| | Grade Five | 6 | 4 | 4 | 6 | 8 | 7 |
| | **Total** | **14** | **19** | **17** | **21** | **19** | **14** |
| Visually Impaired | Grade One | 0 | 1 | 1 | 0 | 0 | 0 |
| | Grade Two | 0 | 0 | 1 | 0 | 0 | 0 |
| | Grade Three | 1 | 0 | 0 | 1 | 0 | 0 |
| | Grade Four | 0 | 1 | 0 | 0 | 1 | 0 |
| | Grade Five | 0 | 0 | 1 | 0 | 0 | 0 |
| | **Total** | **1** | **2** | **3** | **1** | **1** | **0** |
| Hearing Impaired | Grade Three | 0 | 2 | 0 | 0 | 0 | 0 |
| | Grade Four | 1 | 0 | 2 | 0 | 1 | 0 |
| | Grade Five | 0 | 0 | 0 | 1 | 1 | 1 |
| | **Total** | **1** | **2** | **2** | **1** | **2** | **1** |
| Behavior | Grade Five | 1 | 0 | 0 | 0 | 0 | 0 |
| | **Total** | **1** | **0** | **0** | **0** | **0** | **0** |
| Orthopedic Impairment | Grade One | 0 | 0 | 0 | 0 | 1 | 1 |
| | **Total** | **0** | **0** | **0** | **0** | **1** | **1** |
| Other Health Impairment | Kindergarten | 1 | 0 | 0 | 0 | 1 | 1 |
| | Grade One | 0 | 1 | 1 | 0 | 1 | 0 |
| | Grade Two | 1 | 0 | 1 | 0 | 0 | 1 |
| | Grade Three | 0 | 1 | 0 | 1 | 2 | 0 |
| | Grade Four | 0 | 1 | 1 | 0 | 1 | 2 |
| | Grade Five | 1 | 0 | 2 | 1 | 0 | 3 |
| | **Total** | **4** | **5** | **5** | **3** | **7** | **6** |

*Pre-Referral Team (PRT)*

As a part of their RtI system, Somewhere created a Pre-Referral Team (PRT) and process. When children are identified as at risk for failure, a Pre-Referral Team of teachers and other professionals determine appropriate interventions, communicate with a child's parent(s)/guardian(s), and encourage ongoing participation in the pre-referral process.

The Special Education Referral Team (SpERT) is the team of professionals that reviews the interventions used and progress made with an individual student to see if there is support to suspect that this could be a student with a disability; therefore, requiring a complete evaluation. If this is the case, permission to evaluate is sought from the parents, and a Multi-Disciplinary Team (MDT) conducts the evaluation to determine if a disability exists. If the SpERT determines there is not sufficient information to suspect a disability, they will not seek permission to conduct the evaluation, or if permission for an evaluation is denied, then the SpERT generates additional recommendations for the classroom teacher, grade-level team and multi-level-intervention providers to use with the student. Likewise, if the student is not found to have a disability and is not eligible for special education services, the MDT will generate additional recommendations for the classroom teacher, grade-level team, and multi-level-intervention providers to use with the student.

The table in Figure F-23 reflects the number of students reviewed by the PRT at Somewhere to discuss strategies and interventions for addressing student needs for the spring semester of the 2012-13 school year. Following implementation of these strategies and progress monitoring of student performance, some students were referred for consideration of special education evaluation, reflected in the number of referrals to SpERT. Out of 64 students reviewed by the PRT across grades, only 15 (23%) of the students were referred for consideration of special education evaluation. Of those students referred, 11 were evaluated (17%) and all but one was found eligible. This means the pre-referral teams were able to effectively plan and implement interventions for the majority (83%) of the students for whom there were significant concerns about performance and learning.

*Look Fors:* **How many students are referred to Special Education by grade level? How many students are evaluated for Special Education? How many students are determined eligible?**

*Planning Implications:* **How effective is the pre-referral process? Are students referred found eligible (means the team is accurate in referrals)?**

**Are teachers providing appropriate instruction and intervention to effectively intervene for students who do not have a disability so only students who do are referred for evaluation? If not, what professional learning do staff need to better identify and address the needs of students?**

## Figure F-23

### Somewhere Elementary School
### Pre-Referral Effectiveness: January to May 2013
### Number of Students Reviewed, Referred for Evaluation, and Found Eligible

| Grade Level | K | One | Two | Three | Four | Five | Total |
|---|---|---|---|---|---|---|---|
| *Number reviewed by PRT* | 27 | 12 | 10 | 14 | 1 | 0 | **64** |
| *Number of Referrals to SpERT* | 4 | 2 | 1 | 2 | 2 | 4 | **15** |
| *Number of Students Evaluated for SE* | 3 | 1 | 1 | 1 | 1 | 4 | **11** |
| *Number Determined Eligible* | 3 | 1 | 0 | 1 | 1 | 4 | **10** |

Figure F-24 shows who referred the students in 2012-13.

*Look Fors:* Who refers students, by grade level?

*Planning Implications:* What is going on during high referral times, by grade levels, and what can be changed?

### Figure F-24

**Somewhere Elementary School
Staff Referrals: January to May 2013
Number of Students Reviewed, Referred for Evaluation, and Found Eligible**

| Referred By | Kindergarten | Grade One | Grade Two | Grade Three | Grade Four | Grade Five | Total |
|---|---|---|---|---|---|---|---|
| Classroom Teacher | 16 | 14 | 24 | 7 | 5 | 6 | 72 |
| Special Education Teacher | | | | | | | |
| School Psychologist | | | | | | | |
| Instructional Specialist | | | | | | | |
| Principal | 1 | | 2 | 3 | 1 | 3 | 10 |
| Playground Supervisor | 1 | 1 | 3 | 1 | 4 | 1 | 10 |
| Instructional Assistant | | | | | | | |
| District Administrator | | | | | | | |
| Other | | 1 | 4 | | | | 5 |
| **Totals** | **18** | **16** | **33** | **11** | **10** | **10** | **97** |

## Behavior

Figures F-25, F-26, and F-27 show suspension data from 2007-08 to 2012-13. A new principal joined the staff at the beginning of the 2008-09 school year. Somewhere began collecting data differently in 2012-13, so some graphs and table have incomplete or only one year of data. (*Note:* Empty graphs are included for modeling purposes.)

*Look Fors:*  **Increase/decrease in the number of suspensions over time.**

*Planning Implications:*  **Who are the students being suspended? Why and when are the students being suspended? How are the students treated by adults and each other? Are there policy implications?**

### Figure F-25

**Somewhere Elementary School**
**Number of Suspensions, 2007-08 to 2012-13**

Number of Suspensions

| Year | Suspensions |
|------|-------------|
| 2007-08 | 33 |
| 2008-09 | 84 |
| 2009-10 | 102 |
| 2010-11 | 82 |
| 2011-12 | 57 |
| 2012-13 | 41 |

*Look Fors:*     Increase/decrease in the number of suspension over time.

*Planning Implications:*     Who are the students being suspended, by gender and ethnicity?

Figure F-26

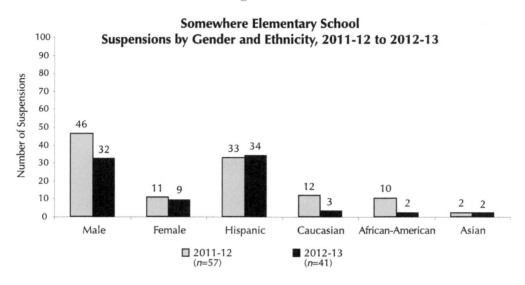

**Somewhere Elementary School**
**Suspensions by Gender and Ethnicity, 2011-12 to 2012-13**

*Look Fors:*     Increase/decrease in suspension, by reason.

*Planning Implications:*     What are the reason students are being suspended?

Figure F-27

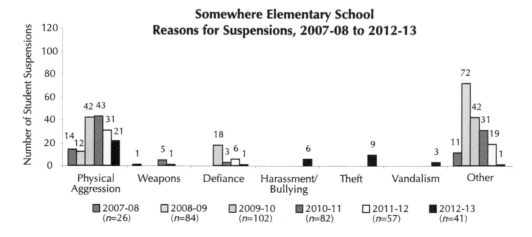

**Somewhere Elementary School**
**Reasons for Suspensions, 2007-08 to 2012-13**

Figure F-28 shows the number of students referred for behavior, by grade level and demographics available. Placeholders are shown for the way the school will gather data in 2012-13.

*Look Fors:* **Behavioral referrals by gender, ethnicity, poverty indicator, special education, and number of years in the school and country.**

*Planning Implications:* **Who is being referred most often? Do teachers need professional learning to address specific populations? Do students or groups of students need direct instruction on behavioral expectations? Does the school need to refine a behavior plan?**

### Figure F-28

## Somewhere Elementary School
## Number of Behavior Referrals by Student Group and Grade Level, 2012-13

| Grade Level | Gender | | Ethnicity | | | | Free/ Reduced Lunch | | IEP | | # Years in the School | # Years in the Country |
|---|---|---|---|---|---|---|---|---|---|---|---|---|
| | Female | Male | African-American | Hispanic/ Latino | Caucasian | Other/ Multiple | Yes | No | Yes | No | | |
| Kindergarten | 6 | 12 | | 13 | 5 | | | | | | | |
| Grade One | 2 | 14 | | 15 | 1 | | | | | | | |
| Grade Two | 12 | 23 | | 13 | 11 | 6 | | | | | | |
| Grade Three | 6 | 6 | 1 | 11 | | | | | | | | |
| Grade Four | 2 | 12 | 1 | 13 | | | | | | | | |
| Grade Five | 0 | 10 | | 8 | 2 | | | | | | | |
| **Total** | **28** | **73** | **2** | **78** | **19** | **6** | | | | | | |

Figure F-29 shows the number of behavior events by demographic.

*Look Fors:* Increase/decrease in number of behavior events, over time, by gender, ethnicity, socio-economic status, English learners and fluent English proficient, and IEP and non-IEP. How many students are contributing to the number of events? How many days of instruction do these students miss?

*Planning Implications:* How many students (and who) are contributing to behavior events? Is this pervasive across many students or a select few? Does the school need a system for addressing repeat offenders that involve teaching/reteaching expectations?

## Figure F-29

### Somewhere Elementary School
### School Behavior Events by Student Group, 2012-13

| Student Group | | Number of Events | | | | |
|---|---|---|---|---|---|---|
| | | 0 | 1 | 2 to 5 | 6 to 10 | 10 or More |
| By Gender | Female | | | | | 28 |
| | Male | | | | | 77 |
| By Ethnicity | African-American | | | 2 | | |
| | Hispanic | | | | | 78 |
| | Caucasian | | | | | 19 |
| | Other | | | | 6 | |
| By Socio-Economic Status | Free | | | | | |
| | Paid | | | | | |
| By English Learners | | | | | | |
| By Fluent English Proficient/English Only | | | | | | |
| IEP | | | | | | |
| Non-IEP | | | | | | |

Figure F-30 shows the number of school behavior referrals by reason and student group for 2012-13.

*Look Fors:* Number of behavior referrals by reason, grade level, gender, ethnicity, free/reduced lunch, IEP and non-IEP.

*Planning Implications:* How many referrals does each subgroup receive? Do teachers need professional learning to address behaviors in diverse populations?

## Figure F-30
## Somewhere Elementary School
## Behavior Referrals by Reason and Student Group, 2012-13

| Reason for Referral | Grade Level | | | | | | Gender | | Ethnicity | | | | Free/ Reduced Lunch | | IEP | Non-IEP | # Years in the School |
|---|---|---|---|---|---|---|---|---|---|---|---|---|---|---|---|---|---|
| | Kindergarten | Grade 1 | Grade 2 | Grade 3 | Grade 4 | Grade 5 | Female | Male | African-American | Hispanic/Latino | Caucasian | Other/Multiple | Yes | No | | | |
| Forgery/theft | | | 6 | 2 | 2 | | 7 | 3 | 2 | 6 | 2 | | | | | | |
| Minor: property misuse | | 1 | | | | | | 1 | 1 | | | | | | | | |
| Property damage/vandalism | | | | | 1 | 2 | 3 | | 3 | | | | | | | | |
| Fighting/physical aggression | 6 | 12 | 15 | 5 | 7 | 5 | 14 | 36 | | 8 | 10 | 2 | | | | | |
| Harassment/bullying | 3 | 1 | 4 | | 3 | 1 | | 12 | | 11 | | 1 | | | | | |
| Abusive language | 2 | 1 | 2 | 4 | | | 1 | 9 | | 6 | 4 | 2 | | | | | |
| Defiance/disrespect/ insubordination/ non-compliance | 2 | 1 | 3 | | | | 3 | 3 | | 4 | 2 | | | | | | |

Figure F-31 shows the location of behavior referrals in 2012-13, while Figure F-32 shows the number of referrals by month.

*Look Fors:* **Where are students when they get behavior referrals?**

*Planning Implications:* **What is going on during high referral times and what can be changed?**

## Figure F-31

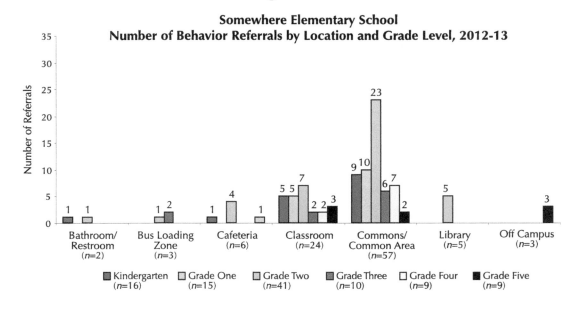

**Somewhere Elementary School**
**Number of Behavior Referrals by Location and Grade Level, 2012-13**

*Look Fors:* **Are there specific months with more behavior referrals than others?**

*Planning Implications:* **What is staff doing for behavior throughout the year?**

## Figure F-32

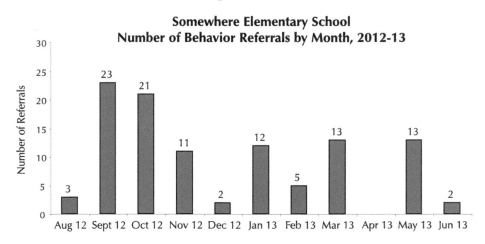

**Somewhere Elementary School**
**Number of Behavior Referrals by Month, 2012-13**

Figure F-33A shows the number of school referrals by time of day for 2012-13. The table that follows in Figure F-33B displays the school day time schedule. Somewhere School staff has begun to monitor these data dynamically so they can do more to prevent behavior issues.

*Look Fors:* **What time of day are most students referred?**

*Planning Implications:* **What is going on during high behavior times and what can be changed?**

### Figure F-33A

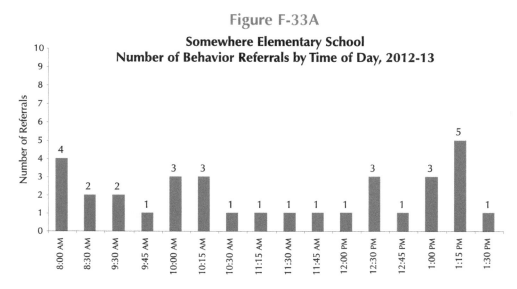

**Somewhere Elementary School**
**Number of Behavior Referrals by Time of Day, 2012-13**

### Figure F-33B

## Somewhere Elementary School Daily Time Schedule, 2012-13

*Daily Schedule*

| | |
|---|---|
| Kindergarten | 8:30 AM to 1:45 PM |
| Grades 1 – 3 | 8:30 AM to 2:40 PM |
| Grades 4 – 5 | 8:30 AM to 2:50 PM |

*Note:* Wednesdays are early release for all grades: 8:30 AM to 1:30 PM

*Recess Schedule*

| | |
|---|---|
| Grades K – 2 | 10:00 AM to 10:15 AM |
| Grades 3 – 5 | 10:30 AM to 10:45 AM |

*Lunch Schedule*

| | |
|---|---|
| Kindergarten | 11:30 AM to 12:10 PM |
| Grade 1 | 11:50 AM to 12:30 PM |
| Grade 2 | 12:00 PM to 12:40 PM |
| Grades 3/4 | 12:35 PM to 1:15 PM |
| Grade 5 | 12:20 PM to 1:00 PM |

## The Staff

During the 2010-11 to 2012-13 school years, the total number of teachers increased at Somewhere Elementary School, up slightly over recent years because of the addition of specialists. The majority of classroom teachers are both female and Caucasian. The 2012-13 pupil/teacher ratio for grades K-3 was 18.5, and for grades 4-5 was 21.5. The maximum class enrollment for K-3 was 20 students, and 25 students for grades 4-5. The number of classroom teachers and specialists is shown below in Figure F-34.

*Look Fors:* **Increases/decreases in number of teachers over time, commensurate with student population.**

*Planning Implications:* **Are there enough teachers to keep class sizes low?**

### Figure F-34

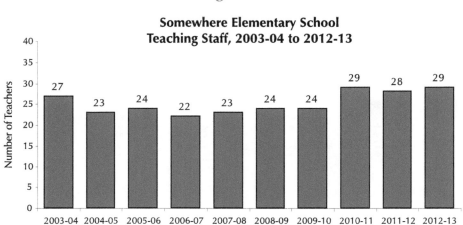

Somewhere Elementary School
Teaching Staff, 2003-04 to 2012-13

Figure F-35 shows the average number of years of teaching experience for Somewhere teachers, compared to the district average, for the past six years for the school and district.

| *Look Fors:* | Number of years teaching experience within and across grade levels. |
| --- | --- |
| *Planning Implications:* | How is the average number of years of teaching experience changing, over time, for the school and district? |

### Figure F-35

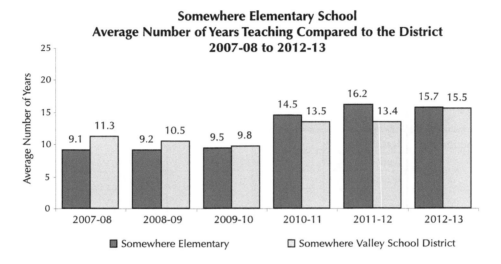

**Somewhere Elementary School**
**Average Number of Years Teaching Compared to the District**
**2007-08 to 2012-13**

Figure F-36 shows the total number of years of teaching experience, by grade taught, for each of the classroom teachers at Somewhere Elementary School for 2012-13. The overall average number of years of teaching experience is just under 16 years. The principal has been the leader of this school since 2008-09.

| *Look Fors:* | Number of years of teaching experience within and across grade levels. |
| *Planning Implications:* | Is a teacher mentoring program required within specific grade levels? Is teaching expertise even across grade levels? |

Figure F-36

**Somewhere Elementary School
Teaching Experience by Grade Level and Teacher, 2012-13**

| Grade Level | Teacher | Years of Experience | Grade Level | Teacher | Years of Experience |
|---|---|---|---|---|---|
| Kindergarten | Teacher A | 11 | Grade Three | Teacher A | 24 |
| | Teacher B | 21 | | Teacher B | 15 |
| | Teacher C | 5 | | Teacher C | 15 |
| | Teacher D | 18 | | Teacher D | 35 |
| | Teacher E | 13 | Grade Four | Teacher A | 11 |
| Grade One | Teacher A | 31 | | Teacher B | 18 |
| | Teacher B | 8 | | Teacher C | 15 |
| | Teacher C | 16 | Grade Five | Teacher A | 41 |
| | Teacher D | 2 | | Teacher B | 3 |
| | Teacher E | 5 | | Teacher C | 10 |
| Grade Two | Teacher A | 15 | Specialists | Science | 7 |
| | Teacher B | 26 | | Science | 12 |
| | Teacher C | 6 | | Resource | 8 |
| | Teacher D | 14 | | Psychologist PT | 20 |
| | Teacher E | 19 | | Title 1 | 32 |
| | | | | Speech PT | 18 |

## PERCEPTIONS

To get a better understanding of the learning environment at Somewhere Elementary School, students, staff, and parents completed *Education for the Future* questionnaires five years in a row in 2009, 2010, 2011, 2012, and 2013. Staff also assessed where they felt the school ranked on the *Education for the Future Continuous Improvement Continuums* (CICs). (Results not shown here.) Summaries of the questionnaire results follow.

### Student Questionnaire Results

Students in kindergarten through grade five at Somewhere Elementary School responded to an online *Education for the Future* questionnaire designed to measure how they feel about their learning environment in June 2009 ($n=490$), May 2010 ($n=479$), June 2011 ($n=455$), April 2012 ($n=446$), and May 2013 ($n=451$). Students in kindergarten and grade one were asked to respond to items using a three-point scale: 1 = disagree; 2 = neutral; and, 3 = agree. Students in grades two through five were asked to respond to items using a five-point scale: 1 = strongly disagree; 2 = disagree; 3 = neutral; 4 = agree; and 5 = strongly agree.

Average responses to each item on the questionnaire were graphed by the totals for the five years and disaggregated by gender, grade level, and ethnicity, for the most recent year.

The icons in the figures that follow show the average responses to each item by the disaggregation indicated in the legend. The lines join the icons to help the reader know the distribution results for each disaggregation. The lines have no other meaning.

*Look Fors:*    **Items which students are in agreement or disagreement.**

*Planning Implications:*    **Where can/should the school provide leadership with respect to school environment?**

### *Kindergarten and Grade One Student Responses*
*Total Student Responses for Five Years*

Overall, the average responses to the items in the student questionnaire were in agreement all five years (June 2009, $n=165$; May 2010, $n=166$; June 2011, $n=170$; April 2012, $n=180$; and May 2013, $n=184$), as shown in Figure F-37.

### Figure F-37

**Somewhere Elementary School Students (Kindergarten–Grade One)
Responses by Year, June 2009, May 2010, June 2011, April 2012, and May 2013**

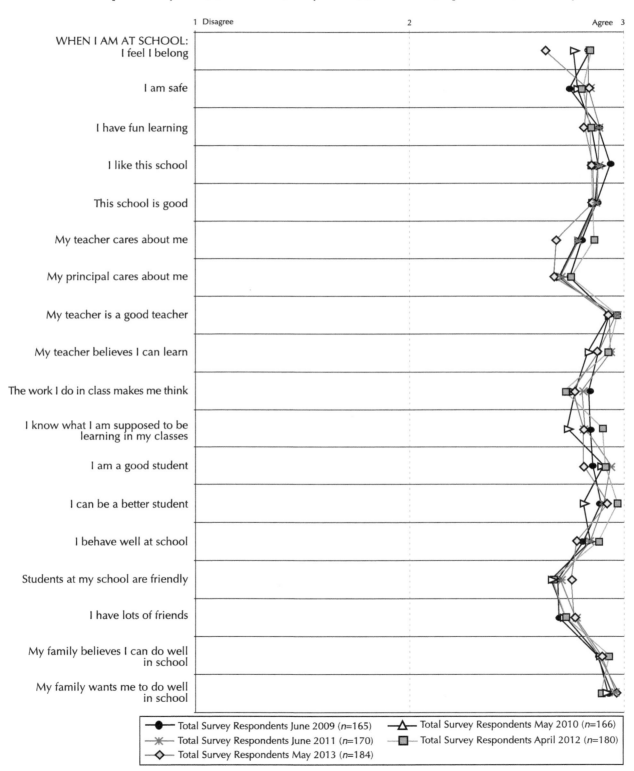

Total Survey Respondents June 2009 (*n*=165)
Total Survey Respondents May 2010 (*n*=166)
Total Survey Respondents June 2011 (*n*=170)
Total Survey Respondents April 2012 (*n*=180)
Total Survey Respondents May 2013 (*n*=184)

## Student Responses by Gender

When the K-1 data were disaggregated by gender (91 female; 93 male), the data revealed that responses were in agreement and clustered around the overall average (graph not shown here).

## Student Responses by Grade Level

The questionnaire results were also disaggregated by grade level. In 2013, there were 95 kindergartners and 89 first graders responding. All students were in agreement with the items on the questionnaire (graph not shown here).

## Student Responses by Ethnicity

When K-1 student questionnaire data were disaggregated by ethnicity: 128 Hispanic/Latino students (70% of the responding population); 39 Caucasian students (21%); 8 Asians (4%); and 8 "Others" (4%) responded. (*Note*: Ethnicity numbers add up to more than the total number of respondents because some students identified themselves by more than one ethnicity.)

While there were slight differences between ethnicities, all students responded in agreement (graph not shown here).

## Student Open-Ended K-1 Responses

Somewhere Elementary School K-1 students were asked to respond to two open-ended questions: *What do you like about your school?* and *What do you wish was different at your school?* Below are the top ten written-in responses for the two questions. (*Note*: When analyzing open-ended results, one must keep in mind the number of responses that were optionally written-in. Open-ended responses often help us understand the multiple choice responses, although caution must be exercised with small numbers of respondents.)

*Look Fors:* **The most often written-in responses to what students like about school and wish was different.**

*Planning Implications:* **Perhaps issues regarding how students are treated?**

## Student Open-Ended Responses (Kindergarten to Grade One)

### What do you like about your school?

| May 2010 (N=165) | May 2011 (N=170) |
|---|---|
| • Learning/classroom activities (66)<br>• Friends (36)<br>• Teachers (33)<br>• Playground (25)<br>• Recess (20)<br>• Computers (15)<br>• Feeling safe (10)<br>• Library (8)<br>• Food/snacks (7)<br>• Principal (4) | • Learning (54)<br>• Recess/playing (50)<br>• Friends (49)<br>• Teachers (41)<br>• School (20)<br>• Classroom (10)<br>• Decision time (10)<br>• Computers (9)<br>• All (8)<br>• Library (6) |

| April 2012 (N=180) | May 2013 (N=184) |
|---|---|
| • I like to play (47)<br>• Good friends (44)<br>• Good teachers (29)<br>• Reading (29)<br>• Learning (24)<br>• Recess (18)<br>• Writing (11)<br>• Math (11)<br>• I like the playground (11)<br>• Self-directed learning time/choice time (9) | • Reading/books (32)<br>• Learning (to draw pictures, write name, work with other kids) (27)<br>• Playing with my friends (27)<br>• I like to play (20)<br>• My teacher (19)<br>• Self-directed learning time (16)<br>• Math timed tests (16)<br>• Computers, computer lab (12)<br>• I like recess (11)<br>• Going to lunch; school is fun (9) |

### What do you wish was different at your school?

| May 2010 (N=165) | May 2011 (N=170) |
|---|---|
| • Playground/swings (38)<br>• Nothing (36)<br>• Food (14)<br>• Friends (11)<br>• Less classroom time (10)<br>• Teachers (5)<br>• Prettier school (4)<br>• More computers (4)<br>• More respect (3)<br>• Classroom (4) | • Playground (25)<br>• Nothing (24)<br>• Free time (11)<br>• Friends (10)<br>• Toys (10)<br>• More recess (9)<br>• Classroom (8)<br>• Curriculum (7)<br>• Lunch/food (7)<br>• Be nice to me (6) |

| April 2012 (N=180) | May 2013 (N=184) |
|---|---|
| • Nothing (28)<br>• Better/more lunch (17)<br>• New/better equipment on the playground (17)<br>• A swimming pool (11)<br>• My friends were nicer to me (9)<br>• More computers/time 8)<br>• We could play more (7)<br>• More nice people (5)<br>• More recess (5)<br>• More books (4) | • Nothing/I like it the way it is (22)<br>• Everybody was nice to each other, no mean people (10)<br>• That the school had more toys/games (10)<br>• We had more time to learn more things/read aloud/more school (9)<br>• More recess/longer (8)<br>• That school had more books (7)<br>• I wish there was swings (6)<br>• More books (5)<br>• I wish I had more friends<br>• Allow pets at school (5) |

*Grades Two through Five Student Responses*

*Total Student Responses for Five Years*

Overall, the average responses to the items in the student questionnaire were in agreement all five years (June 2009, $n=325$; May 2010, $n=313$; June 2011, $n=285$; April 2012, $n=266$; and May 2013, $n=267$), as shown in Figure F-38. Students strongly agreed with all items in 2012, with the following exceptions which were in agreement:

- I have freedom at school.
- I have choices in what I learn.
- I am challenged by the work my teacher asks me to do.
- Students are treated fairly by the people on recess duty.
- Students at my school treat me with respect.
- Students at my school are friendly.

## Figure F-38

### Somewhere Elementary School Students (Grades 2 to 5)
### Responses by Year, June 2009, May 2010, June 2011, April 2012, and May 2013

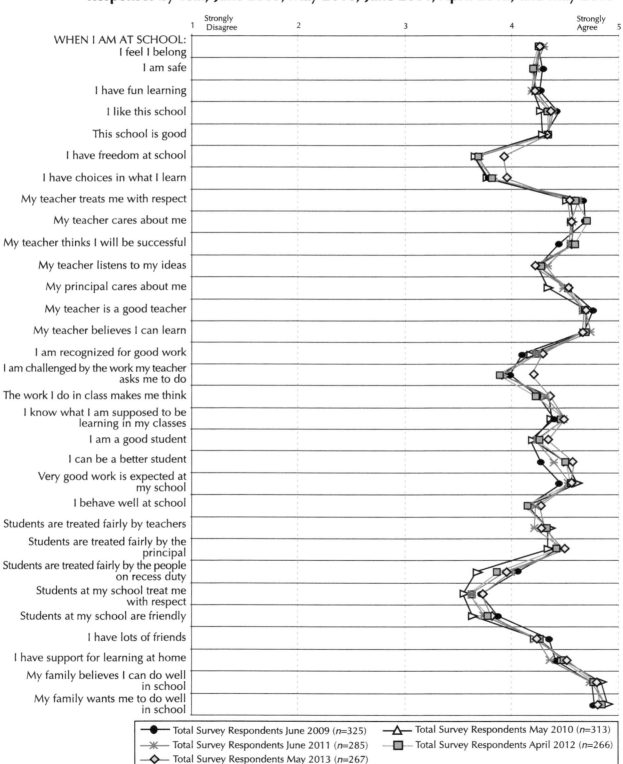

Total Survey Respondents June 2009 (*n*=325)   Total Survey Respondents May 2010 (*n*=313)
Total Survey Respondents June 2011 (*n*=285)   Total Survey Respondents April 2012 (*n*=266)
Total Survey Respondents May 2013 (*n*=267)

*Student Responses by Gender*

When the 2013 results were disaggregated by gender (140 female; 120 male), the data revealed that disaggregated responses were very similar and clustered around the overall average (graph not shown here). (*Note:* Gender numbers do not add up to the total number of respondents because some students did not identify themselves by this demographic.)

*Student Responses by Grade Level*

The 2013 questionnaire results were also disaggregated by grade level (72 second graders, 67 third graders, 62 fourth graders, and 61 fifth graders), as shown in Figure F-39. (*Note:* Grade-level numbers do not add up to the total number of respondents because some students did not identify themselves by this demographic.) All grade levels were in agreement—however, compared to grades two and three, grades four and five students were less positive in their responses.

Figure F-39

## Somewhere Elementary School Students (Grades 2 to 5) Responses by Grade Level, May 2013

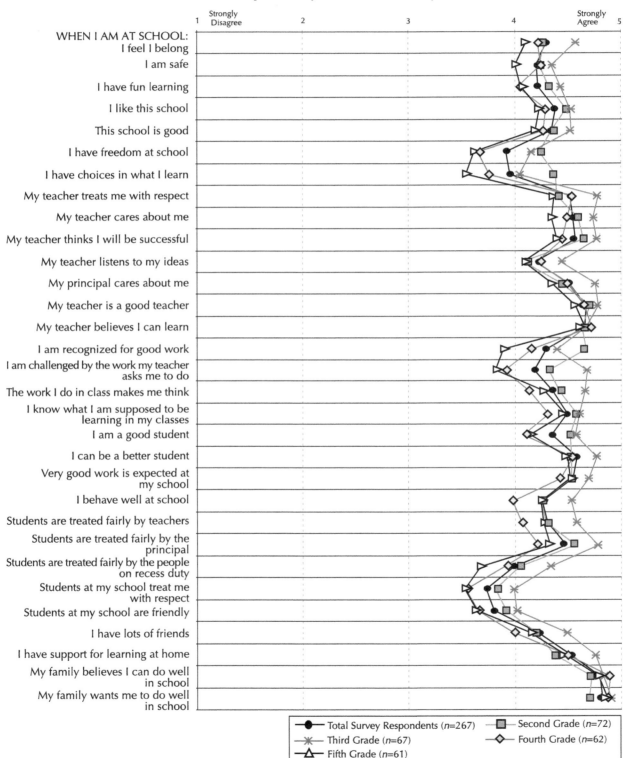

*Student Responses by Ethnicity*

When 2013 student questionnaire data were disaggregated by ethnicity: 183 Hispanic/Latino students (62% of the responding population); 44 Caucasians (15%); 19 Asians (6%); 7 African-Americans (2%); 8 American Indians (3%); and 32 "Others" (12%) responded. (*Note:* Ethnicity numbers add up to more than the total number of respondents because some students identified themselves by more than one ethnicity.)

While there were a few differences between ethnicities (graph not shown here), students mostly responded in agreement, with some exceptions. African-American and American Indian students were the least positive with their responses, in comparison to the other students.

African-American students (*n*=7) were in disagreement with average responses falling between two and three on the five-point scale, about the items:

♦ I have fun learning.

♦ I like this school.

♦ The school is good.

♦ I have freedom at school.

♦ I have choices in what I learn.

♦ My teacher treats me with respect.

♦ Students are treated fairly by teachers.

♦ Students at my school treat me with respect.

♦ Students at my school are friendly.

♦ I have lots of friends.

American Indian students (*n*=8) responded in disagreement to the items:

♦ Students at my school treat me with respect.

♦ Students at my school are friendly.

*Student Open-Ended Grades Two through Five Responses*

Somewhere Elementary School students, grades two through five, were asked to respond to two open-ended questions: *What do you like about your school?* and *What do you wish was different at your school?* Below are the top ten written-in responses for the two questions.

*Look Fors:* **The most often written-in responses to what students like about school and wish was different.**

*Planning Implications:* **Perhaps issues regarding how students are treated?**

## Student Open-Ended Responses (Grades Two to Five)

### *What do you like about your school?*

| May 2010 (*N*=313) | May 2011 (*N*=285) |
|---|---|
| • Teachers (121)<br>• Friends (79)<br>• Classroom (60)<br>• Recess/playground (48)<br>• Computers (33)<br>• Library (24)<br>• P.E. (22)<br>• Everything (20)<br>• Principal (19)<br>• Science (13) | • Teachers (97)<br>• Friends (56)<br>• Recess (55)<br>• Curriculum (37)<br>• Computer (34)<br>• PE (24)<br>• Learning (23)<br>• Library (21)<br>• People (18)<br>• Principal (18) |

| April 2012 (*N*=266) | May 2013 (*N*=267) |
|---|---|
| • Teachers (101)<br>• Friends/Making new friends (48)<br>• Computers (34)<br>• Recess (31)<br>• Everyone is treated with respect/ very nice people/ kids/teachers (27)<br>• The playground/playing outside (25)<br>• I like math (25)<br>• I like to learn (23)<br>• School library (21)<br>• P.E. (20) | • Teachers (73)<br>• Math (53)<br>• Recess (42)<br>• Reading (39)<br>• Computer lab (34)<br>• Friends (32)<br>• Lunch (27)<br>• Friendly atmosphere/respectful/trusting (19)<br>• Learning (17)<br>• Our principal; P.E. (16) |

### *What do you wish was different at your school?*

| May 2010 (*N*=313) | May 2011 (*N*=285) |
|---|---|
| • Better playground/swings (53)<br>• More recess (48)<br>• More respect (43)<br>• Better food (42)<br>• Nothing (27)<br>• Better teachers (13)<br>• Better learning (13)<br>• More fun (9)<br>• Principal (8)<br>• More math (7) | • Nothing (41)<br>• Playground equipment (35)<br>• More recess (35)<br>• Lunch (26)<br>• More respect (24)<br>• Homework (17)<br>• More PE (12)<br>• Curriculum (9)<br>• Freedom (9)<br>• Computers (7) |

| April 2012 (*N*=266) | May 2013 (*N*=267) |
|---|---|
| • The food was better (42)<br>• Bigger playground with more equipment (seesaws, sand, swings) (40)<br>• Nothing, I like it the way it is (38)<br>• Kids/people treated everyone with respect (28)<br>• We had more/longer recess (25)<br>• Nice yard duties (12)<br>• We could have laptops at school (9)<br>• Shorter school time (9)<br>• That there were more books in the library/check-out more at one time (10)<br>• There was a swimming pool (8) | • Better lunch food/snacks (46)<br>• Nothing/everything is good (31)<br>• Longer recess (21)<br>• Bigger/playground slide/swings (16)<br>• Respectful/more friendly/nicer people (15)<br>• Get new soccer goals/bigger field/better soccer balls (14)<br>• We could have brownies/ice cream at lunch (9)<br>• Cleaner bathrooms/dry floors (8)<br>• I wish I could bring my skateboard (8)<br>• Ride our bikes (7) |

## Staff Questionnaire Results

Somewhere Elementary School staff responded to a questionnaire designed to measure their perceptions of the school environment in June 2009 (*n*=36), May 2010 (*n*=38), June 2011 (*n*=45), May 2012 (*n*=48), and May 2013 (*n*=43). Staff members were asked to respond to items using a five-point scale: 1 = strongly disagree; 2 = disagree; 3 = neutral; 4 = agree; and 5 = strongly agree.

Average responses to each item on the questionnaire were graphed by year, and disaggregated by ethnicity, job title, and number of years teaching experience, revealing some differences. The two-page graphs are shown in Figures F-43 and F-45.

The icons in the figures that follow show the average responses to each item by disaggregation indicated in the legend. The lines join the icons to help the reader know the distribution results for each disaggregation. The lines have no other meaning.

| | |
|---|---|
| *Look Fors:* | **Items which staff members are in agreement or disagreement.** |
| *Planning Implications:* | **Where can/should the school provide leadership with respect to school environment?** |

### *Total Staff Responses for Five Years*

Overall, the average responses to the items in the staff questionnaire were mostly in agreement all five years, except for one item: *This school has a good public image* (Figure F-40). Staff responding in 2011 and 2012 were in low agreement, while staff in 2009 and 2010 were in strong disagreement, and closer to neutral in 2008. Responses were in agreement in 2012 and 2013.

In addition to items completed by all staff, the questionnaire contained a set of five statements for teachers and instructional assistants only. The respondents were in agreement, and results are shown in Figure F-41.

Figure F-40

**Somewhere Elementary School Staff Responses by Year
June 2009, May 2010, June 2011, May 2012, and May 2013**

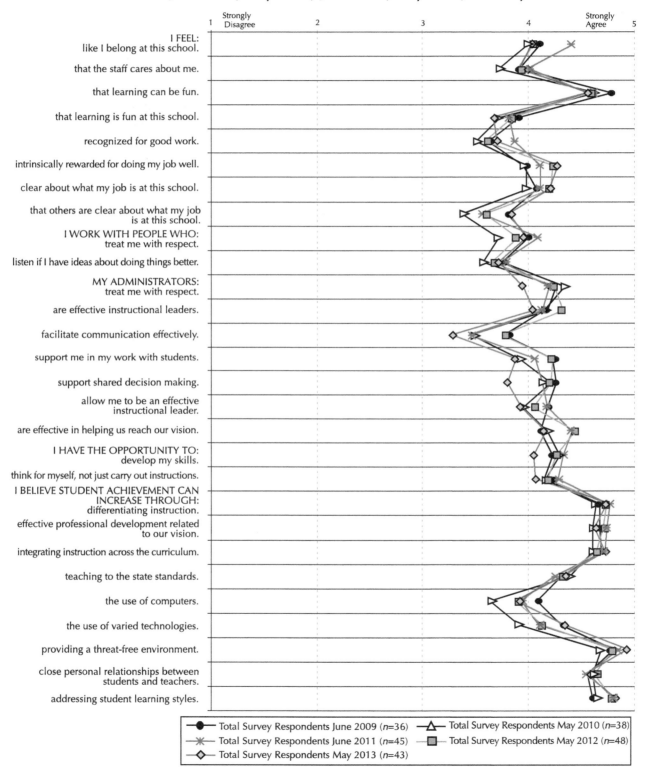

**Figure F-40** (Continued)

## Somewhere Elementary School Staff Responses by Year (Continued)
### June 2009, May 2010, June 2011, May 2012, and May 2013

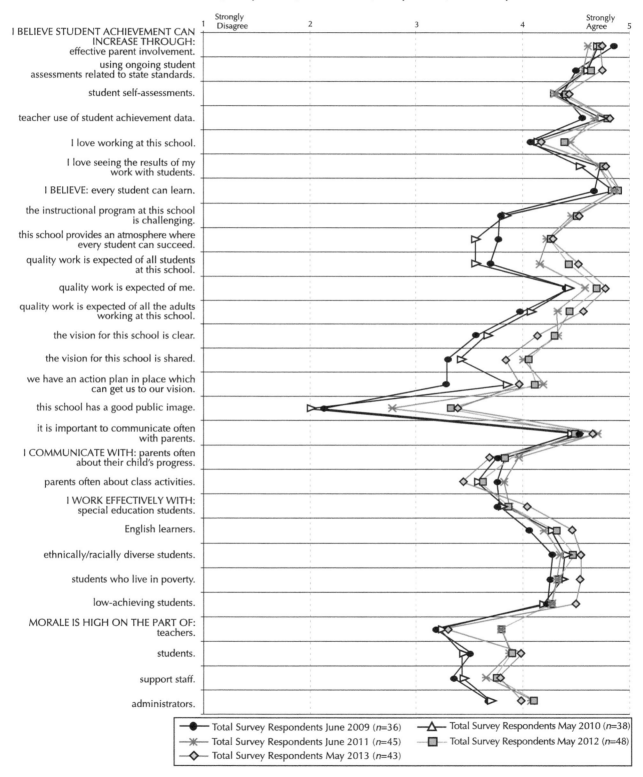

## Figure F-41

### Somewhere Elementary School Staff Responses by Year
### Items for Teachers and Instructional Assistants by Year
### June 2009, May 2010, June 2011, May 2012, and May 2013

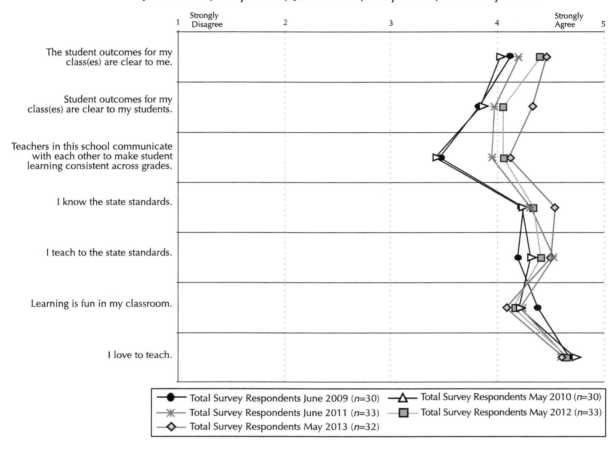

## Staff Responses by Ethnicity

When staff questionnaire data were disaggregated by ethnicity: 30 Caucasians (75% of the responding population); 5 Asians (12.5%); and 5 Hispanic/Latino (12.5%), responded (graph not shown here). (*Note:* Ethnicity numbers do not add up to the total number of respondents because some staff did not identify themselves by this demographic.)

While there were a few differences among ethnicities, staff responded mostly in agreement, except that Hispanic/Latino staff were in disagreement with the item: *My administrators support shared decision making.* Hispanic/Latino staff were neutral (at 3.0 on the five-point scale) about: *My administrators facilitate communication effectively.* Caucasian staff also responded near neutral to this statement. Asian staff were neutral about the item: *I communicate with parents often about class activities.*

## Staff Responses by Job Title

When staff questionnaire data were disaggregated by job title: 25 classroom teachers, 7 instructional staff, 5 certified staff, and 6 classified staff responded (graph not shown here). Most respondents were in agreement, with some exceptions. Classified staff disagreed with the item: *I feel that others are clear about what my job is at this school.* Some staff responded neutral to the following:

♦ My administrators facilitate communication effectively (certificated staff).

♦ I believe this school has a good public image (classified staff).

♦ I believe I communicate with parents often about class activities (certificated staff).

♦ Morale is high on the part of teachers (classroom teachers).

## Staff Responses by Number of Years Teaching

Staff questionnaire data were disaggregated by the number of years teaching experience: four to six years (*n*=8); seven to ten years (*n*=7); and eleven or more years (*n*=21). (*Note:* Numbers do not add up to the total number of respondents because some staff did not identify themselves by this demographic.)

While there were some differences between respondents with respect to the number of years of teaching (Figure F-42), staff responded mostly in agreement. Some staff responded neutral (at 3.0 on the five-point scale), or near neutral, to the three items listed below:

♦ My administrators facilitate communication effectively (seven to ten years; eleven or more years).

♦ This school has a good public image (seven to ten years).

♦ I communicate with parents often about class activities (four to six years; seven to ten years).

♦ Morale is high on the part of teachers (eleven or more years).

Figure F-42

## Somewhere Elementary School Staff
## Responses by Number of Years Teaching, May 2013

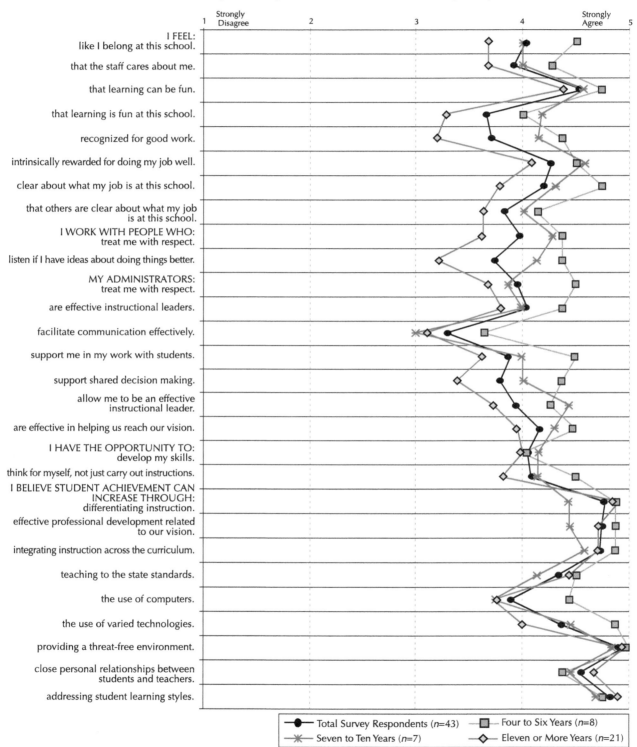

**Figure F-42** (Continued)

## Somewhere Elementary School Staff (Continued)
## Responses by Number of Years Teaching, May 2013

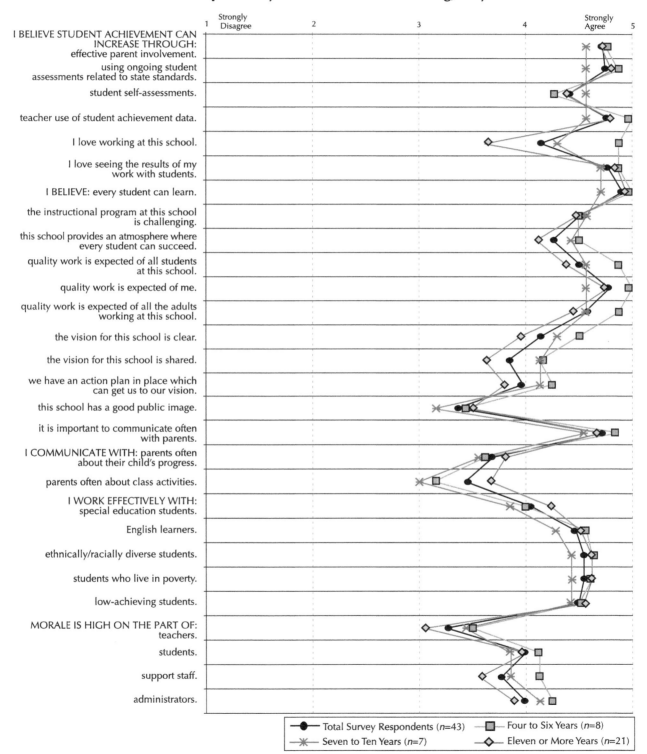

### Staff Open-Ended Responses

Somewhere Elementary School staff completed two open-ended questions: *What are the strengths of this school?* and *What needs to be improved?* The top ten results are shown below.

*Look Fors:* **The most often written-in responses to what staff members like about school and what needs to be improved.**

*Planning Implications:* **Might there be issues regarding communication, climate, vision, data use, etc.?**

## Staff Open-Ended Responses

| What are the strengths of this school? | |
|---|---|
| **May 2010 (*N*=38)** | **May 2011 (*N*=45)** |
| • Staff (17)<br>• Collaboration (14)<br>• Focus of our work on a vision/goals (11)<br>• Classroom practices (8)<br>• Principal (6)<br>• High expectations (5)<br>• Shared leadership (5)<br>• Common, frequent assessments (4)<br>• Use of standards (3)<br>• Diverse student population (2) | • School culture (18)<br>• Collaboration among staff (16)<br>• Administration (9)<br>• Teachers (7)<br>• Instructional practices (6)<br>• Shared leadership (5)<br>• Continuous improvement (5)<br>• Use of data and common formative assessments (4)<br>• Support for bilingual students (2)<br>• Diversity (2) |
| **May 2012 (*N*=34)** | **May 2013 (*N*=43)** |
| • The teachers (13)<br>• Shared leadership/supportive principal (12)<br>• The level of teamwork (9)<br>• Wanting to improve/learn (8)<br>• Enthusiastic students (5)<br>• High expectations (5)<br>• Data driven instruction (5)<br>• Shared vision (5)<br>• Goal to be PLC (2)<br>• Moving on the right path-much has improved over the past 3 years | • Bilingual staff and support staff—very talented/caring/professional (16)<br>• Teachers have high standards/are well qualified/work closely together/collaborate (13)<br>• Collaboration (9)<br>• We use data to drive instruction/data teams (7)<br>• High expectations of students and teachers/rigor/accountability/growth (6)<br>• Shared vision/leadership (3)<br>• Willingness to try new things like CAFE and RTI (3)<br>• The principal/leadership provides a good vision (3)<br>• Achievement is up, and more kids are thriving (2)<br>• Staff development (2) |

## Staff Open-Ended Responses (Continued)

| What needs to be improved? | |
|---|---|
| **May 2010 (N=38)** | **May 2011 (N=45)** |
| • Communication, including staff and parents (15)<br>• Climate including respect and a safe place (9)<br>• Organization (4)<br>• High academic/behavior expectations held by all (4)<br>• Enrichment/fun extras (3)<br>• Vision (2)<br>• Accountability for teachers (2)<br>• Celebrations (2)<br>• Parent participation (2)<br>• More aides (2) | • Communication (10)<br>• Timely office communication (9)<br>• Family involvement (5)<br>• Office procedures (4)<br>• Instructional practices (3)<br>• Keep focus (3)<br>• Expand shared vision (2)<br>• Jobs (2)<br>• Job description (2)<br>• Not following protocol (2) |
| **May 2012 (N=34)** | **May 2013 (N=43)** |
| • Better communication with all involved; parents, students, staff (15)<br>• Respect for everyone's opinion (8)<br>• Work-load (3)<br>• Parent involvement (2)<br>• Funding; state budget<br>• Better follow through<br>• There is a sense of isolation for those that are not tied to a specific team<br>• Still need for all students to buy in to school pride<br>• Continue to insure that all students achieve at high levels<br>• Teaching to the whole child not just test scores | • Communication/from principal/between grade levels/between staff (14)<br>• Equity of listening to ideas, respect for, treatment of staff members by administration (9)<br>• A shared leadership with the entire staff-not just a few chosen ones (6)<br>• The fairness/favoritism among staff needs to be figured out (5)<br>• Staff feeling safe to share opinions (4)<br>• Not all voices are heard (3)<br>• Feel pushed beyond means to accommodate decisions/pace of change (3)<br>• Staff development seems to always be given to the same people (2)<br>• More fun/enrichment in the classrooms (2)<br>• Morale (2) |

## Parent Questionnaire Responses

Parents of students attending Somewhere Elementary School completed a questionnaire designed to measure their perceptions of the school environment in June 2009 ($n=290$), May 2010 ($n=242$), June 2011 ($n=301$), May 2012 ($n=295$), and May 2013 ($n=287$). Parents were asked to respond to items using a five-point scale: 1 = strongly disagree; 2 = disagree; 3 = neutral; 4 = agree; and, 5 = strongly agree.

Average responses to each item on the questionnaire were graphed by year and disaggregated by children's grade levels, ethnicity, native language, number of children in the household, number of children in the school, and person completing the questionnaire.

The icons in the figures that follow, show the average responses to each item by disaggregation indicated in the legend. The lines join the icons to help the reader know the distribution results for each disaggregation. The lines have no other meaning.

| *Look Fors:* | **Items which are in agreement or disagreement.** |
| *Planning Implications:* | **Where can/should the school provide leadership with respect to school environment?** |

### *Total Parent Responses for Five Years*

Overall, the average responses to the items in the parent questionnaire were in agreement all five years, as shown in Figure F-43. They appear to be "happiest" in 2013.

Figure F-43

**Somewhere Elementary School Parent Responses by Year
June 2009, June 2010, June 2011, May 2012, and May 2013**

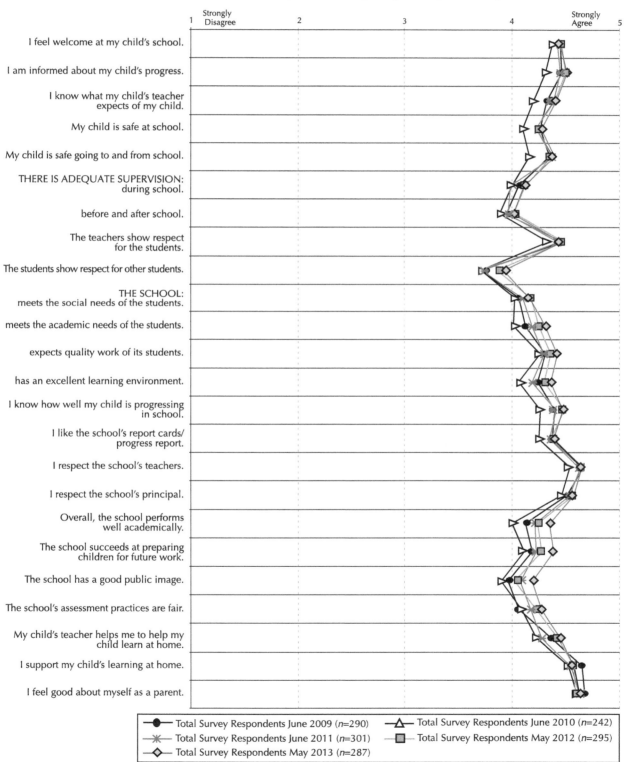

## Parent Responses by Children's Grade Level

Results graphed by children's grade level (kindergarten, $n$=64; first grade, $n$=78; second grade, $n$=63; third grade, $n$=58; fourth grade, $n$=39; and fifth grade, $n$=43), revealed that average responses were very similar and clustered around the overall average (graph not shown here). All respondents were in agreement with the statements on the questionnaire.

(*Note:* Grade-level numbers add up to more than the total number of respondents because some parents identified themselves by more than one demographic.)

## Parent Responses by Ethnicity

Parent questionnaire data were also disaggregated by ethnicity: 203 Hispanic/Latino students (74% of the responding population); 46 Caucasians (17%); 17 Asians (6%); and 9 "Others" (3%) responded. (*Note:* Ethnicity numbers do not add up to the total number of respondents because some parents did not identify themselves by ethnicity.)

While most respondents were in agreement (Figure F-44), parents of "Other" ethnicities were neutral in their response to the item: Students show respect for other students. Also, parents of "Other" ethnicities were less positive to most items, compared to other respondents.

## Figure F-44

### Somewhere Elementary School Parent Responses by Ethnicity
### May 2013

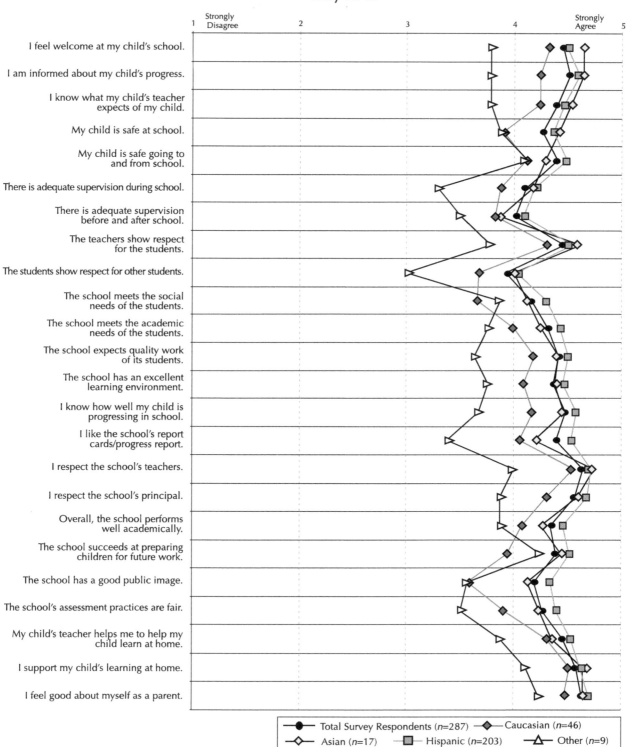

### Parent Responses by Native Language

Parent questionnaire data were also graphed by native language: Spanish language, $n=185$ (70% of the responding population); English language, $n=68$ (26%); and other languages, $n=13$ (5%). Data reveal that average responses were very similar and clustered around the overall average (graph not shown here). All respondents were in agreement with the statements on the questionnaire. (*Note:* Native language numbers do not add up to the total number of respondents because some parents did not identify themselves by this demographic.)

### Parent Responses by Number of Children in the School

Results graphed by the number of children in the school: one child, $n=148$ (66% of the responding population); two children, $n=67$ (30%); and three children, $n=10$ (4%); reveal that average parent responses were very similar and clustered around the overall average (graph not shown here). All respondents were in agreement with the statements on the questionnaire. (*Note:* Number of children in the school do not add up to the total number of respondents because some parents did not identify themselves by this demographic.)

### Parent Responses by Number of Children in the Household

Parent responses were disaggregated by the number of children in the household: one child, $n=40$ (22% of the responding population); two children, $n=76$ (42%); three children, $n=43$ (24%); four children, $n=14$ (8%); and five children, $n=9$ (5%). (*Note:* Numbers do not add up to the total number of respondents because some parents did not identify themselves by this demographic.) Parents were in agreement with all statements on the questionnaire (graph not shown here).

### Parent Responses by Person Completing the Questionnaire

Results graphed by the person completing the questionnaire (Mother, $n=223$; and Father, $n=70$), reveal that average responses were very similar and clustered around the overall average (graph not shown here). All respondents were in agreement with the statements on the questionnaire.

### Parent Open-Ended Responses

Somewhere Elementary School parents completed two open-ended questions: *What are the strengths of this school?* and *What needs to be improved?* The top ten results are shown below.

*Look Fors:* **The most often written-in responses to what parents like about school and what needs to be improved.**

*Planning Implications:* **Are there issues regarding how students are treated or challenged in school?**

## Parent Open-Ended Responses

### What are the strengths of this school?

| May 2010 (N=242) | June 2011 (N=301) |
|---|---|
| • Teachers (49)<br>• Curriculum (13)<br>• Community support (11)<br>• Principal (9)<br>• Safe (9)<br>• Students (6)<br>• Everything (4)<br>• Bilingual program (3)<br>• Teamwork (3)<br>• Communication (3) | • Teachers (84)<br>• Principal (11)<br>• Administration (9)<br>• Climate (10)<br>• Curriculum (9)<br>• Safety (7)<br>• Social skills (6)<br>• Parents (5)<br>• All (4)<br>• Communication (4) |
| **May 2012 (N=295)** | **May 2013 (N=287)** |
| • The teachers the school has (33)<br>• Education/Academics (7)<br>• The principal is excellent (6)<br>• The students (6)<br>• The team work and communication between parents and teachers (6)<br>• That students keep progressing (6)<br>• The school works together as a team (5)<br>• High expectations (4)<br>• The school's rules and behavior policies (4)<br>• The school shows good communication (4) | • Good teachers/caring/supportive/work as a team (39)<br>• We love Somewhere School/very caring/loving environment/great community (9)<br>• Positive academic environment (6)<br>• Excellent communication between teachers and parents (5)<br>• Multi-cultural environment/diversity (4)<br>• Dedication of staff towards students (3)<br>• Teacher/student ratio (2)<br>• Good education (2)<br>• The principal is a parent in the school<br>• Ability to meet families where they are |

### What do you wish was different at your school?

| May 2010 (N=242) | June 2011 (N=301) |
|---|---|
| • Academics (16)<br>• Safety (14)<br>• Nothing (12)<br>• Communication (11)<br>• Yard Duty (7)<br>• Teachers (6)<br>• English only (5)<br>• More after school activities (4)<br>• More differentiation (4)<br>• Principal (4) | • Nothing (29)<br>• Safety (22)<br>• Curriculum (16)<br>• Communication (10)<br>• Activities/whole child (7)<br>• More homework (5)<br>• Parent involvement (5)<br>• After school programs (4)<br>• Lunch (4)<br>• Physical environment (4) |
| **April 2012 (N=295)** | **May 2013 (N=287)** |
| • Nothing/Everything is good (27)<br>• School safety and security (6)<br>• Reading (3)<br>• More variety in lunch (3)<br>• More bilingual teachers (3)<br>• More community and social activities (2)<br>• More parent/student activities with the school (2)<br>• More after school programs (2)<br>• Recess supervision (2)<br>• School image to the public (2) | • Social skills for the students/manners/no bullying (7)<br>• More supervision before and after school/during lunch recess (7)<br>• Need enrichment-learning beyond what is tested (7)<br>• Breakfast and lunch menus need to be more nutritious (3)<br>• Send more homework (2)<br>• Writing programs and spelling programs (2)<br>• Communication-all aspects (2)<br>• More parent involvement (2)<br>• Nothing - everything is great/Can't think of anything (2)<br>• More teacher/parent conferences |

## STUDENT ACHIEVEMENT

The California Standards Tests (CST) show how well students are doing in relation to the state content standards. Student scores are reported as performance levels. The five performance levels are *Advanced* (exceeds state standards), *Proficient* (meets standards), *Basic* (approaching standards), *Below Basic* (below standards), and *Far Below Basic* (well below standards). Students scoring at the *Proficient* or *Advanced* levels have met state standards in that content area. Students are considered "proficient" when they score in the *Proficient* or *Advanced* levels of each test.

The STAR test results by grade level are shown in Figures F-45 through F-48 (English Language Arts) and F-49 through F-52 (Mathematics) for Somewhere students. Test results by cohorts, Figures F-53 through F-56 (English Language Arts) and F-57 through F-60 (Mathematics) follow.

Other data analyzed, but not shown here, included:

+ Individual student growth on CST, over time.

+ Classroom results over time.

+ Students over time, within classrooms.

*Look Fors:* **Overall student achievement gains/losses. The student groups that have the highest and lowest percentage scoring *Proficient*. The gaps.**

*Planning Implications:* **Are there professional learning programs that all teachers need in order to meet the needs of all students? What other services can be provided for student groups that are not scoring *Proficient* or *Advanced*, or to move all students to proficiency?**

## English Language Arts CST Proficiency by Grade Level

### Figure F-45

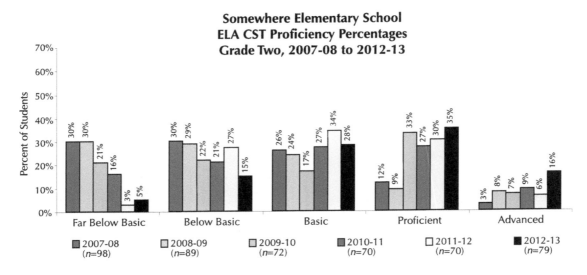

**Somewhere Elementary School**
**ELA CST Proficiency Percentages**
**Grade Two, 2007-08 to 2012-13**

☐ 2007-08 (*n*=98)  ☐ 2008-09 (*n*=89)  ☐ 2009-10 (*n*=72)  ■ 2010-11 (*n*=70)  ☐ 2011-12 (*n*=70)  ■ 2012-13 (*n*=79)

### Figure F-46

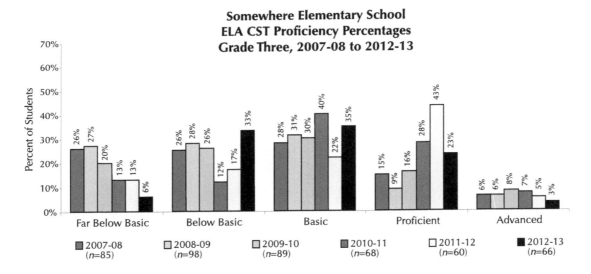

**Somewhere Elementary School**
**ELA CST Proficiency Percentages**
**Grade Three, 2007-08 to 2012-13**

■ 2007-08 (*n*=85)  ☐ 2008-09 (*n*=98)  ☐ 2009-10 (*n*=89)  ■ 2010-11 (*n*=68)  ☐ 2011-12 (*n*=60)  ■ 2012-13 (*n*=66)

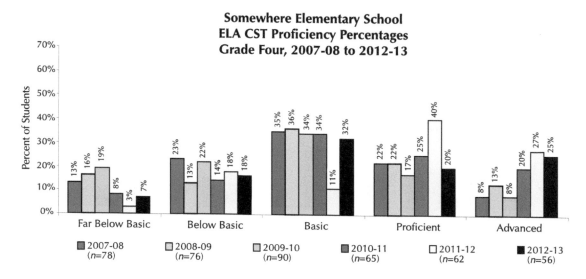

Figure F-47

**Somewhere Elementary School
ELA CST Proficiency Percentages
Grade Four, 2007-08 to 2012-13**

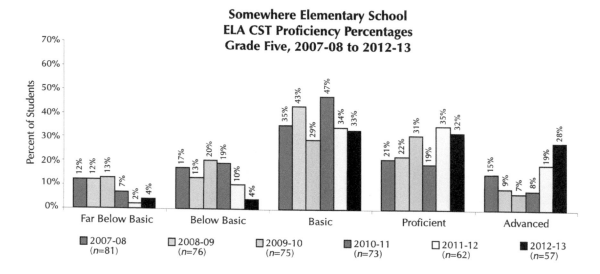

Figure F-48

**Somewhere Elementary School
ELA CST Proficiency Percentages
Grade Five, 2007-08 to 2012-13**

## Mathematics CST Proficiency by Grade Level

### Figure F-49

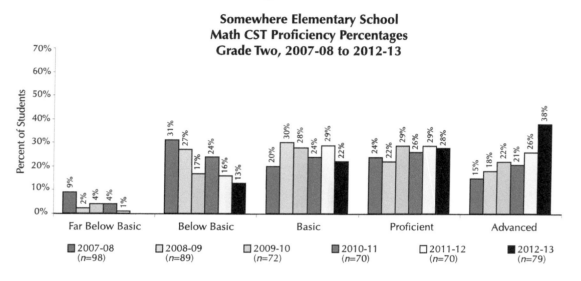

**Somewhere Elementary School**
**Math CST Proficiency Percentages**
**Grade Two, 2007-08 to 2012-13**

- 2007-08 (n=98)
- 2008-09 (n=89)
- 2009-10 (n=72)
- 2010-11 (n=70)
- 2011-12 (n=70)
- 2012-13 (n=79)

### Figure F-50

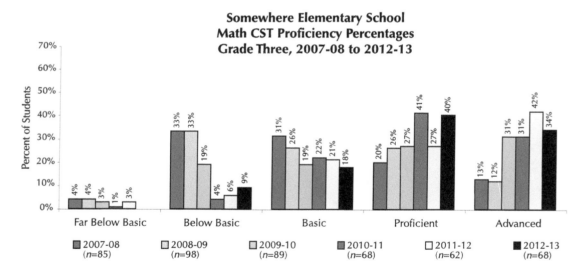

**Somewhere Elementary School**
**Math CST Proficiency Percentages**
**Grade Three, 2007-08 to 2012-13**

- 2007-08 (n=85)
- 2008-09 (n=98)
- 2009-10 (n=89)
- 2010-11 (n=68)
- 2011-12 (n=62)
- 2012-13 (n=68)

## Figure F-51

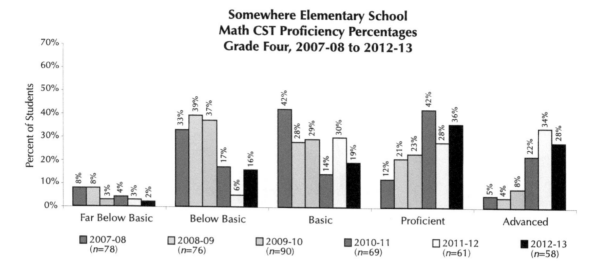

**Somewhere Elementary School**
**Math CST Proficiency Percentages**
**Grade Four, 2007-08 to 2012-13**

## Figure F-52

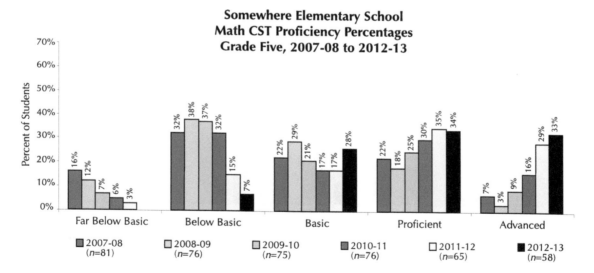

**Somewhere Elementary School**
**Math CST Proficiency Percentages**
**Grade Five, 2007-08 to 2012-13**

## English Language Arts CST Proficiency by Cohorts

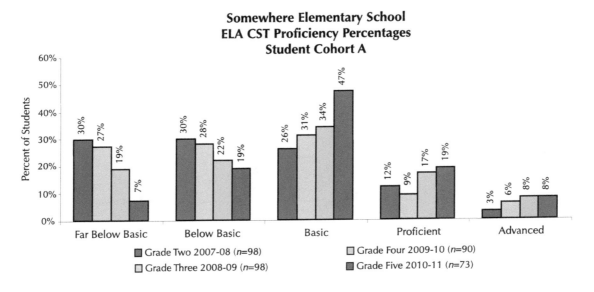

Figure F-53

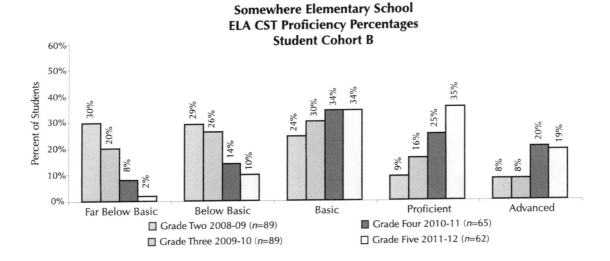

Figure F-54

## Figure F-55

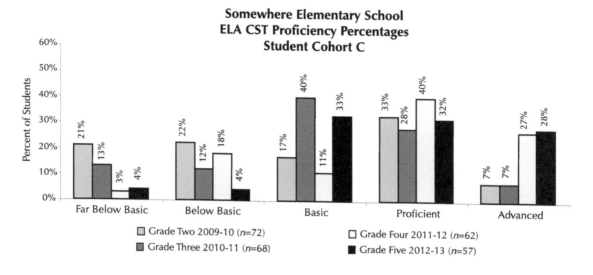

**Somewhere Elementary School**
**ELA CST Proficiency Percentages**
**Student Cohort C**

☐ Grade Two 2009-10 (*n*=72)          ☐ Grade Four 2011-12 (*n*=62)
☐ Grade Three 2010-11 (*n*=68)        ■ Grade Five 2012-13 (*n*=57)

## Figure F-56

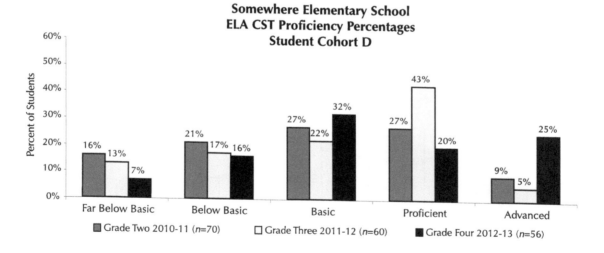

**Somewhere Elementary School**
**ELA CST Proficiency Percentages**
**Student Cohort D**

■ Grade Two 2010-11 (*n*=70)     ☐ Grade Three 2011-12 (*n*=60)     ■ Grade Four 2012-13 (*n*=56)

## Mathematics CST Proficiency by Cohorts

Figure F-57

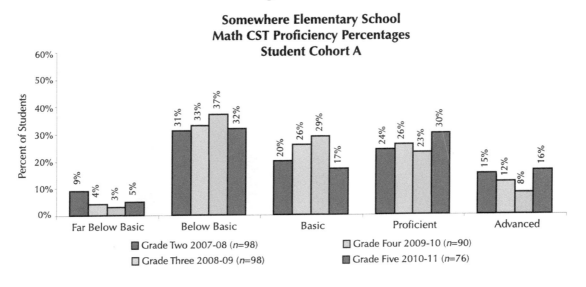

Figure F-58

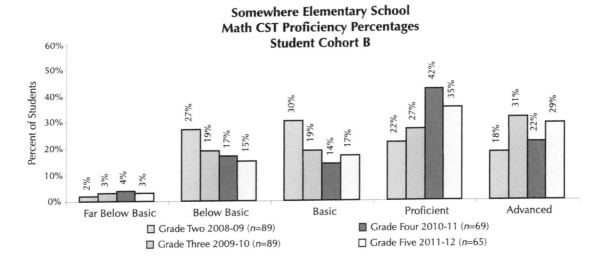

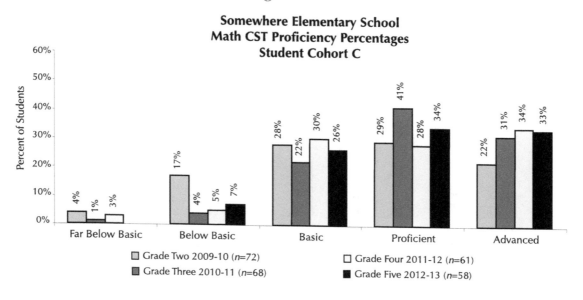

Figure F-59

**Somewhere Elementary School**
**Math CST Proficiency Percentages**
**Student Cohort C**

Grade Two 2009-10 (*n*=72)
Grade Three 2010-11 (*n*=68)
Grade Four 2011-12 (*n*=61)
Grade Five 2012-13 (*n*=58)

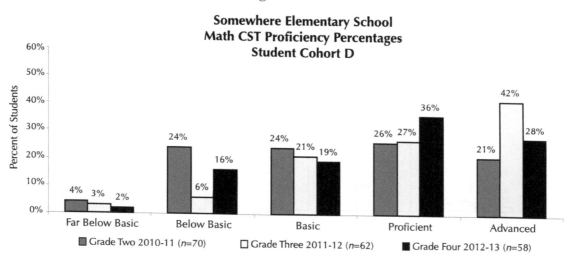

Figure F-60

**Somewhere Elementary School**
**Math CST Proficiency Percentages**
**Student Cohort D**

Grade Two 2010-11 (*n*=70)
Grade Three 2011-12 (*n*=62)
Grade Four 2012-13 (*n*=58)

The CST summary test results by grade level and school total in Figures F61 (English Language Arts) and F-62 (Mathematics) show the number and percentage of Somewhere School students scoring *Proficient* or *Advanced*. Shaded cells represent the student groups and grade levels with 50% or more students scoring *Proficient*.

Figure F-61

## Somewhere Elementary School CST Results for English Language Arts
## Number and Percentage Proficient, 2007-08 to 2012-13

| | | | English Language Arts | | | | | | | | | |
|---|---|---|---|---|---|---|---|---|---|---|---|---|
| | | | Grade 2 | | Grade 3 | | Grade 4 | | Grade 5 | | School | |
| | | | Number | Percent | Number | Percent | Number | Percent | Number | Percent | Number | Percent |
| **Overall** | All Students | 2007-08 | 15 | 15% | 18 | 21% | 23 | 30% | 29 | 36% | 85 | 24% |
| | | 2008-09 | 15 | 17% | 15 | 15% | 27 | 35% | 24 | 31% | 81 | 24% |
| | | 2009-10 | 29 | 40% | 21 | 24% | 23 | 25% | 29 | 38% | 102 | 27% |
| | | 2010-11 | 25 | 36% | 24 | 35% | 29 | 45% | 20 | 27% | 98 | 36% |
| | | 2011-12 | 25 | 36% | 29 | 48% | 42 | **67%** | 33 | **54%** | 129 | **51%** |
| | | 2012-13 | 40 | **51%** | 17 | 26% | 25 | 45% | 34 | **60%** | 117 | 45% |
| **By Gender** | Female | 2007-08 | 8 | 14% | 9 | 20% | 14 | 39% | 13 | 35% | 44 | 25% |
| | | 2008-09 | 9 | 16% | 9 | 16% | 14 | 33% | 12 | 33% | 44 | 23% |
| | | 2009-10 | 18 | 50% | 12 | 23% | 14 | 29% | 15 | 33% | 59 | 32% |
| | | 2010-11 | 14 | 40% | 14 | 37% | 16 | 40% | 13 | 30% | 57 | 36% |
| | | 2011-12 | 14 | 35% | 15 | 45% | 27 | **75%** | 20 | 48% | 76 | **50%** |
| | | 2012-13 | 25 | **57%** | 10 | 27% | 14 | 48% | 19 | **59%** | 68 | 48% |
| | Male | 2007-08 | 7 | 17% | 9 | 23% | 9 | 21% | 16 | 36% | 41 | 25% |
| | | 2008-09 | 6 | 18% | 6 | 15% | 13 | 38% | 12 | 30% | 37 | 25% |
| | | 2009-10 | 11 | 31% | 9 | 24% | 8 | 20% | 13 | 43% | 41 | 28% |
| | | 2010-11 | 11 | 31% | 10 | 33% | 13 | **52%** | 7 | 24% | 41 | 34% |
| | | 2011-12 | 11 | 37% | 14 | **52%** | 15 | **58%** | 14 | **70%** | 54 | **52%** |
| | | 2012-13 | 16 | 46% | 7 | 24% | 11 | 41% | 15 | **60%** | 49 | 42% |
| **By Ethnicity** | Hispanic/Latino | 2007-08 | 5 | 9% | 7 | 13% | 7 | 16% | 6 | 15% | 25 | 13% |
| | | 2008-09 | 2 | 4% | 5 | 8% | 16 | 31% | 9 | 20% | 32 | 15% |
| | | 2009-10 | 17 | 34% | 6 | 11% | 11 | 18% | 14 | 28% | 48 | 22% |
| | | 2010-11 | 14 | 29% | 14 | 30% | 12 | 30% | 13 | 27% | 53 | 29% |
| | | 2011-12 | 16 | 28% | 14 | 37% | 29 | **64%** | 16 | 43% | 75 | 43% |
| | | 2012-13 | 29 | **50%** | 9 | 18% | 15 | 39% | 23 | **58%** | 76 | 41% |
| | Caucasian | 2007-08 | 8 | 36% | 7 | **50%** | 11 | **52%** | 19 | **61%** | 45 | **51%** |
| | | 2008-09 | 9 | 43% | 5 | 33% | 8 | **57%** | 8 | **53%** | 30 | 46% |
| | | 2009-10 | 11 | **69%** | 11 | **55%** | 5 | 45% | 10 | **71%** | 37 | **61%** |
| | | 2010-11 | 9 | **82%** | 10 | **77%** | 11 | **85%** | 3 | 25% | 33 | **67%** |
| | | 2011-12 | 6 | **85%** | 8 | **80%** | 10 | **83%** | 10 | **72%** | 34 | **81%** |
| | | 2012-13 | 9 | **64%** | 3 | 43% | 4 | **67%** | 9 | **69%** | 25 | **63%** |
| **By Free/ Reduced Lunch** | | 2007-08 | 4 | 9% | 3 | 6% | 13 | 28% | 7 | 16% | 27 | 14% |
| | | 2008-09 | 20 | 32% | 19 | 28% | 13 | 25% | 8 | 16% | 60 | 26% |
| | | 2009-10 | 22 | 39% | 6 | 11% | 13 | 20% | 16 | 32% | 56 | 24% |
| | | 2010-11 | 16 | 29% | 14 | 27% | 14 | 33% | 15 | 29% | 59 | 29% |
| | | 2011-12 | 17 | 29% | 21 | 43% | 30 | **60%** | 19 | 45% | 87 | 44% |
| | | 2012-13 | 32 | **50%** | 12 | 21% | 19 | 40% | 22 | **50%** | 85 | 40% |

*Note: Number Proficient* = the number of students who scored *Proficient* or *Advanced* on the test.
  *Percent Proficient* = the number of students who scored *Proficient* or *Advanced* on the test, divided by the number taking the test.

Figure F-61 *(Continued)*

### Somewhere Elementary School CST Results for English Language Arts
### Number and Percentage Proficient, 2007-08 to 2012-13

| | | | English Language Arts | | | | | | | | | |
|---|---|---|---|---|---|---|---|---|---|---|---|---|
| | | | Grade 2 | | Grade 3 | | Grade 4 | | Grade 5 | | School | |
| | | | Number | Percent | Number | Percent | Number | Percent | Number | Percent | Number | Percent |
| **By English Language Learners** | English Learners | 2007-08 | 19 | 4% | 7 | 14% | 6 | 16% | 4 | 13% | 36 | 21% |
| | | 2008-09 | 3 | 6% | 2 | 4% | 9 | 23% | 8 | 21% | 22 | 12% |
| | | 2009-10 | 6 | 19% | 4 | 8% | 7 | 13% | 5 | 15% | 22 | 13% |
| | | 2010-11 | 8 | 20% | 7 | 20% | 9 | 24% | 8 | 18% | 32 | 21% |
| | | 2011-12 | 16 | 31% | 9 | 26% | 15 | **55%** | 12 | 38% | 145 | 36% |
| | | 2012-13 | 24 | 47% | 11 | 23% | 7 | 23% | 10 | 41% | 52 | 34% |
| **Fluent English Proficient/ English Only** | | 2007-08 | 13 | 26% | 11 | 32% | 17 | 41% | 25 | **51%** | 66 | 38% |
| | | 2008-09 | 12 | 34% | 13 | 32% | 18 | **50%** | 16 | 42% | 59 | 39% |
| | | 2009-10 | 23 | **58%** | 17 | 44% | 15 | 41% | 23 | **56%** | 78 | **50%** |
| | | 2010-11 | 17 | **57%** | 17 | **53%** | 20 | **74%** | 12 | 41% | 66 | **56%** |
| | | 2011-12 | 9 | **50%** | 19 | **79%** | 27 | **77%** | 22 | **70%** | 108 | **71%** |
| | | 2012-13 | 17 | **61%** | 6 | 34% | 18 | **69%** | 24 | **70%** | 65 | **61%** |

## Figure F-62

### Somewhere Elementary School CST Results for Mathematics
### Number and Percentage Proficient, 2007-08 to 2012-13

| | | | Mathematics | | | | | | | | | |
|---|---|---|---|---|---|---|---|---|---|---|---|---|
| | | | Grade 2 | | Grade 3 | | Grade 4 | | Grade 5 | | School | |
| | | | Number | Percent | Number | Percent | Number | Percent | Number | Percent | Number | Percent |
| **Overall** | All Students | 2007-08 | 39 | 39% | 28 | 33% | 13 | 17% | 23 | 29% | 102 | 30% |
| | | 2008-09 | 36 | 40% | 37 | 38% | 19 | 25% | 16 | 21% | 108 | 32% |
| | | 2009-10 | 37 | 51% | 52 | 58% | 28 | 31% | 26 | 34% | 143 | 39% |
| | | 2010-11 | 33 | 47% | 50 | 72% | 44 | 64% | 35 | 46% | 162 | 57% |
| | | 2011-12 | 39 | 55% | 43 | 69% | 38 | 62% | 42 | 64% | 162 | 63% |
| | | 2012-13 | 52 | 66% | 50 | 74% | 37 | 64% | 39 | 67% | 178 | 68% |
| **By Gender** | Female | 2007-08 | 18 | 32% | 14 | 30% | 7 | 19% | 9 | 24% | 48 | 27% |
| | | 2008-09 | 20 | 36% | 21 | 36% | 9 | 21% | 8 | 22% | 58 | 30% |
| | | 2009-10 | 20 | 56% | 29 | 56% | 14 | 29% | 13 | 29% | 76 | 42% |
| | | 2010-11 | 18 | 51% | 31 | 81% | 23 | 56% | 21 | 48% | 93 | 59% |
| | | 2011-12 | 19 | 58% | 24 | 72% | 22 | 63% | 25 | 58% | 90 | 64% |
| | | 2012-13 | 33 | 75% | 22 | 58% | 19 | 66% | 24 | 76% | 99 | 69% |
| | Male | 2007-08 | 21 | 51% | 14 | 36% | 6 | 14% | 15 | 34% | 56 | 34% |
| | | 2008-09 | 16 | 47% | 16 | 40% | 10 | 29% | 8 | 20% | 50 | 34% |
| | | 2009-10 | 17 | 47% | 23 | 62% | 14 | 34% | 13 | 43% | 67 | 47% |
| | | 2010-11 | 15 | 43% | 19 | 61% | 21 | 75% | 14 | 44% | 69 | 55% |
| | | 2011-12 | 19 | 66% | 19 | 68% | 16 | 62% | 17 | 77% | 71 | 66% |
| | | 2012-13 | 19 | 54% | 28 | 93% | 18 | 62% | 15 | 58% | 80 | 67% |
| **By Ethnicity** | Hispanic/Latino | 2007-08 | 16 | 28% | 14 | 25% | 6 | 13% | 8 | 21% | 44 | 22% |
| | | 2008-09 | 16 | 29% | 14 | 22% | 11 | 21% | 5 | 11% | 46 | 21% |
| | | 2009-10 | 21 | 42% | 25 | 46% | 13 | 21% | 15 | 30% | 74 | 34% |
| | | 2010-11 | 19 | 40% | 31 | 66% | 24 | 55% | 20 | 40% | 94 | 50% |
| | | 2011-12 | 26 | 46% | 26 | 66% | 27 | 61% | 22 | 55% | 101 | 56% |
| | | 2012-13 | 36 | 62% | 39 | 75% | 25 | 61% | 28 | 69% | 128 | 67% |
| | Caucasian | 2007-08 | 15 | 68% | 6 | 43% | 5 | 24% | 12 | 39% | 38 | 43% |
| | | 2008-09 | 13 | 62% | 10 | 67% | 6 | 43% | 5 | 33% | 34 | 52% |
| | | 2009-10 | 12 | 75% | 16 | 80% | 6 | 55% | 8 | 57% | 42 | 69% |
| | | 2010-11 | 11 | 100% | 11 | 79% | 12 | 92% | 7 | 58% | 41 | 82% |
| | | 2011-12 | 6 | 85% | 8 | 80% | 7 | 58% | 11 | 79% | 32 | 74% |
| | | 2012-13 | 11 | 79% | 3 | 41% | 4 | 67% | 8 | 62% | 26 | 65% |
| **By Free/ Reduced Lunch** | | 2007-08 | 13 | 28% | 9 | 18% | 6 | 13% | 4 | 9% | 32 | 17% |
| | | 2008-09 | 5 | 8% | 6 | 9% | 16 | 31% | 13 | 27% | 40 | 17% |
| | | 2009-10 | 26 | 46% | 31 | 51% | 16 | 24% | 17 | 32% | 90 | 38% |
| | | 2010-11 | 24 | 43% | 34 | 64% | 26 | 55% | 21 | 38% | 105 | 50% |
| | | 2011-12 | 28 | 50% | 35 | 68% | 29 | 60% | 26 | 57% | 118 | 59% |
| | | 2012-13 | 42 | 66% | 44 | 75% | 31 | 63% | 30 | 67% | 148 | 68% |

Note: Number Proficient = the number of students who scored *Proficient* or *Advanced* on the test.
  Percent Proficient = the number of students who scored *Proficient* or *Advanced* on the test, divided by the number taking the test.

**Figure F-62** *(Continued)*

## Somewhere Elementary School CST Results for Mathematics
## Number and Percentage Proficient, 2007-08 to 2012-13

| | | | Mathematics | | | | | | | | | |
|---|---|---|---|---|---|---|---|---|---|---|---|---|
| | | | Grade 2 | | Grade 3 | | Grade 4 | | Grade 5 | | School | |
| | | | Number | Percent | Number | Percent | Number | Percent | Number | Percent | Number | Percent |
| **By English Language Learners** | English Learners | 2007-08 | 12 | 25% | 16 | 31% | 4 | 11% | 4 | 13% | 36 | 21% |
| | | 2008-09 | 17 | 31% | 15 | 27% | 6 | 15% | 5 | 13% | 22 | 12% |
| | | 2009-10 | 10 | 31% | 25 | **50%** | 12 | 23% | 7 | 21% | 54 | 32% |
| | | 2010-11 | 12 | 30% | 22 | **63%** | 20 | 49% | 17 | 36% | 71 | 44% |
| | | 2011-12 | 27 | **52%** | 23 | **64%** | 14 | **52%** | 18 | **54%** | 148 | **55%** |
| | | 2012-13 | 31 | **61%** | 38 | **78%** | 21 | **66%** | 13 | **57%** | 104 | **67%** |
| **Fluent English Proficient/ English Only** | | 2007-08 | 27 | **54%** | 12 | 35% | 9 | 22% | 20 | 41% | 68 | 39% |
| | | 2008-09 | 19 | **54%** | 22 | **54%** | 13 | 36% | 11 | 29% | 65 | 43% |
| | | 2009-10 | 27 | **68%** | 27 | **69%** | 16 | 43% | 19 | 46% | 89 | **57%** |
| | | 2010-11 | 21 | **70%** | 27 | **82%** | 24 | **89%** | 18 | **62%** | 90 | **76%** |
| | | 2011-12 | 11 | **61%** | 19 | **76%** | 24 | **70%** | 24 | **75%** | 109 | **72%** |
| | | 2012-13 | 21 | **75%** | 12 | **63%** | 16 | **62%** | 26 | **74%** | 75 | **69%** |

# CASE STUDY ~ PART 2
# WHAT WE SAW IN THE DATA

To support the analysis of the example case study, the following analysis is shown:

- For each type of data—*demographics, perceptions, student learning,* and *school processes*—we listed *strengths, challenges,* and *implications for the school improvement plan.* We also indicated *other data* we wish the school had—for future data profile updates (Figures G-1 through G-4).

- We lined up the *implications* for each type of data (Figure G-5) and highlighted *commonalities* (Figure G-6). This helps us paint with a broad brush, so the school can make improvements that impact all subject areas. It also helps staff understand how the school is getting its results and what has to change to get different results. Knowing the big picture enables staff to see that there are some things in demographic and perceptions data that need attention in order to ensure student learning increases. The reverse is not true: looking at student learning data will not tell staff what needs to change in other parts of the school.

- After creating the *implication commonalities,* we stood back and determined what needed to be in the continuous school improvement plan with respect to *instruction, assessment, curriculum, standards,* etc. (Figure G-7)

Figure G-1
What We Saw in the Data: DEMOGRAPHICS

## SOMEWHERE ELEMENTARY SCHOOL
### STRENGTHS, CHALLENGES, IMPLICATIONS, AND OTHER DATA

### DEMOGRAPHIC DATA

#### 1. What are Somewhere School's demographic *strengths* and *challenges*?

| Strengths | Challenges |
|---|---|
| • Somewhere School is a diverse, medium-size school serving grades K-5.<br>• Grade-level enrollments seem to be relatively steady, although decreasing in upper grades.<br>• The mobility rate is down from a couple of years ago.<br>• Student attendance is high, although down slightly this year. Great that staff are watching attendance dynamically.<br>• There is a decrease in the number of students retained-only 2 kindergarteners were retained in 2012-13.<br>• The percentage of students by ethnicity identified for special education for the district is compatible with the overall percent enrollment for the district, as well as for the school.<br>• School and district Special Education numbers are consistent over time, by primary disability and ethnicity.<br>• Pre-referral team (PRT) and SpERT (special education referral team) seem to be working well.<br>• There has been a sharp decrease in the number of students suspended over time.<br>• It is great the school is starting to collect more behavior data.<br>• The class size is low.<br>• The average number of years of teaching has increased in the last 3 years, as have the number of teachers.<br>• The grades are pretty balanced by number of years of teaching experience.<br>• The average number of years of teaching was less than the district, then greater than, and now almost equal for Somewhere School. | • There is declining districtwide enrollment in the last few years-up slightly in 2012-13.<br>• Somewhere School is experiencing declining enrollment.<br>• Many different ethnicities are increasing as the Caucasian student population is decreasing. In the school, the Hispanic population has increased from 58% to about 75%, and the Caucasian population decreased from 27% to just under 16%. The Hispanic student population of the district increased from 20% to 26%, while its Caucasian population decreased from 65% to 59%.<br>• Mobility rate is high at about 28%.<br>• Somewhere School's ethnic breakdown is different from the other elementary schools in the district, which are more like the district population.<br>• Almost 61% of the students are English Learners; this percentage has steadily increased over the years. Somewhere School has about 4.5 times more English Learners than the district, with no English Language Development Program.<br>• There has been a steady increase of students qualifying for Free/Reduced Lunch-much higher than the district—82% versus 25%—and close to twice as many as in 2007-08.<br>• The majority of Somewhere School parents do not have high school educations.<br>• The district open enrollment policy could be setting up Somewhere School for a more challenging share of the student population.<br>• The percentage of students qualifying for special education is about 12%. The majority of special education students are male and Hispanic.<br>• The highest percentage of special education students are identified for speech/language (57.4%).<br>• There are a lot of suspensions, but the number is one-half of two years ago, and 40% of what it was three years ago.<br>• The greatest number of behavior referrals are Hispanic and males. The referrals happened mostly in September and October, and at the beginning and end of the day, in 2012-13. Second grade has the largest number of behavior referrals, by grade level.<br>• The school needs a stronger Level 3 RtI structure for the students who need it. |

#### 2. What are some *implications* for the Somewhere continuous school improvement plan?

• Are teachers prepared to teach the changing population? Do teachers know how to teach students with English as a second language, and those who live in poverty? What are the implications of teaching students living in poverty? (Perhaps more male and minority teachers need to be recruited?)
• How are class-size issues dealt with, with mobility?
• Does the school know why the mobility rate is high, and where students go? Do students stay in the district?
• How are new students and their parents welcomed to the school? How do teachers know what the new students know and are able to do?
• Are materials, programs, and library books appropriate for the student population (e.g., EL, poverty, mobile, special education), and for getting students college and career ready? Are there appropriate extra-curricular activities, clubs to meet student interests?
• How does the school help parents know how to help their children learn?
• How are the needs of students who speak English as a second language met? Is there a need for an English Language Development program?
• Why are so many males identified for special education? What is the implemented intention of special education? How effective is the RtI process? Why are so many students identified for Speech and Language?
• A positive, consistent behavior system is needed. Parents need to be a part of the behavior system.
• Instructional assistants, recess and lunch supervisors need professional development in the behavior system.

#### 3. Looking at the data presented, what other demographic data would you want to answer the question *Who are we?* for Somewhere Elementary School?

• How does the district open enrollment policy impact Somewhere Elementary School-and in comparison to the other elementary schools?
• What is the intent of Special Education?
• How does RtI work?
• More data on behavior-especially following individual students dynamically and over time.

## Figure G-2
## What We Saw in the Data: PERCEPTIONS

| SOMEWHERE ELEMENTARY SCHOOL |
| :---: |
| STRENGTHS, CHALLENGES, IMPLICATIONS, AND OTHER DATA |

### PERCEPTUAL DATA

#### 1. What are Somewhere School's perceptual *strengths* and *challenges*?

| Strengths | Challenges |
| --- | --- |
| **Kindergarten-Grade One** <br> • The staff has done a wonderful job of getting student questionnaire responses each year (98.5% in 2013). <br> • It is great to see five years of data. <br> • On the aggregate, all K-1 student responses were in agreement. Not much has changed for them over time. <br> • It is very cool the K-1 students like reading/books the most, followed by learning, and playing with friends. <br> • The second most written-in comment to the questionnaire for K-1 students was about everybody being nice to each other and not mean. <br> **Grades Two-Five** <br> • Overall, the students in grades 2 through 5 are in strong agreement with the items on the questionnaire. <br> • Students in grades 2 to 5 named teachers as what they like most about their school in the past 4 years. <br> • The majority of things students in grades 2-5 liked most were related to the learning. <br> • Four years ago, students talked about wishing the playground and learning were different. In 2012-13, learning is not mentioned as something they wished was different. <br> **Staff** <br> • Staff questionnaire results show that staff, for the most part, continue to be very positive about the school. All items were in agreement or strong agreement in 2012-13. Staff now feel that the school has a good public image. They also feel that their school culture and staff collaboration are the biggest strengths of the school. One can see progress over time. <br> • Staff indicate the talented school staff, staff collaboration, and the use of data are their greatest strengths. <br> **Parents** <br> • Overall, parents continue to be very positive about the school. <br> • Parents, the caring, loving staff, and environment are the strengths of Somewhere Elementary School, according to parents. | **Kindergarten-Grade One** <br> • Someone should follow-up on the lowest scoring items (K-1)— The work I do in class makes me think, Students at my school are friendly, I have lots of friends—even though they are still high. <br> • The second most written-in comment to the questionnaire for K-1 students was about everybody being nice to each other and not mean. <br> **Grades Two-Five** <br> • The lowest items on the grades 2-5 questionnaire are related to students treating each other with respect and being friendly, having freedom and choices at school, and being challenged by the work my teacher asks me to do. <br> • American Indian students (n=8), grades 2-5, were in disagreement with the items, Students at my school are friendly, Students at my school treat me with respect, and I am safe. <br> • There were 8 American Indian students who marked low on several items; however, there is only 1 American Indian student, according to the demographic data. We don't know who these other students are. They may have thought they marked "American." <br> • Seven (7) African-American students were in disagreement to: I have fun learning, I like this school, This school is good, I have freedom at school, I have choices in what I learn, Students are treated fairly by teachers, Students at my school treat me with respect, Students at my school are friendly, and I have lots of friends. <br> **Staff** <br> • The staff members with the most years of experience were the least positive in 2013. <br> • Communication continues to be the most written in comment of what needs to improve, from the perspective of staff. Equity in ideas and favorites needs to be reviewed. <br> **Parents** <br> • Parents, in the ethnic category "Other," were the lowest. <br> • Parents want more social skills for students and more supervision before/after school and during recess. |

#### 2. What are some *implications* for the Somewhere continuous school improvement plan?

• Someone should follow-up on the lowest scoring items (K-1)—*The work I do in class makes me think, Students at my school are friendly, I have lots of friends*—even though they are still high.
• The lowest items on the grades 2-5 questionnaire are related to students treating each other with respect and being friendly, having freedom and choices at school, and being challenged by the work my teacher asks me to do.
• The school personnel might need professional development in behavior/respect and diversity issues, and how they give students freedom and choices.
• Communication and shared leadership need to improve.
• Enrichment in learning.

Figure G-3
What We Saw in the Data: SCHOOL PROCESSES
*(School processes data not shown in Case Study.)*

## SOMEWHERE ELEMENTARY SCHOOL
### STRENGTHS, CHALLENGES, IMPLICATIONS, AND OTHER DATA

### SCHOOL PROCESSES DATA

1. **What are Somewhere School's *strengths* and *challenges* with respect to the *Continuous Improvement Continuums.***

| Strengths | Challenges |
|---|---|
| • Somewhere School has assessed on the Continuous Improvement Continuums five years in a row.<br>• Staff can see the improvements over the years.<br>• Staff have come a long way with data use and developing and implementing a shared vision. Staff understand these two have moved them forward faster than anything.<br>• Staff know the plan and work within it, better, each year. | • Staff need to work hard to respond to each of these issues.<br>• RtI interventions are currently not working for all students.<br>• Time needs to be "created" to allow quality learning on implementing RtI and the Common Core State Standards.<br>• Partnership development is the lowest-rated Continuum.<br>• Staff need win-win partnerships with parents. |

2. **What are some *implications* for the Somewhere continuous school improvement plan?**

*Somewhere School staff need to—*
• Continue using schoolwide data as they have in the past to help them know how the system is doing. Get and keep the database up-to-date so staff can gauge progress.
• Clarify the assessment system to measure the attainment of the Common Core State Standards:
    * Balance it with variety, including performance assessments and student self-assessments.
    * Make sure the assessments that are used are telling them what they need to know to ensure student proficiency.
    * For math and behavior.
    * Streamline the pre-referral process, especially the form completion process.
    * What staff do when students are proficient on benchmarks.

• Improve RtI:
    * Understand why students who have been through interventions are not proficient. Problem-solving cycle can guide this.
    * Continue to provide professional development on RtI for all staff so everyone can understand it and implement it in the same way.
    * Implement a teacher self-assessment and grade-level self-assessment system to help implement the vision and the RtI system with integrity and fidelity throughout the school. Identify internal quality measures.
    * Clarify what the vision and RtI would look like when implemented.
    * Improve the peer coaching system: support and provide guidance for new instruction and assessment strategies. Provide time to develop new skills and improve Level 1.

• Update, improve, and follow the continuous school improvement plan.
• Improve shared decision making and leadership: Define, implement, and communicate.
• Clarify win-win partnerships with parents. Make sure parents know the vision and mission of the school, and learning expectations for their children.
• Ensure cross-grade-level work improves to implement the standards, vision, and RtI consistently, and to ensure that a continuum of learning is in place and makes sense for all students.

## Figure G-4
## What We Saw in the Data: STUDENT LEARNING

### SOMEWHERE ELEMENTARY SCHOOL
### STRENGTHS, CHALLENGES, IMPLICATIONS, AND OTHER DATA

**STUDENT LEARNING DATA**

**1. What are Somewhere School's student learning *strengths* and *challenges*?**

| Strengths | Challenges |
|---|---|
| **English Language Arts (ELA)**<br>• Grades two and five showed increases in the percentages of students Proficient or Advanced overall and for every student group, with the exception of Caucasians in both grade levels and males in grade five.<br>• The cohorts show good progress, for the most part.<br>**Math**<br>• Overall, 2012-13 math scores improved over 2011-12 scores, except with grades two and five males; grade three females; Caucasians, except at grade four; and English only students, except at grade two.<br>• The cohorts show good progress, for the most part.<br>**API**<br>• The overall API scores have been going up since 2008-09.<br>• The API scores increased for all student groups . | **English Language Arts (ELA)**<br>• 2012-13 was a challenging year for Somewhere School with the implementation of RtI. The percentages of students Proficient or Advanced decreased overall, and for every student group in grades three and four.<br>**Math**<br>• Caucasian student scores were down for all grades, except grade four.<br>• English only scores were down for all but grade two.<br>• Males were down in grades two and five; females in grade three. |

**2. What are some *implications* for the Somewhere continuous school improvement plan?**

• How is ELA being taught? How is ELA being measured on an ongoing basis?

• How is Math being taught? How is Math being measured on an ongoing basis?

• Did teachers focus too much on the students not proficient? Do all teachers know what to do when students are proficient?

• We need stronger core instruction for all students.

**3. Looking at the data presented, what other perceptual data would you want to answer the question *How are our students doing?* for Somewhere Elementary School?**

• Individual student growth data-are students improving their achievement over time?

• What is the predictive ability of the formative assessments being used to the California Standards Test (CST).

Figure G-5
What We Saw in the Data: IMPLICATIONS

## SOMEWHERE ELEMENTARY SCHOOL

| DEMOGRAPHICS | STUDENT, STAFF, PARENT QUESTIONNAIRES | STUDENT LEARNING | PROCESS DATA |
|---|---|---|---|
| • Are teachers prepared to teach the changing population? Do teachers know how to teach students with English as a second language, and those who live in poverty? What are the implications of teaching students living in poverty? (Perhaps more male and minority teachers need to be recruited?)<br>• How are class-size issues dealt with, with mobility?<br>• Does the school know why the mobility rate is high, and where students go? Do students stay in the district?<br>• How are new students and their parents welcomed to the school? How do teachers know what the new students know and are able to do?<br>• Are materials, programs, and library books appropriate for the student population (e.g., EL, poverty, mobile, special education), and for getting students college and career ready? Are there appropriate extra-curricular activities, clubs?<br>• How does the school help parents know how to help their children learn?<br>• How are the needs of students who speak English as a second language met? Is there a need for an English Language Development program?<br>• Why are so many males identified for special education? What is the implemented intention of special education? How effective is the RtI process? Why are so many students identified for Speech and Language?<br>• A positive, consistent behavior system is needed. Parents need to be a part of the behavior system.<br>• Instructional assistants, recess and lunch supervisors need professional development in the behavior system. | • Someone should follow-up on the lowest scoring items (K-1)—*The work I do in class makes me think, Students at my school are friendly, I have lots of friends- even though they are still high.*<br>• The lowest items on the grades 2-5 questionnaire are related to students treating each other with respect and being friendly, having freedom and choices at school, and being challenged by the work my teacher asks me to do.<br>• The school personnel might need professional development in behavior/respect and diversity issues, and how they give students freedom and choices.<br>• Communication and shared leadership need to improve.<br>• Enrichment in learning. | • How is ELA being taught? How is ELA being measured on an ongoing basis?<br>• How is Math being taught? How is Math being measured on an ongoing basis?<br>• Did teachers focus too much on the students not proficient? Do all teachers know what to do when students are proficient?<br>• We need stronger core instruction for all students. | *Somewhere School staff need to—*<br>• Continue using schoolwide data as they have in the past to help them know how the system is doing. Get and keep the database up-to-date so staff can gauge progress.<br>• Clarify the assessment system to measure the attainment of the Common Core State Standards.<br>  ＊ Balance it with variety, including performance assessments and student self-assessments.<br>  ＊ Make sure the assessments that are used are telling them what they need to hear to know how to ensure student proficiency.<br>  ＊ For math and behavior.<br>  ＊ Streamline the pre-referral process, especially the form completion process.<br>  ＊ What staff do when students are proficient on benchmarks.<br>• Improve RtI:<br>  ＊ Understand why students who have been through interventions are not proficient. Problem-solving cycle can guide this.<br>  ＊ Continue to provide professional development on RtI for all staff so everyone can understand it and implement it in the same way.<br>  ＊ Implement a teacher self-assessment and grade-level self-assessment system to help implement the vision and the RtI system with integrity and fidelity throughout the school. Identify internal quality measures.<br>  ＊ Clarify what the vision and RtI would look like when implemented.<br>  ＊ Improve the peer coaching system: support and provide guidance for new instruction and assessment strategies. Provide time to develop new skills and improve Level 1.<br>• Update, improve, and follow the continuous school improvement plan.<br>• Improve shared decision making and leadership: Define, implement, and communicate.<br>• Clarify win-win partnerships with parents. Make sure parents know the vision and mission of the school, and learning expectations for their children.<br>• Ensure cross-grade-level work improves to implement the standards, vision, and RtI consistently, and to also ensure that a continuum of learning makes sense for all students. |

Figure G-6

What We Saw in the Data: IMPLICATION COMMONALITIES

## SOMEWHERE ELEMENTARY SCHOOL

| DEMOGRAPHICS | STUDENT, STAFF, PARENT QUESTIONNAIRES | STUDENT LEARNING | PROCESS DATA |
|---|---|---|---|
| • Are teachers prepared to teach the changing population? Do teachers know how to teach students with English as a second language, and those who live in poverty? What are the implications of teaching students living in poverty? (Perhaps more male and minority teachers need to be recruited?) <br><br> • How are class-size issues dealt with, with mobility? <br><br> • Does the school know why the mobility rate is high, and where students go? Do students stay in the district? <br><br> • How are new students and their parents welcomed to the school? How do teachers know what the new students know and are able to do? <br><br> • Are materials, programs, and library books appropriate for the student population (e.g., EL, poverty, mobile, special education), and for getting students college and career ready? Are there appropriate extra-curricular activities, clubs? <br><br> • How does the school help parents know how to help their children learn? <br><br> • How are the needs of students who speak English as a second language met? Is there a need for an English Language Development program? <br><br> • Why are so many males identified for special education? What is the implemented intention of special education? How effective is the RtI process? Why are so many students identified for Speech and Language? <br><br> • A positive, consistent behavior system is needed. Parents need to be a part of the behavior system. Instructional assistants, recess and lunch supervisors need professional development in the behavior system. | • Someone should follow-up on the lowest scoring items (K-1)—*The work I do in class makes me think. Students at my school are friendly, I have lots of friends– even though they are still high.* <br><br> • The school personnel might need professional development in behavior/respect and diversity issues, and how they give students freedom and choices. <br><br> • Communication and shared leadership need to improve. <br><br> • Enrichment in learning. | • How is ELA being taught? How is ELA being measured on an ongoing basis? <br><br> • How is Math being taught? How is Math being measured on an ongoing basis? <br><br> • Did teachers focus too much on the students not proficient? Do all teachers know what to do when students are proficient? <br><br> • We need stronger core instruction for all students. | *Somewhere School staff needs to—* <br> • Continue using schoolwide data as they have in the past to help them know how the system is doing. Get and keep the database up-to-date so staff can gauge progress. <br> • Clarify the assessment system to measure the attainment of the Common Core State Standards. <br> ★ Balance it with variety, including performance assessments and student self-assessments. <br> ★ Make sure the assessments that are used are telling them what they need to hear to know how to ensure student proficiency. <br> ★ For math and behavior. <br> ★ Streamline the pre-referral process, especially the form completion process. <br> ★ What staff do when students are proficient on benchmarks. <br> • Improve RtI: <br> ★ Understand why students who have been through interventions are not proficient. Problem-solving cycle can guide this. <br> ★ Continue to provide professional development on RtI for all staff so everyone can understand it and implement it in the same way. <br> ★ Implement a teacher self-assessment and grade-level self-assessment system to help implement the vision and the RtI system with integrity and fidelity throughout the school. Identify internal quality measures. <br> ★ Clarify what the vision and RtI would look like when implemented. <br> ★ Improve the peer coaching system: support and provide guidance for new instruction and assessment strategies. Provide time to develop new skills and improve Level 1. <br> • Update, improve, and follow the continuous school improvement plan. <br> • Improve shared decision making and leadership: Define, implement, and communicate. <br> • Clarify win-win partnerships with parents. Make sure parents know the vision and mission of the school, and learning expectations for their children. <br> • Ensure cross-grade-level work improves to implement the standards, vision, and RtI consistently, and to also ensure that a continuum of learning makes sense for all students. |

**LEGEND:** *Related to—*

○ Teacher professional development   ◎ Administrative processes   ◉ Parents   ● Data use and standards implementation   ○ Communication

Figure G-7
What We Saw in the Data: AGGREGATED IMPLICATIONS

## SOMEWHERE ELEMENTARY SCHOOL
### AGGREGATED IMPLICATIONS FOR THE CONTINUOUS SCHOOL IMPROVEMENT PLAN

| INSTRUCTION | ASSESSMENT | CURRICULUM | BEHAVIOR | VISION / PLAN | PROFESSIONAL LEARNING |
|---|---|---|---|---|---|
| • Teachers need to strengthen their instructional strategies in ELA, Math, Science, and Social Studies.<br>• There needs to be deeper implementation of RtI.<br>• Continue to ensure that all teachers are teaching to standards and all students are meeting Common Core State Standards (CCSS) in all subject areas.<br>• Clarify what staff do when students are proficient. | • Clarify a balanced assessment system.<br>• We need to make sure teachers know what the new students know and are able to do when they arrive, so we do not lose instructional time.<br>• We need to collect more systematic formative data in all subject areas. | • Are materials, programs, and library books appropriate for the student population? (EL, poverty, mobile, special education)<br>• Will all materials, etc., help us implement the Common Core State Standards (CCSS)?<br>• We need to document and continue to improve RtI implementation. | • We need a positive, consistent behavior system schoolwide.<br>• We need to set-up dynamic data collection for behavior, monitor it, and change as needed. | • The vision needs to be fully implemented.<br>• Staff need to stay focused on the plan; always have next steps in front of them; create and post a graphic organizer to help us stay focused.<br>• We need to systematically include our parents in quality planning. | • Continue our professional learning in meeting the needs of our students, especially students with English as a second language, those who live in poverty, and males, specifically in ELA and Math learning, for RtI, and for implementing the Common Core State Standards (CCSS).<br>• School personnel need consistent training and implementation of behavior and motivation strategies. |

| COLLABORATION | LEADERSHIP | PARTNERSHIPS | DATA | CLIMATE | RtI / SPECIAL EDUCATION | COMMON CORE STATE STANDARDS |
|---|---|---|---|---|---|---|
| • Staff need to strengthen peer coaching and make it and the feedback structure more systematic and defined.<br>• We need to schedule schoolwide articulation more often and make cross-grade-level articulation meetings more systematic.<br>• Staff need to continue cross-grade-level articulation, including agreements about student behavior in terms of motivation, attitude, and effort–also as related to *Students Committed to Excellence*. | • Communication needs to improve among staff and with parents.<br>• Everyone needs to be a part of professional learning and leadership.<br>• We need to improve shared leadership. | • We need to connect student achievement data to partnerships, and look into relationships that might affect student achievement, based on our mission/vision/ plan.<br>• We need to document different ways the community is contributing to the school, and how parent involvement affects student achievement.<br>• We need to make sure parents know how to help meet the learning needs of their children. | • Where do our mobile students go? Do they stay in the district?<br>• We need to gather and monitor behavior data regularly.<br>• We need to continue using schoolwide data teams.<br>• Staff need to become astute in knowing what works so they can predict and ensure successes.<br>• Staff accessibility to data tools needs to be improved. | • We need a system to welcome new students and their parents to the school.<br>• Staff need to continue cross-grade-level articulation, including agreements about student behavior in terms of motivation, attitude, and effort-also as related to *Students Committed to Excellence*.<br>• Staff need to continue to communicate and collaborate. | We need to:<br>• Look into speech and language referrals.<br>• Streamline PRT process.<br>• Get all staff understanding RtI in the same way.<br>• Strengthen core curriculum.<br>• Evaluate and improve RtI implementation. | • Continue to learn more about teaching and assessing the Common Core State Standards (CCSS). |

# ANALYZING DATA FOR CONTINUOUS SCHOOL IMPROVEMENT PLANNING

*Where Are We Now?*

Answering this question is the part of continuous school improvement planning that takes a comprehensive and honest look at all the school's data—not just student learning results—and helps to reflect on how the data implications intersect. There are four sub-questions to answer with data within this category:

♦ Who are we?

♦ How do we do business?

♦ How are our students doing?

♦ What are our programs and processes?

After analyzing each of the four types of data in terms of strengths, challenges, and implications, we can look across implications to understand the common and systemic implications for the continuous school improvement (CSI) plan.

**Strengths, Challenges, Implications, and Other Data**

## Part 1— Comprehensive Data Analysis to School Improvement Implementation

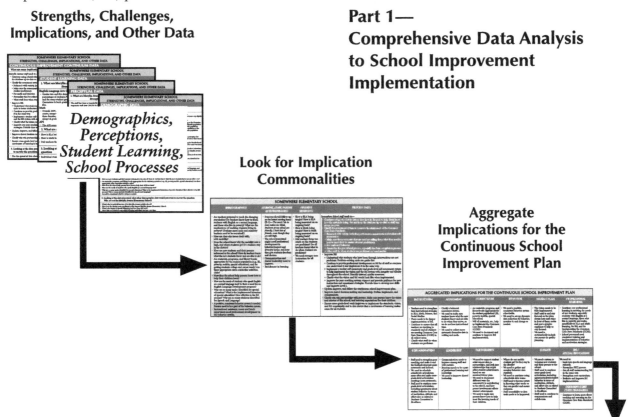

*Demographics, Perceptions, Student Learning, School Processes*

**Look for Implication Commonalities**

**Aggregate Implications for the Continuous School Improvement Plan**

**Purpose**   The purpose of this activity is to guide the analysis of data to inform the school vision and continuous school improvement plan.

**Target Audience**   School staff.

**Time**   Up to three hours, depending upon the number of staff members and the amount of data available.

**Materials**   Chart paper, markers, tape, or push pins to post the chart paper, if necessary. Have the school's data profile printed on paper, or available on technology devices, so each staff member can review the data.

## Process Protocol

**Step 1.**   **Strengths, Challenges, Implications.** Print a *Strengths, Challenges,* and *Implications* worksheet for each staff member (Figures H-1 through H-6).

As individuals, review independently each type of data (e.g., *demographics, perceptions, student learning,* and *school processes*), done separately, have them document what they are seeing as—

♦ *strengths,*

♦ *challenges,*

♦ *implications for the continuous school improvement plan,* and

♦ *other data they wished the school had.*

*Note:* Analyses are much richer if notes about the data are jotted down *as they* are reviewed. **(15-20 minutes)**

**DEMOGRAPHIC DATA**

| 1. What are Somewhere School's demographic *strengths* and *challenges*? | |
|---|---|
| *Strengths* | *Challenges* |
| • Somewhere School is a diverse, medium-size school serving grades K-5. <br> • Grade-level enrollments seem to be relatively steady, although decreasing in upper grades. <br> • The mobility rate is down from a couple of years | • There is declining districtwide enrollment in the last few years-up slightly in 2012-13. <br> • Somewhere School is experiencing declining enrollment. <br> • Many different ethnicities are increasing as the Caucasian student population is decreasing. In the school, the Hispanic population has increased from |
| **2. What are some *implications* for the Somewhere continuous school improvement plan?** | |
| • Are teachers prepared to teach the changing population? Do teachers know how to teach students with English as a second language, and those who live in poverty? What are the implications of teaching students living in poverty? (Perhaps more male and minority teachers need to be recruited?) <br> • How are class-size issues dealt with, with mobility | |
| **3. Looking at the data presented, what other demographic data would you want to answer the question *Who are we?* for Somewhere Elementary School?** | |
| • How does the district open enrollment policy impact Somewhere Elementary School-and in comparison to the other elementary schools? <br> • What is the intent of Special Education? <br> • How does RtI work? <br> • More data on behavior-especially following individual students dynamically and over time. | |

**DEFINITIONS**

*Strengths:* Something positive that can be seen in the data. Often leverage for improving a challenge.

*Challenges:* Data that imply something might need attention, a potential undesirable result, or something out of a school's control.

*Implications for the Continuous School Improvement Plan* are placeholders until all the data are analyzed. Implications are thoughts to not forget to address in the school improvement plan. Implications most often result from challenges.

In small groups, have staff members share what they see as *strengths, challenges, implications for the continuous school improvement plan,* and *other data they wished the school had.* Record commonalities on chart paper. (This makes it easier to combine the small-groups' thinking with full-group thinking in the next step.) **(15 minutes)**

Combine the small group results to get a comprehensive *set of strengths, challenges, implications for the continuous school improvement plan,* and *other data you wished the school had.* This is best done by having a reporter from each small group stand beside her/his group's chart paper ready to mark off items mentioned as each group's reporter indicates what the group saw as *strengths, challenges, implications for the continuous school improvement plan,* and *other data you wished the school had.*

Start on the left and have the first reporter read all the group's strengths. Other reporters check off common elements on their lists. Going to the right, the next reporter reads only what her/his group had on its "strengths" list that has not been read. Continue until all the "strengths" have been read. Have another group read its list of "challenges". You might want to start on the right this time, and go left. Continue with "implications for the school improvement plan," and then "what other data do you wish you had," until you are finished. The result will be a comprehensive list of *Strengths, Challenges, Implications for the school improvement plan,* and *Other Data You Wished the School Had.* **(20 minutes)**

## Process Protocol (Continued)

Repeat the process with the other three types of data.

*Process options:* The process described above is an excellent way to review and combine thinking with demographic data. It is important that all staff members review all the information in at least one area of data.

With perceptions and student learning data, parts of the data work could be delegated to different members of each small group. For example, when a school has student, staff, and parent questionnaires to analyze, one third of each team could review the student questionnaire; another third, the staff questionnaire; and another third, the parent questionnaire. The sub-teams could then report what they saw in the data to their team, who then will combine their thinking with the other teams. With student learning, the data analysis could be delegated by subject area. With process data, divide staff into groups to complete measuring program and processes table for major programs and processes. Your school may also want to use the *Continuous Improvement Continuums* (CICs) to self-assess the entire school.

**Step 2. Implications Across the Data.** After staff members have documented the school's data strengths, challenges, implications for the continuous school improvement plan, and what other data they wished the school had for *demographics, perceptions, student learning, school processes,* review the implications side-by-side.

This alignment is important for seeing commonalities across the different implications (partial example shown below).

**Step 3. Implication Commonalities.** In small groups, look across and highlight commonalities in your *demographics, perceptions, student learning,* and *school process implications.* Share small group thinking with the large group (partial example shown on the following page).

| REVIEW IMPLICATIONS ACROSS DATA | | | |
|---|---|---|---|
| **DEMOGRAPHICS** | **STUDENT, STAFF, PARENT QUESTIONNAIRES** | **STUDENT LEARNING** | **PROCESS DATA** |
| • Are teachers prepared to teach the changing population? Do teachers know how to teach students with English as a second language, and those who live in poverty? What are the implications of teaching students living in poverty? (Perhaps more male and minority teachers need to be recruited?)<br>• How are class-size issues dealt with, with mobility?<br>• Does the school know why the mobility rate is high, and where students go? Do students stay in the district?<br>• How are new students and their parents welcomed to the school? How do teachers know what the new students know and are able to do?<br>• Are materials, programs, and library books appropriate for the student population (e.g., EL, poverty, mobile, special education)? Are there appropriate extra-curricular activities, clubs?<br>• How does the school help parents know how to help their children learn?<br>• How are the needs of students who speak English as a second language met? Is there a need for an English Language Development program?<br>• Why are so many males identified for special education? What is the implemented intention of special education? How effective is the RtI process? Why are so many students identified for Speech and Language?<br>• A positive, consistent behavior system is needed. Parents need to be a part of the behavior system.<br>• Instructional assistants, recess and lunch supervisors need professional development in the behavior system. | • Someone should follow-up on the lowest scoring items (K-1)—*The work I do in class makes me think, Students at my school are friendly, I have lots of friends- even though they are still high.*<br>• The lowest items on the grades 2-5 questionnaire are related to students treating each other with respect and being friendly, having freedom and choices at school, and being challenged by the work my teacher asks me to do.<br>• The school personnel might need professional development in behavior/respect and diversity issues, and how they give students freedom and choices.<br>• Communication and shared leadership need to improve.<br>• Enrichment in learning. | • How is ELA being taught? How is ELA being measured on an ongoing basis?<br>• How is Math being taught? How is Math being measured on an ongoing basis?<br>• Did teachers focus too much on the students not proficient? Do all teachers know what to do when students are proficient?<br>• We need stronger core instruction for all students. | *Somewhere School staff need to—*<br>• Continue using schoolwide data as they have in the past to help them know how the system is doing. Get and keep the database up-to-date so staff can gauge progress.<br>• Clarify the assessment system to measure the attainment of the Common Core State Standards (CCSS).<br>  ∗ Balance it with variety, including performance assessments and student self-assessments.<br>  ∗ Make sure the assessments that are used are telling them what they need to hear to know how to ensure student proficiency.<br>  ∗ For math and behavior.<br>  ∗ Streamline the pre-referral process, especially the form completion process.<br>  ∗ What staff does when students are proficient on benchmarks.<br>• Improve RtI:<br>  ∗ Understand why students who have been through interventions are not proficient. Do a problem-solving cycle to better understand.<br>  ∗ Continue to provide professional development for all staff so everyone can understand it and implement it in the same way.<br>  ∗ Implement a teacher self-assessment and grade level self assessment system to help implement the vision and the RtI system with integrity and fidelity throughout the school. Identify internal quality measures.<br>  ∗ Clarify what the vision and RtI would look like when implemented.<br>  ∗ Improve our peer coaching system: support and provide guidance for new instruction and assessment strategies. Provide time to develop new skills and improve level 1.<br>• Update, improve, and follow the school improvement plan.<br>• Improve shared decision making and leadership: Define, implement, and communicate.<br>• Clarify win-win partnerships with parents. Make sure parents know the vision and mission of the school, and learning expectations for their children.<br>• Ensure cross-grade-level work improves to implement the standards, vision, and RtI consistently, and to also ensure that a continuum of learning makes sense for all students. |

## HIGHLIGHT IMPLICATION COMMONALITIES

| DEMOGRAPHICS | STUDENT, STAFF, PARENT QUESTIONNAIRES | STUDENT LEARNING | PROCESS DATA |
|---|---|---|---|
| • Are teachers prepared to teach the changing population? Do teachers know how to teach students with English as a second language, and those who live in poverty? What are the implications of teaching students living in poverty? (Perhaps more male and minority teachers need to be recruited?)<br>• How are class-size issues dealt with, with mobility?<br>• Does the school know why the mobility rate is high, and where students go? Do students stay in the district?<br>• How are new students and their parents welcomed to the school? How do teachers know what the new students know and are able to do?<br>• Are materials, programs, and library books appropriate for the student population (e.g., EL, poverty, mobile, special education), and for getting students college and career ready? Are there appropriate extra-curricular activities, clubs?<br>• How does the school help parents know how to help their children learn?<br>• How are the needs of students who speak English as a second language met? Is there a need for an English Language Development program?<br>• Why are so many males identified for special education? What is the implemented intention of special education? How effective is the RtI process? Why are so many students identified for Speech and Language?<br>• A positive, consistent behavior system is needed. Parents need to be a part of the behavior system.<br>• Instructional assistants, recess and lunch supervisors need professional development in the behavior system. | • Someone should follow-up on the lowest scoring items (K-1)—*The work I do in class makes me think, Students at my school are friendly, I have lots of friends- even though they are still high.*<br>• The school personnel might need professional development in behavior/respect and diversity issues, and how they give students freedom and choices.<br>• Communication and shared leadership need to improve.<br>• Enrichment in learning. | • How is ELA being taught? How is ELA being measured on an ongoing basis?<br>• How is Math being taught? How is Math being measured on an ongoing basis?<br>• Did teachers focus too much on the students not proficient? Do all teachers know what to do when students are proficient?<br>• We need stronger core instruction for all students. | *Somewhere School staff need to—*<br>• Continue using schoolwide data as they have in the past to help them know how the system is doing. Get and keep the database up-to-date so staff can gauge progress.<br>• Clarify the assessment system to measure the attainment of the Common Core State Standards.<br>　∗ Balance it with variety, including performance assessments and student self-assessments.<br>　∗ Make sure the assessments that are used are telling them what they need to hear to know how to ensure student proficiency.<br>　∗ For math and behavior.<br>　∗ Streamline the pre-referral process, especially the form completion process.<br>　∗ What staff do when students are proficient on benchmarks.<br>• Improve RtI:<br>　∗ Understand why students who have been through interventions are not proficient. Problem-solving cycle can guide this.<br>　∗ Continue to provide professional development on RtI for all staff so everyone can understand it and implement it in the same way.<br>　∗ Implement a teacher self-assessment and grade-level self-assessment system to help implement the vision and the RtI system with integrity and fidelity throughout the school. Identify internal quality measures.<br>　∗ Clarify what the vision and RtI would look like when implemented.<br>　∗ Improve the peer coaching system: support and provide guidance for new instruction and assessment strategies. Provide time to develop new skills and improve Level 1.<br>• Update, improve, and follow the continuous school improvement plan.<br>• Improve shared decision making and leadership: Define, implement, and communicate.<br>• Clarify win-win partnerships with parents. Make sure parents know the vision and mission of the school, and learning expectations for their children.<br>• Ensure cross-grade-level work improves to implement the standards, vision, and RtI consistently, and to also ensure that a continuum of learning makes sense for all students. |

## Process Protocol *(Continued)*

**Step 4. Aggregate Implications for the Continuous School Improvement Plan.** In small groups, or in the large group, if manageable, stand back from the *implication commonalities* and begin a bulleted list of *implications for the plan*, with respect to *leadership, curriculum, instruction, assessment, curriculum, standards, vision/plan, etc.* Use the provided template (Figure H-6), which can be adjusted as needed. (Partial example shown below.) Staff members will be answering the question, *What do the data tell us has to be included in our continuous school improvement plan?*

## AGGREGATED IMPLICATIONS FOR THE CONTINUOUS SCHOOL IMPROVEMENT PLAN

| INSTRUCTION | ASSESSMENT | CURRICULUM | BEHAVIOR | VISION / PLAN | PROFESSIONAL LEARNING |
|---|---|---|---|---|---|
| • Teachers need to strengthen their instructional strategies in ELA, Math, Science, and Social Studies.<br>• There needs to be deeper implementation of RtI.<br>• Continue to ensure that all teachers are teaching to standards and all students are meeting Common Core State Standards (CCSS) in all subject areas.<br>• Clarify what staff do when students are proficient. | • Clarify a balanced assessment system.<br>• We need to make sure teachers know what the new students know and are able to do when they arrive, so we do not lose instructional time.<br>• We need to collect more systematic formative data in all subject areas. | • Are materials, programs, and library books appropriate for the student population? (EL, poverty, mobile, special education)<br>• Will all materials, etc., help us implement the Common Core State Standards (CCSS)?<br>• We need to document and continue to improve RtI implementation. | • We need a positive, consistent behavior system schoolwide.<br>• We need to set-up dynamic data collection for behavior, monitor it, and change as needed. | • The vision needs to be fully implemented.<br>• Staff need to stay focused on the plan; always have next steps in front of them; create and post a graphic organizer to help us stay focused.<br>• We need to systematically include our parents in quality planning. | • Continue our professional learning in meeting the needs of our students, especially students with English as a second language, those who live in poverty, and males, specifically in ELA and Math learning, for RtI, and for implementing the Common Core State Standards (CCSS).<br>• School personnel need consistent training and implementation of behavior and motivation strategies. |

| COLLABORATION | LEADERSHIP | PARTNERSHIPS | DATA | CLIMATE | RtI / SPECIAL EDUCATION |
|---|---|---|---|---|---|
| • Staff need to strengthen peer coaching and make it and the feedback structure more systematic and defined.<br>• We need to schedule schoolwide articulation more often and make cross-grade-level articulation meetings more systematic.<br>• Staff need to continue cross-grade-level articulation, including agreements about student behavior in terms of motivation, attitude, and effort-also as related to *Students Committed to Excellence.* | • Communication needs to improve among staff and with parents.<br>• Everyone needs to be a part of professional learning and leadership.<br>• We need to improve shared leadership. | • We need to connect student achievement data to partnerships, and look into relationships that might affect student achievement, based on our mission/vision/ plan.<br>• We need to document different ways the community is contributing to the school, and how parent involvement affects student achievement.<br>• We need to make sure parents know how to help meet the learning needs of their children. | • Where do our mobile students go? Do they stay in the district?<br>• We need to gather and monitor behavior data regularly.<br>• We need to continue using schoolwide data teams.<br>• Staff need to become astute in knowing what works so they can predict and ensure successes.<br>• Staff accessibility to data tools needs to be improved. | • We need a system to welcome new students and their parents to the school.<br>• Staff need to continue cross-grade-level articulation, including agreements about student behavior in terms of motivation, attitude, and effort-also as related to *Students Committed to Excellence.*<br>• Staff need to continue to communicate and collaborate. | We need to:<br>• Look into speech and language referrals.<br>• Streamline PRT process.<br>• Get all staff understanding RtI in the same way.<br>• Strengthen core curriculum.<br>• Evaluate and improve RtI implementation.<br><br>**COMMON CORE STATE STANDARDS**<br>• Continue to learn more about teaching and assessing the Common Core State Standards (CCSS). |

## Process Protocol *(Continued)*

**Step 5. Create the Plan.** Use this comprehensive data analysis, along with the vision, to create the continuous school improvement plan.

## Comments to the Facilitator

This is an activity to ensure the analysis of all types of comprehensive schoolwide data, to engage all staff members in analyzing the data, and to reach consensus on data implications for the continuous school improvement plan. The important concepts are to have participants:

♦ Review the data independently, writing as they analyze the data.

♦ Combine thinking of staff members.

♦ Look across the different implication analyses to paint with a broad brush.

♦ Create a list of implications for the continuous school improvement plan.

## Figure H-1
## STRENGTHS, CHALLENGES, IMPLICATIONS FOR ANALYZING DEMOGRAPHIC DATA

Use the template below to record your thinking *as you review* your demographic data. Also use these questions for moving individual thoughts to small-group thinking, and then to whole-group thinking.

**DEMOGRAPHIC DATA**

**1. What are the school's demographic *strengths* and *challenges*?**

| *Strengths* | *Challenges* |
|---|---|
|  |  |

**2. What are some *implications* for the continuous school improvement plan?**

**3. Looking at the data presented, what other demographic data would you want to answer the question *Who are we?***

## Figure H-2
## TABLE FOR ANALYZING PERCEPTIONS DATA

Perceptions data are important for continuous school improvement planning because they reveal what students, staff, and parents are thinking about the learning environment. Since humans cannot act differently from what they value, believe, or perceive, it is important to know what each constituency is perceiving about the learning environment to assist with knowing what to change to create a learning environment that everyone perceives as helpful. You may also choose to analyze your perceptions data results using strengths, challenges, and implications (Figure H-1).

| | Student Questionnaire | Staff Questionnaire | Parent Questionnaire | Agreements Across Questionnaires | Disagreements Across Questionnaires |
|---|---|---|---|---|---|
| **General feel of questionnaire (positive, neutral, negative)** | | | | | |
| **Most positive items** | | | | | |
| **Neutral items** | | | | | |
| **Negative items** | | | | | |
| **On which items are there differences in subgroups?** (i.e., disaggregated responses) | | | | | |
| **Implications for the Continuous School Improvement Plan** | | | | | |

## Figure H-3
## STRENGTHS, CHALLENGES, IMPLICATIONS FOR ANALYZING SCHOOL PROCESSES DATA

Use the template below to record your thinking *as you review* your school processes data. Also use this for moving individual thoughts to small-group thinking, and then to whole-group thinking.

| SCHOOL PROCESSES DATA | |
|---|---|
| **1. What are the *strengths* and *challenges* of the school processes?** | |
| *Strengths* | *Challenges* |
| | |
| **2. What are some *implications* for the continuous school improvement plan?** | |
| | |
| **3. Looking at the data presented, what other school process data would you want to answer the question *What are our programs and processes?*** | |
| | |

## Figure H-4
## STRENGTHS, CHALLENGES, IMPLICATIONS FOR ANALYZING STUDENT LEARNING DATA

Use the template below to record your thinking *as you review* your student learning data. Also use this for moving individual thoughts to small-group thinking, and then to whole-group thinking.

| STUDENT LEARNING DATA | |
|---|---|
| **1. What are the school's student learning *strengths* and *challenges*?** | |
| *Strengths* | *Challenges* |
| | |

**2. What are some *implications* for the continuous school improvement plan?**

**3. Looking at the data presented, what other student learning data would you want to answer the question *How are our students doing?***

Figure H-5
LOOK FOR IMPLICATIONS COMMONALITIES

Use this template to look across the implications for the four types of data. Highlight the common implications across the types of data.

| Demographics | Student, Staff, Parent Questionnaires | School Processes | Student Learning |
|---|---|---|---|
|  |  |  |  |

Figure H-6

AGGREGATE IMPLICATIONS FOR THE CONTINUOUS SCHOOL IMPROVEMENT PLAN

Use this template to list implications for the continuous school improvement plan, by major concepts. The headers you see in this template can be changed to reflect your needs.

| INSTRUCTION | ASSESSMENT | CURRICULUM | BEHAVIOR | VISION / PLAN | PROFESSIONAL LEARNING |
|---|---|---|---|---|---|
|  |  |  |  |  |  |

| COLLABORATION | LEADERSHIP | PARTNERSHIPS | DATA | CLIMATE | RtI |
|---|---|---|---|---|---|
|  |  |  |  |  |  |

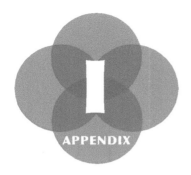

# PROBLEM-SOLVING CYCLE

| | |
|---|---|
| **Purpose** | The purpose of this activity is to get all staff involved in thinking through a problem before jumping to solutions. This activity can also result in a comprehensive data analysis design. By starting with hunches and hypotheses, all staff can get their voices heard. When voices are expressed, there is a better chance of all staff using the information later and being part of the solution. (The first three steps in the problem-solving cycle are *key* and the focus of this activity.) |
| | All staff. Can also be used by teams at any time. |
| **Target Audience** | Twenty minutes for the first three steps of the cycle. |
| **Time** | Chart pad paper, masking tape or push pins, and markers. |
| **Materials** | Handouts for each participant: hunches and hypothesis, and questions and data templates. (Figures I-2 and I-3.) |

## Overview

When schools discover gaps or undesirable results, they naturally want to find solutions immediately to close the gaps. To permanently eliminate the gaps, schools must uncover root causes, or contributing causes (we believe there is more than one cause for undesirable results), and eliminate them, not the surface issues.

The problem-solving cycle is a great activity for getting all staff involved in thinking through undesirable results, or problems, before jumping to solutions. By starting with brainstorming hunches and hypotheses, all staff can be heard. When voices are expressed, there is a better chance of all staff using the information later. During the brainstorming, all staff members hear what they believe are the reasons for the undesirable results, or gaps. Next, staff will need to determine what questions must be answered with data (and what data) before the "problem" can be solved. Deeper data analyses result. (The first three steps in the problem-solving cycle are key and the focus of this activity.)

## Process Protocol

Make sure each person has a copy of the handout and that you are prepared to help small groups identify their problem(s) in objective terms. You will need about one hour to get through the first three steps, if getting the data analysis design is your focus. Analyzing the data will take another two hours—probably at a different time. Developing the action plan will take days with small groups going back to the larger group. (See Appendix L, *Continuous School Improvement Plan.*) Implementing the action plan is the ongoing work of the learning organization, as is evaluating the implementation of the action plan, and improving the processes.

**Step 1.** Establish the size of the group(s) that will be going through this activity. Small groups are beneficial in allowing everyone to participate, even if groups are working on the same problem.

**Step 2.** Start with guidelines or ground rules of acceptable and unacceptable behavior, and how they will be monitored. Make sure it is a "safe" room for threat-free, honest, open discussion.

## Process Protocol *(Continued)*

Step 3.  Have each group clearly identify a problem to be solved, stated in objective terms. For example, *Not all students are reading at grade level by grade three*, as opposed to, *40 percent of our students are not capable of reading by grade three*. The problem should let you find the data.

Step 4.  Brainstorm 20 hunches and hypotheses about why the problem exists (takes about ten minutes). This can spell out what teachers are thinking about the problem currently.

Please resist the urge to "prioritize" or analyze the hunches and hypotheses.

Step 5.  Considering the problem, identify questions that need to be answered, with data, to find out more about the problem (e.g., *How many students have not been reading on grade level by grade three for the past three years?*) Get at least eight questions.

Step 6.  For each question, determine the data that need to be gathered to answer the question. This list becomes the data analysis. Eye balling this list, one can see that for the most part, the data will fall into the four categories of *demographics, student learning, perceptions,* and *school processes*. (At this point, you should have uncovered new ways of looking at the problem. This might be as far as you go on this day.)

Step 7.  Have the groups share their problem-solving cycle, letting others add to them, if appropriate.

Step 8.  Gather and analyze the data. This is often where the schools have the most trouble because they do not have the data readily available. A data team could be assigned to help staff get the data.

Step 9.  Continue with the problem-solving cycle through action planning and implementation.

## Comments to the Facilitator

This is a very action-packed time period. If teams are working on different "problems," you might want to share.

If the hunches and hypotheses are truly brainstormed, the last four or five will be about as close to the contributing causes of the problem as a staff can get.

Some staff will want to use this activity to evaluate programs and processes. Some may want to use this process before a visioning process. The problem-solving cycle will work wherever it is needed.

Figure I-1
STEPS IN SOLVING A PROBLEM

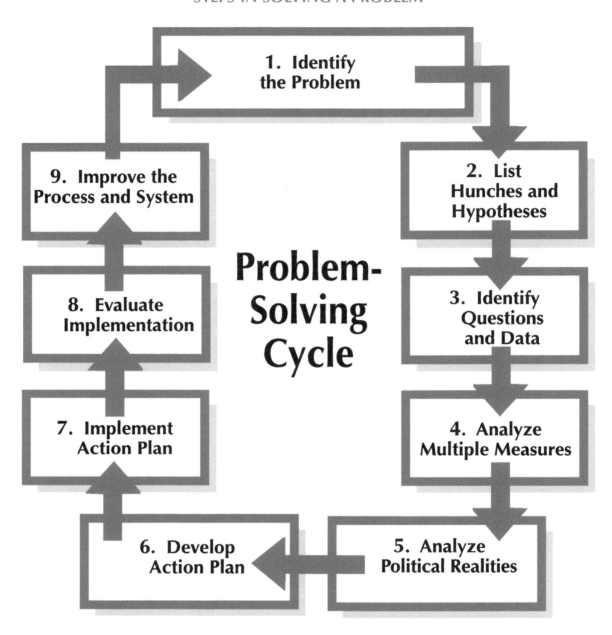

1. Identify the Problem

2. List Hunches and Hypotheses

3. Identify Questions and Data

4. Analyze Multiple Measures

5. Analyze Political Realities

6. Develop Action Plan

7. Implement Action Plan

8. Evaluate Implementation

9. Improve the Process and System

Problem-Solving Cycle

Figure I-2
HUNCHES AND HYPOTHESES

| Identify the problem. |
|---|
| |

| List hunches and hypotheses about why the problem exists. |
|---|
| 1. |
| 2. |
| 3. |
| 4. |
| 5. |
| 6. |
| 7. |
| 8. |
| 9. |
| 10. |
| 11. |
| 12. |
| 13. |
| 14. |
| 15. |
| 16. |
| 17. |
| 18. |
| 19. |
| 20. |

## Figure I-3
## QUESTIONS AND DATA NEEDED

**What questions do you need to answer to know more about the problem, and what data do you need to gather?**

| Questions | Data Needed |
|---|---|
| | |
| | |
| | |
| | |
| | |
| | |
| | |
| | |
| | |
| | |
| | |

# CREATING A SHARED VISION

Schools and districts must have a vision that reflects what the learning organization would *look like, sound like,* and *feel like* when it is carrying out its purpose and mission, and to keep everyone's efforts focused on the target.

To create a vision that is *truly* shared (i.e., agreed upon unanimously and understood in the same way), we must begin with the values and beliefs of individual staff members to create core values and beliefs for the school, and a core purpose and mission for the school. With core values and beliefs, purpose and mission, a vision can be created for the school. *Goals* are the outcomes of the vision.

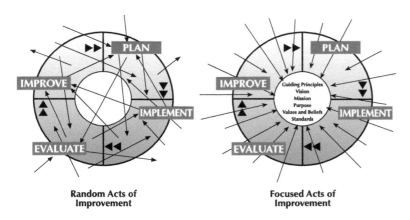

**Random Acts of Improvement**      **Focused Acts of Improvement**

The outcomes are as follows:

Create a vision—

- ◆ everyone can believe in and agree upon;
- ◆ that will lead to student achievement increases;
- ◆ that will lead to continuous improvement across the grades; and
- ◆ to which we all commit.

Prior to the visioning work, it is imperative that staff review comprehensive school data and read Best Practices related to areas of need. If staff members do not learn new ideas of meeting the needs of their students, all they will do is create the same vision—over and over. The end result will be the same.

|  |  |
|---|---|
| **Purpose** | The purpose of this activity is to help staff create a vision that leads to commitment to what we teach, how we teach, how we assess, and how each person treats every other person, that is truly shared (i.e., committed to unanimously and understood in the same way). |
| **Target Audience** | District or school staff. |
| **Time** | Approximately 3.5 to 5 hours. |
| **Materials** | Chart pad paper, material for posting paper on the wall, markers (for each table), scissors, computer, projector, and vision worksheets, attached. |
| **Number of Facilitators** | Preferably two. |

## Overview

To create a vision that is truly shared—committed to unanimously and understood in the same way—we must build on the values and beliefs of the school staff members to create core values and beliefs, a core purpose, and a mission for the school. With core values and beliefs, purpose and mission, a vision can be created for the school.

We must begin with the personal and move to the collective. Systems thinker Peter Senge[1] sums up the rationale:

> *Shared visions emerge from personal visions....*
> *This is how they derive their energy and*
> *how they foster commitment . . . .*
> *If people don't have their own vision,*
> *all they can do is "sign up" for someone else's.*
> *The result is compliance, never commitment.*

## Process Protocol

To create a shared vision, gather all staff members together in a location with tables that seat 5 to 7 people.

Prior to the session, organize seating arrangements to ensure a mixture (grade level/subject area) in the small groups and to ensure that time will be used effectively. Staff members should be well-versed in the literature about what works in schools like theirs.

The steps that follow describe the process in detail. Use the *Creating a Shared Vision Guide* on the day of the vision work to assist with the documentation.

### Step 1. Review Ground Rules.

- This is a safe room.
- There is no rank in this room.
- All ideas are valid.
- Each person gets a chance to speak.
- Each person gets a chance to listen.
- We are here to focus on the future.
- Our purpose is improvement, not blame.

---

[1]Senge, P.M. (2006), *The Fifth Discipline: The art & practice of the learning organization.* New York, NY: The Crown Publishing Group.

## Process Protocol *(Continued)*

Step 2. **Determine Core Values and Beliefs.** Have the members of the group individually brainstorm and document their thoughts about: *What are the curriculum, instruction, assessment, and environmental factors that support effective learning for our students?* **(10 minutes, or longer if needed)**

Compare and merge ideas in small groups. Write the ideas on poster paper. It is okay to add or to agree to ideas that were not on an individual's original list. Stick to the topic. **(15-20 minutes)**

Reconvene as a large group. Someone from each group stands next to the group's posters to note duplicates and to report. Start on one end of the room, for example, and have the reporter for the first group read all of the group's ideas about curriculum. Other groups note duplications on their poster and when it is their turn, report what they have left. Start with a different group for each category and vary the direction so each group gets maximum exposure.

Come to agreement on core values and beliefs for the school. Recorder types on a laptop so statements are displayed on the screen. **(30 minutes)**

There is no limit to the number of core values and beliefs. However, after this day, with staff approval, the Leadership Team might merge some ideas if the list is very long and overlapping.

Step 3. **Determine the Core Purpose.** Have staff members individually brainstorm and document personal ideas about the purpose of the school—do not worry about the wording at this point. **(5 minutes)**

Share individual purposes in small groups and post a common purpose with which everyone in the small group can live. **(10 minutes)**

Look for commonalities across the small group purposes with the large group. Come to agreement on a core purpose for the school. Recorder types the core purpose on the laptop. **(15-20 minutes)**

**Print the core values and beliefs and purpose for each participant to use for the next steps.**

Step 4. **Revisit the Mission.** Review the current mission statement. Either agree that the current mission is fine—that it reflects the purpose of the school—or assign a committee to craft the mission statement at a different time using the core values and beliefs and purpose, and bring it back to the whole staff. As long as the purpose is clear, the process can proceed without the mission statement completely written. It is the purpose that is most important. Determine who will write the mission. Use the existing mission, update it quickly, or delegate the mission to be rewritten. Move on. **(5-10 minutes)**

Step 5. **Create a Vision.** Still assembled in the large group, individuals brainstorm and document personal visions for the school in terms of what the school would *look like, sound like, feel like* if we were doing what we need to do for our children—if we are living our core values and beliefs, purpose, and mission. Identify curriculum, instruction, assessment, and environmental components. (*Note:* If the core values and beliefs are done well, the individuals will say "The vision should be our core values and beliefs," which is what we would like to see happen.) **(10 minutes)**

Share personal visions in small groups and document commonalities. It is okay to add or to agree to ideas that were not on an individual's original list. Post ideas. **(15 minutes—sometimes this step can be skipped if the note about values and beliefs holds true.)**

## Process Protocol *(Continued)*

Come to agreement on the commonalities with the large group. Come to agreement on the elements of the vision for the school. Make sure everyone understands that these agreements become commitments for implementation. **(30 minutes)**

Step 6.   **Determine School Goals—The Outcomes of the Vision.** There should only be two or three school goals. Again, have individuals take time to do their own thinking. **(5 minutes)**

Share individual ideas in small groups and document commonalities. **(10 minutes)**

Small groups share and merge ideas with the large group. **(15 minutes)**

Step 7.   **Draft Vision Narrative and Create a Flowchart.** In addition to the specifics of the vision, it is important to write a narrative and create a flowchart about what it would *look like, sound like, feel like* if the vision was being implemented throughout the school. Brainstorm ideas, at a minimum, if this piece must be delegated to the Leadership Team to finish because of time constraints. (See *Flowcharting School Processes*, Appendix E.)

Again, give individuals a chance to think. **(5 minutes)**

Have individuals compare and combine notes in their small groups. **(15 minutes)**

Compare and combine small group notes to whole group. **(20 minutes)**

Step 8.   **Answer Questions.** You might ask the staff to answer these questions if you have time after you finish the shared vision and school goals.
   ♦ This is a safe room
   ♦ There is no rank in this room
   ♦ All ideas are valid
   ♦ Each person gets a chance to speak
   ♦ Each person gets a chance to listen
   ♦ We are here to focus on the future
   ♦ Our purpose is improvement, not blame

**This is probably where you will end after one day. wherever you are at the end of the day, the following will have to be completed at a later time.**

Step 9.   **Document.** Document the shared vision. Someone can be assigned this task, with review and agreement by the entire staff. Make sure every staff member has a copy of what has been done to this point.

*Suggestion:* Develop a flowchart and an assessment tool that would describe what it would look like when the vision is being implemented in the classroom and across classrooms. This will support the implementation.

Step 10.  **Quality Plan.** Determine a plan to implement the vision. Include the points that follow, especially the professional learning required to implement the vision, materials to purchase, and support mechanisms for implementation, such as peer coaching. (See *Continuous School Improvement Plan,* Appendix H.)

Step 11.  **Curriculum and Instruction.** Grade-level/subject-area teams adapt the vision into real terms for each teacher. Check across grade-level teams to ensure a continuum of learning that makes sense. (Determine a structure and time for grade-level meetings and cross-grade-level meetings.)

## Process Protocol *(Continued)*

Step 12. **Leadership.** Determine a leadership structure to implement and monitor the vision. (See *Leadership Structure*, Appendix N.)

Step 13. **Professional Learning.** Create time in the work week for teachers to collaborate to implement and maintain the vision. Provide professional learning so everyone understands her/his role in implementing the vision and has the support to do it. (See *Professional Learning Calendar*, Appendix O.)

Step 14. **Partnership Development.** Determine how partnerships can help with the implementation of the vision and build them into the vision and the school plan. (See *Creating Partnerships*, Appendix P.)

Step 15. **Continuous Improvement and Evaluation.** Determine an evaluation and monitoring system, specifically to gauge implementation and success. (See *Measuring a Program or Process*, Appendix D.)

## Comments to the Facilitator

This is a very action-packed time period. If you keep within the time estimates, the task will go fast and be productive. If you feel comfortable doing so, consider interspersing the time with team building activities.

An example vision is attached in Figures J-1 and J-2.

Figure J-1

| EXAMPLE: Marylin Avenue Shared Vision, September 2009 | | | |
|---|---|---|---|
| Staff began creating their vision by revisiting their values and beliefs about the *curriculum, instruction, assessment, and environmental* factors that support effective learning for Marylin Avenue students. Core (consensus) values and beliefs follow. | | | |
| MARYLIN AVENUE CORE VALUES AND BELIEFS | | | |
| *Curriculum* | *Instruction* | *Assessment* | *Environment* |
| • Essential standards unwrapped<br>• Meaningful materials are developmentally appropriate<br>• Modified, as appropriate<br>• Curriculum maps<br>• Tools (Open Court)<br>• Vertical and horizontal alignment<br>• Comprehension, Accuracy, Fluency, and Expand Vocabulary (CAFÉ)<br>• Freedom to use district curriculum as a tool<br>• Research based<br>• Use strategies instead of programs<br>• Include fine arts<br>• Choice and independence (social and emotional) | • RtI system<br>• Spiraling—extra time and support because we believe all kids can learn<br>• Focus on the four questions<br>• Students know what they're learning, their individual goals, and why they are important<br>• Whole group, small group, individual<br>• Checking for understanding throughout the lesson<br>• Background knowledge—build on it or develop it<br>• Writing, writing, writing<br>• Increase nonfiction<br>• Manipulatives to build conceptual knowledge<br>• Students on carpet for mini-lessons and guided practice<br>• Data informed<br>• Flexible, modified<br>• Instructional coherence across all grade levels<br>• All learning modalities used<br>• Student centered<br>• Comprehension, Accuracy, Fluency, and Expand Vocabulary (CAFÉ)<br>• Targeted instruction (Level 1)<br>• Team time (Level 2)<br>• Guided Language Acquisition Design (GLAD)<br>• Lucy Calkins<br>• Academic language<br>• Heads Together<br>• Wait Time<br>• Cooperative learning<br>• Math/Language review<br>• Student/individual goals<br>• Differentiated<br>• Daily 5<br>• Literacy Studio<br>• Ample time for guided and individual practice towards mastery<br>• Time for students to communicate and cooperate with each other<br>• Foster thinkers | • Common Formative Assessments (CFAs)<br>• Developmental Reading Assessment (DRA)<br>• Checking for understanding (Explicit Direct Instruction [EDI], pre-planned, non volunteer)<br>• Timely and specific feedback.<br>• Data teams at grade levels<br>• Data wall—staff room<br>• Shared protocols for assessments<br>• Benchmarks<br>• Constant monitoring<br>• Administered by trained staff<br>• Pre-assess<br>• Content valid<br>• Engaging multiple measures<br>• Manageable, meaningful, valuable<br>• Balanced with instruction<br>• Easily supported by technology<br>• Discreet balance with application<br>• Students and Parents informed<br>• Targeting instruction<br>• Individual conferencing<br>• Continuum (Reading, Math, Writing)<br>• Criterion-based (skills)<br>• Standards based | • Caring<br>• Structured<br>• Choice<br>• High expectations<br>• Safe<br>• Void of pre-conceived notions<br>• All staff share in responsibility for all students<br>• Student created<br>• FUN!<br>• Common elements in all classrooms<br>• Parent, Teacher, and Community Connections<br>• Everyone is a teacher and learner<br>• Celebrate student success<br>• High expectations that all students can learn<br>• Sense of urgency<br>• Communication across grade level and within each grade level<br>• Collegial<br>• Collaborative<br>• Frequent use of norms<br>• Students feel ownership<br>• Collaboration on curriculum, instruction, and assessment<br>• Calm<br>• Equitable<br>• Goal oriented<br>• Predictable for adults and children<br>• Respectful for all<br>• Everyone can succeed and grow<br>• Love of learning instilled<br>• Encouraging, positive<br>• Clean, orderly, organized<br>• Adult commitment pushes us toward improvement<br>• Professional reading<br>• Highly qualified teachers<br>• Inviting<br>• Large gathering place<br>• Table groups<br>• Shared materials<br>• Class meetings<br>• Purposeful resources, posters on wall<br>• Awareness of student and staff needs<br>• Basic needs met<br>• Time for reflection |

**Figure J-1** *(Continued)*

| EXAMPLE: Marylin Avenue Shared Vision, September 2009 |
|---|

Staff also revisited their mission and came to consensus on this mission statement:

THE MISSION OF MARYLIN AVENUE ELEMENTARY SCHOOL
*is for **all** to develop the confidence to risk, to accept challenges, and to succeed.*
*We will learn from our experiences, show compassion for others,*
*and grow through the joy of discovery. Learning at Marylin Avenue Elementary School*
*will enable **all** to achieve their personal best and to be respectful, thoughtful, and independent learners.*

Given what their data told them about their current results, what they learned in their research studies, their core values and beliefs, and mission, Marylin Avenue staff agreed that the following curriculum, instruction, assessment, and environmental strategies would assist them in carrying out their mission.

**CURRICULUM:** *Marylin Avenue teachers plan instructional content and learning goals based on California State Standards.*

| COMPONENTS | WHAT IT WOULD LOOK LIKE |
|---|---|
| Curriculum is standards based. | • Teachers plan instruction that meets California state standards for literacy, mathematics, social studies, and science. |
| The collaborative planning of instruction, and the implementation of instruction, for Marylin Avenue students is deep, not just broad. | • All grade-level teams have defined Essential Standards and Super-Power Standards. |
| The collaborative planning of instruction, and the implementation of instruction, for Marylin Avenue students takes into account the prerequisite skills and concepts required for successful learning (unwrapped standards). | • All grade level teams have unwrapped the Essential and Super-Power Standards to feature the needed prerequisite skills and concepts.<br>• As part of instruction, teachers inform students of the standard being taught, the objective of the lesson that addresses the standard, and the importance of the standard. |
| Instruction at Marylin Avenue School is horizontally (agreement among grade level team members) and vertically (agreement across the grades) aligned. | • Grade-level teams come to agreement about the meaning and content of standards, Essential Standards, and Super-Power Standards.<br>• Cross-grade-level teams have aligned the Essential Standards.<br>• Literacy Leads act as the cross-grade-level communication structure for agreement in reading and writing standards. |
| Curriculum is mapped and paced for the school year. | • Grade-level teams draft and agree on year-long curriculum maps to pace instruction. |
| Curriculum implementation is based on researched-based programs and systems. | Literacy programs and resources include:<br>• District-adopted language arts program.<br>• District-adopted Step Up to Writing program.<br>• Systemic Instruction in Phonics and Phonemic Awareness (SIPPS).<br>• Comprehension, Accuracy, Fluency, and Expand Vocabulary (CAFÉ).<br>Mathematics programs and resources include:<br>• District-adopted math program.<br>• Math review.<br>• Specific and agreed-upon grade-level resources may include such strategies as:<br>  * Board language.<br>  * Board math. |

**Figure J-1** *(Continued)*

| EXAMPLE: Marylin Avenue Shared Vision, September 2009 | |
| --- | --- |

**INSTRUCTION:** *Students at Marylin Avenue Elementary School are engaged in intellectually demanding tasks that require higher order and critical thinking skills.*

| COMPONENTS | WHAT IT WOULD LOOK LIKE |
| --- | --- |
| Instruction is based on essential standards. | • Instructional coherence is in place across all grade levels. |
| Instruction is targeted. | • Learning objectives are based on assessments that assess student standards.<br>• Learning objectives are clearly stated.<br>• Students understand the importance of the learning objective.<br>• Teachers frequently check for understanding and adjust instruction as needed. |
| Instruction is differentiated to address needs of students. | • Teachers plan for whole group instruction with students on the carpet for mini-lessons and guided practice.<br>• Classroom teachers plan for small group instruction through invitational groups.<br>• Classroom teachers plan for individual instruction through one-on-one conferences.<br>• Students know their individual goals.<br>• All learning styles are addressed.<br>• Multiple exposure through multi-modality instruction.<br>• Teachers provide additional opportunities to learn and practice essential concepts and skills. |
| A wide variety of instructional strategies are used. | • Effective strategies for English Language Learners include Heads Together, Cooperative Learning, and Wait Time.<br>• Strategies focus on developing schema and building on students' background knowledge.<br>• Tools for developing students' conceptual knowledge include manipulatives, realia, and graphic organizers.<br>• Instruction includes math and language review.<br>• Team time is a structure to provide additional time and support. |
| Schoolwide instructional practices are research based; grade-level teams agree to the levels of use for instructional practices in their collaborative planning. | Classroom practices for literacy include those supported by:<br>• The district-adopted language arts program.<br>• Literacy Studio management (Daily 5, First 20 Days).<br>• Comprehension, Accuracy, Fluency, and Expand Vocabulary (CAFÉ) Strategies.<br>• Lucy Calkins: Units of Study.<br>• Step Up to Writing.<br>• Developmental Reading Assessment (DRA)-Focus for Instruction.<br>• Guided Language Acquisition Design (GLAD) strategies.<br><br>Classroom practices for math include those supported by:<br>• The District-adopted math program.<br>• Math review.<br>• Agreed-upon grade-level specific resources. |
| Instruction is intellectually demanding. | Focus:<br>• Academic language.<br>• Nonfiction reading and writing.<br>• Developing critical-thinking skills. |

**Figure J-1** *(Continued)*

| EXAMPLE: Marylin Avenue Shared Vision, September 2009 | |
|---|---|
| ASSESSMENT: *Marylin Avenue Staff use multiple sources of data from formative and summative assessments to target instruction and measure program effectiveness.* | |
| **COMPONENTS** | **WHAT IT WOULD LOOK LIKE** |
| Our assessments are common, formative, and administered frequently. | • Grade levels agree on which assessments to administer and when.<br>• Grade levels assess each essential standard and conduct data team meetings for most of them.<br>• Teachers use the data from assessments to target instruction for all students.<br>• We look at data from our assessments to determine the effectiveness of instructional strategies and programs.<br>• Our Common Formative Assessments (CFAs) are administered by trained staff every 2 to 3 weeks. |
| All assessments are based on our unwrapped essential standards, and are content valid. | • Grade levels assess and conduct data team meetings for each essential standard.<br>• All concepts and skills of essential standards are assessed.<br>• Teachers will assess essential concepts and skills. |
| Assessments will be supported by technology. | • Data Director and the school server will support classroom teachers to collect and analyze data..<br>• Classroom teachers will receive timely support. |
| Results from assessments will be shared with students and parents. | • Feedback to students will be timely and specific.<br>• Proficiency and growth will be acknowledged and celebrated on a regular basis.<br>• Student goals will be based on assessments, and will be shared with students and parents at goal setting conferences. |
| Assessments must be varied. | • Multiple measures (multiple choice, short answer, essay, etc.) need to be used to accurately assess what students know and don't know. |

Figure J-1 *(Continued)*

| EXAMPLE: Marylin Avenue Shared Vision, September 2009 | |
| --- | --- |
| **ENVIRONMENT:** *The learning environment at Marylin Avenue Elementary School is caring, inviting, and safe. It is achieved as staff members model the way for students, for each other, and for the community.* | |
| **COMPONENTS** | **WHAT IT WOULD LOOK LIKE** |
| Learning environment is structured and predictable. | • Routines that are explicitly taught to students are in place for instructional and non-instructional environments.<br>• Common language is used to teach academic, social, and emotional skills.<br>• Processes and procedures are in place so the operation of the school runs smoothly. These are developed as needed.<br>• Traditions are in place, such as the monthly Students Committed to Excellence (SCE) assembly and perfect attendance awards.<br>• All adults implement the behavior plan so that there is consistency for children.<br>• Days are scheduled so that our students' time is structured and predictable. |
| Interactions are friendly. | • We greet each other.<br>• We greet all students.<br>• We greet parents and members of the community. |
| Interactions are respectful. | • We use calm voices.<br>• We speak quietly in the hallways and walkways.<br>• We listen and seek to understand.<br>• We encourage each other and cheer for each other.<br>• We focus on the positive. |
| Campus is clean, orderly, and organized. | • We keep common areas free of clutter, removing obsolete items for which we are responsible.<br>• We leave common areas cleaner than we found them.<br>• We teach students to care for the classroom and for the campus. |
| Learning is engaging. | • We model the love of learning and the joy of being in school.<br>• A variety of effective instructional strategies are used to address different learning styles.<br>• Students have choices, as guided by teachers. |
| All staff members are teachers. | • We collaborate with a focus on student achievement.<br>• We conduct ourselves in a professional, collegial manner.<br>• We send minutes of meetings to all staff members.<br>• We keep others informed of pertinent information.<br>• We revise, refer to, and use our norms.<br>• We use the issues bin and the anonymous comments envelope to voice concerns; issues are addressed promptly.<br>• We share leadership.<br>• We assume roles that help share the load of work.<br>• We capitalize on and celebrate the strengths of others.<br>• All adults take responsibility for all children. |

## Figure J-1 *(Continued)*

| EXAMPLE: Marylin Avenue Shared Vision, September 2009 | |
|---|---|
| **ENVIRONMENT:** *The learning environment at Marylin Avenue Elementary School is caring, inviting, and safe. It is achieved as staff members model the way for students, for each other, and for the community.* | |
| **COMPONENTS** | **WHAT IT WOULD LOOK LIKE** |
| All staff members are learners. | • We set goals for our students and for ourselves.<br>• We seek feedback from our colleagues.<br>• We provide timely feedback to students and colleagues.<br>• We take time to reflect on our teaching and our actions.<br>• We identify next steps for improvement, using data to objectively guide our work.<br>• We are continuously learning and seeking to improve.<br>• We strive to build the capacity of students and staff. |
| All students can learn. | • We offer a core program, and then provide support through differentiation and flexible groupings.<br>• We hold all students to high expectations. |
| All programs are equitable. | • Marylin Avenue Leadership Team (MALT), Literacy Leads, and grade level teams work towards agreements that benefit all.<br>• Every classroom has a large meeting area, table groupings, and a classroom library.<br>• Purposeful resources that are created with students adorn the walls, without looking like clutter.<br>• Student work is displayed.<br>• Student achievement is celebrated on the walls in classrooms and throughout the school. |
| We have a sense of community. | • Class meetings are held regularly in order to build community and to provide a voice for students.<br>• We engage in group celebrations with student achievement in mind.<br>• We have traditions like the costume parade, the talent show, the softball game, and field day. |
| We value parents. | • We facilitate parent involvement and volunteerism.<br>• We communicate regularly through newsletters, conferences, and report cards that are translated into Spanish.<br>• We share our mission, purpose, shared vision, and action plan with parents.<br>• We offer avenues for feedback: perception surveys, the parent center mailbox, school site council, and meetings held after the monthly Students Committed to Excellence (SCE) assemblies.<br>• We acknowledge and celebrate the languages and cultures that make up our school community. |
| Basic needs are met. | • We ensure that processes are in place through the community outreach worker, the nurse, the Child Welfare and Attendance (CWA), and the office staff. |

Figure J-1 *(Continued)*

| EXAMPLE: Marylin Avenue Shared Vision, September 2009 |
| --- |

Goals are the outcomes of the vision. Given the staff's core values and beliefs, mission, and vision, the following goals represent what staff believe will result from implementing the vision.

| MARYLIN AVENUE SCHOOL GOALS |
| --- |

- All students will exhibit their best effort for themselves, their families, and the community, including a demonstration of respect for their peers and for property.
- We will create an environment where every student, family, staff member, and community member will be excited to be at Marylin Avenue School; and we will be flexible in order to accommodate the educational needs of all.
- All students will be *Proficient* or *Advanced* in Language Arts and Math by the end of fifth grade.

Once the vision was clear and shared, in discussion and on paper, Marylin Avenue staff created a visual of how the parts of the vision work together so all staff can understand it in the same way. The visual of Marylin Avenue's Shared Vision follows.

Figure J-2

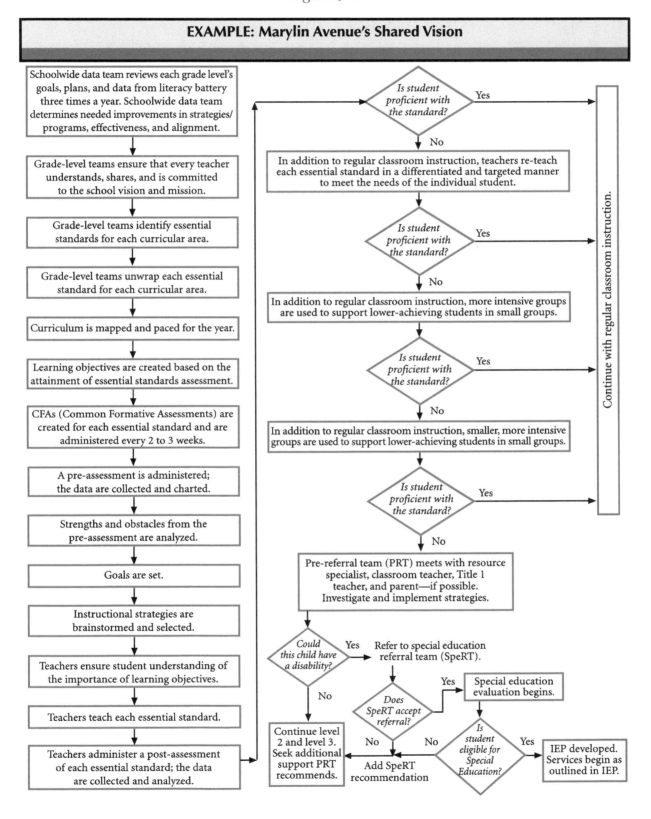

**EXAMPLE: Marylin Avenue's Shared Vision**

# MONITORING VISION IMPLEMENTATION

To know if a vision is truly shared and is making a difference, staff must determine the degree to which the vision is being implemented throughout the school, especially in every classroom. It is almost a guarantee that an instrument to monitor your vision does not exist. Therefore, one must be created.

To create a tool to measure the implementation of your vision, staff need to describe what the program will look like when it is fully implemented. What will the teachers be teaching, and what will the students be learning? What will the curriculum be, what will the instructional practices look like, how will students be assessed, and what will the environment feel like? Staff can list the key elements that reflect the vision and that should be observable in every classroom.

If your vision is one that evolves over time, a rubric that shows how teachers can begin implementing the vision and eventually evolve to one hundred percent implementation might be the approach to take. If your vision is one that should be all or nothing, a scale that will indicate the degree to which these elements are seen in the classroom will be appropriate.

To support your work in monitoring vision implementation (with examples), see Appendices K1 and K2:
   ♦ *Staff Developed Rubric.* (Appendix K1)
   ♦ *Vision Assessment.* (Appendix K2)

The resulting monitoring tools can be used to help teachers know what they are expected to implement. The tools can also be used for teacher self-assessment, for Professional Learning Community discussions, for observations of teachers, and for adjusting the vision. The creation of these tools gives staff members the opportunity to get involved in the development and implementation of their school vision, and to set individual and staff-wide goals for improvement.

# STAFF-DEVELOPED RUBRIC

**Purpose**   The purpose of this activity is to describe how to develop a rubric-like assessment tool for determining the degree of staff implementation of the vision.

**Target Audience**   Leadership team, with grade-level representation.

**Time**   One hour for first draft. Review with staff and refine.

**Materials**   Chart pad paper, markers, self-stick notes, and copies for everyone of core values and beliefs, mission, vision, and continuous school improvement plan.

## Overview

A rubric assessment tool shows teachers how to begin implementing the vision and gradually evolve to one hundred percent implementation. Use this approach when it is expected that the implementation of the vision will evolve over time. The tool helps teachers understand what it will look like, sound like, and feel like when they are implementing the vision in the classroom.

## Process Protocol

Ask the team to:

Step 1.   Review the school vision and continuous school improvement plan, and pull out elements related to what the vision, when implemented, would look like, with respect to:

♦ Curriculum
♦ Instructional strategies
♦ Assessment
♦ Environment
♦ Outcomes

This will become the highest (five) level (the categories can be changed).

Step 2.   Have the team determine what a beginning (one) level would look like.

Step 3.   Think about how staff would logically move from a one to a five level in each of these categories to create levels two, three, and four. What are some of the first things a teacher would do? Consider interviewing those who have begun to implement the vision. How did they start and move ahead, etc.?

Step 4.   Keep refining with full staff review until a tool emerges that contains the elements needed to implement the vision.

## Comments to the Facilitator

The categories and number of levels can be changed. An example follows in Figure K1-1.

Figure K1-1

# Frank Paul School:
## Brain Compatible Education Rubric

| LEVEL ONE |
| --- |

### Physical & Social Values of Environment

- Responsibility to authority is the most important value.
- Social development and interaction is based on external rewards and consequences.
- The environment is agitated.
- Teacher uses loud colors to display items on the bulletin board.
- Students sit in rows.

### Curriculum

- Subject areas and specific skills are taught in isolation.
- Curriculum is textbook driven and teacher centered.

### Instructional Strategies

- Textbook and lecture driven.
- Students working in isolation.

### Assessment

- Publishers' tests are used.

### Outcomes

- Students do not see connections between school and real life and do not understand the interrelationships among concepts common to various subject areas.
- Students are teacher-dependent, passive, authority complacent.
- Students tend not to self-initiate.

Frank Paul School: Brain Compatible Education Rubrics, written by: Vickie Hagan, ITI Coach, Frank Paul School; Jackie Munoz, Restructuring Coordinator, Frank Paul School; Jenne Herrick, Bilingual Education Director, Alisal Union School District; Victoria Bernhardt, Executive Director, Education for the Future Initiative; Mid-California Science Improvement Program (MCSIP) Coaches and Mentors ©1994

Figure K1-1 *(Continued)*

# Frank Paul School:
# Brain Compatible Education Rubric

## LEVEL TWO

### Physical & Social Values of Environment

- Responsibility to authority is the most important value.
- Classroom has calming colors, music, plants, and potpourri.
- Students sit in clusters with individual access to work tools.
- Yearlong theme and life skills are posted.

### Curriculum

- Teacher provides for real-life experiences.
- The curriculum content is aligned with district guidelines.
- Teacher designs a yearlong theme, key points, and inquiries for classroom use which integrate the three areas of science for at least one component of the theme.
- Teacher includes math and science skills essential to the teaching of at least the one component.
- Teacher models and teaches the absence of threat elements as part of the curriculum: life skills, lifelong guidelines, decision making, triune brain, multiple intelligences, written procedures and directions.
- Teacher meets with a professional or peer coach who supports the implementation of ITI in the classroom.

### Instructional Strategies

- Teacher implements a theme-based brain compatible program for at least five hours a week.
- Teacher predominately uses real-life, immersion, hands-on experiences.
- Teacher implements collaborative learning strategies.
- Teacher uses varied instructional strategies such as agendas, direct instruction, mind mapping, discovery process, etc.
- Adequate time is allowed to let students complete their work.
- Limited choices are introduced through inquiries, supplies, time, doing now or doing it later.

### Assessment

- Post-lesson processing about academic or collaborative experiences.
- Use of selected inquiries to assess mastery of key points in such forms as projects, presentations, and some traditional tests.
- Teacher selects work for portfolio folder.

### Outcomes

- Students respond positively to enriched environment by participating in all classroom activities, when there is trust and absence of threat.
- Students are actively participating in the classroom by not being absent, being on time, staying on task, actively listening, responding to teachers' questions, engaging in collaborative interactions, and making connections between the classroom and real life.
- Students do not put others down.
- Students' behavior is absent of threat.

Figure K1-1 *(Continued)*

# Frank Paul School:
## Brain Compatible Education Rubric

| LEVEL THREE |
|---|

### Physical & Social Values of Environment

- Students are beginning to take responsibility for own behavior through the use of the life skills.
- Classroom has calming colors, music, plants, and potpourri.
- The calmness of the teacher's voice contributes to a settled classroom environment.
- Students are beginning to work in cooperative clusters with individual access to work tools.
- Yearlong theme and life skills are posted.

### Curriculum

- Teacher refines the theme and adds at least one additional content area, key points, and inquiries for at least two components of the theme for the year.
- Teacher includes supporting math and language skills which are necessary to the teaching of science.
- Fifty percent (50%) of science curriculum is planned and implemented.
- Absence of threat elements are refined and reinforced.
- Teacher will be supported with implementation by working with a peer or professional coach.

### Instructional Strategies

- Teacher implements ITI for at least ten hours a week.
- Teacher uses "being there" experiences to make learning real for students.
- Teacher engages students in solving problems in a cooperative manner.
- Teacher consistently allows choices for students through presentations—discoveries, explorations, key points, and inquiries based on knowledge of the theory of multiple intelligence and Bloom's Taxonomy.

### Assessment

- Post-lesson about academic or collaborative experiences.
- Use of selected inquiries to assess mastery of key points in such forms as projects, presentations, and some traditional tests.
- Student/teacher selects work for showcase portfolio.
- Assessment of social skills as referred to under absence of threat.

### Outcomes

- Students are self-directed during ITI implementation.
- Students are able to solve problems in a collaborative way.
- Students can make connections between what is learned in science and at least one content area to real life.
- Students master and apply social skills in school and outside of the classroom.
- Students begin to demonstrate the use of life skills.

Figure K1-1 *(Continued)*

# Frank Paul School:
# Brain Compatible Education Rubric

## LEVEL FOUR

### Physical & Social Values of Environment

- Self-responsibility and self-initiated engagement are the most important values
- Classroom has calming colors, music, plants, and potpourri
- The calmness of the teacher's voice contributes to a settled classroom environment
- Students are working in cooperative clusters with individual access to work tools
- Yearlong theme and life skills are posted

### Curriculum

- Teacher refines the yearlong theme and integrates all three areas of science and at least two other content areas, key points, and inquiries for at least 50% of the curriculum for the year
- Curriculum is based predominately on visible locations which provide "being there" experiences and connections with the real world
- Curriculum is designed to enhance pattern-seeking and program building
- The three sciences are integrated for at least 75% of the time
- Curriculum for collaborative assignments is specifically designed for group work

### Instructional Strategies

- Teacher implements integrated thematic instruction for at least ten to fifteen hours a week
- Teacher utilizes explorations and discoveries to make learning real for students
- Students make choices about how they master the key points; including assisting in the development of inquiries
- Learning experiences are predominately based on real life immersion and hands on of real things
- Collaboration is regularly used whenever it would enhance pattern seeking and program building
- Teacher introduces peer and cross-age tutoring to students
- Teacher introduces the idea of outcomes to students

### Assessment

- Implementing culminating performances chosen by the teacher that demonstrate mastery and application of key points
- Students can judge their performance through academic and social skills
- Students select work for showcase portfolio
- Student/parent/teacher conferences led by the student

### Outcomes

- Students take control of their learning and act in a self-directed manner for the entire day
- Students demonstrate more shared leadership while doing collaborative activities
- Peer and cross-age tutoring is being explored
- Students can make connections between what is learned in science and at least two other content areas to real life
- Students participate in the design and evaluation of outcomes
- Students demonstrate life skills throughout the day

Figure K1-1 *(Continued)*

# Frank Paul School:
# Brain Compatible Education Rubric

## LEVEL FIVE*

### Physical & Social Values of Environment

- The sense of responsibility for others and the feeling of the community are the most important values.
- Classroom has calming colors, music, plants, and potpourri.
- The calmness of the teacher's voice contributes to a settled classroom environment.
- Students are working in cooperative clusters with individual access to work tools.
- Yearlong theme is evident throughout classroom environment and life skills are an integral part of the class.

### Curriculum

- Teacher develops and implements a yearlong theme which integrates the three science areas, all content areas, key points, and inquiries for the entire year.
- 100% of science curriculum is planned.

### Instructional Strategies

- Teacher implements integrated thematic instruction all day, all year.
- Collaborative groupings for students.
- Students make choices about the inquiries they do.
- Students help in the selection of key points and take part in writing inquiries.

### Assessment

- Culminating performances chosen by the student that demonstrate mastery and application of key points.
- Performance task assesses original, creative, and problem-solving thinking.
- Students/peers self-assessment.
- Students select best work for showcase portfolio.
- Ongoing student/teacher assessment conferences with the use of rubrics.
- Student/teacher/parent interaction and conferences about portfolio.

### Outcomes

- Students participate in the design and evaluation of outcomes.
- Students take control of their learning and act in a self-directed manner for the entire day.
- Students demonstrate more shared leadership while doing collaborative activities.
- Students participate in peer and cross-age tutoring.
- Students can connect what they are learning in school to real life.
- Students can creatively solve real-life problems through interrelating and connecting what they have learned in various subject areas and the real world.
- Students use life skills as the basis for interacting with others.

(*Level Five was developed for older learners.)

*Note.* Rubrics from *The School Portfolio: A Comprehensive Framework for School Improvement*, Second Edition (p.220-224), by Victoria L. Bernhardt, 1999, Larchmont, NY: Eye On Education. Reprinted with permission.

# VISION ASSESSMENT

**K2**
APPENDIX

|   |   |
|---|---|
| **Purpose** | The purpose of this activity is to help staff develop an assessment tool for determining the degree of implementation of the vision. |
| **Target Audience** | Leadership team, with grade-level representation. |
| **Time** | One hour for first draft. Review with staff and refine. |
| **Materials** | Chart pad paper, markers, self-stick notes, and copies for everyone of core values and beliefs, mission, vision, and continuous school improvement plan. |

## Overview

An assessment tool with a five-point scale can remind teachers of what it takes to implement the vision (from not implementing at all to implementing all the time). Instructional coaches can use this same tool to validate the teachers' self-assessments. The coaches' observations, in collaboration with the teachers, can ensure the implementation of the vision in every classroom. Use this approach when it is expected that all teachers will implement all elements of the vision, as soon as possible. The tool helps teachers understand what it will look like, sound like, and feel like when they are implementing the vision in the classroom.

## Process Protocol

Ask the teachers, in grade-level or subject-area teams, to:

Step 1. Review the school vision and continuous school improvement plan, and pull out elements related to what the vision, when implemented in their classroom, will look like with respect to:

- ♦ Curriculum
- ♦ Instructional strategies
- ♦ Assessment
- ♦ Environment
- ♦ Outcomes

Step 2. Have the teachers determine a scale to indicate the degree of implementation, such as: *1=not at all; 2=some of the time; 3=about half of the time; 4=almost all the time; 5=All the time.*

Step 3. Keep refining with full staff review until a tool emerges that looks like how to implement the vision.

## Comments to the Facilitator

The items and number of levels can be changed. The intent is to get a tool to monitor and measure the degree to which the vision is being implemented. See example of the following page.

## Figure K2-1
## TEACHER ASSESSMENT TOOL FOR IMPLEMENTING
## THE AZALEA MIDDLE SCHOOL VISION

*To what degree are you implementing these processes and strategies in your classroom? Circle the number that represents the degree of implementation right now (1=not at all; 2=some of the time; 3=about half of the time; 4= almost all the time; 5=all the time). Add comments about what would help you implement the different strategies, or notes about what you did that you would like to share with others.*

| *Teachers will—* Implementation | Classroom | Comments |
|---|---|---|
| Create lesson plans and syllabi that address the standards. | 1  2  3  4  5 | |
| Use district pacing guides for grade-level students and adjust pacing and activities as appropriate to accommodate low-performing students, new students, students with special needs, and above-standards-level students. | 1  2  3  4  5 | |
| Maximize instructional time to help every student meet content standards. | 1  2  3  4  5 | |
| Provide students with opportunities to use higher-order thinking and problem-solving skills. | 1  2  3  4  5 | |
| Provide students opportunities to demonstrate knowledge of content in a variety of ways. | 1  2  3  4  5 | |
| Assess student knowledge on an ongoing basis, using multiple strategies. | 1  2  3  4  5 | |
| Use standards-based instruction congruent with what the assessment data say. | 1  2  3  4  5 | |
| Utilize technology for content-area learning and research. | 1  2  3  4  5 | |
| Provide students with opportunities to use technology to support learning. | 1  2  3  4  5 | |
| Provide students with opportunities for sufficient practice of technology skills. | 1  2  3  4  5 | |
| Apply productivity/multimedia tools and peripherals to support individual learning and group collaboration through the state content standards. | 1  2  3  4  5 | |
| Design, develop, publish, and present products (Webpages, videotapes, CDs) using technology resources that demonstrate and communicate curriculum concepts to audiences, both within the school and outside the school. | 1  2  3  4  5 | |
| Collaborate with peers, experts, and others using e-mail to investigate real world problems, issues, and information to develop solutions or products. | 1  2  3  4  5 | |
| Showcase student work on the Intranet by grade and subject. | 1  2  3  4  5 | |
| Create flexible instructional groupings. | 1  2  3  4  5 | |
| Implement *Character Education* concepts in the classroom. | 1  2  3  4  5 | |
| Implement arts-focused strategies that raise student achievement. | 1  2  3  4  5 | |

How many times in the past month have you—
    Observed a colleague teach? _____
    Been observed by a colleague? _____
When will you be willing to provide a demonstration
lesson at a faculty meeting? _____
    Topic?_____
    _____

Comments, needs, or information to share:

_____

_____

_____

_____

# CONTINUOUS SCHOOL IMPROVEMENT (CSI) PLAN

## How Are We Going to Get to Where We Want to Be?

The data profile helps us know *where we are now,* so we can create a plan of action that starts where we are, not where we think we are. Our mission, vision, and goals tell us *where we want to be,* and our gap analysis and problem-solving cycle inform us of *how we got to where we are now.* Our objectives and implication commonalities provide insight into the strategies and activities that will need to take place in order to achieve the vision. All of these pieces are critical for determining *how we are going to get to where we want to be,* as documented in the continuous school improvement (CSI) plan.

CSI plans are different from annual, or typical, school improvement plans as they are written to achieve the vision of the school, not just close a gap, or meet a couple of requirements. This plan is about keeping the entire system together and moving it forward. CSI plans need to be monitored throughout the year and updated as needed, and at least annually.

The CSI plan consists of these items:

♦ Baseline Data
♦ Goals
♦ Objectives
♦ Strategies to implement the vision
♦ Activities to implement the strategies
♦ Person(s) responsible for the activities and strategies
♦ Measurement to know if the activities are being accomplished
♦ Resources needed
♦ Due date
♦ Timeline

Shown here is a flowchart graphic, illustrating the process of *Comprehensive Data Analysis to Continuous School Improvement Implementation.* Start with comprehensive schoolwide data analysis on multiple measures of data, determine strengths, challenges, and implications for the continuous school improvement plan, then line up the implications for the four types of data and highlight commonalities across the data. Staff will soon see there are big concepts that need to be addressed in the plan. These big concepts, recorded as aggregated implications, along with the vision and contributing cause analyses, are used to create a CSI plan to implement the vision.

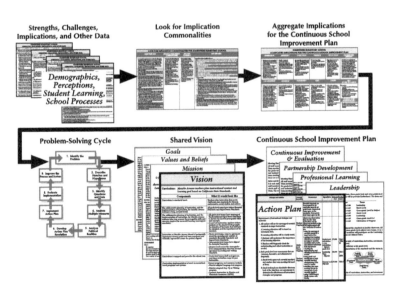

| | |
|---|---|
| **Purpose** | The purpose of this activity is to use the comprehensive data analysis and shared vision to create one continuous school improvement plan for the school. |
| **Target Audience** | A cross-representative team of school staff and school community. |
| **Time** | Overall, this planning activity will stretch over a couple of weeks and will go back and forth to full staff for review and revisions. |
| **Materials** | Self-stick notes (3x3 and 3x5), chart pad paper, masking tape, markers, and a large amount of wall space. Also, computer and projector. |

## Overview

Continuous school improvement planning takes into account implications from comprehensive data analysis, contributing cause analyses, the school vision, and school goals to create the action details for implementing the vision. A continuous school improvement plan is different from an annual school improvement plan; it takes the entire system into consideration and moves it forward to the vision, as opposed to making small adjustments to the status quo.

It is not necessary to have every staff member involved in creating a school improvement plan. While it is important that all staff agree with the strategies, it can become cumbersome and inefficient if too many people are working on the plan at the same time. We recommend that the Leadership Team draft the plan, then take it to staff for review, improvement, acceptance, and commitment to its implementation.

## Process Protocol

**Step 1.** **Enroll a Planning Team.** Enroll a representative group of staff members, not just those who think alike, and not just the leadership team. Include stakeholders such as parents, community, and students. This team will lead the development and draft of the plan, then bring the plan back to the whole staff to review and suggest changes. Although five to eight people is a good size for a functioning team, the more change required of staff to implement the vision and plan, the more individuals need to be involved at the plan creation level.

**Step 2.** **Review the Data.** The action planning team reviews the multiple measures of data analysis (that the entire staff analyzed together) and that answers the question, *Where are we now?*

**Step 3.** **Determine Contributing Causes.** Analyze the underlying reasons for the problems or needs that emerge from reviewing the data. (Use the *Problem-Solving Cycle*, Appendix I.)

**Step 4.** **Learn New Concepts.** The data will show what is not working, as well as if there are subgroup needs not being met. Staff must learn new concepts before creating a vision, or they will find themselves with the same vision.

**Step 5.** **Create/Revisit the School Vision.** If the vision is done well, it will be very clear what needs to be put in the plan and implemented, with respect to *curriculum* (what we teach), *instruction* (how we teach the curriculum), *assessment* (how we assess learning), and *environment* (how each person treats every other person).

**Step 6.** **Set Goals.** Schoolwide goals need to be set with the whole staff before the actual writing of the plan commences. Goals are intended outcomes of the vision. They are stated in broad, general, abstract, and largely measurable terms. We should have only two or three school goals. Write each broad goal on the top of a piece of chart pad paper. Example: *All students will be proficient in all subject areas.* Goals should:

- Give the school a long term vision.
- Be realistic.
- Drive action to the purpose and vision of the school.
- Have at least one objective that describes how the goal will be measured.
- Help the school reach district and state goals.

## Process Protocol *(Continued)*

Goals should not:

- Specify how the schools will achieve the goal.

Benefits of goal setting:

- Achieve more.
- Improve performance.
- Increase motivation to achieve.

Step 7.  **Identify Objectives.** Draft objectives that will close the gap for each of the goals. Objectives are goals that are redrafted in clearly tangible terms, to close gaps. They must be grounded in the data. Objective statements are narrow, specific, concrete, and measurable. When writing objectives, it is important to describe the intended results, rather than the process or means to accomplish them. Write each objective on a large self-stick notes and place under the appropriate goal that is written on the chart pad paper. Objectives are SMART goals: Specific, Measurable, Attainable, Realistic, and Trackable.[1]

Example: *The percentage of grade four students achieving the reading comprehension standard will increase from 80 to 90 by Spring 2014.*

Step 8.  **Determine How the Objectives will be Measured.** Objectives are measurable statements. Determine what assessment tools and strategies will be used to know if the objectives are being met or have been met.

Example: *The percentage of grade four students achieving the reading comprehension standard will increase from 80 to 90 by Spring 2014, as measured by the state reading assessment exam.*

Step 9.  **Identify and Group Strategies to Achieve the Objectives.** Brainstorm and discuss different strategies to reach the objectives, making sure the vision is reviewed and contributing causes of the gap(s) have been analyzed. Your comprehensive data analysis will provide aggregated commonalities to consider as well. Group the strategies under the objectives.

Example: *To increase the number of students reading on grade level by 10 percent, the strategies might include:*

- professional learning in teaching reading for all teachers.
- study how reading is successfully taught in other locations.
- coach each other to implement new strategies.
- determine how to implement standards at every grade level.

Step 10.  **Actions Required to Implement the Strategies.** Below each strategy, list the actions that need to be accomplished to implement the strategies (i.e., *study the learning standards, study the research on reading, review the student-level data*).

Step 11.  **Arrange Strategies and Activities.** Arrange the strategies and activities in chronological order. (Keep the version for later reference and fine-tune the plan in chronological summary form, starting with the action to be taken first.)

Step 12.  **Determine How Achievement of the Actions Will Be Measured.** For each activity, determine how you will know if the action is being implemented and the impact of its implementation.

Step 13.  **Use a Planning Template.** Using a planning template, label columns—strategy/action, person responsible, measurement, resources, due date, and timeline. Place the reorganized strategies

[1]Conzemius, A., & O'Neill, J. (2005). *The power of SMART goals: Using goals to improve student learning.* Bloomington, IN: Solution Tree.

## Process Protocol *(Continued)*

and actions in the action column in a manner that is easiest for staff to utilize later. In the column next to each action, identify the person ultimately responsible for the action. Try not to use team names like Language Arts Action Team in the person responsible column. Accountability is most effective if the responsibility is delegated to an individual. Responsible persons determine how accountability reviews are conducted, and how to talk with one another about fostering and demonstrating accountability (example template is shown at the bottom of Figure L-1)

Step 14. **Establish Due Dates.** In the column next to "person responsible," write in the due dates. For each strategy or activity (depends on the topic and structure for implementation), determine when the activity absolutely must be completed. In the columns that represent months, weeks, and sometimes days, make notations that will indicate when each activity will begin and when it will be completed, by showing an "X" in the cell. Indicate the duration by marking a line between the "Xs" across the months.

Step 15. **Determine Resources.** Determine the resources required of each strategy and activity. This budget, developed in conjunction with the CSI plan, will determine the financial feasibility of the actions for each year. Alterations are made simultaneously and balanced back and forth, while looking for items that can leverage other items. Dollars sometimes limit activities. School staff are often surprised, however, to discover that many times what they have to spend is equivalent to what they can do in a year's time. If the latter does not hold true, the school staff have important and specific information (i.e., the vision, plan, and budget) to utilize in seeking additional support for their efforts. Note that the budget plan is a part of the CSI plan and that all school funds are used with the one resulting CSI plan. Everything in the school should be working toward that one CSI plan and the one school vision. The planning team must have a clear understanding of all budget resources.

Step 16. **Refine the Plan.** With the first draft of the plan complete, review the elements and the big picture of the plan. Below are some guiding questions:
   - Will this plan lead to improved student learning?
   - Will this plan help implement the vision?
   - Are the objectives about improved student learning for *all* students?
   - What evidence do we need to know if the objectives are being met?
   - Will the strategies lead to attainment of the objectives?
   - Do the strategies address contributing causes?
   - Are there strategies/actions that can be further collapsed?
   - Will all staff members know what is expected of them?
   - Does the plan include new learnings required of staff? If so, has training and support been incorporated for each area?
   - Are the time frames realistic?
   - How will you keep the ultimate goal of improved student learning for all students at the forefront of everything you do?
   - How often will the plan and strategies be monitored?
   - Whose job is it to monitor the implementation of the plan?
   - How will new staff members learn about the plan?

Step 17. **Communicate the Plan.** Determine how the continuous school improvement plan will be documented, communicated, reported, and updated. Communicate progress toward the attainment of the school improvement goals and objectives in newsletters, staff bulletins, websites, and bulletin boards.

## Process Protocol *(Continued)*

Step 18. **Monitor the Implementation of the Plan.** A part of refining the continuous school improvement plan is ensuring that everything in the plan is aligned to the implementation of the vision, including the leadership structure, curriculum, instruction, assessment, professional learning, etc. When staff begin to implement the plan, all parts of the plan need to be monitored, regularly. The measurement column for the strategies and activities provide a means for monitoring. We recommend that the Leadership Team check the plan for implementation each month, remembering that implementation of a continuous improvement plan requires collaboration and flexibility on the part of the monitors.

Step 19. **Evaluate the Plan.** The entire continuous school improvement plan must be evaluated, with the vision and school goals as targets. This comprehensive evaluation will evaluate the parts and the whole of the plan to indicate if the goals, objectives, and strategies are leading to the attainment of the vision. (See *Evaluation of Plan*, Appendix U.)

This activity will take many iterations, and is done best with a small group, and reviewed by the larger group. Bring copies of the shared vision, values and beliefs, purpose, mission, goals, and aggregated implications of your data analysis work. You may want to post large versions of these items around the room.

## Comments to the Facilitator

As groups identify actions, the actions will begin to collapse. For example, actions might include *professional learning in integrated instruction, project-based learning*, and *hands-on math and science*. If considered separately, this professional learning could stretch out over years. If considered comprehensively, the professional learning could end up with one facilitator who can help staff translate these elements into grade-level and subject-area implementation.

Figure L-1

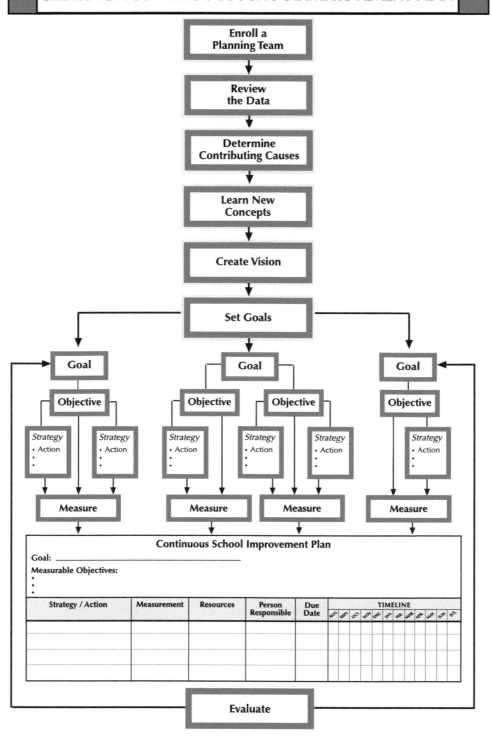

# MONITORING THE IMPLEMENTATION OF THE PLAN

| | |
|---|---|
| **Purpose** | The purpose of this activity is to help staff make sure that all the elements of their continuous school improvement plans are being implemented. |
| **Target Audience** | School staff are the target audience. However, a Leadership Team should accept the primary responsibility for monitoring the implementation of the plan. |
| **Time** | On-going. |
| **Materials** | Vision, continuous school improvement plan, monitoring tools. |

## Overview

After a shared vision and a continuous school improvement plan to implement the vision are developed, it is important to ensure that the plan is implemented, and that the plan is leading to the vision, with its intended results.

## Process Protocol

**Step 1.** Assign the accountability for the monitoring of the continuous school improvement plan to the Leadership Team. Since all staff members should be committed to the vision and its implementation, elements of monitoring the continuous school improvement plan may be shared among the staff.

**Step 2.** Have the Leadership Team establish a regular monthly check on the implementation of the plan. The professional learning calendar and the vision monitoring tools should be a tremendous help. (See *Professional Learning Calendar*, Appendix O, and *Monitoring Vision Implementation*, Appendix K.)

**Step 3.** When the Leadership Team finds that elements of the vision are not being implemented, they need to interview grade level/subject area teams to find out why and to encourage that staff get back on track with implementation.

**Step 4.** If more than one grade-level/subject-area teams are off track and it is determined that all staff need a refresher in how to implement the vision, then the plan will need to be altered to allow for additional professional learning.

## Comments to the Facilitator

The Leadership Team should use whatever it can to make sure that *all* staff are implementing the vision and plan, as intended. It is important that the Principal not be left with this chore. Principals are often pulled out of the school for meetings, and cannot always be in the building to ensure implementation. Staff members may need access to on-going professional learning such as coaching, demonstration lessons, and peer observations to keep their focus on the implementation of the continuous school improvement plan. Resources need to be available to provide necessary professional learning to help staff members sustain their commitment to the vision and implementing the plan.

# LEADERSHIP STRUCTURE

**APPENDIX**

| | |
|---|---|
| **Purpose** | The purpose of this activity is to help staff create a leadership structure to implement the school's shared vision. Usually, this is done by partitioning staff into teams that have specific functions. These teams are most often called Leadership Teams, Data Teams, Grade Level Teams, Subject Area Teams, or Professional Learning Communities. One team can serve multiple functions. |
| **Target Audience** | School staff. |
| **Time** | Approximately two hours. |
| **Materials** | Chart pad paper, material for posting paper on walls, markers, copies of the purpose, mission, vision, and the plan for continuous school improvement. |

## Overview

The important elements of effective leadership structures include:

♦ *Partitioning of all school staff in a manner that makes sense for supporting the implementation of the vision.* For example, in elementary schools, establishing grade-level teams and cross-grade-level teams to implement the vision makes sense. This is especially effective since the focus is to make sure each teacher is implementing grade level standards, and to ensure that standards implementation is calibrated across grade levels. Most traditional high schools and middle schools have departments, which could represent an effective leadership structure—if that structure supports the implementation of the vision. However, if the middle school or high school is trying to integrate subjects, individual subject-specific departments might keep the school from implementing its vision. The leadership structure must reflect the vision. Support staff should be included in the leadership structure in a way that makes sense for implementing the vision.

♦ *Clarifying purposes and roles and responsibilities of all teams.* Team members create and agree on the purpose and roles and responsibilities of each team so everyone knows the intricacies of the team as well as how everyone can contribute to the successful implementation of each team. A part of identifying roles and responsibilities is to set structures for norms, timed agendas, and rotating roles (facilitator, timekeeper, and recorder) to keep the team focus on student learning during team time.

♦ *Identifying times to meet and keeping them sacred.* The teams meet no matter what. There can be no cancellations because of other meetings. It is important to not put the Principal as lead of any team. We find that the Principal is often pulled out at the last minute, and then the team thinks the meeting has to be cancelled. However, the Principal should participate in as many meetings as possible, ensure that the meetings take place, and reinforce the cross-grade level work. To implement the vision with a strong leadership structure, the team meeting times and agendas must be adhered to. At least one hour a week or 90 minutes every other week needs to be dedicated to grade level or subject-area teams to review data and to update instruction.

## Overview *(Continued)*

Additional time needs to be protected for leadership team meetings and other leadership teams that look across grade level/subject matter to ensure instructional coherence. Time must be created. Many schools bank time by extending the school day four days a week, providing an early dismissal or late start for students so teachers can meet part of one day a week. Developing a meeting calendar with dates, times, and locations will help members plan and keep times sacred.

## Process Protocol

Step 1. Gather and randomly arrange staff into small groups of five to seven. Try to find a room with big blank walls to post lots of chart paper.

Step 2. Lead the staff in reviewing the school core values and beliefs, purpose, mission, vision, and continuous improvement plan.

Step 3. Ask staff members to think, independently, about all the purposes leadership teams can meet, with the vision as a "given" target. Have them share with another individual.

Step 4. Provide time for the pairs to share their ideas with their small group. Ask small groups to display their discussion on chart paper. Some of the things staff may want leadership teams to help them with, include—

a. implementation of the vision by all staff—which directs what teachers will teach, how they will teach, and how they will assess student learning.

b. implementation of the vision as intended.

c. implementation of the common core standards, in each classroom, and across classrooms.

d. use of formative assessments.

e. the review of formative assessment data and the discussion of how instruction could be improved to better meet the needs of all students, by grade level, and/or subject area.

f. implementation of strategies that help all students learn.

g. collaboration among all staff.

h. support for the implementation of professional learning.

Step 5. Provide time for each small group to report its ideas to the whole group.

Step 6. As the whole group discusses and merges common ideas into a leadership structure, create a visual for the leadership structure the staff agrees to implement and that everyone understands in the same way.

Step 7. Define team member roles and responsibilities.

Step 8. Establish meeting calendar.

## Comments to the Facilitator

In order to establish a shared decision-making structure to implement the vision, the vision must be crystal clear, and all staff must share the vision. Once you are clear on the vision, it is much easier to engage in scenarios of how decisions should be made throughout the organization, and how staff can collaborate to implement the vision. Try drawing a picture of a leadership structure that would align with the way the vision must be implemented, before people are identified to be on the team, and before the vision is implemented. This can desensitize the whole process and can be a very good way to make the vision actually happen. Four tools, three attached to this activity, will support the leadership team work. They are as follows:

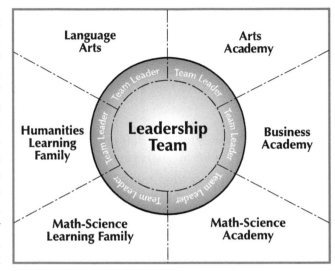

- ♦ *Running Efficient Meetings*
- ♦ *Ground Rules*
- ♦ *Meeting Etiquette*
- ♦ *Norms of Behavior*
- ♦ *Coming to Consensus* (see Appendix A, Figure A-1)

Another helpful activity is the *Communication Protocol,* Appendix Q.

---

## Running Efficient Meetings

The time that shared decision making requires is the most frequently cited disadvantage of the process. Here are some tips on running efficient meetings to help ease the time crunch.

**Running the Meeting**

- ♦ Formalize a meeting time and place (e.g., first Monday of every month in the cafeteria).
- ♦ Set and distribute the agenda before the actual meeting day.
- ♦ Set a time limit for each item on the agenda.
- ♦ Set up a process to make sure that the most important issues (school vision, mission and goals) are addressed, instead of spending time on issues that can be dealt with by one or two people.
- ♦ Assign a facilitator, time-keeper, and record-keeper at each meeting; rotate roles from meeting to meeting.
- ♦ Decisions should be made on the basis of data collected on the issue rather than hunches or "gut feelings," which can obscure the difference between treating the problem or the symptom.
- ♦ Stay on schedule.
- ♦ Make assignments to individuals to follow-up.

# Ground Rules

If ground rules are established, purposes kept clear, and time is focused on the issues at hand, teams can stay away from focusing on individual or group behaviors which usually cause conversations to lose focus.

Example ground rules include:

- This is a safe room
- There is no rank in this room.
- All ideas are valid.
- Each person gets a chance to speak.
- Each person gets a chance to listen.
- We are here to focus on the future.
- Our purpose is improvement, not blame.

# Meeting Etiquette/Norms of Behavior

It might be that your staff members need new ways of behaving as a team. Developing norms of behavior and agreeing on meeting etiquette are ways to get all staff to think about their meeting behavior. It is also a way to monitor the meeting behavior.

### Example Norms of Behavior

- Each member of this school will strive to understand the other person before trying to be understood.
- We will not make assumptions. We will ask for clarification.
- We will not talk behind each other's backs.
- There will be no cross-talk in open meetings.
- Feelings will be expressed openly, without judgment.
- We want to be respected.
- There is no such thing as failure; there are only results.
- There are win-win solutions to every problem. We will find them.
- Our commitment is to help every student succeed. All of our actions are focused on this commitment.
- We value trust and will act with trustworthiness.

We are each accountable to the other to uphold the intent of these guidelines. When we all work together to behave in a manner that will increase our abilities to meet the needs of students, our reward will be the achievement of our outcomes—increased student achievement.

# PROFESSIONAL LEARNING CALENDAR

| Purpose | The purpose of this activity is to guide staff in the creation of a Professional Learning Calendar. A Professional Learning Calendar aligns the dates in the school year to the action spelled out in the school improvement plan, leadership structure, and vision. |
| Target Audience | School staff members are the target audience. However, a Leadership Team can draft the calendar and take it back to the full staff for approval and implementation. |
| Time | Approximately two hours. |
| Materials | Chart pad paper, material for posting paper on the wall, markers (for each table), computer, projector, copies of the purpose, mission, vision, and the continuous school improvement plan. |

## Overview

Once the plan, based on the data analysis, vision, plan, and leadership structure, is completed, school staff can benefit from a Professional Learning Calendar, similar to the example on the next page. A Professional Learning Calendar starts with those agreed upon times for the leadership teams to meet, and then pulls from the plan what the teams should be working on at any point in the school year calendar; thereby setting the topic for each meeting. Many principals and other staff members have found the Professional Learning Calendar to be extremely valuable in keeping the whole school on target with implementing the vision, plan, and leadership structure. Some principals say the use of the calendar makes things happen that have never happened before, even though the activities had been "planned." All the purposes or topics in the calendar are derived from the school improvement plan. If the calendar looks too overwhelming, the plan would need to be changed.

## Process Protocol

Step 1. Using the *Professional Learning Calendar* example, Figure O-1, for guidance, have a small committee of staff members possibly the Leadership Team—lay out the dates of team meetings, as spelled out in the leadership structure, and professional learning commitments. In the second column, indicate who should attend. From the continuous school improvement plan, determine the purpose of the meetings.

Step 2. Adjust the topics and times to ensure full implementation of the vision.

Step 3. If the calendar looks undoable, you will need to revise your school plan.

Step 4. Present the finished product, with revisions to the continuous school improvement plan, to the full staff for approval and implementation.

## Comments to the Facilitator

The main purpose of the *Professional Learning Calendar* is to show how all school structures, like Leadership Teams, professional learning, committees, staff meetings, work to support the implementation of the vision and plan. The second purpose is to make sure all the components of the plan and vision are committed to and get accomplished.

## Figure O-1

| EXAMPLE: Marylin Avenue Professional Learning Calendar |||
|---|---|---|
| **Date** | **Who Should Attend** | **Purpose** |
| July 27-31<br>All day | Leadership Team and Literacy Leads | Attend the *Education for the Future* Summer Data Institute. |
| August 20-21<br>8:00 AM to 4:00 PM | Professional learning for all staff | Expectations for the year. Select team members and team leaders. Review standards. Model how to unwrap standards to feature needed prerequisite skills and concepts, how to vertically align, map, pace for all curricular areas, and review assessment data. Grade-level teams continue with standards. |
| August 25<br>3:05 to 4:15 PM | Cross-Grade-Level Teams | Establish a system to monitor assessment data and ensure the alignment of standards across grade levels. |
| September 1 | All teachers | Conduct literacy assessment. |
| September 1<br>3:00 to 4:00 PM | Literacy Leads | Verify Language Arts standards across grade levels. |
| September 2<br>1:45 to 3:00 PM | Grade-Level Team | Map Language Arts standards to the curriculum. Review assessment data. Create learning objectives. |
| September 2<br>3:15 to 4:30 PM | Leadership Team | Planning for the year. |
| September 9<br>1:45 to 3:00 PM | Grade-Level Team | Map Math standards to the curriculum. Review assessment data. Create learning objectives. |
| September 9<br>3:15 to 4:30 PM | Leadership Team | Continue planning for the year. |
| September 14 | All teachers | Content standards English Language Arts and Math Practice. |
| September 15<br>3:00 to 4:00 PM | Literacy Leads | Verify Language Arts standards across grade levels. |
| September 16<br>1:45 to 3:00 PM | Whole staff | Work on Vision with Vickie and Brad from *Education for the Future*. |
| September 21 | All teachers | District writing assessment. |
| September 22<br>3:05 to 4:15 PM | Cross-Grade-Level Teams | Monitor assessment data and ensure the alignment of standards across grade levels. |
| September 23<br>1:45 to 3:00 PM | Grade-Level Team | Review progress. |
| September 23<br>3:15 to 4:30 PM | Leadership Team | Determine assessment reports that will assist staff in implementing and assessing standards. |
| September 24<br>3:15 to 4:30 PM | Data Team | Determine how to lead staff in developing common formative assessments. |
| September 28<br>3:45 to 4:45 PM | Professional learning for all staff | Inservice on ELA/RtI/Assessments. |
| September 29<br>3:00 to 4:00 PM | Literacy Leads | Translate inservice idea to all grade levels. |

From: V. L. Bernhardt (2011). *Response to Intervention (RtI) and Continuous School Improvement (CSI): Using Data, Vision, and Leadership to Design, Implement, and Evaluate a Schoolwide Prevention System.* Larchmont, NY: Eye on Education, Inc.

# CREATING PARTNERSHIPS

| | |
|---|---|
| **Purpose** | The purpose of this activity is to set up the structure to create partnerships to help students achieve student learning standards, to implement the school vision, and/or to refine current partnerships to better relate to student learning standards. |
| **Target Audience** | Staff and potential or current partners. |
| **Time** | Two hours. |
| **Materials** | Copies of the mission, vision, continuous school improvement plan, data profile, student learning standards, chart pad paper, markers, self-stick notes, computer, and projector. |

## Overview

Many school staff think *partnership* is synonymous with donations, fund-raising events, volunteers, and parents helping with students' homework. They think of the end product being money, "stuff," and homework turned in.

Quality partnerships, where both parties contribute and both parties benefit, can help the school achieve its mission and vision, and help the entire school community prepare students for the 21st Century.

By starting with what we want students to know and be able to do, or a Graduate Profile, school staff and partners can brainstorm appropriate ways to work together to achieve the school's vision.

## Process Protocol

If your school has not worked with partners in meaningful ways to implement the vision, or to help achieve a Graduate Profile, you need to plan to do so. Below are steps in creating partnerships that will help your school accomplish the school vision, and create graduates ready for the 21st Century.

Step 1. Clarify, as a staff, the vision for the school, and what you want students to know and be able to do when they graduate, a Graduate Profile, if you will. It would be ideal to consider the PreK-12 curriculum.

Step 2. Within the continuous school improvement plan to implement the school vision, include partnership involvement to help meet student learning standards.

Step 3. Establish a partnership team whose responsibilities include researching, coordinating, creating, and assuring the implementation of win-win partnerships to help achieve the Graduate Profile.

Step 4. Let the community know that you are looking for win-win partnerships to help achieve the Graduate Profile.

Step 5. Establish a time to meet to with prospective partners.

Step 6. Meet with interested partners to exchange information about student learning standards, the Graduate Profile, the school vision, and the potential partners' organizations, and to determine how each can participate:

- Partnership team describes the school's values and beliefs, mission, vision, student learning standards, Graduate Profile, current operations and processes, and identifies what they need from partners.

## Process Protocol *(Continued)*

- ◆ Prospective partners describe what they need graduates to know and be able to do, why they want a partnership with the school, and how they would like to partner.

- ◆ Set up small groups of staff and partners.

- ◆ Have the small groups pick some standards, brainstorm how teachers, businesses, and parents can help students achieve these standards. Place ideas on self-stick notes. Group the self-stick notes and refine the thinking about what you would like each partner to do, coming to agreement on useful and realistic activities.

- ◆ Have the small groups share their ideas with the larger group.

- ◆ As a group, determine best strategies, by grade level/subject area for a continuum of learning for students.

Step 7.    Prepare an agreement, establish outcomes, and determine how the partnership will be monitored, evaluated, and improved on a continuous basis:

- ◆ Establish regular meeting times.

- ◆ Identify costs and personnel requirements for the partnerships.

Step 8.    Implement the partnerships.

Step 9.    Monitor, evaluate, and improve the partnerships.

Step 10.   Celebrate and thank the partners for their contributions.

## Comments to the Facilitator

Adjust this activity to meet the specific needs of the school, as determined from the comprehensive data analysis work. Consider using the problem-solving cycle (Appendix I) when trying to understand why students are not achieving specific standards and how partnerships can help students achieve the standards.

# COMMUNICATION PROTOCOL

| | |
|---|---|
| **Purpose** | The purpose of this activity is to help educators communicate with each other for improvement by using a communication protocol to examine classroom practices, classroom and schoolwide data, professional learning practices, and/or leadership processes. This protocol provides a structured, formal process of presentation, inquiry, reflection, and action. |
| **Target Audience** | Any education team interested in improving teaching and learning practices. |
| **Time** | This protocol can be used in one and one-half hours to a half-day or full day sessions. |
| **Materials** | Examples of student work, student data, teacher data, schoolwide data, lesson designs, activity protocols, meeting evaluations, case studies, or any other samples of materials for a team to critique. Participants will need note pads for note taking. Timekeeper will need accurate clock or stopwatch. |

## Overview

Staff can appreciate the power of teamwork and collaboration, but often they are not used to working in teams, or asking for support for their continuous improvement. This is a process that can help build a culture of collaborative inquiry, leading to teaching improvement and student learning for all students, without blame or defensiveness.

This communication protocol is based on the *Coalition of Essential Schools' Tuning Protocol.*[1] A protocol is a formal professional learning process that:

- ◆ is job-embedded.
- ◆ promotes reflection and ongoing assessment.
- ◆ focuses on the student as the ultimate beneficiary of the process.
- ◆ honors the strengths of the work.
- ◆ examines areas for improvement relative to the teacher's desire and need to improve.
- ◆ creates an invitational climate for teaching and learning conversations.
- ◆ impacts individual and collaborative practice.
- ◆ empowers all who participate in the process to more thoughtfully consider multiple options for classroom practice.

### PROTOCOL TIMING

**15 min:** *Presenter sets context for the work; uses examples of student work, student data, case studies, lesson plans, etc. Presenter poses two key questions she/he wants colleagues to address.*

**5 min:** *Participants ask clarifying questions.*

**5 min:** *Participants and presenter spend time in reflective writing, organizing notes and thoughts.*

**15 min:** *Participants discuss their observations and thoughts, and begin to explore options, consider gaps, and seek solutions or recommendations among themselves with no input from the presenter.*

**15 min:** *Presenter reflects verbally on participants' discussion while team members silently take notes. Presenter describes next steps.*

**10 min:** *Facilitator debriefs the session.*

[1] *Reference:* Coalition of Essential Schools' Tuning Protocol, *www.essentialschools.org/resources/60#3.* Retrieved 02/25/12.

## Process Protocol

The directions that follow are common for using a communication protocol to gain insight and provide feedback:

Step 1. Enlist your learning teams (i.e., grade level/subject area) to study improvement in program and process implementation to improve student learning. (Team sizes of four to six are usually the most efficient.)

Step 2. Establish a date, time, and location for the team meeting.

Step 3. Explain the purpose, goal, and outcomes of the *protocol process.*

Step 4. Describe the particular process that you will be using, including the steps for using group expertise and the timeline for the process. Assign a timekeeper and a recorder.

Step 5. Determine whether or not the team will be using a "Process Observer," a team member whose job it is to watch and listen to the group dynamics, making sure everyone speaks, that time is adhered to, and that conversations are staying true to the purpose of the meeting.

Step 6. Introduce and facilitate the discussion.

Step 7. Presenter gives a presentation and sets the context for the work, using examples of student work, student data, case study, lesson plan, etc., to be examined with no interruptions from participants. **(15 minutes)**

The presenter poses two key questions she/he is asking colleagues to address. For example: *What other things can I do to help these children learn to read? How can I deal with a whole class of different abilities while helping a very small group of children with specific reading skills?* Secondary question: *How do I help students learn to read so they can learn history? How do I help students learn to read while I am teaching history?*

Step 8. Participants ask clarifying questions. **(5 minutes)**

Step 9. The participants and presenter spend time in reflective writing, organizing notes and thoughts. (The presenter might want to collect these notes later. If so, make sure everyone is aware of this intent at the beginning of the session.) **(5 minutes)**

Step 10. Participants discuss their observations and thoughts, and begin to explore options, consider gaps, and seek solutions or recommendations among themselves with no input at this time from the presenter. The presenter listens and takes notes. **(15 minutes)**

Three types of feedback might be provided, as long as the approaches are agreed to at the beginning of the session:

 ♦ Warm—participants are supportive and describe what they think will work in the process.
 ♦ Cool—participants describe elements of the presentation that deserve further examination, i.e., "have you considered what might happen if you tried _____?"
 ♦ Hard—participants ask more probative questions that go deeper into the presentation.

(Facilitator may want to limit each person's initial response, before a discussion, to two minutes.)

Step 11. Presenter reflects verbally on participants' discussion while team members silently take notes in preparation for debriefing time. Presenter describes next steps. **(15 minutes)**

Step 12. Facilitator debriefs the session with both the presenter and the coaching team by reviewing the process, summarizing the steps, and asking participants to comment on their participation and observations. A process observer may be asked to give reflective comments about the entire group process. **(10 minutes)**

## Comments to the Facilitator

Participants need to be prepared to actively contribute to the discussions with probing questions and/or comments, and be supportive and respectful of the roles of the presenter, facilitator, observer, time keeper, recorder, etc.

The facilitator, or "Process Observer," should make sure that there is a balance of feedback during the process, as well as be willing to coach the presenter and participants in advance about the difference between feedback and evaluation. Feedback is a reaction to the information. Evaluation is an assessment of the value of the information.

When using a "Process Observer," the facilitator may close with the observer's comments on the entire process using detail on the following, for example: how many times group members spoke; to what degree the group members were engaged; group norms that were implemented; at what point the group, as a whole, became a team; how the presenter engaged or disengaged.

| | |
|---|---|
| **Purpose** | The purpose of this activity is to engage staff in discussions about alignment of instruction to standards, within grade levels/subject areas, and across grade levels. |
| **Target Audience** | Grade-level/subject-area teachers and/or cross-grade-level teachers. |
| **Time** | One-half day, with time before for organizing student work. |
| **Materials** | Examples of student work and any appropriate scoring guide, standards frameworks, or assessment rubrics, chart pad paper, and markers. Reserve a room with big blank walls for this activity. |

## Overview

This activity is eye-opening to teachers as they begin to see why students are responding the way they are responding, and to hear about strategies other teachers would use to move an anchor paper or a project from one level on a rubric to a higher level, etc., from a one to a two, or a two to three, etc. The process also spawns a new commitment to teach specific concepts at different grade levels so students will be successful throughout their education.

## Process Protocol

Step 1. Explain that the purpose for looking at student work is to determine how to improve instructional practices to ensure that all students meet the student learning standards.

Step 2. Have grade level teams purposefully choose examples of student work related to a specific content area or standard. A rubric can be used or some other criteria to get a selection of performance levels.

Step 3. On the wall, vertically, place the number 4, under it the number 3, followed by the number 2, and ending with the number 1 (the same as the scoring criteria you are using). Horizontally, across the top, place numbers or descriptions that spell out grade levels. Line up the student work by grade level and achievement level (see photo).

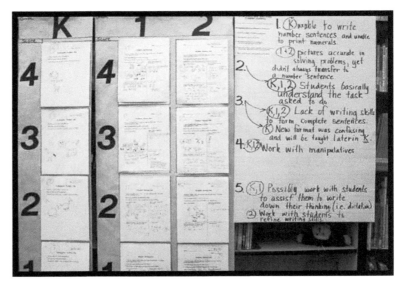

Step 4. After the student work has been posted, have teachers review the work and write on chart paper, answering questions, such as:

♦ What did the student know and understand at this level?

## Process Protocol *(Continued)*

- What did the student not know or not understand?

- What questions would you ask this student to learn more about what she/he understands and knows?

- What strategies would you use to help this student understand the concepts and move to the next level?

Step 5. Have staff members look at the student work at a "4 level" to understand what the standards require across the grade levels. Make sure they look at all the grade levels, not just their grade level.

Step 6. Ask participants to reflect on which concepts need to be taught stronger and determine at which grade level.

## Comments to the Facilitator

One of the goals of continuous school improvement is instructional coherence; in other words, making sure that grade levels and subject areas have horizontal and vertical alignment. There are many ways to ensure this alignment.

The *Examining Students' Work* activity is a very powerful way to assess and ensure alignment, and to engage staff in the conversations about standards, student work, and working together for the benefit of the students.

The more practice in structured settings that teachers have together examining student work as professional development, the more likely it will be that they will spend time informally looking at student work in pairs or in teams. This activity will lead to improved teaching at all levels and in all subject areas.

# ABILITY TO ACHIEVEMENT

| | |
|---:|:---|
| **Purpose** | The purpose of this activity is to engage teachers in discussions with colleagues about how to improve learning for all students in the classroom. |
| **Target Audience** | Teachers, tutors, coaches, etc. |
| **Time** | One to one and one-half hours. |
| **Materials** | Self-stick dots, chart paper, or you could use a couple of computers and projectors. |

## Overview

Teachers often state that some students do not have the ability to achieve, and that the teachers have to work extremely hard to move those students' learning forward.

This activity helps teachers come to grips with their perceptions of students' abilities, then collaboratively consider ways to improve students' achievement.

*Definitions:*

> *Ability:* Perceived aptitude.
>
> *Achievement:* Evidence of attainment of knowledge.

## Process Protocol

**Step 1.** Before the meeting day, by grade levels or subject areas, have teachers choose a subject area, write the names of their students on self-stick dots, and then place the dots in one of the ability achievement quadrants, with respect to teachers' opinions of each student's' ability to do the work and to achieve. Teachers might line up the dots for their class, color code the dots by gender or proficiency levels on an achievement measure, or any other meaningful way.

*Mathematics*
*Ability +*

| | |
|---|---|
| List the names of the students you feel **have the ability to achieve and do *not* achieve.** | List the names of the students you feel **have the ability to achieve and *do* achieve.** |
| *Achievement -* | *Achievement +* |
| List the names of the students you feel **do not have the ability to achieve and do *not* achieve.** | List the names of the students you feel **do not have the ability to achieve, but *do* achieve.** |

*Ability -*

## Process Protocol

Step 2. During the meeting, have teachers discuss and list the common characteristics of the students who fall into each of these quadrants. If possible, add past proficiency levels next to the names of students. An example appears below.

*Ability +*

| *Achievement -* | *Achievement +* |
|---|---|
| Does not do homework. Turns in poor quality work. Missing basic skills. Bored with school. Poor study habits. Attitude is defensive, negative. Distracts others. Lack of consistent parental support. No experience with self-responsibility for learning. "Not cool" with peers. Low self-esteem. | Goal oriented. Good study habits; has career/college in mind. Has good parent support and high expectations. Knows what is expected of her/him. Loves to learn. Positive attitude. Willing to help others. |
| Low IQ—no support from parents; parents don't want interventions. Has a "does not care" attitude. Always has excuses for not having the work done, or not having materials to do the work. Does not do homework. Seeks attention for inappropriate behaviors. Does not know how to read. Excessive Absences. Discouraged. Fear of failure. | Parental support and encouragement. RtI is working. Lacks basic skills. Repeatedly seeking teacher approval. Poor organizational skills. Does not show higher-level thinking. Achieves with one-on one assistance. Does not have a true picture of ability. Gaps in learning. |

*Ability -*

## Process Protocol *(Continued)*

Step 3.  Brainstorm what processes need to be in place in order to help all students achieve. Consider "What can we do in every quadrant to move these students forward." If possible, have the longitudinal individual student growth profile available for each child during this discussion.

*Ability +*

We can—
*   Find out students' interests and make sure the lessons incorporate their interests.
*   Find out what the basic skills gaps are.
*   Provide one-on-one support to get skills up to par.
*   Help students develop study skills and help them get in the practice of doing homework during the school day.
*   Demonstrate value of homework—ensure that it is not "busy" work.

We need to—
*   Keep challenging the students.
*   Get these students to help other students who are having difficulty.
*   Have these students model and describe how they study.
*   Have these students talk and write about careers they want to pursue.

*Achievement -*          *Achievement +*

We can—
*   Find out students' interests and make sure the lessons incorporate their interests.
*   Convince parents of the value of interventions.
*   Find out what the basic skills gaps are.
*   Provide one-on-one support to get skills up to par.
*   Help students develop study skills while helping them get in the practice of doing homework during the school day.
*   Make sure the interventions we use are meeting the learning needs of the students.

We need to—
*   Keep challenging the students.
*   Have these students model and describe how they study.
*   Make sure they interact with the high ability students.

*Ability -*

Step 4.  Determine what needs to be done schoolwide to move all students to the highest quadrant.

*For example:* the teachers in the school, above, determined that they need to clarify their RtI process, and improve their diagnostic assessments so they can have the structures in place to close basic skills gaps for all students.

## Comments to the Facilitator

Done well, this activity will help teachers see what processes need to change to get different results. It will also, hopefully, change some belief systems about student abilities. Perceived abilities might be clouding the teachers' interactions with students and, therefore, students' achievement levels.

As can be seen in the picture below, the axes can be changed for ability/achievement to ability/motivation or any other descriptions that fit your school's issues.

Secondary teachers might want to start with one class.

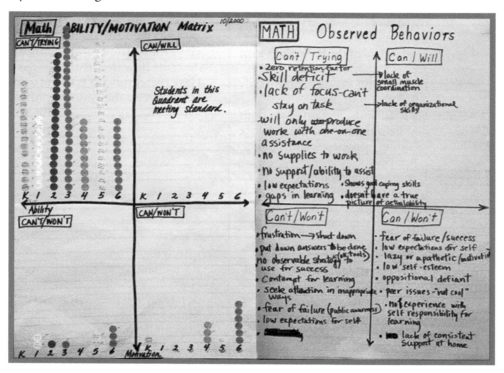

# TIMELINE FOR CONTINUOUS SCHOOL IMPROVEMENT WORK

| | |
|---:|:---|
| Purpose | The purpose of this activity is to guide staff in the creation of a timeline for continuous school improvement by showing them a comprehensive timeline. |
| Target Audience | School staff are the target audience. A Data Leadership Team or School Leadership Team can draft the timeline and take it back to the full staff for approval and implementation. |
| Time | Approximately two hours. |
| Materials | Copies of the school's purpose, mission, vision, school improvement plan, school year calendar, computer, and projector. Chart pad paper and markers might be helpful as well. |

## Overview

If comprehensive data analysis and continuous school improvement are going to be accomplished, the work must be planned throughout the school year. It takes an entire school year to engage in this work in a comprehensive way. After the first year, it will take much less time to update the data and to engage staff in analyzing and using the data.

## Process Protocol

The following process protocol is an example of how the work of continuous school improvement and comprehensive data analysis can be completed the first time. Start wherever you are, with what you have, and move forward. A complete table appears at the end of the activity, Figure T-1. Figure T-2 shows a summary timeline, by roles and time of year, to highlight who needs to be involved in different components of the continuous school improvement process.

We recommend assigning a Data Leadership Team to start the process by organizing the school's data into graphs and a data profile before the school year begins so staff can review the data to set the context for the school year, and so they can create plans for continuous school improvement during the year.

### Before the School Year Begins

Step 1. Long before the first staff meeting, where the data will be reviewed and analyzed, assign a Data Leadership Team (see *Data Leadership Team*, Chapter 11) to learn about the Continuous School Improvement Framework and comprehensive data analysis, and to pull together a data profile that summarizes the schoolwide data currently available. Data most available are demographic and student learning data. Five years of data are preferred, but not necessary to begin. Summer usually is a good time to do this work. In addition to the schoolwide data profile, have the data teams "re-roster" individual student learning data over time by current teachers' classrooms. (Use the data profile example in the case study activities to guide the school data graphing work, Appendices F and G.)

**Process Protocol** (*Continued*)

Step 2.  Have the Data Leadership Team organize a whole-staff meeting to have staff analyze the schoolwide data in the data profile. Provide an overview of the Continuous School Improvement Framework and comprehensive data analysis. Use *Analyzing Data for Continuous School Improvement*, Appendix H, to complete a comprehensive analysis of strengths, challenges, and implications for the school improvement plan. If there is a chance staff members will be jumping to solutions as they are analyzing the data, instead of just recording strengths and challenges, use the case study activity to practice on a data set that is not theirs.

Step 3.  Use the *Problem-solving Cycle*, Appendix I, to understand the contributing causes of undesirable results.

Step 4.  From the comprehensive data analysis and problem-solving cycle, determine—
  ♦ new strategies to get different results and to meet the needs of all students.
  ♦ implications for the school improvement plan and professional learning for the year.
  ♦ what new instructional and assessment strategies staff must learn.
  ♦ time to learn new concepts.

Step 5.  Determine how teachers will work, in teams, with classroom and student level data, during the school year. Have them meet to review student learning results for their grade levels and subject areas, and individual students, over time, and begin working on next steps, such as:
  ♦ Determine what concepts and skills students need to know.
  ♦ Agree on essential standards to teach, when.
  ♦ What do we want students to know and be able to do this year, quarter, month, week? (Review core curriculum standards and update curriculum maps.)
  ♦ How will we know that students know these concepts and skills?
  ♦ Create common formative assessments, including timeline for giving assessments during the year.
  ♦ Determine which instructional strategies will make a difference.
  ♦ Establish plan/flowchart for what teachers will do when students do not know the concepts and do not have the skills, and what teachers will do when students know the concepts and have the skills.
  ♦ Determine times, strategies, and roles and responsibilities for grade-level/subject-area work during the year.

Step 6.  Discuss grade-level/subject-area breakout work with full staff for cross-grade-level congruence.

Step 7.  Assess on the *Education for the Future Continuous Improvement Continuums* to understand what staff members are thinking about where the school is on continuous school improvement. (See *Continuous Improvement Continuums Self-Assessment*, Appendix A.)

Step 8.  Look across the implications that come from the data analysis work for the continuous school improvement plan. Determine new strategies to get different results to meet the needs of *all* students, and determine what has to go into the school improvement plan for the year.

Step 9.  Present the finished product, with recommended revisions for the continuous school improvement plan, to the full staff for approval and implementation.

Step 10.  Determine when and how staff can list programs and processes, their intended/desired results, and what each would look like, separate and together, if they were implemented with 100% integrity and fidelity. (See *Measuring a Program or Process*, Appendix D.)

**Process Protocol** *(Continued)*

**As the School Year Begins**

Step 11.   At the beginning of the year, semester, unit, teachers administer post-assessments as pre-assessments, adjust instructional plans, and then on an on-going basis—

- Monitor student progress.
- Review results.
- Determine how to support students who are not proficient, and students who are proficient in specific skills.
- In teacher teams, review grade-level/subject-area results.
- Determine how teachers will support each other.
- Establish goals for the year, quarter, month, unit.
- Review/update curriculum maps

Step 12.   Data Teams—

- Assist teachers in analyzing student and classroom level data.
- Make sure appropriate reports are available to teachers.

Step 13.   Leadership Teams—

- Review grade-level/subject-area results and teachers' plans to ensure instructional congruence. Discuss needed adjustments with grade-level/subject-area teams.
- Reinforce with staff intentions of programs and interventions, how they are to be implemented, and the results expected.

Step 14.   Determine questionnaires to administer (*Designing Questionnaires*, Appendix C-1).

Step 15.   Administer questionnaires (*Administering Questionnaires*, Appendix C-2).

Step 16.   Analyze questionnaire results, with the other data (*Analyzing Questionnaire Results*, Appendix C-3 and Appendix C-4).

Step 17.   Present and use the questionnaire results (*Presenting and Using Questionnaire Results*, Appendix C-5).

Step 18.   Adjust continuous school improvement plan and vision to improve school climate.

Step 19.   Create/revisit mission and vision (*Creating a Shared Vision*, Appendix J):

- Values and beliefs.
- Purpose and mission.
- Shared vision for curriculum, instruction, assessment, and environment.
- Create flowchart for vision (*Flowcharting School Processes*, Appendix E).
- Determine how the vision will be monitored and evaluated (*Monitoring Vision Implementation*, Appendix K).
- Create/adopt monitoring/evaluation tools.

Step 20.   Program analysis:

- Spell out the intentions of each program/process, expected outcomes, and how the program/ process will be implemented and evaluated (*Measuring a Program or Process*, Appendix D).
- Create flowcharts for programs and processes to support implementation (*Flowcharting School Processes*, Appendix E).

### Process Protocol *(Continued)*

**Step 21.** Create leadership teams to ensure implementation of the vision (*Leadership Structure,* Appendix N):

- Determine roles and responsibilities.
- Establish a partnership plan to include parents, community, and business in achieving the vision.

**Step 22.** Create/update the continuous school improvement plan to implement the vision (*Continuous School Improvement Plan,* Appendix L):

- Determine goals, objectives, strategies, activities, measurement, persons responsible, timelines, and evaluation of the plan.
- Get all staff committed to implementing the plan.
- Get all staff to reflect on the impact of implementing the plan in their classrooms.
- Develop professional learning calendar.

### On-Going During the School Year

**Step 23.** Monitor the implementation of the vision and plan (*Monitoring the Implementation of the Plan,* Appendix M).

### End of the School Year

**Step 24.** Evaluate achievement of goals and the implementation of the vision (See Chapter 13).

- Review data results.
- Clarify new learning required for all teachers over the summer.
- Determine changes required in the vision and plan.

## Comments to the Facilitator

Many schools get excited about starting continuous school improvement work, but they stop the work long before all the work is done. When the work is planned and clear to all staff members, implementation is monitored and evaluated, the work gets done—then continuous school improvement will occur.

Figure T-1
CONTINUOUS SCHOOL IMPROVEMENT AND DATA ANALYSIS TIMELINE

| WHEN | WHO | WHAT | TOOLS | DATA SOURCES | ARTIFACTS |
|---|---|---|---|---|---|
| **Before School Begins.** | *Data leadership team. (AKA Data Team.)* | *Create data leadership team:* At minimum, data leadership team will be responsible for making sure appropriate data reports are available for teachers in a timely fashion. Team members will ensure that teachers in grade-level/subject-matter teams understand how to analyze data and can target instruction based on the data. | *Data Leadership Team.* | School assessment databases. | Identification of members, clarification of roles and responsibilities. |
| | | *Provide data team training:* Data analysis and continuous school improvement (CSI) overview. | Overview of continuous school improvement and data analysis in book. | Student information system. | The beginning of a data profile for the school. |
| | | *Case study:* Practice analyzing schoolwide data and see what it looks like when a school is doing the work and using it for continuous school improvement planning. Model how to do the work with staff. | *Case Study.* | State Longitudinal Data System. | A plan to analyze schoolwide data with staff. |
| | | *Analyze data:* Pull together longitudinal demographic and student learning data for your school. Should be able to get these from your State Longitudinal Data System (SLDS). Add, and plan to add, additional data. | *Analyzing Data for Continuous School Improvement Planning.* | School databases. | Inventories of the school's data, assessments, and programs. |
| | | *Analyze school data and detail observations about next steps:* Analyze the school's demographic and student learning data, along with any process and questionnaire data the school might have. | Introduction to the data tools and how to use them. | | A plan to help staff analyze student learning data during the school year. |
| | | *Inventory* the school's data, assessments, and programs. | Inventories. | | A plan to schedule continuous school improvement work during the year. |
| | | *Re-roster individual student learning data* overtime by current teachers' classrooms, or plan to have grade-level/subject-area teams do this before school starts. | *Timeline for Continuous School Improvement Work.* | | |
| | | *Create a plan* to review data and assess on the *Continuous Improvement Continuums* with staff. | | | |
| | | *Create a plan* to complete this work during the school year. | | | |

**Figure T-1** *(Continued)*
## CONTINUOUS SCHOOL IMPROVEMENT AND DATA ANALYSIS TIMELINE

| WHEN | WHO | WHAT | TOOLS | DATA SOURCES | ARTIFACTS |
|---|---|---|---|---|---|
| As School Begins. | *Entire staff.* | *Data team facilitates,* with staff, the analysis of the school's data.<br>• Provide overview of continuous school improvement and comprehensive data analysis:<br>　*Five essential questions.<br>　*Four types of data.<br>• Analyze schoolwide results, over time (3 to 5 years):<br>　*What are our strengths, challenges, implications for the continuous school improvement plan, and what other data should we be gathering and analyzing?<br>　*How is our student population changing?<br>　*What/where did we do well?<br>　*What/where did we not do well?<br>　*Use contributing cause, prediction, and optimization analyses, to understand how school is getting undesirable results, and to consider how to get different results.<br>• Determine—<br>　*new strategies to get different results and to meet the needs of all students.<br>　*implications for the continuous school improvement plan and professional learning for the year.<br>　*what new instructional and assessment strategies staff must learn.<br>　*time to learn new concepts. | *Continuous School Improvement Framework.*<br><br>*Multiple Measures* chapter.<br><br>*Analyzing Data for Continuous School Improvement Planning.*<br><br>*Problem-Solving Cycle.* | Data profile (created in the summer).<br><br>State Longitudinal Data System.<br><br>Assessment database application. | Data profile completed.<br><br>The consensus analysis of the school's data.<br><br>*Problem-Solving Cycle.*<br><br>Prediction and optimization analyses (if available). |

Figure T-1 *(Continued)*
## CONTINUOUS SCHOOL IMPROVEMENT AND DATA ANALYSIS TIMELINE

| WHEN | WHO | WHAT | TOOLS | DATA SOURCES | ARTIFACTS |
|---|---|---|---|---|---|
| As School Begins. | *Entire staff.* | • Set up Professional Learning Communities/Data Team/Leadership Teams/Grade-Level/Subject-Area Teams.<br>• Grade-level/subject-area breakouts:<br> \*What concepts and skills do students need to know. Agree on essential standards to teach, when.<br> \*What do we want students to know and be able to do this year, quarter, month, week? (Review core curriculum standards and update curriculum maps.)<br> \*How will we know that students know these concepts and skills?<br> \*Create common post-assessments.<br> \*Adopt timelines for giving assessments throughout the year.<br> \*Determine which instructional strategies will make a difference.<br> \*Establish plan/flowchart for what teachers will do when students do not know the concepts and do not have the skills, and what teachers will do when students know the concepts and have the skills.<br> \*Determine times, strategies, and roles and responsibilities for grade-level/subject-area work during the year.<br>• Discuss grade-level/subject-area breakout work with full staff for cross-grade-level congruence.<br>• Reinforce intentions of programs and interventions, how they are to be implemented, and the results expected.<br>• Create flowcharts of processes expected to be used.<br>• Assess on *Continuous Improvement Continuums.*<br>• Look across the implications for the continuous school improvement plan that come from the data analysis work and *Continuous Improvement Continuum* assessment. | *Leadership Structure.*<br>Data Inventories.<br>*Measuring a Program or Process.*<br>*Flowcharting School Processes.*<br>*Continuous Improvement Continuums Self-Assessment.*<br>*Analyzing Data for Continuous Improvement Planning.* | State Longitudinal Data System.<br>Assessment database application. | Professional Learning Community/Data/Leadership Team Structure, including roles and responsibilities.<br>Inventories of school programs and assessments.<br>Flowcharts that show how standards will be implemented, and what teachers will do when students do not know the concepts and do not have the skills, and what teachers will do when students know the concepts and have the skills.<br>Plan for teams to review their students' data throughout the year.<br>*Continuous Improvement Continuums* assessment.<br>Data analysis results with aggregated implications for the continuous school improvement plan. |

**Figure T-1** *(Continued)*
## CONTINUOUS SCHOOL IMPROVEMENT AND DATA ANALYSIS TIMELINE

| WHEN | WHO | WHAT | TOOLS | DATA SOURCES | ARTIFACTS |
|---|---|---|---|---|---|
| On-going. | *Teachers.* | • At the beginning of the year, semester, unit, teachers, in their collaborative teams will want to establish goals, administer post-assessments as pre-assessments, review what they want students to know and be able to do. Figure 13.4 summarizes the when, who, what, tools, data sources, and artifacts for this on-going team work.<br>• Throughout the semester, teachers will—<br>* Monitor student progress.<br>* Review results in collaborative teams.<br>* Determine how to support students who are not proficient, and students who are proficient in specific skills. | *Flowcharting School Processes.*<br>*Analyzing Student Learning Data.* | Data profile.<br>State Longitudinal Data System.<br>Assessment databases. | Pre-assessments of standards knowledge and skills.<br>Flowcharts that show what teachers will do when students do not know the concepts and do not have the skills, and what teachers will do when students know the concepts and have the skills. |
| | *Data team.* | • Assist teachers in analyzing student and classroom level data.<br>• Make sure appropriate reports are available to teachers. | *Analyzing Student Learning Data.* | Assessment database application. | Assessment reports. |
| | *Grade-level/ subject-area teams.* | • Review/share grade-level/subject-area results.<br>• Determine how teachers will support each other.<br>• Establish goals for the year, quarter, month, unit.<br>• Review/update curriculum maps.<br>• Ensure the implementation of programs/vision. | *Analyzing Student Learning Data.*<br>Strategies for teachers to support each other.<br>*Communication Protocol.* | Data profile.<br>Data warehouse/ State Longitudinal Data System.<br>Assessment databases. | Student achievement results graphed by teachers, students, grade-level/subject-area/leadership teams/school.<br>Analysis of student learning results by grade levels and across grade levels. |
| | *School Leadership Team.* | • Review/share grade-level/subject-area results and teachers' plans to ensure instructional congruence.<br>Discuss adjustments required with grade level/subject-area teams.<br>• Reinforce with staff the intentions of programs and interventions, how they are to be implemented, and the results expected. | *Analyzing Student Learning Data.*<br>Strategies for teachers to support each other.<br>*Measuring a Program or Process.* | Data profile.<br>Data warehouse/ State Longitudinal Data System.<br>Assessment databases. | Plan to ensure instructional coherence.<br>Evidence of instructional coherence. |

**Figure T-1** *(Continued)*
## CONTINUOUS SCHOOL IMPROVEMENT AND DATA ANALYSIS TIMELINE

| WHEN | WHO | WHAT | TOOLS | DATA SOURCES | ARTIFACTS |
|---|---|---|---|---|---|
| **After School Begins.** *Administer no earlier than a month into the school year.* | *Data Team.* | Determine questionnaires to administer to students, staff, and parents. Research existing, adapt, or create questionnaires. Review with staff and approve to administer. | *Designing Questionnaires.* | Research. | Questionnaires to administer. |
| | *Staff.* | Administer staff school improvement questionnaires. (Staff meeting, 20 minutes.) | Questionnaires. *Administering Questionnaires.* | Questionnaire administration, analysis, presentation tool (online). | Questionnaire. |
| | *Students: Strategic administration.* | Administer student school improvement questionnaires. (Organized class time, 20 minutes.) | Questionnaires. *Administering Questionnaires.* | | Questionnaire. |
| | *Parent-Teacher Conference. In person.* | Administer parent school improvement questionnaires. (20 minutes.) | Questionnaires. *Administering Questionnaires.* | Questionnaire administration, analysis, presentation tool (online). | Questionnaire. |
| | *Data teams(s).* | Merge open-ended results. | *Analyzing Open-Ended Responses.* | | |
| | *Entire staff.* | Review/share questionnaire results, along with the data profile and analysis, and current assessment results. Adjust school improvement plan and vision to improve school climate. | *Analyzing Data for Continuous School Improvement Planning. Analyzing Questionnaire Results.* | | Questionnaire analysis, with other data. Adjustments to the school improvement plan. |

## Figure T-1 *(Continued)*
## CONTINUOUS SCHOOL IMPROVEMENT AND DATA ANALYSIS TIMELINE

| WHEN | WHO | WHAT | TOOLS | DATA SOURCES | ARTIFACTS |
|---|---|---|---|---|---|
| Professional Learning Day. | *Entire staff.* | • Revisit/create the school vision.<br>*Values and beliefs.<br>*Purpose and mission.<br>*Shared vision for curriculum, instruction, assessment, and environment.<br>• Create flowchart for vision.<br>• Determine how the vision will be monitored and evaluated.<br>• Create monitoring/evaluation tools. | *Creating a Shared Vision.*<br>*Flowcharting School Processes.*<br>*Monitoring Vision Implementation.*<br>Assessment and Program Inventories. | Data profile.<br>State Longitudinal Data System.<br>Assessment tools. | Core values and beliefs, mission, vision for the school.<br>Flowchart of the vision.<br>Monitoring and evaluation plan for vision.<br>Updated inventory of assessments and programs. |
| Delegated or staff meeting. | *Staff members.* | • Spell out the intention of each program/process, expected outcomes, and how the program/process will be implemented and evaluated.<br>• Create flowcharts for programs and processes to support implementation, within the context of the vision. | *Measuring a Program or Process.*<br>*Flowcharting School Processes.* | Data profile.<br>State Longitudinal Data System.<br>Assessment tools. | Program intention and assessment plan established for programs.<br>Program flowcharts. |
| Professional Learning Day, unless it can be done during the vision process. | *Entire staff.* | Create structures to implement the vision.<br>• Review all the implications from the data.<br>• Review purpose, mission, vision, and values and beliefs.<br>• Revisit leadership structure.<br>• Determine roles and responsibilities.<br>• Establish a relationship plan to include parents, community, and business in achieving the vision.<br>• Begin the school improvement plan for the year. | *Leadership Structure.*<br>*Creating Partnerships.* | Data profile.<br>State Longitudinal Data System. | Leadership structure.<br>Plan for building relationships, with parents, community, and business. |
| Create and Use a Continuous School Improvement Plan. | *Work with Leadership Team to create and bring back to staff.* | • Create/update the continuous school improvement plan to implement the vision.<br>• Determine goals, objectives, strategies, activities, measurement, persons responsible, timelines, and evaluation of the plan.<br>• Get all staff committed to implementing the plan.<br>• Develop professional learning calendar. | *Continuous School Improvement Plan.*<br>*Professional Learning Calendar.* | Data profile.<br>State Longitudinal Data System. | School improvement plan.<br>Professional learning calendar. |
| On-going. | *Leadership Team.* | • Assess the implementation of the vision and plan, and make adjustments to implement better. | *Evaluating a Continuous School Improvement Vision and Plan.* | Vision monitoring tool. | On-going monitoring of the vision and plan reports and analysis. |
| End of Year. | *Data team or data analysis personnel, with staff.* | • Review/share data results:<br>• Clarify new learning required for all teachers over the summer.<br>• Determine changes required in the vision and plan. | *Analyzing Data for Continuous School Improvement Planning.* | Data profile.<br>State Longitudinal Data System.<br>Assessment database application. | Analysis of data and analysis of changes required. |

## Figure T-2

## TIMELINE FOR CONTINUOUS SCHOOL IMPROVEMENT WORK

| | DATA LEADERSHIP TEAM | WHOLE STAFF | TEACHER TEAMS | LEADERSHIP TEAM |
|---|---|---|---|---|
| **BEFORE THE SCHOOL YEAR BEGINS** | **Before First Staff Meeting**<br>Assign a data leadership team to—<br>• understand the concepts of continuous school improvement and comprehensive data analysis.<br>• pull together a data profile that summarizes the schoolwide data currently available.<br>• re-roster individual student learning data, over time, by current teachers' classrooms.<br>• inventory assessments, data, and programs.<br>• create a plan to do this work with staff. | **Whole-Staff Meeting**<br>• Provide overview of continuous school improvement framework and comprehensive data analysis.<br>• Analyze the schoolwide data in the data profile.<br>• Use the Problem-Solving Cycle Activity to understand the contributing causes of undesirable results.<br>• Determine how teachers will work, in teams, with classroom and student-level data during the school year.<br>• Allow time for grade-level/subject-area teams to work.<br>• Discuss grade-level/subject-area breakout work with full staff for cross-grade-level congruence.<br>• Assess on the CICs to understand what staff members are thinking about where the school is on continuous school improvement.<br>• Look across the implications that come from the data analysis work for the school improvement plan.<br>• Determine new strategies to get different results to meet the needs of *all* students, and determine what has to go into the school improvement plan for the year.<br>• Determine when and how staff can list programs and processes, their intended/desired results, and what each would look like, separate and together, if they were implemented with 100% integrity and fidelity. | **Grade-Level/Subject-Area Team/PLC Breakout Session**<br>Determine—<br>• what concepts and skills students need to know.<br>• agree on essential standards to teach, when.<br>• what do we want students to know and be able to do this year, quarter, month, week?<br>• core curriculum standards and update curriculum maps.<br>• how we will know that students know these concepts and skills.<br>• common assessments, including timeline for giving assessments during the year.<br>• which instructional strategies will make the difference.<br>• an established plan/flowchart for what teachers will do when students do not know the concepts and do not have the skills, and what teachers will do when students know the concepts and have the skills.<br>• times, strategies, and roles and responsibilities for grade-level and subject-area work during the year. | |
| **ON-GOING** | **On-Going**<br>Help teachers review student learning data by—<br>• creating reports.<br>• coaching their interpretation of results.<br>• listening to, and creating, others ways teachers may want the data displayed. | **Create/Revisit a Mission and Vision**<br>• Review implications from all the data.<br>• Values and beliefs.<br>• Purpose and mission.<br>• Shared vision for curriculum, instruction, assessment, and environment.<br>• Determine school goals and objectives.<br>• Create flowchart for vision.<br>• Get staff to reflect on the impact of implementing the vision in her/his classroom.<br>• Determine how the vision will be monitored and evaluated.<br>• Create/adopt monitoring/evaluation tools. (Leadership Team may have to finish and bring it back to staff.)<br>• Create Leadership Teams to implement the vision.<br>• Determine roles and responsibilities for Leadership Teams.<br>• Establish a partnership plan to include parents, community, and business in achieving the vision.<br>• Begin the school improvement plan for the year. (Leadership Team can finish and bring back to staff.)<br>**Program Analysis**<br>• List the programs operating in the school.<br>• Spell-out the intentions of each program/process, expected outcomes, and how the program/process will be implemented and evaluated.<br>• Create flowcharts for programs and processes to support implementation.<br>• *Analyze Program results* with the other data.<br>**Professional Learning**<br>• Engage all staff in appropriate professional learning. | **At the Beginning of the Year**, semester, unit, administer post-assessments as pre-assessments.<br>**On-Going**<br>• Monitor student progress.<br>• Review results.<br>• Determine how to support students who are not proficient, and students who are proficient in specific skills.<br>• Determine how teachers will support each other.<br>• Establish goals for the year, quarter, month, unit.<br>• Review/update curriculum map.<br>• Monitor the implementation of the vision and plan. | **Regularly Scheduled Meetings**<br>• Review grade-level/subject-area results and teachers plans to ensure instructional congruence.<br>• Discuss needed adjustments with grade-level/subject-area teams.<br>• Reinforce with staff the intentions of programs and interventions, how they are to be implemented, and the results expected.<br>• Monitor the implementation of the vision and plan.<br><br>**Create a School Improvement Plan to Implement the Vision**<br>• Get all staff committed to implementing the vision and plan.<br>• Develop professional learning calendar from the plan.<br>• Get staff approval of plan and professional learning calendar.<br>• Ensure all staff have appropriate professional learning. |
| **QUESTIONNAIRE WORK** | **Questionnaires**<br>• Research existing questionnaires.<br>• Adopt or develop questionnaires to administer.<br>• Gain staff approval to administer questionnaires.<br>• Organize and administer questionnaires. | | **Administer Questionnaires**<br>• Support the administration of questionnaires.<br>• Review results with respect to grade level/subject areas. | **Use Results**<br>• Adjust school improvement plan and vision to improve school climate.<br>• Clarify new learning required for all teachers over the summer. |
| **END OF SCHOOL YEAR** | **Evaluate Achievement of Continuous School Improvement** goals and the implementation of the vision.<br>• Review data results.<br>• Clarify new learning required for all teachers over the summer.<br>• Determine changes required in the vision and plan. | | | **Evaluate Achievement of Continuous School Improvement** goals and the implementation of the vision.<br>• Review data results.<br>• Clarify new learning required for all teachers over the summer.<br>• Determine changes required in the vision and plan. |

# REFERENCES AND RESOURCES

Alkin, M.C. (2013). *Evaluation roots: A wider perspective of theorists' views and influences.* Second Edition. Thousand Oaks, CA: Sage Publications.

Allen, D. (1995). The tuning protocol: A process for reflection. *Studies on Exhibitions* No. 15. Providence, RI: Coalition of Essential Schools. Retrieved February 25, 2012, from *www.essentialschools.org/resources/60#3.*

Allensworth, E. & Easton, J.Q. (2007). *What matters for staying on-track and graduating in Chicago Public High Schools: A close look at course grades, failures, and attendance in the freshman year.* Chicago: Consortium on Chicago School Research.

Allensworth, E. & Easton, J. (2005). *The on-track indicator as a predictor of high school graduation.* Chicago: Consortium on Chicago School Research.

Angoff, W.H. (1988). *Scales, norms, and equivalent scores.* Princeton, New Jersey: Educational Testing Service (ETS).

Balfanz, R. & Herzog, L. (2005, March). *Keeping middle grades students on-track to graduation: Initial analysis and implications.* Presentation at the second Regional Middle Grades Symposium, Philadelphia.

Barker, J.A. (1993). *Paradigms: The business of discovering the future.* New York: HarperBusiness.

Bernhardt, V.L. & Geise, B.J. (2009). *From Questions to Actions: Using Questionnaire Data for Continuous School Improvement.* Larchmont, NY: Eye On Education, Inc.

Bernhardt, V.L. & Hérbert, C.L. (2011). *Response to intervention (RtI) and continuous school improvement (CSI): Using data, vision, and leadership to design, implement, and evaluate a schoolwide prevention system.* Larchmont, NY: Eye On Education.

Bernhardt, V.L. (2000). Intersections: New routes open when one type of data crosses another. *Journal of Staff Development,* 21(1), 33-36.

Bernhardt, V.L. (2003). *Using data to improve student learning in elementary schools.* Larchmont, NY: Eye On Education.

Bernhardt, V.L. (2004). *Using data to improve student learning in middle schools.* Larchmont, NY: Eye On Education.

Bernhardt, V.L. (2005). *Using data to improve student learning in high schools.* Larchmont, NY: Eye On Education.

Bernhardt, V.L. (2006). *Using data to improve student learning in school districts.* Larchmont, NY: Eye On Education.

Black, P.J. & Wiliam, D. (1998). *Inside the black box: Raising standards through classroom assessment.* Phi Delta Kappan, 80(2), 139-148. Retrieved from: *http://www.pdkintl.org/kappan/kbla9810.htm.*

Blankstein, A.M., Houston, P.D., Cole, R.W., Earl, L.M., Katz, S., Hill, P.W., et al. (2010). *Data-enhanced leadership.* Thousand Oaks, CA: Corwin Press.

Blase, J., Blase, J., & Phillips, D.Y. (2010). *Handbook of school improvement: How high-performing principals create high-performing schools.* Thousand Oaks, CA: Corwin Press.

Bloom. B. (May, 1968). *UCLA CSEIP Evaluation* Comment, 1(2).

Boudett, K.P., City, E.A., & Murnane, R.J. (2005). *Data wise: A step-by-step guide to using assessment results to improve teaching and learning.* Cambridge, MA: Harvard Education Press.

Collins, J. & Hansen, M. (2011). *Great by choice: Uncertainty, chaos, and luck—Why some thrive despite them all.* New York: Harper Business.

Conzemius, A. & O'Neill, J. (2005). *The power of SMART goals: Using goals to improve student learning.* Bloomington, IN: Solution Tree.

Darling-Hammond, L. (2010). *The flat world and education: How America's commitment to equity will determine our future (multicultural education).* New York: Teachers College Press.

Deming, W.E. (1982). *Quality productivity and competitive position.* Cambridge, MA: MIT Press.

Deming, W.E. (1991). *Out of the crisis.* Cambridge, MA: MIT Press.

Depka, E. (2006). *The data guidebook for teachers and leaders: Tools for continuous improvement.* Thousand Oaks, CA: Corwin Press.

Doyle, M. & Straus. D. (1993). *How to make meetings work: The new interaction method.* New York: Berkley Publishing Group.

DuFour, R., DuFour, R., Eaker, R., & Thomas, M. (2010). *Learning by doing: A handbook for professional communities at work.* Bloomington, IN: Solution Tree.

DuFour, R. & Marzano, R.J. (2011). *Leaders of learning: How district, school, and classroom leaders improve student achievement.* Bloomington, IN: Solution Tree.

Earl, L. & Katz, S. (2002). Leading schools in a data rich world. In K. Leithwood, Pl. Hallinger, G. Furman, P. Gronn, J. MacBeath, B. Mulforld & K. Riley (Eds.), *The second international handbook of educational leadership and administration.* Dordrecht, Netherlands: Kluwer.

Easton, L. (2011). *Professional learning communities by design: Putting the learning back into PLCs.* (Pap/Cdr Edition). Thousand Oaks, CA: Corwin Press.

Easton, L.B. (2008). *Powerful designs for professional learning.* Second Edition. Oxford, OH: National Staff Development Council.

Elmore, R.F. (2011). *I used to think…and now I think…: Twenty leading educators reflect on the work of school reform.* Second Edition. Cambridge, MA: Harvard Education Press.

Epstein, J.L. & Associates (2009). *School, family, and community partnerships: Your handbook for action* (Third Edition). Thousand Oaks, CA: Corwin Press.

Faria, A.M., Heppen, J., Li, J., Stachel, S., Jones, W., Sawyer, K., et al. (2012). *Creating success: Data use and student achievement in urban schools.* Washington, DC: Council of the Great City Schools and the American Institutes for Research.

Fitzpatrick, J.L., Sanders, J.R., & Worthen, B.R. (2010). *Program evaluation: Alternative approaches and practical guidelines* (Fourth Edition). New York: Pearson.

Fullan, M. (2003). *The moral imperative of school leadership.* Thousand Oaks, CA: Corwin Press.

Fullan, M. (2009). *The challenge of change: Start school improvement now!* Second Edition. Thousand Oaks, CA: Corwin Press.

Fullan, M. (2010). *All systems go: The change imperative for whole system reform.* Thousand Oaks, CA: Corwin Press.

Fullan, M. (2011). *Choosing the wrong drivers for whole system reform.* East Melbourne, Australia: Centre for Strategic Education.

Gabor, A. (1992). *The man who discovered quality: How W. Edwards Deming brought the quality revolution to America.* New York: Penguin Books.

Goldring, E.B. & Berends, M. (2008). *Leading with data: Pathways to improve your school (leadership with learning series).* Thousand Oaks, CA: Corwin Press.

Grudens-Schuck, N., Lundy Allen, B., & Larson, K., (5/2004). Focus Group Fundamentals. *Iowa State University Methodology Brief.* p.8.

Hargreaves, A. & Shirley, D. (2009). *The fourth way: The inspiring future for educational change.* Thousand Oaks, CA: Corwin Press.

Hawley, W.D. (2006). *The keys to effective schools: Educational reform as continuous improvement.* Second Edition. Thousand Oaks, CA: Corwin Press.

Heppen, J.B. & Therriault, S.B. (2008, July). *Developing early warning systems to identify potential high school dropouts.* Washington, DC: The National High School Center at the American Institutes for Research.

Hiatt, J.M. (2006). *ADKAR: A model for change in business, government and our community: How to implement successful change in our personal lives and professional careers.* Loveland, CO: Prosci Learning Center Publications.

Jensen, E. (2009). *Teaching with poverty in mind.* Alexandria, VA: Association for Supervision and Curriculum Development (ASCD).

Jerald, C. (2006). *Identifying potential dropouts: Key lessons for building an early warning data system.* Washington, DC: Achieve, Inc.

Joyce, B. & Calhoun, E. (2012). *Realizing the promise of 21st-century education: An owner's manual.* Thousand Oaks, CA: Corwin Press.

Katz, S. (June 2012). *The learning-driven school: Towards a culture of inquiry.* Keynote presentation given at Compass for Success Conference, Mississauga, Ontario.

Katz, S., Earl, L.M., & Jaafar, S.B. (2009). *Building and connecting learning communities: The power of networks for school improvement.* Thousand Oaks, CA: Corwin Press.

Kaufman, T.E., Grimm, E.D., & Miller, A.E. (2012). *Collaborative school improvement: Eight practices for district-school partnerships to transform teaching and learning.* Cambridge, MA: Harvard Education Press.

Kennedy, K., Peters, M., & Thomas, M. (2011). *How to use value-added analysis to improve student learning: A field guide for school and district leaders.* Thousand Oaks, CA: Corwin Press.

Kennelly, L. & Monrad, M. (2007). *Approaches to dropout prevention: Heeding early warning signs with appropriate interventions.* Washington, DC: National High School Center, American Institutes for Research.

Killion, J. (2007). *Assessing impact: Evaluating staff development.* Second Edition. Thousand Oaks, CA: Corwin Press.

Knowlton, L.W. & Phillips, C.C. (2012). *The logic model guidebook: Better strategies for great results.* Second Edition edition. Thousand Oaks, CA: Sage Publications.

Kouzes, J. & Posner, B. (2008). *The leadership challenge.* Fourth Edition. San Francisco: Jossey-Bass.

Lipton, L & Wellman, B. (2012) *Got data? Now what?: Creating and leading Cultures of Inquiry.* Bloomington IN: Solution Tree.

Love, N. (2008). *Using data to improve learning for all: A collaborative inquiry approach.* Thousand Oaks, CA: Corwin Press.

Manitoba Education, Citizen and Youth. (2006). *Rethinking classroom assessment with purpose in mind.* Retrieved from *http://www.edu.gov.mb.ca/k12/assess/wncp/rethinking_assess_mb.pdf.*

Manitoba Education. *The role of assessment in learning.* Assessment and Evaluation. Retrieved from *http://www.edu.gov.mb.ca/k12/assess/role.html* (January 2013).

Marzano, R.J. (2007). *The art and science of teaching: A comprehensive framework for effective instruction.* Alexandria, VA: Association for Supervision and Curriculum Development (ASCD).

Marzano, R.J. (2009). *Formative assessment & standards-based grading: Classroom strategies that work.* Alexandria, VA: Association for Supervision and Curriculum Development (ASCD).

Marzano, R.J., Frontier, T., & Livingston, D. (2011). *Effective supervision: Supporting the art and science of teaching.* Alexandria, VA: ASCD.

McDonald, J.P., Mohr, N., Dichter, A., & McDonald, E. (2003). *The power of protocols: An educator's guide to better practice.* New York: Teachers College Press.

Mitchell, R. (1999). Examining student work. *Journal of Staff Development,* 20(3), 32-33.

Patton, M.Q. (2011). *Developmental evaluation: Applying complexity concepts to enhance innovation and use.* New York: Guilford Press.

Patton, M.Q. (2012). *Essentials of Utilization-Focused Evaluation.* Thousand Oaks, CA: Sage Publications.

Pfeffer, P. & Sutton, R. (2000). *The knowing-doing gap.* Boston: Harvard Business School Press.

Pinkus, L. (2008, August). *Using early-warning data to improve graduation rates: Closing cracks in the education system.* Policy Brief. Washington, DC: Alliance for Excellent Education.

Popham, W.J. (2008). *Transformative assessment.* Alexandria, VA: Association for Supervision and Curriculum Development (ASCD).

Popper, K.R. (2002). *Conjectures and refutations: The growth of scientific knowledge.* (Vol. 2). London: Routledge.

Ontario Principals' Council (2008). *The principal as data-driven leader (Leading student achievement series).* Thousand Oaks, CA: Corwin Press.

Saginor, N. (2008). *Diagnostic classroom observation: Moving beyond best practice.* Thousand Oaks, CA: Corwin Press.

Sagor, R. (1993). *How to conduct collaborative action research.* Alexandria, VA: Association for Supervision and Curriculum Development (ASCD).

Sagor, R. (2000). *Guiding school improvement with action research.* Alexandria, VA: Association for Supervision and Curriculum Development (ASCD).

Senge, P.M. (2006). *The fifth discipline: The art & practice of the learning organization.* New York: The Crown Publishing Group.

Schmoker, M. (2006). *Results now: How we can achieve unprecedented improvements in teaching and learning.* Alexandria, VA: Association for Supervision and Curriculum Development (ASCD).

Schmoker, M. (2011). *Focus: Elevating the essentials to radically improve student learning.* Alexandria, VA: Association for Supervision and Curriculum Development (ASCD).

Sharratt, L. & Fullan, M. (2012). *Putting faces on the data: What great leaders do.* Thousand Oaks, CA: Corwin Press.

Smylie, M.A. (2009). *Continuous school improvement* (Leadership for Learning Series). Thousand Oaks, CA: Corwin Press.

Stiggins, R.J. (1999). Teams. *Journal of Staff Development,* 20(3), 17-21.

Stronge, J.H. & Grant, L.W. (2009). *Student achievement goal setting: Using data to improve teaching and learning.* Larchmont, NY: Eye On Education.

Trilling, B. & Fadel, C. (2012). *21st Century skills: Learning for life in our times.* San Francisco: Jossey-Bass.

Wayman, J.C., Cho, V., Jimerson, J.B., & Spikes, D.D. (2012). District-wide effects on data use in the classroom. *Education Policy Analysis Archives,* 20 (25). Retrieved from *http://epaa.asu.edu/ojs/article/view/979.*

Whitmire, T. (2012). *Engaging families to improve student achievement.* (White paper from Stand for Children Leadership Center.) Retrieved from *http://standleadershipcenter.org/ what-we-stand-principals.*

Wholey, J.S., Hatry, H.P., & Newcome, K.E. (2010). *Handbook of practical program evaluation (essential texts for nonprofit and public leadership and management).* San Francisco: Jossey-Bass.

Wiliam. D. (2007). Content then process: Teaching learning communities in the service of formative assessment. In D. Reeves (Ed.), *Ahead of the curve: The power of assessment to transform teaching and learning* (pp. 182-204). Bloomington IN: Solution Tree.

Wiliam, D. (2011). *Embedded formative assessment.* Bloomington, IN: Solution Tree.

Zachary, L.J. (2011). *The mentor's guide: Facilitating effective learning relationships.* San Francisco: Jossey-Bass.

# INDEX